ENGLISH MONEY
AND
IRISH LAND

The 'Adventurers' in the
Cromwellian Settlement of Ireland

BY

KARL S. BOTTIGHEIMER

STATE UNIVERSITY OF NEW YORK
STONYBROOK, NEW YORK

OXFORD
AT THE CLARENDON PRESS
1971

Oxford University Press, Ely House, London W. 1

GLASGOW NEW YORK TORONTO MELBOURNE WELLINGTON
CAPE TOWN SALISBURY IBADAN NAIROBI DAR ES SALAAM LUSAKA ADDIS ABABA
BOMBAY CALCUTTA MADRAS KARACHI LAHORE DACCA
KUALA LUMPUR SINGAPORE HONG KONG TOKYO

PRINTED IN GREAT BRITAIN
AT THE UNIVERSITY PRESS, OXFORD
BY VIVIAN RIDLER
PRINTER TO THE UNIVERSITY

PREFACE

THIS book is a composite of literary and quantitative methods of historical inquiry. Chapters I, II, IV, and V will be found to be for the most part conventional attempts to describe from documentary evidence the origins, nature, and development of the Cromwellian Settlement of Ireland. Chapters III and VI, and the two lengthy Appendices, A and B, are quantitative, in that they treat a body of some two thousand persons and attempt various measurements and generalizations on the basis of statistical evidence. Use of a computer made possible the manipulation of an otherwise forbidding amount of data.

Every attempt has been made to keep the quantitative methodology unobtrusive; in part, because it is frequently more overwhelming than informing, but more importantly, because the subject has been treated thoroughly in Theodore K. Rabb's *Enterprise and Empire* (Harvard University Press, Cambridge, Mass., 1967). Little mention will be found here of the mechanics by which data is computerized, except where a procedural decision would appear to invite controversy.

In this study the computer functioned as little more than an inexhaustible book-keeper. It did nothing that a scholar with a bank-clerk's knowledge of simple arithmetic could not have done in several thousand tedious hours. It answered simple questions about a sizeable body of people, such as 'how many were women?', 'what percentage came from Essex?', or 'how many acres of land did members of the group receive in Leinster?' Thus it made it possible to arrive reasonably quickly at a notion of the characteristics and tendencies of the group as a whole. Such a capacity is of utility wherever one desires to study numbers of subjects rather than individuals.

On the other hand, quantitative history is in some ways inimical, or at best, uncongenial, to the severe, individualistic criteria of modern historical scholarship. The historian is a trained guardian of the discrete datum. If one of his colleagues says 'here is a group of ten people from London', he will be quick to point out that three were actually born in the country and only moved later in life to London; that three were born in London but moved later to the country; and that the remaining four lived half the year in London and the remainder elsewhere. His criticisms dissolve the group as a conceptual entity, and nothing more can be said about it collectively. But without the licence to merge the individual into the group by the process of categorization it is impossible to address a host of important historical problems, not least among which are land and property settlements. To answer the question 'who owned what?', it is usually necessary to count; and once counting begins, some of the individuality of the subjects is inevitably sacrificed.

Every quantitative historian must ask the indulgence of critics who will quite easily detect the inadequacies of the quantitative method with regard to specific individuals and cases. He must ask them to consider whether the inaccuracies they discover are abundant and basic enough to overturn the conclusions to which the quantitative study leads. This is not to say that the quantitative historian is indifferent to error, but rather that he has had to accept a certain amount of it as unavoidable, in order to go about what he believes and hopes to be useful work.

It remains to thank those who assisted most directly in the effort. The Research Foundation of the State University of New York provided the Fellowships that released the author's time, and through a grant-in-aid also financed the computer costs. The Stony Brook Computer Centre provided the skills and equipment necessary to carry out the desired operations. My colleagues in the Department of History were always a source of stimulation, and I am particularly indebted to Bernard Semmel, from whose wide knowledge and warm encouragement I so often benefited. Sonia Sbarge was a valued research assistant. Jacqueline Willis Liebl typed the manuscript with care, and Mark Kishlansky and Francis Rivelin Pratt offered generous and thoughtful editorial assistance. C. P. Bateman executed the map.

A number of scholars, English, Irish, and American, have contributed to the work, albeit sometimes unwittingly. Theodore Rabb, J. W. Stoye, Valerie Pearl, H. R. Trevor-Roper, William O'Sullivan, L. P. Curtis, Jr., and David Underdown have given me the benefit of their advice at various stages of the proceedings. So, in a most helpful sense, has the anonymous advisor of the Clarendon Press. One of my greatest debts is to my friend, Walter Love, whose premature death sadly interrupted a promising line of inquiry into Anglo–Irish historiography. My interest in quantification is only a small part of my legacy from Thomas G. Barnes of the University of California at Berkeley, the supervisor of my doctoral studies and the friend, benefactor, and mentor of a decade. Of all my debts, those to my parents and my wife are least adequately expressed by their mention here.

CONTENTS

List of Tables   xi

Abbreviations and Notes   xiii

I. THE EVOLUTION OF 'PLANTATION' IN IRISH HISTORY   1

II. ORIGINS OF THE ADVENTURE FOR IRISH LANDS   30

III. A PROFILE OF INVESTORS AND INVESTMENT   54

IV. PARLIAMENT'S IRISH POLICY, 1642–9   76

V. THE ENACTMENT AND IMPLEMENTATION OF THE CROMWELLIAN SETTLEMENT   115

VI. THE ANATOMY OF THE ADVENTURERS' SETTLEMENT   145

CODES FOR APPENDICES A AND B   164
(*a*) Christian Names
(*b*) Place Names
(*c*) Professions
(*d*) Miscellaneous

Appendix A. COMPOSITE LIST OF INVESTORS IN IRISH LAND   170
Introduction
List

Appendix B. ADVENTURERS WHO DREW IRISH LAND   196
Introduction
List

Appendix C. MAP: DISTRIBUTION OF LAND
    CONFISCATED IN THE CROMWELLIAN
    SETTLEMENT   214

Select Bibliography   216

Index   223

LIST OF TABLES

1. Comparison of Names on Three Adventurer Lists   60

2. Allocation of Adventurers' Debt by the Act of 1653   144

3. Returns of the Gross Survey for the Ten Counties   145

4. Returns in Irish Acres of the Gross and Down Surveys for the Adventurers' Baronies of the Ten Counties   148

5. Debts Assigned and Acres Encumbered in the Ten Counties by 26 October 1658   150

6. Deficiencies and Surpluses of Land in the Ten Counties   151

ABBREVIATIONS AND NOTES

Add. MS.	Additional Manuscript, British Museum
BM	British Museum
CJ	*Journals of the House of Commons* [England]
CSPD	*Calendar of State Papers, Domestic*
CSPI	*Calendar of State Papers, Irish*
DNB	*Dictionary of National Biography*
EcHR	*Economic History Review*
EHR	*English Historical Review*
EUQ	*Emory University Quarterly* [Atlanta, Georgia]
HMC	Historical Manuscripts Commission
IHS	*Irish Historical Studies*
JBS	*Journal of British Studies*
JCHAS	*Journal of the Cork Historical and Archaeological Society*
LJ	*Journals of the House of Lords* [England]
PRO	Public Record Office, London
TRIA	*Transactions of the Royal Irish Academy* [Dublin]

NOTES

All spelling and capitalization has been modernized.

All fractional sums of money and land have been rounded to the nearest whole pound or acre.

An Irish acre is 7,840 square yards; an English acre is 4,840 square yards.

I

THE EVOLUTION OF 'PLANTATION' IN IRISH HISTORY

INTRODUCTION

'HISTORY is a fable agreed upon' Napoleon once commented, and he might have added that it was usually at the command of the triumphant. There are moments when the debt of 'history' to 'power' is particularly glaring, and the dramatic revision of the role of the Negro in America is an example of the lacunae and distortions which generations of historians are capable of tolerating. In colonial history, too, it is the triumphant whose version of events most often provides the basic contours of received history. Take, for instance, the differing connotations of the word *colonist* in Ireland and in North America. In American history the *colonist* of North America is a brave man who dared to seek his fortune or follow his conscience in a wild and distant land. Above all he is the founder of the states which came into being : Mexico, Canada, and the United States. The colonies succeeded. The stock which planted them soon dominated, making enfeebled minorities of the original Indian inhabitants. In the nationalist history of Ireland, by contrast, a *colonist* is an unwanted stranger; an intruder from an alien culture, a predatory Protestant. In Ireland the Anglo-Protestant colony failed. The natives were not extirpated. Repressed for over two hundred years, they nevertheless succeeded in asserting their identity in the nation which emerged. The descendants and compatriots of the colonists wrote a defensive history of their efforts, an apologia for their failure rather than a paean to their success.[1]

Because the colonization of Ireland 'failed' it received relatively little attention in England, where it was more

[1] The best example, perhaps, is J. A. Froude, *The English in Ireland*, 3 vols., London, 1881.

conveniently forgotten than memorialized. Because in a nationalist perspective it represented the incursion of an alien nation-
ality, it has received equally little attention in Ireland. Addressing
the Cork Historical and Archaeological Society in 1966, Professor
D. B. Quinn felt compelled to point out gently that the Society
has 'not done very much to help forward the study of the history
of the plantation [of Munster] . . .'.[1] And perhaps even in
Ireland's 'new' history, there lingers a feeling that the history of
what failed, of what was successfully resisted and extinguished,
deserves little attention. And yet the contrary is true. Not
because the English colony in Ireland failed, but because it was
of great importance in its own time, the colonization of Ireland
needs to be studied. Quinn placed it in proper perspective when
he wrote that 'From the aspect of comparative colonisation, the
English plantations in Ireland, both in Munster and Ulster, are
amongst the largest population movements of their time.'[2] If
the phenomenon of imperialism is to be treated analytically, it
must be treated wherever it occurred and not exclusively where
it succeeded. The expansion of England in the sixteenth and
seventeenth centuries is too important a theme in Early Modern
History to be subjected to jingoistic preferences; and Ireland,
however unfruitfully, absorbed an immense amount of that
expanding society's energy, attention, and wealth.

This study is concerned with the mechanics of English
expansion into Ireland during the seventeenth century. Both
English and Irish historians have tended to regard that process
as inevitable, a mark, perhaps, of their indifference towards it;
for what is 'inevitable' hardly requires scrutiny. In order to
perceive more clearly how this phase of English expansion
came about it has been necessary to assume that it was not at all
inevitable, that it was not even the result of a distinct colonizing
urge or a general land-hunger, but rather that it was a by-product
of specific political and economic developments within England.
If the concept of inevitability is thus suspended, and English
Protestants are assumed to have been no more and no less
inherently rapacious than other men in other times, there
remains the hypothesis that the colonization of Ireland is compre-

---

[1] 'The Munster Plantation: Problems and Opportunities', *JCHAS*, 1966, p. 19.
[2] Ibid., p. 39.

hensible, and that it occurred because of identifiable forces within English society. What those forces were and how they operated is the general concern of this work. How they produced the Cromwellian Settlement of Ireland is the more specific subject, while the minute operation and effect of the so-called 'Adventure for Irish Land' is the pinnacle upon which this inverted pyramid stands and from which more general ideas were developed.

Between 1640 and 1688 the amount of land held by English and Scottish Protestants in Ireland nearly doubled. Their share of Irish land rose from 41 to 78 per cent, an increment of the order of 7,000,000 English acres.[1] The Catholic share of Ireland declined correspondingly, thus providing an economic and agrarian foundation for a Protestant ascendancy, which was well established by 1719. Although 1641 and 1688 are the most convenient termini for measuring this change, in fact it took place almost entirely in the eight years between 1652 and 1660. Except by main force, little land changed hands before the Cromwellian acts of 1652–3; and the Restoration modified, but in no significant sense reversed, the verdict which had been brought against Catholic Ireland by the recent conquest and settlement.

How did so drastic a land revolution come about? What were its precedents and what were the forces that produced it? Ireland was not, like America, a *terra incognita* suddenly assaulted by Englishmen in the sixteenth and seventeenth centuries. The two societies had common origins in the Celtic migrations of the second and first centuries B.C. But from that point onward there operated what J. C. Beckett has called 'the most significant factor in the political geography of Ireland, the position of Great Britain as a barrier between Ireland and the continent'.[2]

The Romans knew of Ireland and traded there, but they did not invade or leave upon Ireland the imprint of their institutions. Ireland was also spared the invasions of the Anglo-Saxons. Not until the late eighth and ninth centuries were the Gaels seriously disturbed, and then it was by the Danes who founded the first

---

[1] J. G. Simms, *The Williamite Confiscations in Ireland, 1690–1703*, London, 1956, p. 195.

[2] J. C. Beckett, *A Short History of Ireland*, New York, 1968, p. 9.

cities of Ireland (Cork, Dublin, Wexford, Waterford, and Limerick), before being checked in their progress at the battle of Clontarf in 1014. Their Christianized and gallicized brethren, the Normans, first moved upon Ireland in 1170 under the aegis of Henry II, sponsor of the claims of Richard de Clare ('Strongbow'), Second Earl of Pembroke.

Exploiting the historic divisions among the Irish kings Henry II added the Lordship of Ireland to his polyglot holdings, and in the treaty of Windsor of 1175, formalized a dual government in which he and his successors were to rule over one part of Ireland (The kingdoms of Leinster and Meath, and the Norse cities and kingdoms of Dublin, Wexford, and Waterford) while the Gaelic *árd rí* (or High King) was to preserve certain prerogatives over the remainder of the island to the extent that they were enforceable. The almost continual absence of the Norman kings, together with the historic feebleness of central administrative organs in Ireland, conduced to endemic baronial warfare. Skilled warriors, possessing the sympathy and support of their king, the Norman settlers slowly expanded their holdings until, by the early fourteenth century, they controlled nearly two-thirds of the land of Ireland.[1] Anglo-Norman law and institutions proliferated in the Norman precincts. Counties, sheriffs, knights of the shire, and parliaments, all made their appearance. But the accretive Anglo-Normanization of Ireland came to a halt in the fourteenth century. The occasion was the invasion of Ireland in 1315 by the Scot, Edward Bruce, and the warfare of Gaels and Scots against Normans which it inspired. But the underlying cause was the small number of Anglo-Normans who had migrated to Ireland. The Normans were too few. Moreover, whereas in England they had extirpated and supplanted the Anglo-Saxon aristocracy, in Ireland the native aristocracy had been left in existence to dwell in sporadic enmity with the invaders. In the fourteenth century that aristocracy provided the leadership for a native population which far outnumbered the Normans, and which Hibernicized them in peacetime as it overwhelmed them in war.

The Norman policy of conquest that had only been carried out in a piecemeal fashion was gradually replaced by the policy

[1] J. C. Beckett, *A Short History of Ireland*, p. 22.

of colonization: the conscious maintenance and nourishment of a compact, Norman-settled, area in the midst of a hostile native population. This was the English Pale, a fluctuating area of Norman settlement surrounding Dublin, the centre of Anglo-Norman government; and under the pressure of Gaelic incursions it shrank in the fourteenth and fifteenth centuries to little more than a foothold upon the island, the shrivelled beach-head of a once ambitious conquest.[1]

The late Middle Ages saw a necessary narrowing of English ambitions in Ireland, as English military energies were diverted into the wars in France and the struggles between York and Lancaster. Claims to the lordship of Ireland were passed from monarch to monarch, but without any major attempt to rule beyond the Pale. By the reign of Henry VII it was sufficient if Ireland could be prevented from harbouring and supporting the rival claimants to the Tudor throne. Even the notorious legislation of Henry's deputy, Sir Edward Poynings, was intended less to extend the area of English power in Ireland than to prevent future lapses from loyalty in the Yorkist-leaning Pale. About 1534 Henry VIII abandoned this passive policy and resurrected the objective of thorough subjugation. He was moved by the fear that England's expanding Continental rivals, France and Spain, would seek to entrench themselves in Ireland; and this fear was reinforced by the progress of the Henrician Reformation in the English Church and its failure in Ireland. In a sense, the 'Expansion of Europe' and the developing 'European State System' gave to Ireland an importance in the eyes of English rulers that it had not previously had, and that it was to retain at least up to the conclusion of the Second World War. As the religious animosities of the post-Reformation era developed, an unconquered Ireland was increasingly feared as a spear-head of the Counter-Reformation.

[1] By 1641 the Old English (as the Anglo-Normans and, indeed, all Catholics not of Gaelic descent came to be called) held an estimated third of Ireland's profitable land, approximately 2·3 out of 6·4 million Irish acres. This was half the total land held by Catholics in that year. The Gaels' share of Ireland in 1641 was thus about what it had been in 1315, one third, the acquisitions of Celtic families like the O'Briens and the O'Sullivans in the late sixteenth century having been balanced by the losses of the Ulster chieftains in the early seventeenth. See Aidan Clarke, *The Old English in Ireland, 1625–1642*, London, 1966, p. 236, and J. G. Simms, op. cit.

But it was no longer simply the Gaels who resisted the extension of English authority, for they were joined by great Anglo-Norman families, the Butlers, Fitzgeralds, Burkes, and others, jealous of the privileges they came to enjoy under English monarchs whose indifference to Ireland allowed their subjects there a considerable measure of autonomy.

By 1540 Henry VIII had broken the power of the Geraldine League, an awkward alliance of native Irish and Old English. Thereafter he applied the policy of Surrender and Regrant, an attempt to make every Gaelic and Old English lord acknowledge a feudal relationship to the English king. The policy was applied indiscriminately to native Gaels and Anglo-Normans, and had, therefore, the fusionist objective of creating an integrated feudal aristocracy. But it failed, as previous 'native' policy had, because it attributed to Gaelic lords rights over their lands which, in Irish custom, they did not have. Their followers and clansmen, instead of supporting their lords' allegiance to the English king, turned against them as betrayers of traditional and tribal responsibilities.

Henry's policies were continued, for the most part, under Edward VI—but their failure was visible in the growing cost of government. In 1542 the Dublin government required £4,000 more than the £3,000 it was able to raise in Ireland. Between 1547 and 1553 the differential averaged £25,000 p.a., and in 1553 was actually closer to £50,000.[1] The outlook was either one of protracted heavy expenditure, abandonment of Ireland, or the discovery of some better way of maintaining order. The Plantation movement, which provides the immediate background to the theme of this book, was a conscious attempt at a better way. All previous Anglo-Norman expedients had accepted the suitability of the natives as permanent inhabitants. There had been no serious attempt to liquidate them, or even to deprive them as a race, like the Anglo-Saxons in England, of wealth and power. That such harsh and ambitious measures should have recommended themselves to Queen Elizabeth was the result of changing circumstance. Gaelic and Anglo-Saxon law had never harmonized in Ireland, but before the sixteenth century there had been little necessity for them to do so. It was the

[1] Dean G. White, 'The Reign of Edward VI in Ireland', *IHS*, 1965, p. 208.

failure of Henry's policy of Surrender and Regrant that exposed as a fallacy the supposition that the Gaels could be brought into compliance with the law of England. In the second place, the Old English (historically the pillars of English rule) had revealed the extent to which their interests could diverge from those of the government, and their preference for Rome in matters ecclesiastical undermined the trust which a Protestant state could place in them. If the Gaelic lords could not be brought into a feudal relationship with the monarchy and the Old English lords could not be trusted to force them into subjection; if the fear of some Continental Catholic power in Ireland made vital the maintenance of order there, then some scheme for introducing a new and more tractable population was capable of recommending itself.

THE PLANTATION OF LEIX AND OFFALY

The first attempt to implement a scheme based on the idea of an implanted population was made in the reign of Queen Mary. The districts of Leix and Offaly, which lay on the western borders of the Pale, had long been the seat of two marauding clans, the O'Mores and the O'Connors. Repeated attempts to garrison them had failed. As early as the 1530s Sir Anthony St. Leger, later Lord Deputy of Ireland, had suggested to Thomas Cromwell that 'unless . . . [Leix and Offaly] be peopled with others than be there already, and also certain fortresses there builded and warded, if it be gotten the one day it is lost the next'.[1] A new concept had appeared : the idea that a submissive population was essential to successful rule; and its corollary, that if such a population did not exist, it was necessary to import it. This was the axiom of the Plantation movement and the basis of the elaborate plan of 1556 for the confiscation and plantation of all land in the two districts. According to the plan a small class of native owners was to be settled in the western third of the area—at the greatest remove from County Kildare and the Pale. Its members were to hold in free socage at a quit rent of 2*d*. per acre p.a. to the Crown. The remaining two-thirds of the land was to be distributed to English subjects, who were also to hold in free socage at 2*d*. per acre, but were required to maintain for

---

[1] Robert Dunlop, 'The Plantation of Leix and Offaly', *EHR*, 1891, p. 61.

every ploughland 'one man at the least of English birth, a native and he to be an archer'. No Irishman was to hold more than two ploughlands (240 acres), and no Englishman more than three ploughlands (360 acres). Non-residence for English planters was to result in forfeiture. The recipe, then, was for a 'mixed' plantation, the Irish within it being reduced to a minority, holding a minor share of the land, and this formula, it was suggested, could be applied to all additional lands in Ireland taken from 'rebels, traitors, and enemies'.[1] An act of the Irish Parliament of Philip and Mary erected the two districts as the shire ground of Queen's and King's Counties.[2]

The definition of 'English subjects' was interestingly vague. For the purposes of settling Leix and Offaly, English subjects were 'as well such as be born in England as Ireland, having respect to men of honesty and good service, and such as have most need and be likeliest to do good thereon'.[3] Neither place of birth nor Protestant faith made an Englishman, but rather a certain well-affectedness combined with freedom from Gaelic blood. Catholics born in England as well as Old English in Ireland might both be included in this spacious category.

Progress was made slowly. Some settlers, both English and Irish were planted in 1563 and 1564. But the O'Connors and O'Mores dug in their heels and effectively impeded the plantation. New, more hibernophobic terms of plantation were imposed in 1563, and included demands, common in medieval legislation, for adherence to English language, manners, and dress, as well as prohibitions against marriage to rebellious Irish.[4]

The plantation suffered from two basic problems: the first was the need to keep in subjection, or expel from the counties, the native O'Connors and O'Mores. Time and again they rebelled. Time and again they were repressed. The second problem was finding suitable 'English' planters to take over two-thirds of the land and then ensuring that they fulfilled their various burdensome obligations. How the plantation fared at any particular moment is almost impossible to determine. The

[1] BM Cotton MS. Titus B XI, 413–17. Queen Mary to the Earl of Sussex, Lord Deputy of Ireland, cited in Dunlop, 'The Plantation of Leix and Offaly'.
[2] III and IV, cap. 8, cited in Dunlop, 'The Plantation of Leix and Offaly', p. 69.
[3] BM Cotton MS. Titus B XI, 413–17.
[4] Dunlop, 'The Plantation of Leix and Offaly', p. 72.

more violent of the rebellions produced numerous abandon-ments and hasty transfers of holdings. Yet a commission in 1622 found the English Plantation well rooted and for the most part consisting of resident owners.[1] What distinguished the planta-tion of Leix and Offaly was not its success, but the fact that it was, in the words of W. F. T. Butler, the first case of 'confiscation accompanied by the dispossession of the occupants of the land' since the Norman Conquest.[2]

THE MUNSTER PLANTATION

The most important of the Tudor plantations was that in Munster.[3] As early as 1551 Sir James Croft had proposed to Edward VI the establishment of an English colony at Baltimore in west Cork, more or less on the model of the enclave in France at Calais.[4] The late 1560s witnessed an unprecedented migration of West-Country Englishmen to Southern Ireland, the illus-trious Walter Raleigh, Humphrey Gilbert, and Richard Gren-ville among them. Military prowess had every hope of winning immense wealth, either through service to the great Irish chief-tains, or to the English government in suppressing whichever of them was deemed rebellious at any given moment. We do not know precisely how numerous or successful these knights errant were, but one of them, alone, succeeded in shaking the foundations of Irish property.

Sir Peter Carew of Devonshire, a minor courtier of ancient family, put forward a claim to most of county Carlow and half of the former 'Kingdom of Cork' (the greater part of Cork, Kerry, and portions of Waterford). He was aspiring to an estate of one to 2,000,000 English acres, between 5 and 10 per

---

[1] A list of proprietors anno 1622 is in an appendix to Dunlop's article. It lists only a few dozen planters in each county and shows their holdings to have totalled 22,690 acres, a minuscule fraction of counties which later surveys showed to contain nearly 1,000,000 English acres.

[2] *Confiscation in Irish History*, 2nd edn., London, 1918, p. 12. A Ph.D. thesis on the early Tudor plantations was completed in 1967 by Dean G. White, under the supervision of T. W. Moody of Trinity College, Dublin, and is a mine of information regarding Leix and Offaly.

[3] Recent work on the Munster Plantation has been done by D. B. Quinn of the University of Liverpool, and several of his students. An introduction to it is Quinn, 'The Munster Plantation: Problems and Opportunities'.

[4] Richard Bagwell, *Ireland under the Tudors*, London, 1885, i. 360.

cent of all the land of Ireland, all on the strength of what one historian calls 'a curious bit of antiquarian buccaneering', which linked him with a family of Irish Carews who had probably expired in the fourteenth century.[1] Carew's claims were taken seriously by the governing Council in Ireland and his title to parts of his claim was affirmed, over the protests of Irish chieftains that their ancestors had been seised of the property before the Norman Conquest and ever since. Carew's success was a dramatic demonstration of the way in which the application of English feudal law could devastate the customary system of property in Ireland. There is little direct evidence to explain the waves of disorder that occurred in Ireland during the sixteenth and seventeenth centuries, but the insecurity of land titles was among the underlying causes of the predominantly Old English Desmond rebellions which ravaged Ireland, and particularly Munster, between 1569 and 1583.

If West-Country Englishmen by their incursions into Munster contributed to the Desmond rebellion, its aftermath was their reward. The rebels, the Munster Fitzgeralds and their retainers, were convicted of treason, and 574,645 acres of their former lands in Cork, Waterford, Limerick, Kerry, and Tipperary were placed at the disposal of the Crown.[2] The Desmond wars, and the religious element which had inflamed them, undoubtedly hardened English opinion toward Ireland. In 1581—midway between the outbreak of the second Desmond rebellion in 1579 and its suppression in 1583—Sir John Perrot, former Lord-President of Munster and future Lord Deputy, called for an end to conciliatory methods of dealing with rebellion in his 'Discourse touching the Reformation of Ireland'.[3] D. B. Quinn has compared its harsh attitude with the similar one of the Spaniards towards the heathens of the New World.[4] The war ended with very little concern for elimination of its causes, but an obsessive zeal to protect against its recurrence. Indeed, one of the war's

[1] Edmund Curtis, *A History of Ireland*, London, 1936, p. 190.
[2] Robert Dunlop, 'The Plantation of Munster, 1584–1589', *EHR*, 1888, p. 250; and M. J. Bonn, *Die Englische Kolonisation in Irland*, Stuttgart, 1906, i. 288.
[3] BM Add. MS. 48017 (formerly Yelverton–Calthorpe MS. XVII, ff. 86–9). Cited by D. B. Quinn, 'Ireland and Sixteenth-Century Expansion', *Historical Studies*, i, ed. by T. Desmond Williams, London, 1958, p. 28 and note 14.
[4] Quinn, 'Ireland and Sixteenth-Century Expansion', p. 27.

principal causes—the settlement of new English in Munster—was envisaged as the principal means of preventing rebellion in the future.

A scheme of Plantation, far more elaborate and systematic than that in Leix and Offaly, was drawn up for the confiscated Desmond lands of Munster. Removal of native Irish and their replacement by English-born Protestants was a cardinal feature of the scheme, in which it was unlike that of Leix, where religious considerations were irrelevant and greater emphasis was put upon the qualities of individual planters than upon their origins. A plan for the peopling of Munster drawn up in December 1585 described with geometric precision how the Desmond lands were to be divided up into seignories of twelve, ten, eight, six, and four thousand acres, each full seignory to be planted with 86 families, 42 of them copyholders (at 100 acres each), 6 freeholders (at 300 acres each), 6 farmers (at 400 acres each), and 36 families as tenants on 1500 acres of demesne.[1] 4,200 colonists were hoped for in the first year of settlement, and 21,000 after seven years. The intended function of the settlers was to Anglicize the province. The articles of Plantation demanded that no settler should convey any property to the 'mere' Irish, or permit them its use or occupation. All the English were to be planted as close together as the geography of the confiscated estates allowed. The head of every planting family was to be born of English parents, and daughters, in order to inherit, had to marry men of like parentage.[2]

The 12,000-acre limit of the seignories is proof that the government wished to avoid the mere substitution of an English baronage for an Irish one. That method had failed since the advent of Strongbow. A colonizing gentry and yeomanry were desired instead, but Ireland had a bad name among those productive classes in England, who well realized how easily

[1] Dunlop, 'The Plantation of Munster', p. 254 and *Ireland from the Earliest Times to the Present Day*, Oxford, 1922, p. 78. It has frequently been pointed out that the tenures offered the New English, copyholds, common socage, etc., were less burdensome than that of knight service offered to or imposed upon the native Irish and Old English under the policy of Surrender and Regrant.

[2] Articles for the Plantation of Munster, 21 June 1586, *CSPI*, 1586–1588, pp. 84–9.

they and their investments could be wiped out by an Irish rising. The government was compelled to beat the bushes for colonists, eventually concentrating its efforts in the south and north-west, where colonizing companies of a sort were formed (one for Somerset and Dorset; another for Lancashire and Cheshire) to promote interest and recruit settlers.[1]

Despite the government's attempts at encouragement and propaganda the Plantation failed to realize its goals. By 1592, nine years after its inception, there were only 32 seignories, 20 of which belonged to absentee owners. The 32 seignories occupied 202,000 acres, an average of about 6,300 acres; but the 12,000-acre limit had necessarily been abandoned. Raleigh acquired at least 42,000 acres by 1598. Richard Boyle, later First Earl of Cork, buying Raleigh's complete holdings in 1602, made them the cornerstone of an immense Munster empire. But as estates accumulated, immigration of English tenants failed to keep pace. By 1598 the English population of the plantation numbered in the hundreds rather than in the thousands. Irish labour was cheap and available. The short-term interest of the magnate was to escape the conditions of plantation and employ native labour. The combination of the scarcity of willing English settlers and the vociferous insistence of many of the Earl of Desmond's clients that they were not, under Irish landholding practices, mere tenants of the attainted rebels but the equivalent of freeholders, caused a drastic reduction in the size of the plantation. The government sought to establish that these followers were strictly dependent tenants without any right to the land they formerly held. The followers claimed to be freeholders who, not having been attainted, had every right to their land. The government proceeded harshly against some; more leniently with others. The size of the plantation shrank by 1592 from the originally envisaged 577,645 acres to a mere 202,099.[2]

The Munster Plantation was virtually swept away by rebellion in October 1598. Contemporaries agreed upon the cause.

---

[1] M. J. Bonn, op. cit., p. 290.
[2] Ibid., p. 299. The most spectacularly successful of the English colonists in Munster, is treated in T. Ranger, 'The Career of Richard Boyle, first Earl of Cork, in Ireland, 1588–1643', Oxford, D.Phil. thesis, 1958.

According to one, the 'worser sort' of planters had found 'such profit from their Irish tenants who give them the fourth sheaf of all their corn and 16d yearly for their beasts' grain, so . . . [the planters] care not though they never plant an Englishman there'.[1] In his *View of the Present State of Ireland*, written in 1596, Edmund Spenser complained that 'instead of keeping out the Irish, the undertakers did not only make the Irish their tenants in these lands, but thrust out the English'.[2] A more judicious lament was that of Sir William Herbert to Lord Burghley in a letter written ten years before the rebellion: 'Our pretence in the enterprise of plantation was to establish in these parts piety, justice, inhabitation and civility, with comfort and good example to the parts adjacent. Our drift now is, being here possessed of land, to extort, make the state of things turbulent, and live by prey and pay.'[3]

It was Spenser who pointed the way to the future in his *Brief Note of Ireland* (1598). The basic problem with the plantation had not—according to him—been with the planters. It had been the failure of England to clear out the human and institutional rubble of one civilization before implanting another. As he put it, metaphorically, 'before new buildings were erected, the old should have been plucked down'. The Irish could not but hate the English who were settling their former lands. For the settlement to survive the Irish had to be rendered powerless. 'How then, should the Irish have been quite rooted out? That were too bloody a course; and yet their continual rebellious deeds deserve little better.' Spenser left his own question unanswered. Instead he recommended a garrison of three or four thousand men to watch over the plantation in the future and protect it from its Irish neighbours.[4] It was for a later generation to answer the question squarely, a generation which experienced in 1641 yet another undoing of English colonization in Ireland, a generation driven by Protestant martyrology down the path Spenser called 'too bloody a course'. The final

---

[1] From Robert Payne, *A Brief Description of Ireland* (1590) cited by George O'Brien, *The Economic History of Ireland in the Seventeenth Century*, Dublin, 1919, p. 27.

[2] Cited ibid.

[3] *CSPI, 1588–1592*, p. 62.

[4] Cited in Constantia Maxwell, ed., *Irish History from Contemporary Sources, 1509–1610*, London, 1923, p. 251.

elaboration of plantation theory, the 'plucking down' of the old edifice, the 'rooting out' of the native inhabitants, was to be the endeavour of the Cromwellian conquest.[1]

SIXTEENTH-CENTURY ULSTER

While Munster was the main theatre of Tudor plantation in Ireland, there were recurrent efforts at settlement in Ulster as well. Here, however, the situation was somewhat different. The province was still almost exclusively inhabited by native Irish, and such intruders as there were came from Scotland and were often regarded as a greater threat than the Irish. Queen Mary's Lord Deputy, the Third Earl of Sussex, had suggested sending 1,000 English settlers into Antrim to expel the Scots and keep the Irish quiet. Elizabeth, viewing the Scots more as Protestant brethren than rivals, acquiesced in their presence.[2] When, in the 1570s, she was persuaded to allow colonization in Ulster, her first concern was that the undertakers should defray all the costs.[3] She was especially drawn to the schemes proposed by Captain Thomas Chatterton and her own Secretary, Sir Thomas Smith. Chatterton contracted with Elizabeth in 1571 to plant several parts of Ulster by 1579. A military expedition was to pacify the country, whereupon the soldiers would, in the words of Robert Dunlop, 'subside into husbandmen and colonists'.[4] Smith's venture dates from the same period. Given a grant of 144,000 acres of profitable land in the Ards district of County Down, 'the nearest part of all Ireland to Lancashire', he too intended to carry out his plantation by means of a military expedition. He envisaged his soldier-planters as latter-day Romans bringing law, peace, and civilization to a savage land.[5] In Munster the colonists were planters first and soldiers only if need arose. In Ulster they were soldiers first and settlers second,

---

[1] Dunlop pointed out that Elizabeth despaired of the Munster Plantation even before its overthrow in 1598. When Hugh Roe MacMahon of County Monaghan was executed as a rebel in 1591, she rejected the obvious opportunity for plantation, and instead had his lands divided among the principal members of his clan (*Ireland from the Earliest Times to the Present Day*, p. 78).

[2] Robert Dunlop, 'Sixteenth-Century Schemes for the Plantation of Ulster', *Scottish Historical Review*, 1925, p. 52.

[3] Ibid., p. 116.   [4] Ibid., p. 117.

[5] D. B. Quinn, 'Sir Thomas Smith and the Beginnings of English Colonial Theory', *Proceedings of the American Philosophical Society*, vol. 89, no. 4 (1945), p. 547.

wherever victorious.[1] Only by intensive use of misleading propaganda did Smith get together an expedition of some seven to eight hundred 'adventurers' by May of 1572.[2] The actual departure of the expedition was delayed and many of the adventurers drifted away. Smith claimed that his colony 'neither sought to expel [n]or destroy the Irish race, but to keep them in quiet, in order, in virtuous labour, and in justice, and to teach them English laws and civility'.[3] When, however, Smith's son was murdered by the Irish in 1573, he realized that 'the facile hopes of exploiting and reforming the Irish were too lightly grounded'.[4] In particular, his plantation had been insufficiently capitalized from the first and—because of the Queen's frugality—almost entirely dependent upon its own resources. He had needed a minimum of £13,000 for the first year,[5] and had hoped to raise most of this from the recruits themselves: £20 from each horseman, £10 from each footman; but most of the men who came had only their bodies to venture.

Yet another military expedition with colonizing ambitions was that of Walter Devereux, First Earl of Essex, who undertook to conquer Ulster in 1573, partly to relieve pressure on Smith's colony in Down. The Queen was to bear half the expense and receive half the dividends. Horsemen who served two years with Essex were to receive 400 acres of conquered Irish land; foot soldiers, half that amount. On those terms 212 horse and 228 foot were recruited, but the expedition was a failure almost from the start and Elizabeth, despairing of the expense, withdrew her support from it in 1575.[6]

Most societies contain both expansive and contractionist elements, usually very nearly in balance. A period of aggressive imperialism is frequently the result of the victory of one over the other. The efforts at plantation in the sixteenth century lacked both the enthusiastic commitment of a planter rank and file, and adequate capitalization from either private or public sources. D. B. Quinn has observed 'a current of anti-Imperialism in Elizabethan England' connected with an essentially correct

---

[1] Both approaches appear in the Cromwellian Settlement: the 'adventurers' are there the planter-militia; the 'soldiers' the embryonic farmers.
[2] Quinn, 'Sir Thomas Smith . . .', p. 547.
[3] Ibid., p. 553.   [4] Ibid., p. 554.   [5] Ibid., p. 555.
[6] Dunlop, '. . . The Plantation of Ulster', pp. 125 and 211.

notion of the immense cost of subjugating and Anglicizing Ireland.[1] Sixteenth-century English government happened upon plantation as a means of keeping Ireland in order, but the costs proved to be higher than the state was willing to bear. It had been hoped that confiscated Irish land could provide the capital out of which a para-military English gentry could be maintained. But, without adequate security for the lives and goods of its inhabitants, the land proved incapable of attracting the English settlers the scheme required. The more it failed of this vital purpose, the more conditions the government imposed upon the planters. The more conditions the planters bore, the more unattractive the plantation became.

The constant tendency of plantations, both in Ulster and Munster, was to run rapidly down hill, with fewer and fewer planters on the land and more and more property in the hands of a few magnates who were more assiduous in evading the proliferating conditions of plantation than in fulfilling them. Quinn saw in the Munster Plantation 'an excellent example of the ideas of a sixteenth-century government out-running its capacity for performance'.[2] Sir John Davies was despairing of the sixteenth-century plantations in Ireland as a whole when he wrote: 'There have been sundry plantations in this kingdom whereof the first plantation of the English Pale was the best and the last plantation of the undertakers in Munster was the worst.'[3]

SEVENTEENTH-CENTURY ULSTER

The wars of Tyrone which devastated Ireland between 1594 and 1603 ended with the surrender of the last great Gaelic Chiefs, the Ulster Earls of Tyrone and Tyrconnell. While their power was strictly curtailed, no attempt was made initially to

[1] D. B. Quinn, ed., ' "A Discourse of Ireland" (*circa* 1599)', *Proceedings of the Royal Irish Academy*, 1942, p. 154.

[2] 'The Planter was told exactly how much he should spend, precisely how many tenants of various categories he should establish, and yet, when it came to the point, he found the greatest difficulty in locating the lands assigned to him, establishing their boundaries, and discovering what rival claims might be in existence to their ownership' ('The Munster Plantation: Problems and Opportunities', p. 24).

[3] In a letter to Salisbury of 5 Aug. 1608, cited in George Hill, *An Historical Account of the Plantation of Ulster, 1608–1620*, Belfast, 1877, p. 69.

confiscate their vast lands—a reminder, perhaps, of the disfavour into which Plantation had briefly fallen as a means of maintaining order in Ireland. In August 1607 the two earls, despairing of their emasculated positions in Ireland, fled the island with nearly a hundred of their followers. Their departure was interpreted by the government as a confession of treason, and the whole area over which the earls had ruled was treated as liable to confiscation. Of the nine counties of Ulster, Monaghan had been settled with loyal members of the MacMahon clan in 1591.[1] Antrim and Down, the two counties geographically most accessible from Scotland had been and continued to be *de facto* areas of gradual Scottish colonization. The six remaining counties of Ulster—Armagh, Cavan, Coleraine (later Londonderry), Donegal, Fermanagh, and Tyrone—were all found to be in the King's hands and open to colonization.

Plans for a plantation flowed from the pens of the Lord Deputy, Sir Arthur Chichester; the elderly Irish Secretary, Sir Geoffrey Fenton; and the Lord Chancellor, Sir Francis Bacon.[2] It is mystifying that so much enthusiasm should have been expressed for a situation essentially similar to that in Munster on the eve of its plantation. Why, for instance, in his most frequently quoted remark on the subject, should Chichester have said he would rather 'labor with his hands in the Plantation of Ulster than dance or play in that of Virginia', given the inglorious history of the previous half-century of Irish plantation?[3] Bacon's tract on the subject took cognizance of the shortcomings of the Munster Plantation and suggested ways of remedying them in Ulster—but not with any sober sense of the difficulties involved.[4] It was easy enough to say that the state should pay for the building of towns, churches, bridges, causeways, and highways, for the greater security and comfort of the settlers—but it was entirely another matter to persuade the state to do so. The Attorney-General for Ireland, Sir John Davies, was more realistic when he warned that, if in a few years 'the number of civil persons to be planted do not exceed the

---

[1] See n. 1, p. 14, above.
[2] Richard Bagwell, *Ireland Under the Stuarts*, London, 1909, i. 66.
[3] *CSPI, 1608–1610*, p. 520.
[4] *Considerations Touching the Plantation of Ireland*, 1 Jan. 1608–9 in James Spedding, ed., *Collected Works of Sir Francis Bacon*, London, 1857, iv. 123–5.

number of the natives', the fate of the Munster Plantation would overtake them.[1]

Chichester put forward a scheme the principal distinction of which was that it called for the plantation of native Irish before the allocation of land to servitors (Scotch and English soldiers who had served in Ireland) and immigrant planters. The abortive rebellion of Cahir O'Doherty in the spring of 1608 may have discouraged the government from implementing the lenient policy of Chichester's plan. According to his modern biographer, James I deliberately rejected Chichester's recommendations, contemplating rather a plantation which favoured first the new planters, secondly the servitors, and finally the native Irish. 'It would, he believed, civilize Ulster quickly, . . . secure the British interest, and . . . provide a welcome means of rewarding importunate suitors without expense to the crown.'[2]

The conditions of Plantation were drawn up by a committee in London and published in January 1609. In Munster an attempt had been made to plant only former Desmond acres lying within the southern counties, but to settle those lands exclusively with English. In Ulster, by contrast, virtually the whole of the six confiscated counties was to be settled, but with a mixture of new settlers, old soldiers, and old Irish. The geographical magnitude of the Ulster Plantation was therefore much greater, as it was capable of disturbing all property relationships in the North —not just those on lands planted with new settlers.[3] To each class of planters in Ulster specific conditions applied. They were most rigorous for the new settlers and most lenient for the Irish. The former could plant only Protestants on their lands and could employ only Protestant tenants. The Irish were under no such strictures, nor were they obliged to build costly defensive buildings as their Protestant counterparts were. Only in the matter of rents were they discriminated against, for they paid nearly double the rent charged to the new planters.[4]

The conceptual innovations of the new plantation in Ulster

---

[1] Cited in Hill, *Plantation of Ulster*, p. 70.

[2] D. H. Willson, *James VI and I*, London, Jonathan Cape, paperback edn., 1963, p. 325.

[3] This may help to explain why rebellion spread with great rapidity in the northern plantation in 1641, but very slowly in the southern one.

[4] T. W. Moody, *The Londonderry Plantation, 1609–1641*, Belfast, 1939, p. 33.

are seen most clearly in the writings of the Irish Attorney-General, Sir John Davies. Challenged by the Irish while implementing the plantation, he attributed to it an almost luminous virtue. Dismissing Irish, or Brehon, law as 'abolished and adjudged no law but a lewd custom', Davies easily demonstrated that the Irish subjects of the rebellious Ulster earls 'had no estates in law' and could 'make no title against his Majesty or his patentees'. But it was in considering whether 'in conscience, or honour' the King might 'remove the ancient tenants and bring in strangers among them' that Davies surpassed himself. The King, he argued, was 'bound in conscience to use all lawful and just courses to reduce his people from barbarism to civility'.

Now civility cannot possibly be planted among them, but by this mixed plantation of civil men, which likewise could not be without removal and transplantation of some of the natives and settling of their possessions in a course of common law : for if themselves were suffered to possess the whole country, as their septs have done for many hundreds of years past, they would never (to the end of the world) build houses, make townships, or villages, or improve the land as it ought to be.[1]

Davies was emphatic in asserting that the Crown intended no *extirpation*, but only the *civilization* of the native Irish. They and their island were to be forcefully improved. But the progress of the plantation, with its increasing cost in land to the Irish, revealed the hypocrisy of such sentiments, as the failure of the plantation to 'civilize' the Irish revealed its futility. The arguments for 'a mixed plantation of British and Irish, that they might grow up together in one nation', would not soon again convince either party.

The most important novelty of the Ulster Plantation was its association with the City of London, dating from May 1609. Previous Irish plantations had drawn both their personnel and financing primarily from the provincial and agricultural sector of English society. Several scholars have detected elsewhere the tendency of sixteenth- and seventeenth-century colonizing schemes to attract their financial support from rural and gentry groups, as distinct from mercantile and trading ventures, which

---

[1] Cited in *Irish History from Contemporary Sources*, p. 277.

tended to attract urban and merchant capital.[1] It is an attractive thesis, suggesting as it does an organic and traditional element in embryonic capitalism. Money made from trade is seen being reinvested in trade, while capital drawn from the soil is observed being reinvested in agrarian schemes, whether domestic (estate management) or foreign (colonization). But if this tendency should prove the rule, the seventeenth-century plantation of Ulster must stand as an exception. The opportunities for trade in northern Ireland were minimal, and the investing companies of the City were soon to find themselves immersed in the minutiae of agriculture—an unaccustomed calling. How did it happen that urban capital, accumulated by grocers, tailors, haberdashers, and their fellows in trade, was channelled into the establishment of a remote and agrarian plantation?

It is arguable—and the City long argued—that it was *induced*, or even coerced, by the King to play a role in Ulster. Professor Moody called attention to the fact that the City had lent large sums of money to the Crown for the repression of Tyrone's rebellion, and concluded that 'In the history of the City's Relationship with the Crown, there was ample precedent for the action of James . . . in seeking support for . . . the Plantation in Ulster.'[2] If, indeed, the City's involvement in Ulster was a consequence of its loans to Elizabeth, it presents an almost classic case of imperial receivership: the money-lender finding himself increasingly managing the affairs of his debtor and being drawn into affairs in which he had formerly neither expertise nor interest. In any event, it would be surprising to find much genuine enthusiasm in the City for a project so distant, so unaccustomed, and so obviously fraught with financial perils.[3]

Whatever its impulses, the City took over one of the six escheated counties, Coleraine, soon to be called Londonderry. The Crown sought to unload upon the City those expensive obligations for civil and military construction which Bacon had suggested should be taken over by the state. The City, for its part, wished to minimize its expenditure in Ulster and maxi-

---

[1] For intimations of such a thesis see T. K. Rabb, *Enterprise and Empire*, Cambridge, Mass., 1967, and an unpublished Oxford D.Phil. thesis: R. G. Lang, 'The Greater Merchants of London in the Early Seventeenth Century', 1963.

[2] Moody, op. cit., p. 62.   [3] Ibid., p. 72.

mize its profits. The most influential piece of promotional literature for the plantation, *Motives and Reasons to Induce the City of London to Undertake Plantation in the North of Ireland*, probably written by Sir Thomas Philips, and appearing in July 1609, also placed great emphasis, as had promotional literature for earlier plantations, upon the overcrowding in England and particularly London. The precedent of the involvement of Bristol in the re-peopling of Dublin in the reign of Henry II was also adduced.[1] The outcome of negotiations between the City and the Crown over Coleraine was the completion of articles of agreement signed on 28 January 1610. They were explicit as to what the City was to have of the Crown, but vague as to what the Crown was to have of the City. Moody commented of their bargain: 'If the Crown had inveigled the City into Ulster for its own purposes, the City had made the most of its unsought compact with the Crown.'[2] The City gained 'extensive privileges including the patronage of all churches within their territory, the fisheries of the Foyle and the Bann, and a long lease of the customs at a nominal rent'.[3] In return the City was obliged to expend no less than £20,000, to plant with English and Scots settlers some 400,000 acres of Coleraine, and to fortify the two main towns, Derry and Coleraine. The financial burden was distributed among the City's major companies, the companies determining for themselves how to raise the necessary funds from their memberships.[4]

The affairs of the Plantation were to be directed by a governor, a deputy governor, and twenty-four assistants, responsible as a

---

[1] Reprinted in Hill, *Plantation of Ulster*, p. 362.
[2] Moody, op. cit., p. 77.
[3] J. C. Beckett, *The Making of Modern Ireland, 1603–1923*, London, 1966, p. 46.
[4] By 13 Dec. 1610 the following twelve London companies had made major contributions to the Plantation in the amounts shown:

	£			£
Merchant-Tailors	3,885	Fishmongers	. .	2,260
Grocers	3,873	Clothworkers	. .	2,260
Haberdashers	3,124	Skinners	. .	1,963
Goldsmiths	2,999	Salters	. .	1,954
Mercers	2,680	Vintners	. .	2,080
Drapers	3,072	Ironmongers	. .	1,514

Smaller companies also had made less significant contributions (Hill, *Plantation of Ulster*, p. 433).

management to the Common Council of London. This constitution was similar to that of the East India Company drawn up in 1600, but differed in making the managers responsible to London's Common Council rather than to the individual City companies which were the true stockholders.[1] T. W. Moody has argued that the Irish Society, as the Governor and his twenty-four Assistants were called, also differed from other contemporary colonizing companies, like the Virginia, Somers Island, and Massachusetts Bay and Providence Companies, in that the latter, 'while encouraged by the Crown, were promoted by private individuals for motives of profit, and the capital was voluntarily subscribed. The former was initiated by the Crown as a means of carrying out part of its programme for the Anglicization of Ulster and was foisted on the City as the most capable body for that purpose.'[2] But the City *did* attempt to make the best of its plight, and it is probable that there were hidden coercive forces at work in other colonial ventures as well.

In a sense, the state learned from the failure of the sixteenth-century Irish plantations. It became more aware of the need for capital in colonization and the difficulty of obtaining it from private sources, at least for the uses of Ireland. At the same time it declined to underwrite the capital costs of plantation itself, and turned instead to the much plumbed coffers of London. The tragedy of the Londonderry venture was that the City was no more willing than the Crown to make extensive long-term investments in Ulster. When the costs of plantation multiplied beyond what the City companies had been led to expect, their instinct was one of retreat from the venture altogether. It was 'not a work for men who seek a present profit', according to Lord Deputy Chichester.[3]

The clash of interests between Crown and City over Ulster culminated in the Star Chamber proceedings of 1633–5, at the end of which the City was sentenced to a fine of £70,000 (much of it never levied) and the loss of the Ulster Charter. The Crown tried to demonstrate that the City had made £98,000 in profits from the Plantation, and had failed to plant the county with

---

[1] Moody, op. cit., p. 81.   [2] Ibid., p. 96.

[3] In a letter of 31 Oct. 1610 to the Earl of Nottingham. Cited in Hill, *The Plantation of Ulster*, p. 445.

Protestants. The City asserted that it had never desired the Ulster concession in the first place, that it had managed—under the most burdensome conditions—to plant 2,000 arms-bearing Protestants, and that it had expended more than seven times the originally envisaged £20,000.[1] The Irish Society may be seen either as a predatory, proto-capitalist, institution, which drained Ulster of its wealth at the expense of the Crown as well as of the displaced native Irish; or as the innocent victim of Stuart fiscal tyranny.[2] More relevant to the history of colonialism than the innocence or guilt of the Irish Society is the mere involvement of London, Londoners, and London money.

We know less, to date, about the progress of the plantation in the five counties outside Coleraine where matters were less in dispute. The survey of Captain Pynnar carried out in late 1618 and 1619 showed a total of 6,215 'British Armed' men to have been planted: 642 in Armagh, 642 in Londonderry, 645 in Fermanagh, 711 in Cavan, 1,106 in Donegal, and 2,469 in Tyrone.[3] Perhaps the most spectacular but least well recorded progress was made in Antrim and Down, two Ulster counties outside the Plantation, where the Scots under the leadership of Hugh Montgomery of Braidstane and James Hamilton were energetically colonizing.[4] The character of modern Ulster may be due more to their efforts than to any of those in London. If we ask how the Scots capitalized *their* settlement of two counties, when scores of thousands of pounds from London did not suffice for the settlement of one, a possible answer would be that a supply of eager colonists from Scotland substantially reduced the amount of capital needed. In Londonderry, capital was needed to attract settlers, to assure them of their security and their ability to improve their fortunes. Many of those settled by the Londoners were Scots, but apparently they streamed in greater numbers to Antrim and Down, where there already existed a transplanted Scottish culture and society. Such

[1] Moody, op. cit., p. 365.

[2] The latter view is found in Moody, the former in, E. G., Constantia Maxwell, 'The Colonization of Ulster', *History*, 1916.

[3] Printed in Hill, *Plantation of Ulster*, p. 288. Donegal and Tyrone are the largest, if not the most fertile, counties in Ulster. Armagh is the smallest. Londonderry and Cavan are middle-sized.

[4] Beckett, *Making of Modern Ireland*, p. 47.

colonial phenomena are perhaps more susceptible of sociological than economic explanation.

MISCELLANEOUS PLANTATIONS, 1615–41

Under both James I and Charles I the state attempted to use plantation as a means of 'recovering' for the Crown revenues it was supposed at one time to have enjoyed. This had always been a secondary feature of Tudor plantation, but as the Stuarts experienced increasing fiscal pressure at home they transmitted it to Ireland. And if the Crown could not find a sufficient number of Protestants to plant on recovered lands, or if rebellion was not a continuous enough process to throw the needed amount of land into the Crown's hands, then the government, like the City, would simply have to accept Irish-Catholic tenants. After 1615 a rash of minor plantations were instituted up and down Ireland: in Longford (Leinster), Leitrim (Connaught), Wexford and parts of Kings County. In north Wexford, for instance, 22,000 acres of land was 'discovered' in 1610 to be held under defective title and therefore available for plantation. Litigation ensued as the native owners attempted to protect their claims. In March 1615, acting on orders from London, Lord Deputy Chichester imprisoned the leaders of the opposition and distributed 23,300 acres to 18 new undertakers, all English and all Protestants.[1] One hundred and fifty of the old chief inhabitants received estates now valid at law, but 200–500 smaller holders were deprived of their lands entirely. The Old English proprietors were treated more leniently than the Celts, but these new confiscations in peace time 'struck at the root of Tudor policy, which had in the main recognized the occupier as the equitable owner of lands; they upset or at least rendered insecure all grants by Elizabeth or even by James in early years based on surrender by the occupier.'[2]

A similar plantation was carried out in Longford. Again small landowners were swept away and again confiscation was limited to a portion of the county, in this case the lands of the O'Ferralls.[3] In Kings county the policy was applied to the territory of Ely O'Carroll, and in Leitrim more generally throughout the

[1] Butler, *Confiscation in Irish History*, pp. 63–7.
[2] Ibid., p. 75.　　　[3] Ibid., p. 82.

county. Rarely did these plantations succeed either in substantially improving the revenue of the Crown or in establishing a strong Protestant population.[1] In retrospect they seem to have contributed principally to the insecurity and disillusionment which nurtured the rebellion of 1641.

The last of the pre-Cromwellian plantations was that of Connaught, closely identified with the career of Strafford. It was the only province in which recent English settlement had not taken place, and beginning in 1624 rumours of its imminent plantation circulated. The principal obstacle was the historic loyalty of the province under its Irish O'Brien, Earl of Thomond, and Old English de Burgh, Earl of Clanricarde. Throughout the uprising of Tyrone (1598–1607), and at the battle of Kinsale (1604), the men of Connaught had fought on the side of the English. Now, with the power of Ulster presumed to be broken, the loyalty of Connaught was less crucial and its discontent more easily afforded.

The Plantation of Munster had been erected principally upon the former lands of the Fitzgeralds, an Old English rather than Celtic family. Indeed the Crown has been served nobly by many Celtic families, such as the O'Briens of Thomond. But the seventeenth-century plantations, beginning with that in Ulster, devoured almost exclusively Celtic lands, often to the profit of Old English.[2] In Connaught, by contrast, the Old English de Burghs were threatened along with the Gaelic O'Briens by the contemplated plantation, particularly in Clanricarde's county of Galway. Until 1634 the scheme languished, but in that year it was taken up by the new Lord Deputy, Sir Thomas Wentworth, later Earl of Strafford and Lord Lieutenant. The advocates of the Connaught Plantation, mostly New English, had been willing to spare Galway, the county in which the greater part of Clanricarde's estates lay. Thus they hoped to reduce the opposition of the Old English to the scheme.

Wentworth made the crucial decision to include Galway in the Plantation.[3] After a long struggle with Clanricarde, and

---

[1] Beckett, *The Making of Modern Ireland*, p. 55.

[2] The Old English Earl of Westmeath, e.g., received one of the largest grants in the Plantation of Longford (Hugh F. Kearney, *Strafford in Ireland*, Manchester, 1959, p. 87. I am in debt to this work for my treatment of the Connaught Plantation).   [3] *Ibid.*, p. 90.

the Galway jury impanelled for the purpose, the King's title to Galway was acknowledged in 1637, and title to other portions of Connaught was obtained with little difficulty. The Old English for the first time began to feel the weight of the policy of confiscation for defective title. Previously only open rebellion had exposed them to such harsh treatment. It was the implications of the plantation rather than its actuality which was unsettling, for Ireland was swept by rebellion before any extensive colonization could take place. Even before Strafford's trial it was evident that the plantation was proceeding slowly. Settlers were scarce, as they had been in the previous plantations, and even scarcer owing to Strafford's refusal to plant Scots and his forbidding Anglicanism. As Kearney comments: 'A puritan fleeing from what he considered the tyranny of Laud in the province of Canterbury would be unlikely to emigrate to Connaught to endure the more efficient control of Wentworth.'[1] Galway and Mayo were almost untouched by 1640. Some English plantation was perceivable in Sligo and Roscommon, but principally

The significance of the plantation of Connacht lay in the fear which it created. It formed part of the same story as the court of wards and the commission of defective titles in the way in which it threatened to cause large-scale changes in the ownership of land. For the first time, old English proprietors and those Gaelic Irish who had come to terms with the English government during Elizabeth's reign were faced with the threat of Plantation.[2]

CONCLUSION

The practice and nature of Plantation in Ireland underwent important changes between its initiation in Leix and its application in Connaught. In a sense, it had come full circle. In the beginning it had been a specific response to rebellion. Confiscation had been limited to the estates of those found in rebellion, the principal object of plantation being the settlement of a more loyal population. With the Munster Plantation 'Protestant'

[1] Kearney, Strafford in Ireland, p. 101.
[2] Ibid., p. 102. For a controversy over some of the other consequences of Strafford's policies, particularly as they affected the New English, see T. Ranger, 'Strafford in Ireland: A Revaluation', Past and Present, 1961, pp. 26–45; and J. P. Cooper, 'Wentworth and the Byrnes' County', IHS, 1966, pp. 1–20.

and 'English' came to be equated with 'loyal' and the infusion of New English into Ireland dates mainly from that settlement. After the wars of Tyrone, a much more ambitious policy was applied to Ulster. The principle of confiscation was expanded so as to apply not merely to the lands of the chief rebels, but to all the land of the six counties over which they had held sway. Accordingly, some adjustment was made to allow the resettling of thousands of Irish who would otherwise have been left landless; they were relegated instead to an inferior status. The lesser plantations of James and Charles I abandoned such grand ambitions and returned to the piecemeal confiscations of the earlier period. For the first time, however, they abandoned rebellion as the sole justification for confiscation and plantation. In effect the policy of Plantation adapted itself to the absence of rebellions between 1607 and 1641 by evolving new justifications for confiscation. Had revolution and rebellion not overtaken England and Ireland respectively, further plantations on the Connaught model would have been likely.[1]

Although the respective plantations since the mid sixteenth century had differing effects upon their particular localities, the Plantation phenomenon had certain common consequences. It established in Ireland a new element in the population distinguished from the old by its novelty, its Protestantism, and its Englishness. Its very presence introduced yet another, religious excuse for confiscation of Irish land. This is not to suggest that the New English were purposely placed in Ireland as bait to a trap, but that they sometimes inadvertently and sometimes consciously performed such a function. The rebellion of 1641 was the first in which crimes against Protestants as such received any great publicity, and the moral energy of the Cromwellian conquest derived less from the act of rebellion (which after all was directed against the same monarch as the English rebellion) than from a desire to revenge Protestant sufferings. Thus the new colonial class, though not great in numbers, provided what was in effect the thin edge of a wedge. They were a potential *cause célèbre* and an active political lobby for further expansion of English interests in Ireland.

[1] In fact, the area of South Leinster was already under consideration (Kearney, *Strafford in Ireland*, p. 99).

The Plantation movement accomplished pacification in only a most superficial sense. Rebels were more often moved from their land than destroyed, and frequently became tenants of New English proprietors. The dispossessed and their descendants naturally nourished hopes of reconquest. Those who did not lose lands during the plantations feared that they might, in some subsequent Protestant expansion. Gaels and Old English alike were shown by Strafford that their claims to land could be successfully challenged by the government, even in times of peaceful obedience to law.

Chronic insecurity among Gaelic and Norman Irish was compounded by the rise to power in 1640 of an English Parliament which regarded Strafford as a virtual papist and successfully sought his head. A Plantation policy which might previously have been seen by Catholic Irish as cruel but inadvertent suddenly became comprehensible only as a conscious Protestant plot. The New English seemed a fifth column awaiting the bidding of a puritanical English parliament, to complete the confiscation of Catholic Ireland.

The situation was further exacerbated by the capacity of the Plantation movement for self generation. Vocal and influential support for extension of the plantations came from the New English who had already settled in Ireland. They saw further plantation both as a road to self enrichment and as an increment to their security. When the rebellion broke out in 1641, it was the Lord Justices in Dublin and the Earl of Cork in Munster who perceived some cause for jubilation in the midst of the holocaust. They never doubted, indeed they overestimated, the certainty and ease with which England could repress disorder in Ireland, and they envisaged a final Plantation which would carry to their ultimate conclusion principles inherent in a century of colonization.

On the one hand Plantation created an appetite for new appropriations by the English, while on the other it undermined the land tenure system of Ireland and stimulated new rebellions, which in turn justified further plantation. The process was without logical end until all Ireland had been planted by Protestants. Ironically, the enthusiasm of the New English was not necessarily shared by the English in England, large numbers of whom were needed for complete colonization of the island. By 1641 the risks of Irish Plantation were well known. However desirable the subjugation and reformation of Romish Ireland might seem, it had to be weighed, by the prospective colonist, against the probability that this most recent and terrible rebellion would not be the last.

II

ORIGINS OF THE ADVENTURE FOR IRISH LANDS

ABOUT the events of the year preceding the Irish rebellion, there is little controversy. Almost exactly twelve months before, on 3 November 1640, the Long Parliament had convened and begun to dismantle the personal government of Charles I. Triumph followed triumph. Strafford and Laud were impeached, the former to be attainted and executed in May 1641. The prerogative courts of Star Chamber and High Commission were abolished, and a number of acts were passed to ensure the future dependence of Crown upon Parliament. By October 1641 the destruction of Caroline absolutism was virtually complete, and among the parliamentary revolutionaries a mood of euphoria prevailed. 'It was then', Professor Trevor-Roper has written, 'that Milton's great pamphlets were written, then that Dury and Comenius met in England to plan the new social reformation for which the political basis, it now seemed, was secure. The disillusion caused by the Irish rebellion and its consequences was therefore profound.'[1]

Rebellion broke out in Ireland on 24 October 1641. It was altogether unanticipated both in England and Ireland, and it transformed the political situation instantly. Among the English revolutionaries one has a sense of men whose assiduous and promising attempt to control events was suddenly, disastrously, upset. By contrast the Prayer Book rebellion in Scotland had been the long prophesied and deserved reward of Stuart folly. Spontaneous though its origins may have been, the Scottish resistance to Charles I was a protest with which the English opponents of the King could sympathize, in which they could connive, and which they successfully exploited to force the calling of a parliament. The uprising in Ulster was not the response

[1] 'The Fast Sermons of the Long Parliament', *Essays in British History Presented to Sir Keith Feiling*, ed. by H. R. Trevor-Roper, London, 1964, p. 96.

to some specific English act or policy but rather an outburst against immemorial grievances. If so amorphous an uprising was aimed at any party outside of Ireland (where its targets were quite simply the Protestant planters), it was not at the King, but at the English Parliament whose triumphs in the previous year threatened to destroy the already rickety protection which Caroline authority afforded Catholic Ireland.

The genesis and nature of the Irish rebellion are still obscure. Virtually every theory imaginable has been advanced about it, except that it did not happen at all. All that can be said with certainty is that a conspiracy to overthrow the English government in Ireland was hatched in October 1641, that its principal locus was Ulster, and its principal participants Irish gentry who had suffered by the plantation of their province. The conspirators had been encouraged to believe that they would be aided by Catholic Europe, or even that they might find their activities sanctioned by the King. They believed they would be joined in rebellion by the discontented Old English Lords of the Pale, and that Dublin would fall into their hands on the first day of the rising. Their motives were as vague as their plans. Clearly they wished to regain their lands and re-establish their religion. Much as they had detested Strafford, the spectacle of his destruction at the bidding of the English Parliament augured ill for the few liberties Catholics retained in Ireland. On 23 October their attempt at seizing Dublin was frustrated by disclosure of their plans, but the conspirators launched an extensive insurrection in Ulster. The fires, once lit, were to burn for over a decade.

The King, who was in Edinburgh, learned of the rebellion on 27 October. On 1 November the news reached Westminster, where it was described in the Commons *Journal* as 'certain intelligences that were lately come, of a *great* treason and *general* rebellion of the Irish papists in Ireland; and a design of cutting off *all* the Protestants in Ireland; and seizing *all* the kings forts there'.[1] The italicized words (my emphasis) reveal the histrionic atmosphere with which the event was instantly invested. How had the newswriters determined so quickly that the rebellion was general? There were no reports of disorder in Munster, Leinster, or Connaught. Probably they concluded general rebellion

[1] *CJ*, ii, 300.

from the fact that many places in Ulster were simultaneously affected, that Dublin had been threatened, and that its saviour, a drunken Irish informer named Owen O'Connolly, had revealed the magnitude of the conspiracy. Yet the use of the words 'great', 'general', and 'all' in the Commons *Journal* recorded a semantic transformation, in which the specifics of uprising in Ulster, together with the allegedly grand intentions of the malefactors, were converted into a crime on the part of the entire Irish nation; and this total criminality later became the foundation of the Cromwellian Settlement.

The response of Parliament was hardly equal to its great alarm. Little more was done on the day the news arrived than to prepare to acquaint the City of London that the lending of £50,000 would be 'an acceptable service to the Commonwealth'. On 2 November twenty-six Lords and fifty-two M.P.s were appointed commissioners for Ireland, and on the third the City of London conveyed various grievances which might discourage it from lending the requested money for Ireland. The new commissioners were ordered to consider how 'to make use of the friendship and assistance of Scotland'.[1] On the 5th John Pym warned that he and his followers would not feel obliged to support the King against the rebels in Ireland, unless Charles put away his evil counsellors and took only 'such as might be approved by Parliament'.[2] Either Pym did not believe in the seriousness of the rebellion—which is unlikely—or he was prepared to sacrifice the Protestants of Ireland to his political interests in England.

S. R. Gardiner believed that Pym's doctrinaire position cost him the support of some of his followers and forced him to modify and moderate his tactics. In a motion of 8 November Charles was again urged to employ as counsellors only those approved by Parliament. This time, however, he was not warned that Ireland would be left to its fate if he failed to comply, but rather that Parliament would

resolve upon some such way of defending Ireland from the rebels as may concur to the securing of ourselves from such mischievous counsels and designs as have lately been and still are in practice and agitation against us . . . and to commend those aids and contributions

---

[1] *CJ*, ii, 304.
[2] S. R. Gardiner, *History of England, 1603–1642*, London, 1884, x. 53.

which this great necessity shall require, to the custody and disposing of such persons of honour and fidelity as we have cause to confide in'.[1]

'No proposal of so distinctly revolutionary a character had yet been adopted by the Commons', Gardiner commented, yet it was passed by 151 votes to 110, over the objections of Culpepper and others who argued that Protestant Ireland deserved the unquestioning assistance to which any part of England would be entitled.[2]

In Gardiner's interpretation, Pym's resolution 'seized upon the executive power itself, so far, at least, as Ireland was concerned', but was justified by the demonstrated untrustworthiness of the King.[3] Gardiner saw quite clearly that the outbreak of the Irish rebellion brought the dispute between Crown and Parliament to a critical stage. Either the rebellion in Ireland had to run its course, or an army had to be raised to put it down. If the latter, the jealousy and fear of both parties over control of the army was almost certain to produce a military confrontation.

Through the pages of his diary Sir Simonds D'Ewes repeatedly lamented that fact. To D'Ewes the rebellion in Ireland was paramount and deserved to eclipse the animosities between King and Parliament. Why, he asked, could not the natural and traditional thing be done and an army sent to Ireland to repress the rebellion? This was the first major rebellion in Irish history specifically and exclusively aimed at Protestants, and its outbreak and greatest progress occurred in heavily Protestant-colonized Ulster. The Counter-Reformation could hardly have struck British Protestantism a more telling blow. Yet the response of England was a mixture of agony and paralysis. The press teemed with accounts of atrocities upon Protestants. Prayers were offered and funds solicited in virtually every parish. Monthly fasts were initiated in February 1642, and the lamentable closing of the theatres was carried out in 1643, in the name of compassion for the suffering Protestants of Ireland.[4] But schemes of repression languished as the rebellion was converted into a political football in the consuming struggle between King and Parliament. Indeed from 1641 to 1649 there was no attempt to deal with the Irish rebellion in a frontal way. Parliamentary policy

---

[1] *LJ*, iv. 431.   [2] Gardiner, op. cit. x. 57.   [3] Ibid.
[4] John Rushworth, ed., *Historical Collections*, London, 1659–1701, III. i. 494.

darted from expedient to expedient, and the colonial future of Ireland was determined by the forms which the expedients happened to take.[1]

There were other than political reasons for Parliament's inaction. Parliament did not witness the rebellion, but merely the dim shadows it cast upon the walls at Westminster. A flood of pamphlet literature appeared describing the progress of the rebellion, a multitude of atrocities committed in connection with it, and the heroic efforts of the Protestants of Ireland in resisting their fate. An examination of this literature reveals it to have been unbelievably muddled. Non-existent personages were reported to be in non-existent places. Battles that never occurred were described in the most minute detail. 'The treacherous Earl of Care' was the favourite figment of the late Walter Love, who made so diligent and perceptive a study of the pamphlet literature.[2] Amidst conflicting, often fictitious, reports it was impossible to determine what was occurring in Ireland. Even if there was general agreement that there were serious disturbances in Ulster, few men in England could perceive the state of affairs in Connaught, Leinster, or Munster. Was the rebellion general, or limited to one area? Were all Catholics involved, or merely some? How did the Old English Lords of the Pale stand? And so on. To none of these questions was a firm answer immediately available, and many men, especially but not exclusively royalists, doubted its truth, as the growing tide of unsubstantiated bad news flowed in from Ireland. '. . . ofttimes we have much more printed [here] than is true, especially when anything concerns the papists whom, though they are bad enough, our Preciser sort strive to make yet worse'[3] commented one correspondent. In any event, Parliament did not, in 1641 and 1642, suppose it was dealing with the massacre of 200,000 to 400,000 poor Protestants, an exaggeration which propagandists were later to concoct and shamefully to defend for several centuries. It was not known what the extent of the rebellion was, or what, therefore, the probable cost of repressing it would be.

---

[1] Chapter IV is, in effect, an extended defence of this point of view.

[2] It was the Earl of Clare to whom the pamphlet intended to refer. Walter Love left his study unfinished. Some of his initial conclusions are in 'Civil War in Ireland: Appearances in Three Centuries of Historical Writing', *EUQ*, Summer, 1966.   [3] *CSPD, 1641–3*, p. 162.

Secondly, and perhaps less nobly, Parliament regarded Ireland—even a rebellious Ireland—as rather remote. The same callousness visible in the mercantile legislation of the late seventeenth and eighteenth centuries operated in this earlier period to impede prompt, strong, and costly restoration of order and Protestant hegemony. An elemental nationalism was responsible. However Protestant their faith or English their blood, the Protestants of Ireland were brethren only to a degree. Their bond to the nation was diluted by the waters of St. George's Channel and the Irish Sea. As refugees from a barbarous island frontier they had claims upon the charity and sympathy of their homeland, but not to the extent of commanding the expedition necessary to re-establish them. The Irish Protestant in 1641 found himself pitied when he was in London but little supported when in Dublin or Cork. This was one-half of a classic colonial reflex: on the one hand, the reluctance of the 'homeland' to support the brethren abroad; on the other, the great proclivity of the colonists to flee 'home' when adversity knocked. It is clear that a widespread phenomenon of the Irish rebellion was the departure of thousands of colonists for England, where they remained until the Cromwellian conquest. It was only with great difficulty that men could be raised for service in Ireland, even on those rare occasions when there were sufficient funds. Not only the women and children, but many of the men, departed from the land.

The cumulative result of doubt, faintness of heart, and political impasse, was a disjointed, halting, and thoroughly Lilliputian response to the Irish rebellion. It brought out the meanest in everyone: a niggling, unco-operative, suspicious, and ungenerous attitude which, admittedly, was part of the legacy of the personal rule of Charles I. Visionary ideas for repressing the rebellion were advanced daily in and out of Parliament, but they were mainly distinguished for their cheapness. A few thousand pounds might be sent; Lord Lieutenant Leicester might be urged to go over; the rebellion might be repressed by the Protestants of Ireland themselves; or help might be got from the Scots. The scale of all such suggestions paled beside the estimates received on 11 November, from the Irish Lords Justices, Sir William Parsons and Sir John Borlase, according to which there was immediate need of £100,000, and of 10,000 fresh foot and 1,000 horse. D'Ewes, lamenting Parliament's parsimony in his diary, recorded that he advocated meeting these needs and more, by fining the delinquent bishops and judges, levying a £160,000 scutage, and passing the £400,000 subsidy bill which had been before Parliament since May.[1] D'Ewes was prepared to pay for Ireland's rebellion out of England's wealth, even though he would saddle knights and delinquents with a major share of the burden.

It was instead a policy of temporizing that prevailed. Pym argued that Ireland should wait at least until the passage of the Grand Remonstrance. The City followed his example of obstinacy by refusing to lend the requested £50,000 until its grievances over 'protections' for members of Parliament had been satisfied. The Lords refused to see Parliament accept 10,000 soldiers whom the Scots had offered to send to Ireland at English expense, unless the Commons would agree to send 10,000 English soldiers to join them. The Commons would not agree to send 10,000 English, and the Scots would not agree to maintain at their own expense the soldiers they offered to raise and transport. The net result of these unreconcilable positions was the merest trickle of men and supplies to Ireland in the closing months of 1641.

The King was no less willing to exploit the situation than were Parliament, the City, or the Scots. On the one hand, he could chide Parliament for its dilatory behaviour, as he did in his speech to both Houses on 14 December:

> The last time that I was in this place, and the last thing that I recommended unto you was the business of Ireland; whereby I was in good hope that I should not have need again to put you in mind of that business. But, still seeing the slow proceedings therein, and the daily dispatches that I have out of Ireland of the lamentable estate of my Protestant subjects there, I cannot but again earnestly recommend the despatch of that expedition unto you: for it is the chief business that at this time I take to heart; and there cannot (almost) be any business that I can have more care of.[2]

On the other hand, Charles could equivocate, as he did until

[1] *The Journal of Sir Simonds D'Ewes*, ed. by Willson H. Coates, New Haven, 1942, p. 118.
[2] Thomas May, *The History of the Long Parliament*, Oxford, 1854, p. 362.

1 January 1642, over declaring the Irish rebels and traitors, and he could obtrude his prerogative, as he did in refusing Pym's impressment bill, which he declared would be acceptable only if it came to him 'as it may not infringe or diminish my prerogative'.[1] The rebellion placed Charles in a relatively strong position, for it demanded a military force over which he would, by all tradition, have command. He was far from ready to throw away this high card which fortune had placed in his hand. He defied Parliament to attempt a military solution in Ireland without him, and this Parliament declined to do, preferring to remain on guard in England rather than risk overreaching itself in stormy Ireland.

Nothing is more basic to the developing Irish crisis than the reluctance of Parliament to finance a solution through taxation. The onus has often been put upon the Lords Justices and the Council in Dublin for the decision to finance the repression out of the wealth of Ireland; but that suggestion was only an obvious response to the evident unwillingness of Parliament to do anything else. In a frequently-quoted letter to Lord Lieutenant Leicester, for instance, the Lords Justices described the December defection of the Anglo-Irish Lords of the Pale with more delight than remorse, pointing out that as a result '. . . those great counties of Leinster, Ulster, and the Pale now lie the more open to his Majesty's free disposal, and to a general settlement of peace and religion by introducing of English'.[2] But this letter was not written until 14 December, seven weeks after the rebellion's outbreak, and more than long enough for the Lords Justices to comprehend Parliament's inaction.

As long as the rebellion had been confined to Ulster, the pickings for any would-be repressor appeared lean. Ulster was by far the most heavily colonized of the four provinces, and the one in which least remained to enrich a yet newer colonial class. After the plundered lands had been restored to their Protestant owners, there would be little left to confiscate. The defection of the Pale, on the other hand, awakened dreams of new riches. If the news of it was intended to stimulate Protestant greed and animate a repression, it may have succeeded, for the first mention of the

---

[1] Loc. cit. and p. 152.
[2] Robert Dunlop, *Ireland under the Commonwealth*, Manchester, 1913, i. cxxi; and Thomas Carte, *The Life of James Duke of Ormond*, Oxford, 1851, i, 260.

merchants of London as having any special connection with the rebellion dates from a few days after the presumed arrival of the Lord Justices' news. On Christmas Eve, D'Ewes tells us, 'certain merchants and citizens of London trading into Ireland' attended Parliament with a petition showing that 'a great part of their estates now lay in Ireland' and desiring Parliament's support of the poor Protestants there.[1] Sir Robert Pye was quick to suggest that the petitioners themselves should lend some money for Ireland, since their interest was concerned, but D'Ewes argued that the merchants' losses might disable them from lending, and that it was rather the responsibility of the Lords and Commons to make 'timely supply' for Ireland.[2]

It may have been these same merchants who, according to Sir Philip Perceval, made 'certain propositions as if they would undertake the charge of the war, but it did not take effect'.[3] The germ of an idea was there: that a special and wealthy segment of the realm might take financial responsibility (and an undetermined amount of military and organizational responsibility) for repression of the rebellion, in return for yet unstated opportunities in Ireland. That the special segment should have been London can be no surprise. In addition to merchants 'trading into Ireland' and owed money for goods already delivered, the City's Londonderry Plantation had left numerous connections with Ireland. The City had been evicted from its Jacobean plantation in Ulster by the unpopular Star Chamber verdict of 1635, but a committee of the Long Parliament appointed for the purpose had re-examined the evidence and, not surprisingly, vindicated the Londoners, recommending their restoration to all they had previously held in Ulster. In the words of T. W. Moody, 'The prospect of complete restitution lay before the City, and already the Londonderry tenants were not only refusing to pay rent to the royal receivers, but in menacing fashion, were demanding the return of what they had previously paid.'[4]

The month of December 1641 may have been a turning point. Not only did official news of the defection of the Pale arrive, and

---

[1] 'The Irish owe the London Merchants £120,000', Sir Philip Perceval wrote some weeks later, 'and they are continual and earnest suitors to dispatch aid away . . .' (HMC, *Egmont Papers*, 1st Ser. i. 164).

[2] *D'Ewes Diary*, p. 342.   [3] HMC, *Egmont*, 1st Ser. i. 614.

[4] T. W. Moody, *The Londonderry Plantation*, Belfast, 1939, p. 416.

petitioners appear from the City on behalf of themselves and
Protestant Ireland; but the Grand Remonstrance, laden with
accusations over Ireland, was presented to the King. The
Remonstrance viewed the rebellion in Ireland as part of a popish
plot which threatened all three kingdoms, but which, 'by God's
wonderful providence', had come close to succeeding only in Ireland. Even there, the rebels' 'main enterprise upon the City and
castle of Dublin' had been detected, so that the loss of the Kingdom as a whole had been prevented.[1] While acknowledging and
decrying 'such a fire [in Ireland], as nothing but God's infinite
blessing upon the wisdom and endeavours of this State will be
able to quench . . .', the Commons more or less professed their
impotence : 'But what can we, the Commons, without the conjunction of the House of Lords, and what conjunction can we
expect there, when the Bishops and recusant lords are so numerous and prevalent that they are able to cross and interrupt our
best endeavours for reformation . . . ?'[2] The Commons were thus
setting a price for their co-operation in restoring order in Ireland. It was the old tune of 'grievances before supply', played
over a prostrate Ireland.

In a petition which accompanied the Grand Remonstrance the
Commons asked the King 'to forbear to alienate any of the forfeited and escheated lands in Ireland which shall accrue to your
Crown by reason of this rebellion, that out of them the Crown
may be better supported, and some satisfaction made to your
subjects of this kingdom for the great expenses they are like to
undergo [in] this war'.[3] This was the foundation stone of the
fiscal expedient which was to follow: the hypothecation of the
potentially confiscable land of Ireland.

Some such step was apparently necessary to break the financial
deadlock. Moneyed Londoners were evidently interested in
pursuing their profit in Irish schemes, but were far from ready
to bear the financial burden of a reconquest, even at 8 per cent
p.a. When the Mayor, Aldermen, and Common Council were
asked in January 1642 to lend £100,000, they replied that they had
'no power to raise any sums by way of tax for foreign use'. They

---

[1] S. R. Gardiner, *Constitutional Documents of the Puritan Revolution*, Oxford,
1906, p. 228.   [2] Ibid.
   [3] Ibid., p. 205.

complained that the £50,000 they had lent a few months earlier had not yet carried the Lord Lieutenant to Ireland, that Parliament had not relieved the siege of Derry, and that offers of Scottish assistance had not yet been accepted. Most crucially, they lamented Parliament's failure to pass a bill for pressing soldiers in England, deducing that 'there may be some design rather to lose . . . [Ireland], and to consume this [kingdom] in the losing of Ireland, than to preserve either the one or the other'.[1] Some means had to be discovered of depoliticizing the Irish problem and attracting financial support to it.

On 11 February 1642, in the House of Commons, 'divers worthy and well affected citizens of London' put forward proposals 'for the speedy and effectual reducing of Ireland'.[2] The rebellion, they observed, had 'spread over almost the whole face of the kingdom', and the authors of it were 'encouraged by the weak opposition hitherto made against them'. The treasury of England was 'wonderfully exhausted, so that such sums as will be required . . . will hardly be drawn out of the subjects purses . . . without much murmuring and repining'. The petitioners themselves offered to undertake the expenses of repressing the rebellion, upon four conditions : that they have the right to name their own officers; that arms and ammunition be supplied at the expense of the state; that they have power to enlist soldiers in England and, 'if need be, the benefit of the desired act to impress'; and finally, but most importantly, that they have 'satisfaction out of the rebels estates (the war being ended) as shall be thought reasonable by the honorable houses, upon their present humble demands and future merits'.[3]

These proposals were entrusted to the Parliament's commissioners for Irish affairs, and emerged, after considerable metamorphosis, as a measure which received the King's assent on 24 February, and was formally recorded on 19 March as 'An Act for the speedy and effectual reducing of the rebels in His Majesty's Kingdom of Ireland'.[4]

Most of what we know about the act—hereafter called 'the

[1] Rushworth, *Historical Collections*, iv. 504.
[2] Dunlop, *Ireland under the Commonwealth*, i. cxxiii.
[3] *CJ*, ii. 425.
[4] Dunlop, *Ireland under the Commonwealth*, i. cxxiii; and *Statutes of the Realm*, 16 Car. i, c. 33.

act for adventurers'—we learn from the wording of the statute itself. Part of the preamble runs as follows:

Whereas the Lords and Commons taking into their serious considerations as well the necessity of a speedy reducing of the rebels of Ireland to their due obedience as also the great sums of money that the Commons of this realm have of late paid for the public and necessary affairs of this kingdom whereof the Lords and Commons are very sensible and desirous to embrace all good and honourable ways tending to his Majesty's greatness and profit the settling of that realm and the ease of his Majesty's subjects of England. And whereas diverse worthy and well affected persons perceiving that many millions of acres of the rebels lands of that kingdom which go under the name of profitable lands will be confiscate and to be disposed of. And that in case two millions and [an] half of those acres to be equally taken out of the four provinces of that kingdom may be allotted for the satisfaction of such persons as shall disburse any sums of money for the reducing of the rebels there would effectually accomplish the same have made these propositions ensuing (viz.) . . .[1]

Several noteworthy assumptions are built into this language: first, Parliament's solicitude for the 'Ease of his majesties Subjects of England', its sensibility of the financial burdens of England, its reluctance to tax England in order to repress Ireland. Second, there is the assumption, or rather the 'perception' by 'divers worthy and well-affected persons', that so much Irish land would be subject to confiscation, that 2,500,000 profitable acres could easily be allotted as security for those who lent money to finance the repression. That is to say, approximately 18 per cent of the total profitable land of Ireland was to be so used.[2] It should also be noted that the 2,500,000 acres were 'to be taken equally out of the four Provinces of that Kingdom'. These assumptions, viewed through the fog of several centuries of Anglo-Irish recriminations, have seldom been questioned. Or rather, it has been assumed that all the bad things which

---

[1] *Statutes of the Realm*, 16 Car. 1, c. 33.

[2] See W. H. Hardinge, 'Circumstances Attending the Civil War in Ireland', *TRIA* (Antiquities), vol. 24, Appendix I. According to Hardinge, 7,700,000 of 11,000,000 forfeited acres (English measure) were 'profitable', i.e. about 70 per cent. 70 per cent of Ireland's whole contents of 20,000,000 English acres is about 14,000,000 acres, of which the adventurers' 2,500,000 constituted 18 per cent.

Protestant propagandists were to say about the Irish rebellion had already been said by 11 February, when these propositions were made. Indeed, they had not. Little more was known about the rebellion than that it was violent, and that it was spreading out of the North, where it had begun. As Robert Dunlop wrote of atrocities against Protestants: 'Considering all the talk about the depositions [of atrocities] as evidence, it was startling enough to find that, so far as I could gather, the Long Parliament had no cognizance of their existence. In the circumstances the only conclusion I could come to was that the Rebellion in itself was regarded by the Long Parliament as a sufficient ground for the sale of Ireland.'[1] How else could Parliament have agreed that 2,500,000 acres was to be taken equally out of the four Provinces, except upon the assumption that all Catholic Ireland was equally culpable, and that Munster, Connaught, and Leinster were as guilty as Ulster? These were extraordinary assumptions to make in the almost total absence of facts, and before even rudimentary attempts had been made to ascertain the facts.[2] A massive land settlement was implicit in such assumptions.

The act set up a scale of land values whereby one acre of Ulster was allowed to secure four shillings of 'adventure', one acre of Connaught six shillings, one acre of Munster ten shillings, and one acre of Leinster twelve shillings. Where did such a scale come from? Why was land in Ulster valued at one-third the value of land in Leinster? Was it because Ulster was expected to be so much more wasted by war? When the land was actually distributed after 1653 these relative valuations were found to be wholly inappropriate. Parts of low-valued Ulster, for instance, were worth ten times parts of high-valued Leinster. The remainder of the act elaborated the machinery by which the adventure was to be taken up, the additional advantages which the adventurers would enjoy, the means by which the adventurers were ultimately to be planted upon the confiscated soil, and the conditions under which they would hold.

The effect of the act was immense. It heartened those who

---

[1] Dunlop, *Ireland under the Commonwealth*, i. vii.

[2] The act did state that if 625,000 acres of profitable land could not be found confiscated in any one province, however much was lacking might be taken from the superfluity (the amount available *over* 625,000 acres) in another province.

wished the rebellion to be repressed by force and discouraged those who hoped to see a compromise. Foremost among the latter was the King. One of Charles's great hopes was for Irish support of his cause. The constitutional conflicts which divided Englishman from Englishman hardly existed in Ireland, where an abundance of grievances did not weaken a primitive but fundamental respect for the Crown. Irish Protestants and Catholics feared each other more than they feared the King. But if Charles was to become titular head of a crusade against the Catholics of Ireland, allying himself with a weak, refugee, Protestant minority, this Irish base of support would be lost. On the other hand, the King had apparently been mortified by the rebels' profession to be acting in his name, and Phelim O'Neil's flaunting of an alleged commission under the Great Seal.[1] In order to restore the confidence of Protestants in England that he was not involved in a vast popish plot against them, Charles had to appear to be resisting the Irish rebels, and was obliged to consent to the act for adventurers.

Thus, [wrote Clarendon] His Majesty was necessitated to consent to that bill by which too great a latitude is given for the disposal of land in the several provinces of that kingdom, to those who have adventured money in the war, which without the interposition, shelter, and mercy of the sovereign power, would give up almost all that whole people and their fortunes, to the disposal of their cruel enemies.[2]

'Ireland', Clarendon wrote later, 'was the great capital out of which all debts were paid, all services rewarded, and all acts of bounty performed.'[3] The only protection which Charles had against the act for adventurers being turned against him was the specific requirement written into it that all money raised was to be used exclusively 'for the reducing of the said rebels'. The act was a compromise between King and Parliament at the expense of Ireland. It theoretically resolved the deadlock between the two parties by bringing into existence an independent,

[1] See Gardiner, *History of England*, x. 92 for details.
[2] Edward Hyde, Earl of Clarendon, *The History of the Rebellion and Civil Wars in Ireland*, Dublin, 1719–20, p. 13.
[3] *The Life of Edward, Earl of Clarendon*, Oxford, 1888 edn., ii, 218.

nominally non-partisan, agency to finance the restoration of order in Ireland.

For his own selfish reasons Charles regretted the act, and he perceived both its dire consequences and the absurdity upon which it was based. In replying to the request which accompanied the Grand Remonstrance that the Crown should not alienate any of the Irish lands forfeited to it as a result of the rebellion, he had expressed the doubt 'whether it be seasonable to declare resolutions of that nature before the events of a war be seen'.[1] This was precisely the point. Because Parliament was reluctant, for political reasons, to mount the reconquering expedition, it concentrated its energies upon abusing the rebels vocally and dreaming idyllic reconquests of the future. One of these dreams, of an Ireland Anglicized, virtually incarnated itself in the minds of certain moneyed men, and made its legal appearance in the act for adventurers. 'As we look upon . . . [Ireland]', Charles declared, 'so our unhappiness is increased, in that by the distempers at home, so early remedies have not been applied to those growing evils as the expectation and necessity there requires.'[2] The King's assertions of his own innocence in this process is unconvincing, but his observation was correct. The act for adventurers was conceived in frustration and bears all the signs of that kind of excess which so frequently follows repression.

The financial arrangements of the act resembled those of a joint stock company; and in his work on the subject W. R. Scott dutifully puzzled over them: 'In this enterprise the plantation element is strongly marked,' he said, 'while the corporate one is less important and of an accidental character'; and finally he concluded that the scheme was closer to a 'lottery' than to anything else.[3] For another assumption built into the act for adventurers was that the rebels would unquestionably be defeated. Indeed, they would have to be defeated, almost unconditionally, because any negotiated settlement with them would prejudice the ability of the adventurers to take over their 2,500,000 acres

---

[1] May, *History of the Long Parliament*, p. 395.
[2] Ibid., p. 402.
[3] W. R. Scott, *The Constitution and Finance of English, Scottish and Irish Joint-Stock Companies to 1720*, Cambridge, 1912, ii. 343.

of 'confiscable' land. And were the Irish to triumph, the adventurers would lose all.

But who were the adventurers to be? There is one hint that they were originally intended to be wealthy Londoners. The Earl of Warwick, writing in late February or early March 1642, described the act as 'a brave proposition in London that 2000 citizens will lay down £500 apiece'[1] (thereby producing the £1,000,000 envisaged by the Act). But the adventurers did not evolve in such form. There was no compact body of willing investors waiting in the wings, as there was fifty years later when capital was taken up for the Bank of England. Instead, the subscription lists were thrown open to M.P.s, Londoners, provincials, and eventually foreign Protestants, with very little idea how many adventurers would come forward or how much money would be raised. The act called for 2,500,000 acres to be set aside, and at the rates published, that amount of Irish land, drawn equally from the four Provinces, would secure £1,000,000 of adventure. Yet there was no certainty that such an amount could be raised, or if raised, that it would be sufficient to suppress the rebellion. Raising money in London for Ireland was a little like cutting diamonds in a den of thieves. Both the King and the fiercer elements of Parliament could think of uses for the money nearer home, and were equally apprehensive, each lest it should fall into the hands of the other. From a colonizing point of view the whole scheme was fraught with perils. And like previous Irish colonization schemes, it did not sell itself, but had to be aggressively sold. Even the land rates were not notably favourable. From an investor's point of view, what the scheme meant was an opportunity (with a certain risk) to buy Irish land at rates ranging from four to twelve shillings an acre, and averaging 7s. 9d.[2] In addition to the risk of an Irish triumph or a negotiated settlement, there was the danger that the rebels would not be defeated, or the land parcelled out, for many years. By that time the land might be terribly wasted. By contrast, land in North America had been offered thirty years earlier by the Virginia

---

[1] Earl of Warwick to Earl of Cork, in *The Lismore Papers*, ed. by A. B. Grosart, London, 1886–8, 2nd Ser., vol. iv, p. 288.

[2] The adventurer had no control over which province his lot fell into, and therefore, no knowledge of how much he would be paying per acre.

Company at 2*s*. 6*d*. per acre, less than one-third the average cost of the Irish land now offered for occupancy at some unspecified point in the future in unspecified condition.[1]

The taking up of subscriptions was accompanied by an out-pouring of propaganda of both a material and a spiritual orientation. As early as 8 March M.P.s were announcing their intended subscriptions, even though the machinery for taking up money was not in operation until the end of that month, and some never paid the amounts they announced.[2] Subscriptions by M.P.s, over 100 of whom eventually became involved, were intended to inspire the public to a like performance.[3]

By March 1642 Parliament had been a long while bombarded with tales of suffering in Ireland and pleas for assistance. Some of these were ordered to be printed, such as that of the Earl of Cork, who allegedly wrote from Munster in January: 'We have been a long while flattered with hopes of relief from England, and other countries, but we find them too slow in their succour, that if we feed ourselves any longer with such or the like expectations, it is to be justly feared that ruin will overtake and overwhelm us.' He warned that if the Catholic conflagration was not stopped in Ireland, its flames would spread to England.[4]

Much of what reached Parliament's ears from Ireland was hearsay: frightening and horrible, but less than conclusive. On 21 March viva-voce evidence was heard from Dean Henry Jones of Kilmore, later Bishop of Clogher, who was about to publish his lengthy pamphlet, *A Remonstrance of Divers Remarkable Passages Concerning the Church and Kingdom of Ireland*. Jones and seven other clergymen had been given a commission to take depositions from refugees in Dublin, and his report contained their conclusions, supported by extracts from eighty-five depositions. Walter Love made a careful study of Jones's *Remonstrance*, and came to interesting conclusions:

The *Remonstrance* was no sober account of mere events in Ireland. It was a collection of everything the deponents said that would reveal

---

[1] Scott, *Joint Stock Companies*, ii. 343.

[2] Thomason Tracts, BM, 669. f. 5 (3), a printed list of M.P. adventurers.

[3] See the important article of J. R. MacCormack, 'The Irish Adventurers and the English Civil War', *IHS*, 1956, 21–58. MacCormack finds 136 M.P. adventurers, but includes recruiters and M.P.s who held shares only briefly. My figures, excluding both, show 119.   [4] Thomason Tracts, BM, E. 133 (2).

the *intentions* and thus the full form and character of the great Catholic plot. This supposed plot Jones drew up in his history as the cause from which had 'proceeded' everything the deponents swore to. But for Jones, *acts* reported in the deponents' sworn statements were of an interest only secondary to what they *heard*. Jones insisted that 'we find the hearts of these men in their tongues'. It was the hearts of the rebels that he wanted to display in his report, and he displayed them through their words first, and their actions second.[1]

The *Remonstrance* was 'in fact a collection of rumors' which 'must have been conceived as provocation for arousing people to contribute [to the cause of Protestant Ireland, in some form]'.

It may have been thought of as particularly valuable in assuring investors that there would be plenty of land to reward them, because it showed the extent of the rebellious character by attributing it to all Irish and Catholics. If all of them would eventually rebel in act because of the rebellion in their hearts (and that—rebellion in their hearts—is what the pamphlet was designed to prove), a vast amount of property would be available.[2]

It may be excessive to accuse Jones of cynically setting out to write a sanguine prospectus for the adventure, but his findings conduced to that end by emphasizing the *generality* of the rebellion, with its corollary implication of massive confiscations.

The prevailing sentiment of the adventure was one of self-interested colonialism, but it was alloyed with elements of charity and even fear. Pure charity, however, had other outlets. Under the 'act for a speedy contribution and loan towards the relief of H.M.'s distressed subjects of the Kingdom of Ireland' of January 1642 (16 Car. I, c.30), £45,931 was raised from thirty-six counties and literally thousands of small donors. Although loans—as opposed to gifts—were to receive the usual 8 per cent p.a. interest, this was the obvious channel for wholly disinterested philanthropy.[3] Those who preferred instead to contribute through the adventure were thinking as much of Irish land as of Protestant suffering.

It was never intended that members of Parliament should undertake the adventure alone. The Commons was merely to

---

[1] Love, 'Civil War in Ireland', p. 61.   [2] Ibid., p. 64.
[3] Hugh Hazlett, 'The Financing of British Armies in Ireland, 1641–9', *IHS*, 1938, 26.

set an example for the nation to follow. According to J. R. MacCormack, by 10 April 1642 approximately 80 M.P.s had subscribed, or announced that they *would* subscribe, £55,000.[1] This was but one-twentieth of what was envisaged in the act.

As Jones exhorted Parliament, the adventurer M.P.s exhorted the public, sometimes urging self-interest, sometimes the unity of Protestantism. Pym blasted the 'impudence' of the rebels and assured all would-be adventurers that 'nothing but the sword must decide the controversy . . . [for] not one particular [of the rebels' demands] can be granted, neither with safety nor honour to his majesty and his kingdom'.[2] Thus he sought to allay fears that Parliament would accept some kind of compromise with the rebels, a solution which reason, but never feeling, might promote.

In another hortatory pamphlet, Bulstrode Whitelocke, who later adventured £400, looked at the rebellion, and perceived the Counter-Reformation rampant. 'Reducing of Ireland', he asserted, 'concerns not only the civil power, but the existence of our religion.' Former rebellion in Ireland had been largely conflict with sovereignty, but 'the present revolt goes to the extirpation of our nation and religion amongst them', and would eventually lead to an assault upon the Protestant faith in England. More to the point, perhaps, was Whitelocke's contention that adoption and support of the adventure scheme would conduce to 'the ease of the people of England'. 'The great and heavy payments they have lately undergone', together with 'the present general decay of trade', had 'brought the people very low'. taxation was an unwelcome remedy even for a situation so perilous as that in Ireland. The burdens of England were contrasted with the wealth of Ireland, which in his opinion hardly deserved to remain in the hands of papists and rebels.

Whitelocke gave some clue to the thought of those responsible for the details of the adventure when he conceded that 'the propositions [i.e. 2,500,000 acres to be disposed of] may seem at the first very large and difficult'; but then he allayed such misgivings, explaining that 'by computation of men of great experience of that country . . . the content of this island [Ireland] is

---

[1] MacCormack, 'The Irish Adventurers', p. 34.
[2] Speech of John Pym, 19 Feb. 1642, Thomason Tracts, BM, E. 200 (13).

above fifteen millions of acres of profitable land, whereof five millions of acres are estimated to belong to the King's good subjects there: out of the ten millions remaining they ask but two millions and a half; and yet three parts of four of that Kingdom are out in rebellion.'[1] Whitelocke made it appear to be a highly conservative intrusion into Irish land. But where had his figure of 10,000,000 confiscable profitable acres come from? And with what justice did he assert that three-quarters of the land-holding population was in rebellion? These conclusions were spun out of such thin stuff as the atrocity stories of Dean Henry Jones, and such assertions as those of the Earl of Cork, who wrote from Munster in late February: 'I do beseech your Lordship [the Earl of Warwick] believe this great truth from me, that there is not many, (nay I may more truly say) very few or none, that is a native of Ireland and of the Romish religion, but he is either publicly in this action, or privately in his heart, an assistant or well-wisher unto it.'[2]

Like Dean Jones, Cork divided the Irish into active rebels and passive rebels, hardly distinguishing between the culpability of the two. It was guilt by blood. Anglo-Irish magnates like Cork had their own reasons for wanting the adventure scheme implemented. In the short run they hoped it would finance the speedy repression which Parliament was so unwilling to support by taxation. In the long run, they saw it as 'a fit opportunity . . . to root the popish party of the natives out of the kingdom, and to plant it with English Protestants', on the theory that '. . . so long as English and Irish protestants and papists live here intermingled together, we can never have firm and assured peace. . . .'[2]

The arrangements which had emerged to meet the Irish crisis were remarkable, indeed frivolous. The rebellion, about which little was known, was to be repressed by forces financed through the hypothecation of land which, it was supposed, could be confiscated in the course of the repression.

In the very propaganda which sought to promote the adventure lie the clues to its less then immediate success. 'One would

[1] Speech of Bulstrode Whitelocke at a conference of Lords and Commons, 17 Feb. 1642, Thomason Tracts, BM, E. 200 (30).
[2] Cork to Warwick, 25 Feb. 1642, BM Egerton MS. 80, f. 33.

think', commented an anonymous pamphlet, 'that in matters of profit men should not need to be persuaded much; but yet it hath so happened since the first presenting of the propositions for the levying of money for Ireland, that many, conceiving it a troublesome and improbable adventure, have been slow to subscribe any sum, although masters of great store of coin.'[1] Subscriptions, the same author admitted, were coming in more slowly than had been expected. 'Troublesome' and 'improbable' were adjectives which, when applied to the adventure, could mean either that the war was likely to be over too soon for very many of the Irish to perish in it, or, more charitably, 'that this way is cruel, and tends not to a reformation, but to an utter extirpation, that it doth involve the nocent and innocent in the same punishment, that it were better to offer conditions of peace, and then let the obstinate suffer'.[2]

J. R. MacCormack reminds us that Sir Simonds D'Ewes, 'A Parliamentarian and a good Puritan', evinced concern for Irish women and children, and noted that doubts on this subject did 'discourage some from venturing lest there were an intent to destroy them all . . .'. When, later, he offered fifty pounds to the cause it was 'without expecting any part of the rebel lands in that Kingdom . . .'.[3] The King himself had implied dissatisfaction with the adventure even as he gave it formal approval, writing that he did 'consent to every proposition made to him, without taking time to examine, whether this course may not retard the reducing of that Kingdom, by exasperating the rebels, and rendering them desperate of being received into grace, if they shall return to their obedience'.[4]

The scheme, which had been intended to break the political deadlock preventing aid to Ireland, rapidly degenerated into a suspect partisan effort. MacCormack believed it was a partisan

[1] 'Motives to Incite All Men of Ability to Subscribe to the Propositions for Ireland', Thomason Tracts, BM, E. 136 (28).

[2] 'That Great Expedition for Ireland', Thomason Tracts, BM, E. 137 (3). Feb./Mar., 1642.

[3] BM Harley MS. 163, f. 28 r., and *CJ*, ii, 544, cited by MacCormack, 'The Irish Adventurers', p. 33. Mr. Mark Kishlansky reminds me that J. H. Hexter insists on the essential royalism of D'Ewes in his *The Reign of King Pym*, Cambridge, Mass., 1941, p. 52.

[4] 'Propositions Made to the Parliament . . . and His Majesty's Gracious Reply Thereto', Thomason Tracts, BM, E. 136 (9).

scheme all along, brilliantly engineered by Pym. 'If all went well [i.e. no civil war in England], the Ireland of Irish papists would soon be a thing of the past and the gentry of England would have received another massive transfusion of landed wealth. If, as men were now fearing, there should be civil war in England, the Parliament would have a treasury, men under arms, and the support both of London and the Scots.'[1] MacCormack's own figures tend to corroborate these conclusions by revealing that only 8·8 per cent of all adventurer M.P.s were, in the categories of Brunton and Pennington, royalists. But this is a comment upon the repute of the scheme essentially *after* March 1642, as is the statistic furnished by MacCormack that, of the 80 M.P.s who had adventured by 10 April, 95 per cent were 'future parliamentarians'.[2]

Pym could not have his cake and eat it too. If money was to be drawn to the adventurers' treasury, the scheme would have to appear genuinely bi-partisan and Irish-oriented. Land is ordinarily a more attractive investment than revolution, and most of those who adventured for Irish land wanted to believe that their investments would expedite conquest abroad, not revolution at home. Apparently the adventure failed to project that image, and it was evident from a very early point that nowhere near the desired £1,000,000 was likely to be raised. It had been thought in February that the Londoners alone could subscribe the full amount, but by early April M.P.s were being pressed to subscribe 'as may best stand with your own occasions', and the sheriffs of each county were ordered to approach the men 'of the best quality of your county'.[3]

Hardly had the original act been passed when additional acts were rushed through to enhance its terms or open them to more investors. By 16 Car. I, c. 34 the act's operation was extended to persons wishing to subscribe from Holland. By c. 35 the terms were thrown open to 'cities, boroughs, towns, corporate companies, guilds and fraternities'. Chapter 35 also extended the time limit for accepting subscriptions, and offered Irish measure

[1] MacCormack, 'The Irish Adventurers', p. 34.
[2] Ibid., and D. Brunton and D. H. Pennington, *Members of the Long Parliament*, London, 1954.
[3] MacCormack, 'The Irish Adventurers', p. 33, citing Thomason Tracts, BM, 669, f5/5 (13).

—a 60 per cent increase—to those who paid in their full subscriptions by 20 July.[1]

The ink was scarcely dry on these 'explanatory' acts when in mid April further proposals were made to Parliament, and enacted without the King's approval as an ordinance 'for the sea adventure to Ireland'.[2] Fifteen named Londoners and 'their associates', including the royalist adventurer Sir Nicholas Crispe, offered to set forth an expedition of twelve ships and six pinnaces, 'with a convenient number of land forces, horse and foot', as 'a good means to further the reducing of the said realm of Ireland and the rebels therein'. Parliament accepted this offer, licensing the petitioners to 'invade the said rebels, in any ports, harbors, creeks, havens, islands, castles, forts, towns, or any other places in the possession of the said rebels', and 'to take, surprise, vanquish, destroy, or kill' any rebels they should encounter. They were given further extensive powers to prey upon all rebel shipping, in effect, letters of marque. In return for those services the petitioners were to have all the booty they should take, and their expenses in this enterprise were to be treated 'as an additional increase of their former adventure'.[3] Many, but not all of the sea adventurers had formerly adventured under the act of 19 March, but the prospect of pillage apparently revitalized their interest. 171 adventurers ultimately put forth £43,000 for this expedition.[4]

The basic framework for financing the repression of the Irish rebellion had now been laid down, and was not without a measure of limited success. Money, though less than hoped for, was being taken up by the treasurers for the adventure, and in June the City agreed to lend £100,000 for Ireland's reconquest, abandoning the parsimonious course it had pursued since January.[5] This was an indication of the City's greater confidence and satisfaction in Parliament's Irish policy, now that Irish land had been opened

---

[1] 'Irish measure' see note p. xiii above.

[2] These were accepted by the Commons on 16 Apr., by the Lords on 29 Apr., and were printed on 17 June 1642.

[3] C. H. Firth and R. S. Rait, eds., *Acts and Ordinances of the Interregnum*, London, 1911, i. 9.

[4] These figures are drawn from J. P. Prendergast, *The Cromwellian Settlement of Ireland*, Dublin, 1875, Appendix V, the only extant source of information about sea adventure subscriptions. For further discussion of Prendergast's list see below, pp. 59–63.

[5] Charles M. Clode, ed., *London During the Great Rebellion*, London, 1892, p. 18.

to exploitation. Few doubted that England could reconquer Ireland, if sufficiently committed to the task; and the designation of Irish land as fiscal security for the reconquest insured that commitment and determined the form it would take.

The germ of the Cromwellian Settlement was planted by the act for adventurers, for it initiated a financial debt which could only conveniently be satisfied with Irish land. Ireland had thereafter not only to be conquered, but a significant chunk of it confiscated. The chunk grew in size as the English and Irish civil wars progressed. It was the fiscal needs of the Long Parliament and the Commonwealth, rather than the culpability of the Irish, which ultimately determined the extent of the Settlement.[1] The acts defining the guilt of the Irish were passed in 1652 and 1653, and were administered to put at the government's disposal sufficient land to satisfy its obligations. But this was only the consequence and outgrowth of a dependence upon Irish land which was initiated on the eve of the English civil war.

[1] An important description of the financial straits of the Commonwealth is H. J. Habakkuk, 'Public Finance and the Sale of Forfeited Property during the Interregnum', *EcHR*, 1962, pp. 70–88.

III

A PROFILE OF INVESTORS AND INVESTMENT

(i)

THE foundation of the Cromwellian Settlement of Ireland was laid in the spring of 1642 by the legislation of the Long Parliament.[1] The major features of that legislation were its assignment of Irish land to pay the ultimate costs of repressing the rebellion, and its postulation of a large group of English investors to undertake the immediate expenses of defending the English interest there. These investors, or adventurers, were eventually to be repaid in Irish land and to constitute a new colonial class in Ireland. It is of interest to determine how many persons responded to that opportunity, what kinds of people they were, why they became involved, and what influence they had upon the development of Parliament's policy towards Ireland and the rebellion. All such information is relevant to the central question of Colonialism or Imperialism: why and by what means one society expands into another.

In the spring of 1652, with the rebellion in Ireland all but extinguished, the adventurers claimed to have lent the state a total of £293,072 under the acts and ordinances of 1642, £12,283 under the 'doubling ordinance' of 1643, and, under a special provision of the same ordinance, £1,363 for rebel houses in the cities of Limerick, Galway, Waterford, and Wexford.[2] Altogether they reckoned the adventure to have brought in £306,718, a considerable amount of capital, even if only one-third of the amount hoped for by the framers of the scheme.

---

[1] This foundation was modified, but not significantly changed, by ordinances in 1643 and 1647 which simply liberalized the terms of investment and so sought to encourage further subscription. Those ordinances are discussed at greater length in Ch. IV.

[2] 'The Humble Petition of the Committee of Adventurers for Lands in Ireland', 6 Apr. 1652, Bodleian Carte MS. 67, f. 230; available, printed, in HMC, *Portland Manuscripts*, i. 639, and *CJ*, vii. 115.

If we compare the adventure with the joint-stock companies of the early seventeenth century we find that its total capital dwarfed all but that of the East India Company (£2,887,000). In his *Enterprise and Empire*, T. K. Rabb provides a convenient digest of the working capital of the principal trade and colonizing ventures of the period, 1575–1630. Only the Virginia Company, with £200,000, came close to the Irish adventure of the 1640s, while the various Irish ventures of the sixteenth and early seventeenth century were minuscule in comparison. £70,000, for instance, is Rabb's estimate of the capital invested in the Londonderry Plantation, while £30,000 is his rough guess at the amount invested in Munster.[1] It seems likely that the amount raised by the adventurers for Ireland exceeded by two and possibly three times what had been invested in Irish land during the whole of the Elizabethan and Jacobean reigns.

£306,718 also represented a substantial contribution to the cost of the war against the King, for none of the funds raised fell into royalist hands, despite the fact that the King was legally qualified to receive them.

In comparison with the other financial expedients of Parliament, the adventurers' capital shrinks to a more humble significance. The Commonwealth had realized by 1653 :

£108,990	from the King's goods,
£676,387	from Bishops' lands,
£1,170,000	from Dean and Chapter lands,
£816,834	from fee farms,
£1,434,000	from Crown lands, and
£1,224,916	from compositions with royalists.[2]

Between 1649 and 1656, something on the order of £3,500,000 was expended upon the subjugation of Ireland, over £2,000,000

[1] T. K. Rabb, *Enterprise and Empire*, Cambridge, Mass., 1967, pp. 57–9.

[2] Maurice Ashley, *Financial and Commercial Policy under the Cromwellian Protectorate*, 2nd edn., 1962, p. 41; and H. J. Habakkuk, 'Public Finance and the Sale of Confiscated Property during the Interregnum', *EcHR*, 1962. Whereas the adventure for Irish lands actually raised in 'hard cash' more than £300,000, the other lands in the disposal of the state were, for the most part, used to satisfy already existing debt, and at rates seldom advantageous to the creditors. The process is discussed by Habakkuk, and below, pp. 118–19, where its effects on the soldiers' settlement in Ireland are examined.

of that amount being raised and sent from England, while the remainder was derived from rents, assessments, and taxes collected in Ireland.[1] The total costs of the conquest included, also, the sporadic efforts at aid between 1642 and 1649. Those must have amounted to no less than £500,000, so that repressing the rebellion required a total of between £2,500,000 and £3,000,000 from English sources up to 1656, and that figure is exclusive of the £1,750,000 owed to the Cromwellian army and its creditors in Ireland, and intended to be satisfied in Irish land. The costs of the rebellion to England, then, proved at least three times the £1,000,000 the adventurers had estimated in 1642, and nearly ten times the amount the adventurers actually succeeded in raising. Nevertheless, the adventure was the initial legislative response to the Irish rebellion, and the Settlement which developed behind it preserved its basic assumptions and objectives.

For the English public the adventure possessed various attractions. First, as a speculation it offered possible increase of capital. Land selling at an average price of eight shillings per acre was, by any historical view, underpriced. If the rebellion were quickly repressed and title taken to Irish real estate, the possibilities of selling at a great profit were good. In contrast, a conventional loan to the state would yield only 8 per cent; but everything hinged upon the rapidity of the reconquest. The act of 1642 provided no form of repayment alternative to that of Irish land, so that, once in on the adventure, an investor was out of pocket for the duration, unless he managed (as many did, at a loss) to sell his shares to a secondary investor.[2] In a sense, the real value of his putative land was at its height the moment he subscribed. Prolongation of the war increased the likelihood of the lands' being wasted, and lessened any ultimate capital gain. For example, if an adventurer procured a claim on land at eight shillings an acre, which in 1640 was worth twelve shillings an acre, he would have a potential profit of fifty per cent. But if, after ten years of civil war, he was still able to sell it at only its 1640 price of twelve shillings per acre, his money would have earned only

[1] C. H. Firth, 'Account of Money Spent in the Cromwellian Reconquest and Settlement of Ireland, 1649–1656', *EHR*, 1899, pp. 105–9.

[2] According to a document in the Carte Papers, £11,249 of adventure money *was* paid back out of English Dean and Chapter lands, prior to 1652. This seems the only case of repayment in any form other than Irish land (Carte 67, f. 230).

5 per cent p.a. over the intervening period, considerably less than an 8 per cent conventional loan.

Secondly, as we have already shown, there was a religious and emotional attraction in the adventure. Money lent to the state for the repression of papist uprisings was money put to a good cause. The rebellion caused a shudder of fear and repulsion in most Englishmen and inspired investment in many who would not otherwise have become involved.

Finally, there was a 'colonial incentive' to participate in the adventure for those with a real enthusiasm to plant themselves or part of their family on new lands in Ireland. As one piece of propaganda put it, 'He that hath many children may raise his younger sons to as great a fortune by £200 purchase in this way, as £2000 in trade . . .', an argument plainly aimed at merchants rather than gentry.[1]

It is tempting to postulate certain types of economic behaviour appropriate to each of the three hypothetical types of investors: the 'zealot', the 'materialist', and the 'colonist'. The zealot ought to be an early investor—anxious to lend his money to the sacred cause of putting down the rebellion—and willing to hold on to his shares regardless of the prospects for speedy victory. By the same token he ought not to speculate in the deflated shares of other adventurers, for money so invested might serve himself but not the reconquest. The materialist, on the other hand, uninterested either in the cause or in settling in Ireland, would be tempted simply to speculate, to buy shares of adventure when *de*flated and sell them when *in*flated. Finally, the colonist, little concerned for the cause and unwilling to speculate, might invest in the original shares or buy them up later at deflated prices, but in either event he would hold the shares in the hope of some day claiming the land to which they entitled him. Obviously, such a model of behaviour is over-simplified, but the patterns, however difficult to explain, do exist. Analysing such economic behaviour, however, is the last rather than the first step in dealing with the adventurers.

The first step is to compile the data which makes such an

[1] 'A Declaration of Both Houses', Thomason Tracts, BM E. 136 (20), cited by J. R. MacCormack, 'The Irish Adventurers and the English Civil War', *IHS*, 1956, p. 31.

analysis possible, and for this purpose it is useful to regard the total number of adventurers between 1642 and 1658 as participants in a parade. They can be counted as they issue from the marshalling area, or as they cross the finishing line, or at some mid point in their march. In a conventional and well-disciplined parade the number should be the same, regardless of where the counter is placed; but in a disorderly parade, where participants are entering and leaving the procession over its entire course, measurements will vary drastically. Even if the number of participants remains the same, the paraders who finish may not be the same paraders as began.

The adventurers constitute such a 'disorderly' parade. They came into existence with the act of Charles I, but their composition was thereafter constantly changing. To be an adventurer was to possess a claim to Irish land under the acts and ordinances which designated Irish land as security for loans of money to the state. There were two ways to acquire such a claim: First, by subscribing funds with treasurers appointed for the purpose by Parliament. Certificates were issued showing how much the adventurer had invested. But as the war in Ireland dragged on without conclusion these vague 'futures' in Irish land were increasingly available from the original adventurers at a discount, so that secondary classes of adventurers came into existence. A considerable amount of traffic must have existed in these futures as the fortunes of men fluctuated along with the price of land. Early adventurers sold out or reduced their holdings, while new money came forward to buy them out or profit by their demise.

A census was taken of the adventurers three times, that is to say at three different points in their history. The first census is the collection of certificates of subscription preserved in the State Papers Ireland. These are not the records of the original treasurers appointed for receiving moneys, for those seem to have perished. Instead, they are records compiled by men that examined in 1653 and 1654 the claims of adventurers or their assignees who wished to 'draw' Irish land. The adventurers brought in the receipts for money issued by the treasurers between 1642 and 1647, or, in lieu of the receipts, they brought in affidavits certifying their subscription. If they were heirs or assignees of original adventurers, they brought in documents which would corroborate their claim as well: wills, letters, assignments, partnership instruments, and so forth. All of these were carefully preserved in the State Papers Ireland, and provide an initial census, though at one remove, of the original investors and their investments.[1]

The second complete census of the adventurers was taken between 1654 and 1658. It is a census not of those who invested as adventurers but of those who drew Irish land in the lotteries of 1653 and after. These 'drawers' were in many cases original investors, but some were heirs of original adventurers, while others were assignees or their heirs. There are several such lists, very nearly identical in form. They are sometimes referred to as 'barony tables', because they list by Irish barony the adventurers who had drawn land therein. All the adventurers who had drawn in a given barony were listed with the value or 'credit' of their adventure (it could be greater or less than the actual amount they had invested), the number of Irish and English acres to which this entitled them, and the quarter and subsections of the barony in which the lot was to be located. Such lists are to be found in the Public Record Office, but more complete and later lists (1658) are in Marsh's Library, Dublin, and an almost exact copy of that list is in the Irish Record Office, where no one seems previously to have noticed it.[2]

The third census is in many ways the most puzzling. It is the only printed list that purports to be of all the adventurers, and appeared as an appendix in the 1875 and subsequent editions of *The Cromwellian Settlement of Ireland* by J. P. Prendergast. Because of its relative accessibility Prendergast's list has been the most frequently used source regarding the adventures. Prendergast took this list 'from the collection of papers relating to the execution of the Act of Settlement made in 1675, by order of the Earl of Essex, Lord Lieutenant of Ireland, and preserved in nine folio volumes in the Record Tower, Dublin Castle'.[3] These papers were later transferred to the Irish Record Office, where they

---

[1] These documents are to be found in State Papers 63, vols. 289–302. They are calendared, though not always adequately, in the volume of *State Papers, Ireland: Adventurers for Land, 1642–1659*, ed. by R. P. Mahaffy, 1903.

[2] The PRO lists are in S.P. 63/300. That in Marsh's Library, Dublin, is catalogued Z. 2. 1. 5. The Irish Record Office Copy is marked 2A. 12. 43.

[3] J. P. Prendergast, *The Cromwellian Settlement of Ireland*, Dublin, 1875, p. 401.

perished in the fire of 1922. Prendergast's list has 1,360 entries, 1,188 of them subscriptions under 'the act' (i.e. of 19 March 1642), and 172 of them under the 'Ordinance for the Sea Service' of June 1642. There are 1,360 'adventures' rather than 'adventurers', because many of those listed as investing under 'the act' are also listed as investing under the sea ordinance. Actually there are 1,281 names.[1]

The questions about the list are: when was it compiled, from what records, by whom, and for what purpose? According to Prendergast the list could not be later than 1675. It contains no information about land, only about men and their investments. In form, therefore, it is closer to the certificates of subscription in the State Papers Ireland (S.P. 63) than to the barony tables in Marsh's Library. It is also closer in size. Prendergast's list contains 1,281 names, the papers in S.P. 63, 1,293. Marsh's barony tables, by contrast, contain but 1,043. Finally, the overlap of names in Prendergast and S.P. 63 is much greater than that between any other two lists. Of the 1,281 names on Prendergast's list, 1,041 of them (A and B in Table 1) appear also in S.P. 63. Only 549 (A and E) of the 1,281 also appear on Marsh's list. This seems to establish the closer relationship of Prendergast's list with S.P. 63 than with Marsh's barony tables.

TABLE I

Comparison of Names on Three Adventurer Lists

A	Investors who appear on all three lists	548
B	Investors who appear on S.P. 63 and Prendergast only	493
C	Investors who appear on S.P. 63 only	137
D	Investors who appear on Prendergast only	239
E	Investors who appear on Marsh and Prendergast only	1
F	Investors who appear on S.P. 63 and Marsh only	115
		1,533
G	Total no. of names appearing in S.P. 63 (A plus B plus C plus F)	1,293
H	Total no. of names on Prendergast (A plus B plus D plus E)	1,281
I	Total no. of names on Marsh's list plus at least one other (A plus E plus F)	664
J	Total no. of names on Marsh's list	1,043
K	Number of names peculiar to Marsh's list (J minus I)	379

[1] That is to say, the numeration shows 1,360 adventures. In fact, numbers 333 and 909 are missing, owing to lacunae in the original manuscript, and no. 588 is missing without explanation.

What, then, is the exact relationship between these two kindred lists? S.P. 63 is a slightly larger list (1,293 compared with 1,281). It contains 252 names (C and F) not listed in Prendergast, compared with 240 names (D and E) which appear in Prendergast and not in S.P. 63. Nearly half (115 out of 252) of the names in S.P. 63 and *not* in Prendergast appear in Marsh's list. But only 1 of the 240 names in Prendergast and *not* in S.P. 63 appears in Marsh's list. This means there are 239 names unique to Prendergast's list, and that fact strongly suggests that some source other than Marsh and S.P. 63 was used by the compiler of Prendergast's list. The 239 unique to Prendergast's list are a puzzling group. They include prominent M.P.s like Oliver St. John, Samuel Vassal, Sir Arthur Haselrigge, and the future Fourth Earl of Pembroke (Phillip Herbert), as well as Thomas Adams, John Warner, and Laurence Halstead, Aldermen of the City. It is easy to think of a reason why they did not get into Marsh's list: they had, presumably, assigned their land to others prior to the lottery. But why are they not found in S.P. 63—at least among the subscription certificates? There are two possibilities: first that they were intermediate investors, who bought from original adventurers and sold to subsequent ones before the land lotteries of 1653–4. More likely, however, the 239 were original investors whose certificates are unaccountably missing from S.P. 63. This thesis is confirmed, at least with regard to the M.P.s among the 239, nearly all of whom are shown as original and early investors by a list printed in 1642.[1] It is thus more likely that the 239 *were* original adventurers who ought to have been included in S.P. 63, but that, if so, the certificates of subscription have not survived. S.P. 63 then, cannot stand alone. Prendergast is more than its pale shadow, and includes information which complements that in the public records.

What of the 115 names which appear in S.P. 63 *and* Marsh—but *not* in Prendergast? These are partially the result of changing nomenclature. John French is shown in S.P. 63 to have adventured £200 under the act and £50 under the doubling ordinance in partnership with Richard Darnelly and William Frith. Neither his name nor Frith's appears in Prendergast, but their standing

---

[1] The printed list is in Thomason Tracts, BM, 669 f. 5 (3) and John Rushworth, ed., *Historical Collections*, London, 1659–1701, iv. f. 563ᵛ.

is obviously described under entry 227, 'Richard Dornelly and Co-partners' [*sic*]. S.P. 63 is often more complete in the sense that all partners are named in any given venture. Most of the 115 names, along with many of the 137 names found only in S.P. 63, belong to adventurers from corporations, like Exeter, which are given but one entry in Prendergast's list, but which actually represent the contributions of many individuals (over 100 in the case of Exeter). There are other important differences between these two lists. Prendergast's list distinguishes between adventure under the act and adventure under the sea ordinance. The documents in S.P. 63 do not. This too suggests that Prendergast's list was compiled by someone with access to material not now in S.P. 63. On the other hand, S.P. 63 identifies adventure under the later 'doubling' ordinances, while all information relating to the doubling ordinances was omitted from Prendergast's list.[1]

That no subscriptions subsequent to the sea ordinances were recorded in Prendergast constitutes an important clue. For why should a list—the compilers of which apparently had at their disposal records more complete than those at present in S.P. 63 —omit the £14,000 (approximately) raised under the additional ordinances? The answer must be that the list was compiled *after* the Caroline acts of settlement and explanation disallowed all claims to Irish land under the doubling ordinances. Hence the list was made up in the 1660s by someone who wanted a complete list of the *original* adventurers and their investments under the only laws which the Restoration Settlement recognized as entitling adventurers, their heirs or assigns, to Irish land. For those purposes the barony tables were useless, for they did not indicate the actual amount invested by the claimant, but only the *value* of his claim as established by the examiners in 1653 and 1654. It was no easy job to distinguish legitimate claims from the inflated ones of the doubling ordinance, and every acre claimed had to be traced back to determine whether it derived from a legitimate investment, as defined by the new acts of settlement.

[1] Prendergast did not realize this. 'It is evidently', he wrote, 'a list of the original adventurers under the various Acts and Ordinances of subscription, commencing with the Act of 17 Charles I . . ., and ending in 1646, when all further subscription ceased' (*The Cromwellian Settlement*, p. 401). Subscription did not cease in 1646. Officially it was ended by an ordinance of 13 Nov. 1647, but was reopened, with little effect, in 1652 and 1653.

Prendergast's list, then, is the latest of the three lists, but it attempted to recreate the roster of original investors as it might have stood in 1643 on the eve of the doubling ordinance. In doing so, it incorporated some information which appears not to have survived in any other form. Used carefully, it is an important supplement to the information in S.P. 63.

It is necessary to add that, despite its structural soundness, Prendergast's list is a mass of errors. Some of these, no doubt, were part of the manuscript which Prendergast found—but a great many more were due to Prendergast or his publisher. One can hardly blame J. R. MacCormack for failing to find an entry for Gilbert Millington, a regicide M.P. who adventured £1,275, together with several partners. He is listed under Gilbert Willington. Manifold misspellings in the list are further obscured by an index which is incomplete, frequently incorrect, oblivious of alphabetical order, and which passed through three editions without corrections of any kind. In the 'disorderly parade' of adventurers from England to Ireland, S.P. 63 is an account close to the origin. Marsh's barony tables give the state of the adventure in the lottery stage, that is, from 1654 to 1658. Prendergast's list supplements S.P. 63 and is based upon sources no longer extant.

From these three sources a list of 1,533 investor-adventurers has been compiled (Appendix A). 1,293 of them were taken from S.P. 63, the basic component of the list and the remainder were derived from Prendergast. *No* names were added from Marsh's list (which includes 379 names not on the other two lists), because it is essentially a list of *drawers* of land as of 1658, not of investors. Investor-adventurers have been defined as those who subscribed for Irish land prior to 1653, whose subscriptions were recorded either in S.P. 63 or in Prendergast's list. It may be objected that this is an arbitrary definition and that it is either too narrow or too broad. Purists might argue that the 240 names from Prendergast's list cannot be proved to have been *original* adventurers, because certificates of subscription are not to be found for them in S.P. 63. Advocates of a broader definition could reply that anyone who either invested in or claimed a share of adventure, or drew a lot in Ireland by virtue of some share, ought to be regarded as an adventurer. Use of these criteria would add all 379 of the names peculiar to Marsh's list, plus a host of 'intermediary' adventurers who populate the records of S.P. 63. I have chosen what seemed the middle course of including only those persons who could reasonably be assumed to have been original investors: men who loaned their money to the state upon security of Irish land rather than men whose involvement was essentially secondary and speculative.

(ii)

In order to understand either the development of capitalist society or the economic roots of colonial expansion, it is necessary to identify the sectors of the society from which investment sprang. Modern business machinery—with the computer at its apex—is ideally adapted to examining economic activity, whether recent or historic. Only the quality and quantity of data gathered in a pre-statistical era limits the possibilities of such an examination. In the case of the adventurers, that data includes the amounts they contributed, their places of residence, their statuses, and their professions. Sex is ordinarily ascertainable from Christian names. Of course there are large lacunae. Status, residence, and profession are not to be found for all adventurers. The political and religious affiliations of only a few adventurers are known, and they, for the most part, are members of Parliament. J. R. MacCormack examined the M.P. adventurer as a group in his article 'The Irish Adventurers and the English Civil War'.[1] His conclusions are discussed below (p. 71), together with the difficulties of extrapolating from them to the adventurers as a whole. In examining all 1,533 persons we have classified as investor adventurers, we are confined for the most part to social, geographical, and professional considerations, of which the geographical are the most basic.

Of the 1,533 adventurers it is possible to attribute a geographical location to all but 202. Of the 1,331 who can be classified, 750 prove to have been from London. These 750, collectively, contributed over £170,000 toward the adventure, a little more than half of the total collected. Londoners subscribed approximately half the £258,000 raised under the original

[1] *IHS*, 1956, pp. 22–58.

act, more than three-fifths of the £43,000 raised by the sea ordinance of June 1642, and nearly nine-tenths of the money raised on the doubling ordinance of 1643. Both in numbers and in total investment they were the clearly preponderant geographical group in the adventure. Their statistically heavy role helps to explain the involvement of London in adventurer affairs during the 1640s, and the tendency of 'the adventurers in London' to act as the executive of the body as a whole.

The remaining adventure money came from all over the country. The Home Counties produced a substantial share. Eighteen adventurers from Buckinghamshire advanced £4,709, 22 from Essex £3,614, 14 from Middlesex £2,693. Like numbers and sums came from Sussex, Surrey, Hertfordshire, Suffolk, and Norfolk. Investment from the north, though light, was not rare. £1,110 came from 10 investors in Lancashire, £3,418 from 13 in Yorkshire, £1,285 from 15 in Derbyshire. Such outposts as Durham and Cumberland were, not surprisingly, unrepresented. The one area, outside of London, where there was a striking amount of investor interest was the West Country. In Somerset 44 adventurers advanced £3,953. In Bristol (in addition) three adventurers alone subscribed £2,050. In Dorset 6 subscribed £3,350. But the outstanding example is Devon, where something of the order of 200 adventurers put forward approximately £17,500. The data for Devon is confusing because the City of Exeter (under the Act of 16 Car. I. c. 35) maintained its own records, which overlap awkwardly with those in S.P. 63, but it is clear that the West Country as a whole generated an amount of capital and a number of investors unmatched by any other provincial area. The West had long been identified with Irish colonization, particularly with the plantation of Munster in the late sixteenth century, but this is not necessarily an adequate explanation of the enthusiasm of Devon. In addition, the phenomenon of small investment is nowhere more visible than in Exeter, where 132 persons contributed £5,553 (an average investment of £42), a strikingly lower figure than the £220 average for the 1,533 adventurers as a whole.[1] The adventure in Exeter was therefore markedly different from

[1] See below, pp. 158–60, for a more detailed examination of the Exeter subscription.

the adventure in London, where it was largely the province of very rich men.[1] In Exeter there appeared the phenomenon of 'popular' colonialism, in which relatively humble people sought security and increments of wealth from the nearby lands of Ireland.

The dominance of London remains the salient geographic characteristic of the adventure, and is visible, also, in a profile of the adventurers' vocations. Seventy-one vocational 'labels' were applied to the adventurers by the keepers of their records. Some of these, such as 'lord', 'yeoman', or 'esquire', are more properly 'status' than vocational appellations. Nevertheless, they make it possible to distinguish roughly between 'trade' and 'land'. Only roughly, of course, because a butcher or draper could also be a wealthy guildsman with manors in Essex. Nevertheless, out of the seventy-one categories, seven seem predominantly 'non-urban': cleric, esquire, gentleman, knight, lady, lawyer, and yeoman. It is true that any one (except yeoman and esquire), and especially lawyer or cleric, could be found in a thriving town, but as a group they seem less inherently urban than the pewterers, plasterers, painter-stainers, and the like who make up the remaining sixty-four categories. If, then, the seven excepted categories are treated as a 'gentry' group and the sixty-three others as a 'merchant' group, a further analysis of the 1,533 adventurers can be attempted. Of the adventurers 928 have vocational designations. There is no reason to assume that those who do not would be more likely to be in one group than the other; so the 928 should constitute a reasonably fair sample. Of these 928, 239 fall into the 'country' or 'gentry' category, and account for £72,996 of adventure; 689 fall into the 'merchant' or 'urban' category, and account for £139,333. The average investment of the 'gentry' investors is £305; that of the 'urban' investors £200. Once again the evidence thus arranged points to the predominance of urban and merchant money, though not to the exclusion of a substantial and well-heeled rural or gentry involvement.

---

[1] The average London investor contributed approximately the same amount—£200—as the average investor from the group as a whole. There were many small investors from London but not nearly so many, proportionately, as from Exeter.

The picture is not dissimilar to that presented by T. K. Rabb, who has recently examined gentry involvement in trading and colonizing ventures of the period 1575–1630. Rabb found some twenty companies in which gentry investors constituted more than one-quarter of the classifiable members. The Irish plantations of the period—treated as one group of 762 persons— appeared to have 26·5 per cent gentry members.[1] My figures for the adventurers suggest a similar numerical level of participation (25·7 per cent), but a slightly larger participation in terms of money (33·9 per cent). Faced with a lack of individual invest- ment data, Rabb assumed the percentage of investment would be proportional to the percentage of involvement, a sometimes misleading supposition.[2] The mixture of gentry and merchant involvement delineated by Rabb in the earlier period is obviously still an important factor, as is the predominance of merchants. Both R. G. Lang and Rabb have noted that gentry tended to be attracted more strongly to colonizing than to trading companies, and for that reason they might have been expected to make a strong showing in the Irish adventure of the 1640s.[3] But the dominance of the urban and merchant investment—whether measured in the dominance of London over the provinces or of merchant vocations over country statuses—seems an indisput- able characteristic of the Irish adventure.

The preponderance of the City places the Irish adventure squarely in the tradition of the Plantation of Ulster, and reveals it to have been a successor to the ill-starred involvement of the City in Londonderry. For both plantations had turned very early in their course to London for capital, and in so doing acquired an entrepreneurial cast. That is to say, the men who

[1] *Enterprise and Empire*, p. 30, Table 2. Rabb distinguished basically between 'gentlemen' whose 'income originally came from land' and 'merchants' whose 'income originally came from commerce' (p. 12).

[2] Ibid., p. 55.

[3] R. G. Lang, 'The Greater Merchants of London in the Early Seventeenth Century', Oxford D.Phil. thesis, 1963, p. 265. None of the 140 greater merchants in his sample participated in the colonizing of New England in the 1620s. Lang depicts the merchants as highly conservative, and wary of the hidden costs of colonizing ventures. Trade was more to their liking. The gentry, on the other hand, familiar with land and its management, were more disposed to schemes of overseas land settlement. In this sense both the Ulster and Cromwellian settle- ments were exceptions in which the nearness of the new lands seems to have drawn merchants to an unwonted involvement.

financed the plantation had, themselves, little desire to participate in it. What fishmonger with capital of £200 would have condemned himself to the wilds of Ireland? The settling of some hapless younger son might rather have been his objective, or the turning of a profit when the rebellion was over and land values returned. Can one envisage Pym settling down to his £600 worth, or many of the other adventurer M.P.s having done so? Nor was absentee landlordism necessarily a more promising solution, conducing, as it did, to dwindling revenues and the deterioration of the English plantation. It is at least arguable that many of the adventurers were investing not in land but in 'futures', that is to say, in claims upon a commodity which they would never enjoy in their own names, but which they hoped to dispose of profitably to others. Such a mercantile outlook toward land would seem least surprising in the adventurers from urban and commercial backgrounds.

Some such explanation is necessary to account for the 'volatility' of the original adventurers, their gradual disappearance from the adventurers' records. To employ the metaphor used above, many who began the parade did not finish it, and a high number of new men took up their places at the finishing-line. The latest, chronologically, of the existing adventurer lists is the set of barony tables in Marsh's Library, Dublin. The 1,043 persons named on that list each claimed Irish land in 1653 and 1654. But of that 1,043, only 664 (A plus E plus F, in Table 1) can be found in S.P. 63 or Prendergast, the sources for the names of original adventurers. 379 (K) were newcomers who, at some point between 1642 and 1658, had bought into the adventure, taking over the claims and certificates of original subscribers.

If 36 per cent (379 of 1,043) of the men who drew land were not original investors, 67 per cent (869—B plus C plus D—of 1533) of the original investors failed to claim land in 1653. These 869 had dropped from sight, and, for the most part, their shares had been bought up or inherited by the 379 newcomers. This reduction in the numbers of men involved, without a corresponding reduction of the claims outstanding, indicates a consolidating tendency within the adventure, a phenomenon surely connected with the tendency in Irish Plantation history of small holders to sell and large holders to buy.

If we investigate the group of categories that we have identified with gentry, we find it made up of:

68 clerics	investing	£8,561	(average £126)
36 esquires	„	£11,730	(average £326)
48 gentlemen	„	£13,043	(average £274)
53 knights	„	£33,503	(average £632)
3 ladies	„	£270	(average £90)
12 lawyers	„	£4,060	(average £338)
19 yeomen	„	£1,829	(average £96)
239		£72,996	

The peerage played a minor role. Philip Herbert, Fourth Earl of Pembroke, advanced £600, but does not appear on the barony lists. Edward, First Baron Littleton, advanced £150. William Lord Mounson invested £600. Thomas, Second Viscount Wenman, successor to an Irish barony in 1640, invested £600 and drew the full amount in Kings County. These four peers make up the total aristocratic complement. Their four persons and collective investment of £1,950 would add very little to the percentage of 'gentry' involvement if they were added, for purposes of computation, to the 'gentry' category. They do, however, glaringly demonstrate the negative: that the Irish adventure was anathema among the peerage, very probably because the King's assent to the act of 19 March 1642 was known to be a grudging concession, and because the adventure as a whole was heavily tinged with partisan and parliamentary considerations.

An analysis of the sixty-four 'urban' categories is less revealing. 'Merchants' constitute the single largest group (the label was obviously applied widely), with 117 members investing £36,169 (average: £309). Of the guildsmen, merchant-tailors are the largest group (62 subscribing £13,272—average: £214), followed by the grocers (60 subscribing £15,091—average: £251) and the haberdashers (49 subscribing £6,820—average: £139). The goldsmiths, apothecaries, brewers, clothworkers, drapers, feltmongers, girdlers, ironmongers, leathersellers, mercers, pewterers, salters, skinners, stationers, and tallow-chandlers, all had more than ten members subscribing a total of £1,000 or more. Not all these guildsmen were Londoners (though most of them certainly were), and it would require a more discrete study of Londoners alone to determine the relative roles of the London companies. It is unlikely that such a study would reveal anything other than that the larger and richer companies, the same companies as had been heavily involved in the Londonderry Plantation, played the leading roles.[1] Examination of the guild and vocational background of the 'urban' group of investors also emphasizes the breadth and variety of that sector. Great and small guildsmen rubbed shoulders with mariners, shoemakers, and whitebakers. One cannot find that within the urban group any single element predominated to the exclusion of others.

A significant portion of the total adventure money was raised from members of the Long Parliament. Before the books were closed, 119 M.P.s had subscribed £69,982, more than a fifth of the total raised by 1653.[2] The M.P. adventurers averaged nearly £600 apiece. They contributed nearly one-quarter of the money raised under the original act, only 12 per cent of the money raised under the sea ordinance, and 15 per cent of that on the 'doubling' ordinance. Their prominence was most notable in the scheme's early months, and it was repeatedly urged that their involvement should serve as an example to the nation.

The most prominent members of the parliamentary opposition were, not surprisingly, in the vanguard of the adventure. John Pym invested £600, John Hampden £1,000, and Oliver St. John £300. Cromwell subscribed £300 for the original adventure, £300 for the sea adventure—and perhaps acquired £250 more before the 1653 drawings for land by which he acquired 1,257 Irish acres in Kings County. Sir Arthur Haselrigge appears to have subscribed £1,000 and £600 to land and sea adventures respectively. Denzil Holles is credited with £1,000 in an early printed list (Thomason Tracts, BM, 669, f. 3), but is

---

[1] See above, p. 21, footnote 4, for a list of contributions of London companies to the Londonderry Plantation. The similarity is striking.

[2] MacCormack counted 136 M.P. adventurers, because he included some who appear neither in S.P. 63 or Prendergast. I have regarded such M.P.s as 'secondary' adventurers and have excluded them.

otherwise invisible. The largest single M.P. adventurer was the royalist Sir Nicholas Crispe, with £2,600. Gregory Clement, the London regicide recruited to Parliament only in 1647, was a close second, with £2,100. More than two dozen M.P.s subscribed and paid amounts of £1,000 or more, thus comprising about 50 per cent of all investors in that category (see table below p. 73). Some allowance must be made, however, for the practice of M.P.s subscribing in their own names money which had been taken up from relatives, friends, constituents, or commercial associates. Thus Dennis Bond, a woollen draper who sat for Dorchester, subscribed £2,000 in trust for citizens of that town.

J. R. MacCormack examined the M.P. adventurers as a group and found only 8·8 per cent of them classifiable as royalists. If anything, his computation over-estimates the royalist role, and my own calculations would place it closer to 7·5 per cent, or 10 out of 119 M.P.s. Most of the ten were middling adventurers who advanced less than the £600 average for adventurer M.P.s. One, Sir Edward Littleton, appeared also as one of our four peerage adventurers, with an investment of £150. By far the most impressive was the monopolist, Sir Nicholas Crispe, who invested £900 in the original adventure and a further £1,700 in the adventure under the sea ordinance. On the barony lists he is shown to have drawn 2,000 acres in Limerick—though whether he retained or ever occupied the land is not known. How he reconciled his ardent royalism with so markedly parliamentary a scheme as the adventure is equally obscure, but the paucity of his royalist colleagues suggests that it was not easily or frequently done. To judge from the House of Commons, future royalists, like peers, were able to resist the economic attractions of the venture into Irish land.

MacCormack also attempted to calculate the relative roles of 'Independents' and 'Presbyterians'. He found that 41·1 per cent of the M.P. adventurers were 'Independents' (by the criteria of Brunton and Pennington), that 26·4 per cent were 'Presbyterians', and that 23·7 per cent were 'Parliamentarians but not readily classifiable'. The remaining 8·8 per cent were, of course, royalists.[1] MacCormack inferred that the future Independents

[1] MacCormack, 'The Irish Adventurers', p. 39.

were the major force behind the adventure—or, at any rate, that they responded most enthusiastically to it. MacCormack was also able to show that Independent M.P.s were slightly larger investors on the average than Presbyterian M.P.s, a further proof, he believed, of their deeper commitment to the cause. I have not attempted to re-do MacCormack's computations, even though my list of the adventures differs on a number of details, and the limitations of Brunton and Pennington's categories have been demonstrated.[1] My conclusions would almost certainly be similar, and the heavy role of Independent M.P.s would certainly remain.

Two important questions suggest themselves, but are not easily answered. (1) Were the 1,414 adventurers who did not sit in Parliament as sympathetic to Independency as the 119 who did? and (2) Why were M.P. Independents so attracted to the adventure? There is really no way of knowing the answer to the first. That embryonic Independents were attracted to the adventure in greater number than other parliament men would seem explicable in terms of their greater disaffection from conventional policies. To accept the adventure they had to reject all thought of compromise with the rebels in Ireland, all thought of conciliation or of a 'political' solution. To some the Irish rebellion of 1641 was a regrettable disaster, but to others it was flaming proof of Catholic perfidy. The adventure accorded best with this latter group, for implicit in it was the presumption of Irish criminality on a national scale. The less disaffected Presbyterians—eager to negotiate with the King for specific political and religious objectives—were not inclined to make Ireland an obstacle to that achievement by rendering its settlement non-negotiable. For that was precisely what the adventure

---

[1] A whole literature exists on the meaning of the word 'Independent'. See David Underdown, 'The Independents Again', *JBS*, viii (1968), 83–93.

In an article, 'Political Affiliations in the House of Commons after Pym's Death' (*Bulletin of the Institute of Historical Research*, xxxviii (1965)), Dr. Lotte Glow argued that after 1644 'the Irish investors found themselves largely backing the forces of peace in England', the implication being that they leaned to moderation or Presbyterianism. I agreed with this view at one point, and it may well be true on the whole of adventurers who were *not* M.P.s. But in the late 1640s M.P. adventurers appeared in both war and peace parties, and perhaps predominantly in the former, their interest in Ireland leading them to no unanimous political position in England.

did: it created an economic barrier to negotiations over Ireland.
It gave birth to a claim on Irish land which could be satisfied
only by a drastic and punitive settlement.

In a crude sense, we have now determined that the collective
character of the adventurers was more London than country,
more merchant than gentry, more parliament than royalist, and
more Independent than Presbyterian (at least within Parliament).
We should look also at some of the patterns of investment, and
particularly at the question of whether the adventure money
came preponderantly from small investors or large ones. We
know that the average adventurer subscribed £220, but it would
be misleading to assume that there were 1,533 such 'average'
investors. The following table indicates the dispersion of
investments of various sizes.

Investors who adventured		Total of their investment:
£1000 or more:	50	£73,624
£500–£999:	125	£78,839
£100–£499:	755	£138,233
£25–£99:	440	£20,247
less than £25:	163	£1,940
	1,533	£312,883

It reveals that only 7 per cent of the money raised came from the
40 per cent of the investors whose investments amounted to less
than £100. The mainstay of the adventure was obviously the
numerous class of investors who advanced between £100 and
£499, while those who advanced £500 or over, though only
176 in number, contributed nearly 50 per cent of the total
amount collected. Only two adventurers appear to have invested more than £2,500, although many other speculators
acquired claims to that amount by buying up discounted shares.
One of the former was Sir David Watkins, a London merchant
who subscribed £2,025 for the original adventure in April
1642. In June he subscribed and paid an additional £375 for the
sea adventure, and in 1646 he availed himself of the 'doubling
ordinance' by paying in an additional £600 (¼ the sum of his
original investment). This entitled him, under the existing
legislation, to draw land to the value of £6,000, and he did so,
according to the barony tables, for 10,000 Irish acres in the

counties of Queens and Eastmeath. The other 'super-adventurer' was the mysterious Lewis Dyke whose name appears only in Prendergast's list, where he is credited with an imposing investment of £5,200 in the sea adventure. No information is given about his place of residence, vocation, or status, and neither his name nor any reasonable variation of it appears in the other records of the adventure. Conceivably he is one of Prendergast's many misprints. If he actually existed and actually invested more than £5,000, he managed thereafter to creep inconspicuously from the annals of Plantation.[1] The greater part of the adventure money came from men who had advanced it in sizeable parcels, but not from a limited number of tycoons who had each made massive investments. In so far as the adventure failed by nearly two-thirds to reach its goal of £1,000,000, its failure was to recruit more large investments. It was not that those who invested, invested too little, but that not enough large adventurers came forward. Unless we assume that only those who *did* adventure *could* adventure, that is, that those who did not subscribe simply could not afford to, we are left with the opposite conclusion: that a great number of wealthy men hung back and refused, on mainly political grounds, to be associated with the enterprise. The very profile of adventure investment we have drawn leads us to ask: where was the country money, the gentry money, the royalist money, the Presbyterian money? No economic theory equips us to believe that only the urban, merchant, Independent and Parliament-supporting citizenry was wealthy enough to invest in the adventure, so that we are forced to account for the absence of that major part of the *richesse*. The answer to which our data points is that the economic

---

[1] Since writing the above I have discovered lengthy litigation involving Lewis Dyke in the 1660s. At the Restoration Alderman William Barker of London, an original adventurer and Long Parliament M.P., claimed 15,550 acres in Limerick and Tipperary as assignee of two alleged adventurers, Dyke for £5200, and Thomas Cunningham for £1800. The *bona fide* character of Dyke and Cunningham's adventure was challenged by a set of plaintiffs led by one Joseph Ruthorne who contended that the two 'adventurers' never paid in the amounts they claimed, but that in 1649 they had been given certificates of subscription in return for sea services performed (against the King) in 1642 in English waters. Thus, Ruthorne argued, the adventure of Dyke and Cunningham was bogus and not entitled to confirmation by Charles II. In 1667 the Irish Council Board upheld Ruthorne's challenge, and Barker seems to have lost the lands. *CSPI*, 1663–65 and 1666–69, *sub* Dyke, Cunningham, and Barker.

attractions of the adventure tended to be persuasive only when reinforced by political, social, and religious considerations. The adventure did not exist in an idealized free market in which materialism could function as the sole efficient cause.

(iii)

The profile of the adventurers as a group reveals their essential narrowness. Though not without royalists, Anglicans, gentry, and country-folk, the adventurers were predominantly their opposites. The faint-hearted endorsement which Charles I gave the act for adventurers was evidently reflected, even magnified, in the purses of his people. Perhaps the burning outrage of Protestant England has been over-estimated, and insufficient allowance made for the propagandist nature of much that was said and written of Ireland in 1641 and 1642.

In the long run the adventure was a two-fold failure. In a fiscal sense it failed to raise the amount of money necessary to repress Catholic Ireland. In a colonial sense it failed to find and tap an aggressive, expansive, and enterprising stream within English society. It did not rouse any abiding interest in the colonization of Ireland, comparable to seventeenth-century emigration to North America. No doubt Ireland, with its sad history of uprooted plantations and war-torn land, was partially responsible, but the partisan quality of the adventure played its part. It must have been more obvious to contemporaries than to us that the primary beneficiaries of the adventure were the opponents of Charles I. Even if the moneys raised *were* used in Ireland—as many feared they would not be—they would promote Parliament's independence of the Crown. The adventure was conceived as a response to the Irish crisis. But all the marks of the English crisis are upon it. If it was to expand the former Plantation policy in Ireland to a new magnitude, this was less because that seemed a sensible solution to the Irish problem than because no other response was compatible with the ambition of the parliamentary opposition. What seems most tragic about the Irish Settlement of the seventeenth century is not its heroic sternness—but rather the almost frivolous series of financial and political expedients which brought it into being.

IV

PARLIAMENT'S IRISH POLICY
1642-9

WE have now examined the genesis of the adventure and the character, so far as it can be determined, of the investors who participated in it. But a seven-year hiatus existed between the inception of the adventure in 1642 and the Cromwellian conquest of 1649 which began its fulfilment. During those years the adventure was inseparably tied to Parliament, the body which had fostered it. The subject of this chapter is Parliamentary policy towards Ireland, the way in which it interacted with the adventure, and the way in which it contributed to the development of the Cromwellian Settlement. 'Policy' is perhaps too grand a word, suggesting as it does a comprehensive programme or ideology. Neither King nor Parliament had a policy, as such, for Ireland. Each was struggling for its own survival and viewed Ireland and Irish problems only as they bore upon the English struggle.

The Crown's Irish dealings have historically attracted a certain amount of attention, for Charles's fortunes depended heavily upon Ireland.[1] His Irish policy was crucial to his cause. Had he been able to restore order there and knit together an Irish coalition in support of his cause, the military victory of Parliament and its Scottish allies might have been prevented.

Ireland's importance to Parliament was by contrast entirely negative: Ireland could lend little assistance, but could cause immense difficulties. It was therefore the axiom of Parliamentary policy to prevent the Crown from deriving any benefit from Ireland, and as a corollary to support Protestant New English resistance to the Irish rebellion. If the Protestant inhabitants of Ireland laid down their arms or accepted an

---

[1] See, for instance, John Lowe, 'Charles I and the Confederation of Kilkenny', an unpublished London Ph.D. thesis, and an article of the same name in *IHS*, 1964, pp. 1–19.

accommodation with the rebels, the Catholic Irish would be free to stream to the support of the King, or so it was assumed. On the other hand, the Protestants of Ireland had little alternative to accommodation of some kind, unless they received massive support from Parliament, and such support, as we shall see, Parliament was unwilling or unable to lend.

Parliament's policy towards Ireland in the years 1642–9 revolved around several questions, the foremost of which was *when* a reconquering expedition would be dispatched. Secondary, but highly controversial, were the questions of who should lead such an expedition, how large it should be, and by what means it could be financed. Finally, and for seven years more relevant, Parliament had to determine what to do for Ireland pending reconquest.

The adventurers were involved in all these considerations, both as members of the House of Commons and as members of extra-parliamentary committees appointed to handle aspects of the Irish effort. Did they, as a group, have a distinct policy for Ireland based upon their economic interest, and if so, what success did they have in urging it upon Parliament? To what extent, in other words, did the adventure and the adventurers determine the course which Parliament followed with regard to Ireland? What role, beyond the mere promulgation of the adventure scheme, did the investors play in the unfolding Cromwellian Settlement?

The adventurers, it should be recalled, had originally seen themselves as something like corporate *condottieri*. In their petition to Parliament of 11 February 1642 they had demanded the right to name the officers in the military forces for Ireland, and, implicitly, the right to manage and supervise the war effort there.[1] This was partly a political move to assure would-be adventurers that their moneys would be employed in Ireland and not in political struggles at home; but there was, apart from this, a distinctly proprietary attitude toward the Irish rebellion, as if, in effect, the adventurers were purchasing a concession to repress it and collect whatever profits accrued. As the act was finally passed it contained no disposition of military responsibilities to the adventurers, and substituted for that

---

[1] *CJ*, ii. 425.

guarantee a mere assurance 'that no part of the money which shall be paid in according to this Act shall be imployed to any other purpose than the reducing of the said Rebels [in Ireland] . . .'[1] Actual authority over the sums collected by the treasurers of the adventure remained vested in Parliament, a heavy blow to the non-partisan pretensions of the scheme.

From its enactment, if not its inception, the adventure was an *appannage* of Parliament, which had erected the initial machinery for dealing with the rebellion. On 1 November 1641 the House of Lords had appointed twenty-six of its members to be 'commissioners for Irish Affairs' (a title which had been employed by both James I and Charles I previously), and on the following day the Commons had appointed fifty-two of its body to serve with them.[2] Thereafter the commissioners reported from time to time to the House of Commons, often through John Pym, one of their members.

For the most part, the work of the commissioners is observable only in the records of the House of Commons, where their activity is inconspicuous among the functions of numerous *ad hoc* committees treating various aspects of the Irish crisis. A glimpse of its workings is found in the diary of Sir Simonds D'Ewes, one of the Commons' fifty-two commissioners. On 13 November 1641, for instance, the commissioners were discussing with the Lord Lieutenant, the Earl of Leicester, whether a winter war could be successfully prosecuted in Ireland. The Lord Lieutenant, probably hesitant more for political than strategical reasons, argued that it could not. D'Ewes, anxious to see the rebellion repressed, rather than exploited for political reasons, countered that between 1600 and 1603 Mountjoy had proved the contrary: the feasibility, even necessity, of carrying out winter operations against Irish rebels.[3]

In April 1642 we find the commissioners proposing that a

---

[1] *Statutes of the Realm*, 16 Car. i. c. 33, article x.

[2] Robert Dunlop, review article in *EHR*, 1906, p. 589. Twenty-two of the Commons commissioners later became adventurers, but a number, most notably Hyde and Falkland, were royalists and separated themselves soon there after from Parliament.

[3] *The Journal of Sir Simonds D'Ewes*, ed. Willson H. Coates, New Haven, 1942, p. 132.

brigade of 5,000 men should be sent into Munster.[1] They agreed also to ask the adventurers—now in the midst of raising their funds—whether they would pay for this Munster expedition. By the next day the adventurers had agreed, thus initiating the special relationship between themselves and the Munster expedition which was to persist until midsummer. By late May, and probably earlier, the adventurers had crystallized some committees of their own. In particular the adventurers who were members of Parliament constituted one such body, while a committee 'chosen in London of the adventurers themselves' constituted another.[2] The M.P. adventurers were acting as liaison between the House of Commons as a whole and the adventurers collectively.

In late May we catch a glimpse of the London adventurers complaining to the M.P. adventurers thay they were not being given a sufficient role in the naming of officers for the Munster expedition.[2] In mid June and early July the adventurers were attempting to speed up the preparation of the expedition, which, under the direction of the Parliamentary commissioners, was making but slow progress toward embarkation for Ireland.[3] The brigade, under the command of Philip, Fourth Baron Wharton, was intended to take ship at Chester; but on 28 July a letter was addressed to the committee for the Irish adventurers [in London] by the committee for the defence of the kingdom. It spoke of 'the distresses of the Kingdom' and of 'disbursements . . . so great that greater sums are now necessary . . . than the Lords and Commons can for the present raise'. In short, the adventurers were desired to advance to Parliament from their funds £100,000 'by way of loan, upon the public faith, to be repaid in so short a time that it shall not be diverted from the purpose for which it was intended, or any way frustrate the acts already made on behalf of that adventure'.[4] Two days later, on 30 July, saying that the consent of the committee for adventurers had already been obtained, the House of Commons authorized £100,000 to be borrowed from the adventurers 'for

---

[1] Propositions of the Lords and other Commissioners for Irish Affairs, 18 Apr. 1642, PRO, S.P. 63/260, no. 66.
[2] Ibid., 26 May 1642.   [3] Ibid., 15 June 1642.
[4] HMC, *5th Report: House of Lords Manuscripts*, p. 40.

the supply of the public necessity, for the defence of the King, Parliament and Kingdom'.[1] At the same time the officers of the brigade for Munster were ordered to serve in England until 'there shall be occasion to send any more forces into Ireland'.[1] In effect the adventurers' money and forces were requisitioned for use against the King. Wharton's brigade was to serve at Edgehill, the first battle of the English civil war, rather than in the repression of Ireland. Whether the committee for adventurers really consented to this diversion of its funds or not it is impossible to say. In all probability it yielded to an irresistible demand. Those adventurers alarmed at the King's recruitment of an army in the North looked upon the 'loan' with sorry resignation. Others despaired that money raised to repress rebellion abroad was being used rather to fuel it at home.

The diversion of funds from Ireland was, in any event, a turning point in the history of the adventure, for very little additional money was subscribed after 30 July 1642 and before the doubling ordinance of July 1643. The diversion cast a pall over the adventure and betrayed its slender pretentions to non-partisan and wholly Irish objectives. Even before 30 July the adventure was encountering heavy weather. 'The Million comes in not so fast as was expected' wrote a correspondent of Lord Mountagu in early June, and he described the preparations of an act which would allow those who paid in their subscriptions before 20 July to have repayment in Irish instead of English acres.[2] As early as mid May a son of Sir John Coke wrote to him: 'It is hard pressed that all men of ability should in some sort come in upon the adventure',[3] but added gratuitously that he did not think much of the adventure as an investment, though it might be politic for his father to adventure three or four hundred pounds. His father evidently thought otherwise, for his name does not appear among the lists. The forced loan of 30 July simply confirmed the scepticism of those who had looked upon the adventure as a ruse established to serve the enemies of the King.

[1] *CJ*, ii. 702.

[2] HMC, *Buccleuch & Queensbury Manuscripts*, i. 304. An Irish or Plantation acre was the equivalent of 1·62 English acres.

[3] HMC, *12th Report: The Coke MSS. at Melbourne Hall*, p. 314.

The only part of the adventurers' military plans which proceeded in 1642 was the inglorious 'sea adventure' which descended on the southern coasts of Ireland in July, a floating mockery of the conquering expedition the adventurers had desired. £43,000 had been raised under the sea adventure ordinance of June 1642, much of it from men who were also heavily involved in the adventure under the act of 19 March. It was due to the brainstorm of a group of Londoners, and its largest supporter was ironically, Sir Nicholas Crispe, the royalist monopolist who had been expelled from Parliament in 1641. The sea adventurers were guaranteed repayment of their subscriptions, eventually, in confiscated Irish land—but they were also entitled by ordinance to whatever rebel property they could seize.

Under the command of the Scot, Alexander, Lord Forbes, ten ships, eight barges, and 1,000 men reached the shores of Munster in early July 1642. Heedlessly and impetuously Forbes plunged into the Munster war, seemingly more interested in pillage than in rescuing the beleaguered Protestants. The Protestant military commander of Munster, the Earl of Inchiquin, complained that Forbes 'did not . . . vouchsafe me that civil respect as to acquaint me either with his design, commission or intent, and hath . . . thought good without my privity to land part of his force [at Kinsale, on 8 July] and to march into the country'.[1] When several of his companies were ambushed by the Irish at Cloghnakilty, Forbes beat a retreat to Kinsale, where he embarked for the relative safety of coastal waters. Sailing on to Galway, he attempted to persuade Clanricarde, the Lord President of Connaught, to wage a war of utter extirpation against the Irish. Clanricarde demurred and attempted to convince Forbes that the only policy which could prevent the rebellion from being lengthened and worsened was 'a just distinction between practick and passive rebels, with severity to the one and moderation to the other'.[2] Forbes would have no such hair-splitting, and pointlessly, though possibly profitably, ravaged the coasts

---

[1] Inchiquin to the Lords of the Council, 25 July 1642, Carte MS. 3, f. 361.

[2] Richard Bagwell, *Ireland under the Stuarts*, London, 1909-16, ii. 39, quoting from the Memoirs of the Earl of Clanricarde, who may have overstated his own moderation.

of Clare and Galway without attempting to assist the genuinely distressed English garrison at Tralee in Kerry, which soon after capitulated.[1] Autumn brought the sea adventure to a close, though remnants of the flotilla were reported in Irish waters as late as February 1643. In any event, it would seem to have exacerbated the rebellion in Ireland without having brought it any closer to a conclusion. In that sense, the sea adventure was a special instance of the adventure as a whole, of which much the same could be said.

The summer of 1642 was palpably a period of diminishing English interest in Ireland, as all thoughts turned to the war which was looming in England. This fact itself was exploited by the King who could, and did, make the charge that the Parliament which had lamented so theatrically the fate of the Protestants of Ireland was now callous to their needs. The King had urged a moderate and conciliatory policy in Ireland. Parliament had merely inflamed the situation without being prepared to proceed to a cure. The diversion of the first £100,000 raised by the adventurers was the most concrete example of this hypocrisy.[2] These charges cut to the quick, judging from the shrill reply they drew from the House of Commons on 5 September. Two days earlier, and perhaps as part of Parliament's reaction, a new committee was appointed in the House of Commons 'to take care of the affairs of Ireland'. Twenty-three M.P.s were nominated to the committee, of whom twelve were adventurers, but it was ordered that all the fifty-two 'commissioners' for Ireland appointed the previous November should also be members of the new committee, as should all the adventurers sitting in the House. Only six of the fifty-two former 'commissioners' were actually named to the new committee, however, and five of them were adventurers.[3] At the same time, a 'select committee of adventurers for Ireland chosen in London' made its appearance, consisting of twenty men, none of them M.P.s[3]

---

[1] Bagwell, *Ireland under the Stuarts*, ii. 41.

[2] 'His Majesty's Message to the House of Commons . . .', Thomason Tracts, BM, E. 115 (16).

[3] The five were Robert Reynolds, Sergeant Wilde, William Strickland, John Pym, and Sir Thomas Barrington. The sixth was Henry Lucas. (Minutes of the committee for Irish affairs from 3 Sept. 1642 to 7 May 1646; BM, Add. MS. 4771, f. 3.)

Some kind of co-operation was obviously intended between the two groups, the London adventurers handling contracts and provisions for the forces in Ireland, however few they might be.[1] This intruded a new economic interest into the adventure. Trade-oriented Londoners might make more profit on war contracts, Irish or otherwise, than they could ever hope for from the ravaged lands of Ireland. Thus, the London committee of adventurers was capable of a dual interest in Ireland. On the one hand, by virtue of the investments each of its members had in the adventure, it desired the rapid reconquest of Ireland, with the confiscation and redistribution of rebel land. On the other hand, numerous opportunities for profit existed in the contracts which proliferated with the continuation of the war. In the Westminster committee, as well, the main concerns were logistical: how many hogsheads of peas should go to Youghal, how many tuns of butter to Dublin. By 17 October 1642 £142,781, nearly half of the total funds the adventure would raise, had been expended by the various Parliamentary committees—but victory in Ireland was nowhere in sight.[2] Whether that sum included the £100,000 'borrowed' from the treasurers of the adventure by the order of 30 July we do not know, though Parliament was later to claim that all that was borrowed was shortly repaid.[3]

King Charles took the position in the spring of 1643 that Parliament had lost the right to take up money from the adventurers. By diverting £100,000 from Ireland, Parliament had betrayed the purposes of the act for adventurers to which Charles had given his assent; purposes which were explicitly stated in the statute. The King now made a feeble attempt to collect money from the adventurers through his own agents—though with no greater assurance that the money would find its way to Ireland. Parliament replied with a juggled version of the

---

[1] See, for instance, the entry in the Commons committee's records for 24 Nov. 1642: 'Forasmuch as this committee have formerly recommended to the Committee of Irish Adventurers chosen in London the contracting for and providing of several propositions of victuals, clothing, ammunition, and other necessaries for the army and soldiers in Munster, Galway, and at Athlone . . .' (Orders passed by the committee of adventurers for Ireland from 4 Oct. 1642 to 29 Sept. 1643; BM, Add. MS. 4782, f. 29).

[2] BM, Add. MS. 4782, f. 64.   [3] Ibid., f. 176.

books. Not £100,000, but only £73,000, had actually been removed from the adventurers' treasury. Furthermore, 'by the same order [of 30 July 1642] it is provided that the issuing of this money shall no way frustrate the acts already made in behalf of that adventure, in pursuance whereof they have since sent thither very great proportions of ammunition, victuals, and clothes, amounting to £123,382'.[1] By its own account, therefore, Parliament had not subtracted £100,000 from the Protestant cause in Ireland, but added over £50,000. To reassure the faint-hearted the Commons 'solemnly profess[ed] to all the world, never to divert any penny raised or to be raised for the relief of Ireland, to any other use, upon any occasion whatsoever'.[2] An only slightly less solemn pledge had been contained in the act for adventurers.

By June of 1643 approximately 42,000 troops in Ireland were nominally in the pay of Parliament; 6,000 in Munster, 15,000 in Leinster, 20,000 in Ulster—at least half of them Scots—and 1,000 in Connaught.[3] In November of 1641 John Pym had reported to the House of Commons that the cost per annum of maintaining a regiment of 1,000 men in Ireland was £19,201, and that of a regiment of 600 horse £37,310.[4] If 4,200 of the forces in Ireland were horse, and the remainder foot, the total cost of maintaining the establishment there would have amounted to something over £930,000 p.a. It is inconceivable that sums of this magnitude were actually being disbursed by Parliament. On the contrary, the records of the committee for Irish affairs at Westminster suggest that minuscule amounts were being doled out; quite frequently, just enough to keep a particular regiment from disbandment. If, then, the estimate of the number of troops in Ireland is roughly correct, and Pym's estimate of the cost of maintaining them is equally accurate, we must assume that the Irish forces went largely unpaid, or that they were expected to live almost entirely off the land. Neither circumstance was unusual in the seventeenth century. The immensity of the costs involved reminds us that even had

[1] BM, Add. MS. 4782, f. 175ᵛ.
[2] Ibid., and John Rushworth, ed., *Historical Collections*, v. 541.
[3] BM, Add. MS. 4782, f. 212ᵛ.
[4] *CJ*, ii. 313.

the adventurers succeeded in raising the full £1,000,000 they expected, such a sum would have sufficed only to pay the costs of the first year of the war, a year which brought little progress to the Protestant cause. The money raised by the adventure had been intended to finance repression of the Irish rebellion, but while it tied Parliament to a policy of confiscation in Ireland it offered only a minuscule contribution to the staggering costs of repression.

An attempt was made in midsummer 1643 to squeeze further funds from the adventure. The so-called 'doubling ordinance' was passed on 14 July, and stipulated that any adventurer who paid in an additional fourth of his original subscription (assuming the original subscription had already been paid in full) would receive double the measure of Irish land originally due to him, and in Irish rather than English acres. Thus, a man whose £600 original subscription would have entitled him to 1,000 English acres in Leinster could pay an additional £150 and be due to receive double the actual amounts he had paid in, or £1,500. This would entitle him to 2,500 English acres at the 'act rates', but he would be given 2,500 Irish acres, the equivalent of 4,050 English acres. Such a scheme meant that land in Leinster could be purchased, in effect, for a little over three shillings an acre, and in Ulster, for a third of that. Yet the doubling ordinance was an almost total failure. Only 171 adventurers took advantage of it and subscribed somewhere between ten and twelve thousand pounds.[1] The ordinance's failure to raise substantial sums is testimony to the low repute into which the adventure had fallen—and the hopelessness of reviving it while the civil war raged in England. If land would not sell at one to three shillings an acre, it was virtually unsaleable; but, of course, the ordinance did not have the assent of the King, and its operation was doubtful if the civil war ended in royal victory or compromise.

Parliament's refusal to divert major funds from its war effort in England to the struggle in Ireland, combined with the failure of the adventure to yield anything like the sums of money needed to support Protestant forces there, led predictably to a military

[1] My computations show the doubling ordinance to have raised £10,554, but the adventurers' own reckoning in 1652 stated £12,283 (Carte MS. 67, f. 230).

crisis. From the moment of rebellion's outbreak in October 1641 Parliament had followed a policy of extreme parsimony in supporting the Protestant resistance. In Leinster the Lords Justices had received too little too late. Of the 10,000 men they requested, less than a quarter were sent, and none before the last day of December 1641.[1] In Ulster 10,000 Scots took the field in mid 1642 but were continually under-supplied and in arrears.[2]

A close study of Munster reveals an atrocious state of affairs, with organized military units melting away almost more rapidly than they could be assembled.[3] The military commander in the south, Inchiquin, was driven into a conciliatory position *vis-à-vis* the Irish by the paucity of support which reached him. The fact of his Irish descent (he was Murrough O'Brien, First Earl and Sixth Baron) was later used by Parliament to prove that he had betrayed the Protestant interest; but it was the failure of Parliament to support Protestant Munster which forced him to agree to the cessation of hostilities signed in September 1643 between Ormond and the confederate Catholics.[4]

Withdrawal of the Munster forces from the war made the Irish once again, as in 1640, a threat to the enemies of the King. The cessation, basically an instrument of royalist policy, was intended to free thousands of Irish troops for service in England against the Parliament. Only the British forces in Ulster remained available to tie down Irish troops and prevent this much-feared transfusion of royalist support. The crisis of the cessation stirred another alteration in the management of Irish affairs. On 27 November, the Commons committee and the adventurers committee in London were joined into one, by an order of the House of Commons that also urged solicitude for the needs of the forces in Ulster.[5]

---

[1] Richard Bagwell, *Ireland under the Stuarts*, London, 1916, i. 332.

[2] See Hugh Hazlett, 'The Recruitment and Organization of the Scottish Army in Ulster', *Essays in British and Irish History in Honour of James Eadie Todd*, ed. by H. A. Cronne, T. W. Moody, and D. B. Quinn, London, 1941, pp. 107–31.

[3] See K. S. Bottigheimer, 'The English Interest in Southern Ireland, 1641–1650', Ph.D. thesis, University of California, Berkeley, 1965.

[4] 'Is this cessation just to the spoiled Protestants or *to the English Adventurers?*' [my emphasis], asked a resolution in the House of Lords (HMC, *5th Report: Lords Manuscripts*, p. 113).

[5] BM, Add. MS. 4771, f. 3ᵛ.

The adventurers hoped for greater influence in these new councils, but their options were limited, and no major campaign could be urged in Ireland while the fate of the civil war in England hung in the balance. Ireland had become a secondary theatre. Management of that theatre was gradually in late 1643 and 1644 assumed by the committee of both kingdoms. The combined committee of Parliamentary and London adventurers did not cease to meet, but it dealt with increasingly trivial matters, and after June 1644 convened only rarely.[1] A joint Scottish and English command for the Irish war was long overdue. Scottish and English forces had been operating side by side in Ireland since 1642 with little formal apparatus to co-ordinate their efforts. The Scottish role in Ulster has gone largely unrecorded and unremembered. Ironically, one of the possibilities in the autumn and winter of 1643-4 was that Anglo-Scottish co-operation might lead to a complete, if temporary, abandonment of Ireland. With all but the Scottish forces in Ulster pledged to cessation of hostilities, it made a certain amount of military sense to let Ireland be, until the confrontation between the King and the Anglo-Scottish covenant had been resolved in the latter's favour.

Such a possibility horrified the adventurers, who preferred to see Ireland reduced forthwith as a *means* of undermining royalist strength. In December 1643 the London adventurers produced a paper arguing that 'the Scottish army in the province of Ulster . . . and the other British regiments there should be continued and maintained under one command for to oppose the Cessation with such means as they humbly conceive may do the same'.[2] The adventurers argued that to do otherwise would 'dishearten the Protestant party throughout Christendom' and discourage further loans toward repression of the rebellion. Closest to their hearts, perhaps, was the thought that 'an army now to be continued there will hinder and interrupt that state [the confederate Catholics] now devising by acts of Parliament and otherwise to clear and acquit those from the forfeitures which

[1] The concluding pages of its records are in BM, Add. MS. 4771, ff. 60-5.
[2] Charles McNeill, ed., *The Tanner Letters*, Dublin, Irish Manuscript Commission, 1943, pp. 169-70.

they have incurred both of their lives and estates'.[1] The Scots forces were, as it turned out, kept in Ulster, but on a minimal footing and with little opportunity to function as anything other than a beachhead for some later conquest.

The committee of both kingdoms evolved in March 1644 a special subcommittee for Ireland, with power to consult both the adventurers' committee in London and the Parliamentary committee for Ireland at Westminster.[2] The committee consisted of the Earl of Northumberland, Sir Henry Vane, Oliver St. John, Philip Stapleton, Robert Wallop, and the Scottish commissioners. St. John was the only adventurer among them (for £300). The subcommittee introduced a new principle into the financing of the Irish war by proposing what it called 'a settled course' for the British forces in Ireland, an assessment of £4,000 p.m. exclusively for the uses of Ireland.[3]

When it is recalled that in June 1643 there were approximately 20,000 British soldiers supposedly in Ulster, and that the estimated cost of their upkeep was in the vicinity of £400,000 p.a., an assessment of £48,000 p.a. seems less than bountiful. Presumably it was intended to do no more than keep a kernel of these forces from disbanding, but for that reason the assessment had the support of the adventurers who preferred financial assistance from any quarter to capitulation. The assessment was not passed until October 1644, and by then it had been raised, though not very significantly, to £80,000 p.a.[4] Still, the principle of public financing had been intruded into an area where private and proprietary financing had predominated. The immense and continuing expenses of the Irish war, together with the poverty of the adventure, were forcing the state to turn to public revenues, burdensome and politically undesirable as they were.

In July 1644 the Munster commander, Inchiquin, defected

---

[1] As an afterthought the adventurers proposed that the plundered Protestants of Ireland should 'have land of the rebels for their losses, when the war shall be ended and *after* [my emphasis] all the adventurers shall be first satisfied . . .: This will draw all of them away from the other [royalist] side and strengthen the parliament exceedingly in their party there . . .' (McNeill, ed., *The Tanner Letters*, pp. 169–70).   [2] *CSPD, 1644*, p. 61.   [3] Ibid., p. 79.
[4] C. H. Firth and R. S. Rait, eds., *Acts and Ordinances of the Interregnum*, London, 1911, i. 551.

from the cessation of hostilities which he had signed the previous September, and the committee of both kingdoms urged the adventurers' committee in London to sit daily until means could be found 'for supplying the wants of Munster and Ulster'.[1] The October ordinance for £80,000 was its only evident accomplishment. The return of Munster to the fold, though much applauded, added another hungry mouth to an already impoverished nest. For the next four years Inchiquin was to regret his alliance with Parliament almost as much as his brief, uncongenial, cessation with the Irish.

Only a thin stream of funds was allowed to reach Munster. In March 1645 Inchiquin reported 4,000 men under his command (2,000 less than were estimated in Munster two years earlier), a force which would have required something like £80,000 p.a. to maintain.[2] But £10,000 was all that was voted for Munster between October 1644 and March 1645, and of that amount, only £750 came over in specie.[3] The scarcity of specie may have been more the result of policy than necessity. In the first place, the adventurers were eager to control all contracts for supplies in London. They argued that they were best placed to secure the lowest bids, and that their interest in Irish land motivated them to resist profiteering. In fact a greedy self interest may have been responsible, as in the case of Sir John Clotworthy, the noted M.P. adventurer (for £1,000), who was charged with shameless profiteering in supplies intended for Ireland. Secondly, Parliament wished to keep the Protestant forces in Ireland fighting, but not to pay their swelling arrears, especially for the nine months during which they had observed the cessation. Parliament was fearful that specie sent to Ireland would disappear into the pockets of the plundered Irish Protestants who made up the bulk of the forces there. The most efficient way to support the war was to send the forces what they needed to exist, but in a form which they could not hoard. Inchiquin's compensation for such mean treatment was the title of Lord President of Munster, which Parliament conferred upon him in January

[1] *CSPD, 1644*, p. 454.
[2] Ibid., *1644–5*, p. 339.
[3] Ibid., p. 61, and Inchiquin to the committee of Both Kingdoms, mid May 1645, *LJ*, vii. 410.

1645.[1] His instructions urged him 'by example and persuasion
. . . [to] draw the officers and soldiers of Munster to subscribe
for lands in satisfaction of all or part of their arrears'.[2]
Economy was the overriding consideration in Parliamentary
policy for Ireland at this juncture, and the Protestant forces
there suffered heavily as a result. When the committee of both
kingdoms wished to send a few thousand pounds to Ireland, it
usually commissioned the adventurers' committee in London
to find an expedient by which the sum could be raised. In April
1645 the adventurers replied despairingly:

Until some such course be taken that the subscriber may be satisfied
and see a way laid before him to support that war, and that the
Parliament is resolved to go on with it, the expense of their former
disbursements for the service with so little fruit have put them out
of all comfort that any good will be done by any such supplies which
are only small—as we say—from hand to mouth. . . .[3]

The doubling ordinance had amply demonstrated how little
additional money could be raised on the security of Irish land.
With money from the £80,000 October assessment coming in
slowly, and, more than that already uselessly expended,
statutory revenue was proving an almost equally unattractive
form of security. It seemed possible that Protestant Munster
—providentially rescued from compliance with the hated
cessation—might succumb for lack of support to the Catholic
armies assaulting her in the summer of 1645.
    The pivotal importance of the Protestants in Munster drew

[1] *CJ*, iv. 19, 27. The manner in which the title was denied to Inchiquin by the
King is a case-study of Caroline inefficiency. The Presidency of Munster had
been promised needlessly to Jerome Weston, Second Earl of Portland, a man
who had no ability to serve the King's cause in Ireland. When Inchiquin went
to Oxford in Jan. 1644, he was put off with vague promises and returned to
Ireland convinced that the King intended him no substantial reward for his
considerable services. If he wished to be Lord President of Munster, it would
have to be as Parliament's Lord President. Portland never even attempted to
take up his important command, and there were rumours from time to time that
he intended to sell it to Richard Boyle, Second Earl of Cork.
[2] Instructions of 14 Jan. 1644/5, in BM, Egerton MS. 1048, f. 29. The doubling
ordinance of 14 July 1643 had allowed for soldiers to convert their arrears into
shares of adventure at 'the act rates'. There is no way of knowing how many
of them chose to do so.
[3] Letter of 10 Apr. 1645, HMC, *Portland*, i. 220.

the adventurers' attention increasingly to the South. The original aborted adventurers' brigade under Lord Wharton had been intended for Munster. The sea adventure had shown a similar preference for southern waters. And this predilection grew into a distinct adventurer policy with Inchiquin's defection from the cessation in 1644. On 10 June 1645 a committee of M.P. adventurers was appointed to look into the possibility of providing relief for Munster, and on 20 June the committee of adventurers in London petitioned Parliament to send additional forces to Inchiquin, 'else that the province of Munster and the Protestants there will all be destroyed'.[1] On 1 July a new committee of the Lords and Commons for Ireland was created, ostensibly as a result of 'late informations . . . come from several parts of Ireland, and more particularly from Munster, importing the great extremities and danger that kingdom is reduced unto . . .'[2] Indeed, Munster had been invaded by Catholic forces under the Earl of Castlehaven, and Youghal, one of the few strong-points remaining in Protestant hands, was besieged and on the verge of surrender.

The membership of the new committee fluctuated. The first meeting was attended by the Earl of Kent, Alexander Rigby, Sir John Clotworthy, William Jephson, Richard Knightley, Richard Whitehead, and Sir Robert Goodwin.[3] Clotworthy and Goodwin were the only adventurers; Jephson, M.P. for Stockbridge, had estates in Ireland and was adjutant to Inchiquin. Often, between 1644 and 1648, he served as the Munster commander's liaison with Parliament and its Irish committees. In its early meetings the committee dealt mainly with the plight of Munster, spurred on by the warnings of Jephson and Roger Boyle, Baron Broghill, that without aid the Munster Protestants would be compelled to surrender the province to the Irish, evacuating it for the comparative safety of England. Little of

[1] HMC, *Portland*, i. 227; *LJ*, vii. 440; and *CJ*, iv. 181.

[2] *CSPD, 1645–7*, p. 1. The complete minutes of the committee, beginning 1 July 1645, and running to 11 Sept. 1648, may be found in State Papers Ireland (S.P. 63), vol. 261, nos. 9 and 30; vol. 262, no. 9; and vol. 266, no. 6. An original minute book of more than 200 pages was thus cut up arbitrarily into four fascicles when the State Papers were bound, and, in effect, was further 'cut up' when the *Calendars* were constructed on strictly chronological principles.

[3] S.P. 63/261, no. 9.

substance was accomplished by the committee. The port towns of Munster weathered the summer, owing partly to the timely arrival of a detachment of Parliament ships under Admiral William Penn, partly to the military failings of Castlehaven, and partly to supplies sent to Munster by Lord Fairfax out of the provisions of his own New Model Army.[1] It was the slender maritime life-line which sustained the few thousand holed-up Protestants of Southern Ireland.

In August Parliament extended for six months the £80,000 p.a. assessment first passed the previous October.[2] But in September the committee of 1 July 1645 again turned to the adventurers for financing; this time requesting £14,850 for the use of the forces in Munster.[3] On 24 October the London adventurers committee at Grocers' Hall adopted a vigorous refusal, and incorporated a lengthy denunciation of Parliament's handling of the Irish war and its treatment of the citizen-adventurers who had first financed it.[4] The indictment began with Parliament's decision of 30 July 1642 to 'borrow' £100,000 from the recently raised adventurers' funds, and the consequent dissolution of the brigade under Lord Wharton intended for the rescue of Ireland in the spring of 1642:

When they had well nigh raised and armed all these forces, and made all other provisions fit for transportation, both their money and men and provisions were upon an unavoidable occasion made use of by the state here, upon a sudden and unexpected breaking forth of the distractions here at home; and the remains of what was not thus employed or that hath come into . . . [the adventurers'] treasuries since, have likewise been made use of by the state here, wherewith to content the Irish officers who have done very little or no service for all that they have had since.[5]

---

[1] For Penn's advent see 'Extracts from William Penn's Journals', *JCHAS*, 1904, 106–14. For Castlehaven see *Commentarius Rinuccinianus*, Irish Manuscript Commission, i. 570. For Fairfax, a letter of Thomas Herbert, 17 Nov. 1645, in *The Tanner Letters*, p. 197. The situation in Munster is treated at greater length in Bottigheimer, 'The English Interest in Southern Ireland, 1641–1650'.

[2] Firth and Rait, *Acts and Ordinances*, i. 746.

[3] *CSPI, 1633–47*, p. 415.

[4] 'Reasons for their refusal to lend moneys upon the security of the ordinance of 15th August last . . .' (BM, Egerton MS. 1048, ff. 36–7, published in Thomason Tracts, BM, E. 314 (7)).

[5] BM, Egerton MS. 1048, f. 36.

Wharton's brigade had been intended for Munster and its failure to materialize there had contributed to the virtual triumph of rebel arms in the South, and the decision of Inchiquin to join the cessation of September 1643. When, thereafter, forces in Ulster remained the sole survivors of Parliamentary authority in Ireland, the adventurers were pressed to take over their financing 'upon promise that . . . [the forces in Ulster] should . . . march out of that province against the rebels, into other parts of the kingdom . . .'.[1] Reluctantly, the adventurers at Grocers' Hall had contributed, but to no good purpose, for the Ulster forces accomplished little towards the reduction of Ireland. The adventurers complained that they had been effectively displaced from management of the moneys they had raised and the enterprise which they believed their own.

The tangle of Parliamentary committees that had managed the Irish war had

cooled and withdrawn the zeal and affections of the adventurers and others to bring in any more money upon the said ordinance of the 14th of July 1643 seeing their committee set aside, and to have no oversight . . . of the disposal of their moneys; that great sum of £300,000 or thereabouts, which they have formerly brought in, having been employed as aforesaid, without adding to them the least hope to possess their adventures.[1]

The failure of the extravagant 'doubling ordinance' was proof of the demoralization of the adventurers. In their declaration of 24 October 1645 they made explicit grievances which had been long-standing but unexpressed.

The adventurers could not simply withdraw from the Irish war, and their 'refusal' to lend money upon the ordinance of 15 August 1645 was an attempt to extort concessions from Parliament. As early as August 1644 they had made certain proposals for the revivification of the adventure.[2] The doubling ordinance was to be made retroactive to those who adventured before 14 July 1643; new subscriptions were to be extracted by ordinance from men of plentiful estates who had done little

---

[1] Ibid.
[2] 'The State of the Irish Affairs for the Members of Parliament . . .' (Thomason Tracts, BM, E. 314 (7)).

for Parliament and commonwealth; and so much of Cork, Kinsale, and Youghal as belonged to Irish rebels was to be put up for sale at four times its 1640 value.¹ If those conditions were met, the adventurers would immediately advance '£20,000 in money, and such provisions as should be ordered to be sent for relief of those forces [in Munster], and they did not doubt but thereby to make all further supplies for carrying on that war in Munster, and that those forces being well supplied and maintained (under God) might be a great and ready means quickly to reduce all that kingdom'. By such a course of action 'the lives of many thousands of poor Protestants, our friends and brethren, will thus be there preserved, and this kingdom delivered from a blood-thirsty enemy'.²

By refusing to lend money upon the assessment, and by pressing their own proposals, the adventurers were forcing a confrontation with Parliament. Their implicit argument was that the principle of confiscation had not been carried far enough, that Irish land should be made to pay for Irish war irrespective of the justification for further confiscation. Why should loyal Englishmen pay for repressing rebellious Celts? The adventurers depicted a post-war Ireland entirely occupied and owned by a new mass of Protestant freeholders. Adventurers, soldiers, foreign Protestants, and London merchants who had advanced credit, were all to be satisfied, in that order, with Irish land. Irish Protestants were to be restored to their plundered estates, and Irish Catholics were to be 're-educated' to Protestant-ism by the removal of their children to England.³

Thus the adventurers expanded the concept of confiscation and dovetailed it with that of massive and systematic coloniza-tion. They brought together into an enduring amalgam the two conceptions which lay at the heart of the Cromwellian Settle-ment. Their purpose in doing so was neither entrepreneurial

---

¹ The doubling ordinance had put the first Irish towns on the auction block. Rebel property in Limerick and Waterford was up for sale at £30,000 per town. Galway and Wexford could be had for a little less, but all four towns were rebel-held, and the date of taking possession was therefore highly uncertain. With Inchiquin's 'rendition' to Parliament in July 1644 the wealthy old port towns of Munster seemed within reach of the adventurers' hands.

² Thomason Tracts, BM, E. 314 (7).

³ An undated appendix to the adventurers' statement of 24 Oct. 1645 (Thomason Tracts, BM, E. 314 (7)).

nor evangelical. Undoubtedly they intended to profit by their own propositions in the form of larger Irish estates, but after how many fruitless years! Their immediate problem was to speed up the reconquest of Ireland, and only in massive confiscation could they see any hope. With the aftermath of Parliament's victory at Naseby still uncertain, Parliament was unwilling to pass large assessments for Ireland. The meagre £80,000 assessment had only been extended for six months. The adventurers claimed that only a fraction of what was due the first year had been paid in, and that even less was likely to be collected in subsequent years.[1] In November 1645 the House of Commons resolved to double the assessment to £160,000, but no ordinance to that effect was brought in.[2] If public money was so unlikely to be forthcoming, and if Ireland could not be subdued without immense quantities of money from some source, further exploitation of Irish land was inevitable. When the London merchant and adventurer (of £2,562), William Hawkins, addressed the Parliamentary committee for Ireland in early November 1645, he added to the Grocers' Hall proposals the suggestion that all officers and men in Ireland should be assured that they would be paid in Irish land, and that they should receive no more and no less than three years' pay, regardless of whether the war lasted for that or a longer period.[3] Thus they would have an incentive to end the war as soon as possible and a good reason for not letting it linger.

It was a proposal incredibly prodigal of Irish land. According to records of 20 November 1645, the forces in Ireland nominally in Parliament's pay were costing £1,387 *per diem*, nearly £500,000 p.a. or £1,500,000 for three years. It had originally been calculated by the framers of the adventure that 2,500,000 acres of Irish land would have to be confiscated to raise £1,000,000 in adventure at the 'act rates'. Another 3,750,000 acres would be necessary simply to implement William Hawkins's proposal.

Hawkins's proposal, like the clause of the doubling ordinance which permitted soldiers in Ireland to receive their pay in the

---

[1] BM, Egerton MS. 1048, f. 3.   [2] *CJ*, iv. 352, 22 Nov. 1645.
[3] *CSPI, 1633–47*, p. 418. Also HMC, *6th Report: Lords Manuscripts*, p. 84. It may have been this William Hawkins who was solicitor to the Earl of Leicester, the ephemeral Lord Lieutenant of 1642–3. See HMC, *Portland*, i. 133–4; and *De L'Isle and Dudley*, vi. 47 *et passim*.

form of adventure at the act rates, and the instructions to Inchiquin to urge as many of his men as possible to elect this form of payment, were merely the stepping-stones along the path from repression and selective confiscation, the traditional English response to Irish rebellion, to repression and massive confiscation, the response ultimately delivered by the Cromwellian state.[1]

It is interesting that the adventurers' proposals were rejected at this time by Parliament. Instead of acquiescing in a further hypothecation of Irish land, Parliament appointed a committee to investigate the adventurers' refusal to lend money, and on 11 December 1645 subpoenaed the adventurers' records.[2] Co-operation between the two overlapping bodies had all but broken down. But in the New Model Army there were indications in late 1645 of considerable sympathy for the adventurers and their frustration with the slowness of the Irish war. Fairfax, for instance, had been instrumental in obtaining supplies for Youghal during the autumn.[3] In December the Munster officer, Sir Hardress Waller, was in England arranging for the shipment of more supplies directly from the Army, and he commented that he found 'great inclinations in some eminent men of this army to the business of Ireland'. Indeed he was 'certain our greatest hope for Ireland is from this army'.[4]

Waller said he had discussed the prospect of the Irish war at length with Lieutenant General Cromwell, 'whose spirit leads much that way, and especially for the support of Munster and to begin the war there'. Were Cromwell sent over to Ireland, Waller prophesied, 'I should look upon the work [of reconquest] as done'. He urged Sir Philip Perceval in London to see if Parliament could be persuaded to make Cromwell Lord Lieutenant. This was in early December 1645. Perceval replied that

---

[1] In 1642 the Scots had requested that the terms of the act for adventurers should be extended to the Scottish forces serving in Ulster. At that stage the English had refused on the grounds that the adventure scheme was not open to English soldiers. The pressure of mounting expenses must have persuaded Parliament to change its position, and the resulting extension of the settlement to the soldiery ultimately multiplied by several times the scope of the Cromwellian Settlement. See Hazlett, 'The Recruitment and Organization of the Scottish Army in Ulster', p. 116.

[2] Thomason Tracts, BM, E. 314 (7).   [3] See above, p. 92.

[4] Waller to Sir Philip Perceval, 4 Dec. 1645, HMC, *Egmont*, i. 264.

until recently the Scottish Earl of Leven had been rumoured to be a candidate for the command, but the post had been left vacant by Parliament since November 1643, when the King had forced the resignation of the last tenant, the Earl of Leicester. Now, however, the name of Leicester's son, Robert Sydney, Lord Lisle, was being put forward.

The very first of William Hawkins's proposals from the adventurers, the naming of a commander-in-chief in Ireland,[1] was hotly debated in January 1646. Two parties were in contention over the nomination, those who favoured Lisle and those who opposed him. His opponents pushed through a resolution limiting his tenure to one year.[2] His supporters defeated a move to put the Lord Lieutenancy into commission.[3] Finally, on 21 January 1645/6 Lord Lisle was appointed Lord Lieutenant, his authority to run for one year from 9 April 1646. It would appear that Lisle was the candidate of Parliament-men and that his opponents believed him the do-nothing figurehead of a do-nothing Irish policy. The year of his tenure proved them correct.

The Lieutenancy of Lord Lisle was a rebuff to the adventurers, the Army, and the Protestants of Munster, all of whom, in 1646, longed for rapid progress in winning the Irish war. Protestant Ireland had waited in vain throughout 1642 for the promised expedition of the former Lord Lieutenant, the Earl of Leicester. Now it awaited, through 1646, the salvation promised by his son. 'There is a fatality in the business of that unhappy country,' Perceval wrote to Broghill in the spring, 'everything suffering delays which in many cases are as bad as denials.'[4] The jealousies between the Scots and English seemed daily to heighten. Lord Lisle spited the adventurers by selecting as his provisioner John Davies, a man whom they had repeatedly charged with profiteering and peculation. Nothing seemed less likely than that a formidable military expedition would evolve out of such strife.[4]

Despite the journeying of Inchiquin to London in early 1646 with pleas for military support, the summer of 1646 found the Protestants of Munster in as perilous a position as in 1645. On

---

[1] *CSPI, 1633–47*, p. 417.   [2] *CJ*, iv. 369.   [3] Ibid., p. 397.
[4] 7 Apr. 1646, HMC, *Egmont*, i. 286.

the last day of July a proposal which would have enabled 1,000 horse and 2,000 foot to be raised immediately for service in Munster was tabled in the House of Commons by a vote of 98 to 78. An alternative proposal to detach and send to Ireland four regiments of foot and two of horse from Fairfax's army was defeated by the narrower margin of 91 to 90. The only scheme for raising troops for Ireland that the Commons would accept called for the Committee of 1 July 1645 to negotiate with the separate county committees for the collection of any county forces regarded as superfluous. By 4 August 2,300 foot and 700 horse had been volunteered, but this polyglot force of remaindered soldiers was viewed as a much less promising contribution to Munster than the two schemes voted down.[1]

Inchiquin was increasingly resentful of the new Lord Lieutenant and of Parliament's indifference to Ireland in general. A libellous pamphlet accusing Inchiquin of leniency towards the Catholics and peculation with Parliament funds appeared in London during the summer.[2] He heard that his reputation was under discussion in the House of Commons, and that objections were being raised to his compliance with the royalist cessation between September 1643 and July 1644.[3] He suspected —correctly, it appears—that an attempt was being made to discredit him, so that the new Lord Lieutenant could assume command of Munster. This was the policy of a Lord Lieutenant who intended not a reconquest—that was not in his feeble commission—but merely the assumption of the most attractive bridgehead from its present commander.

Inchiquin found himself increasingly in the shadow of the Lord Lieutenant, who yet remained in England. When the President of Munster deferentially suggested some reorganization of his own forces, Lord Lisle replied, 'not having a perfect knowledge of your affairs in Munster I shall not for the present prescribe any alteration of what hath been done'.[4] All things were contingent upon the Lord Lieutenant's pleasure, which would not be signified until his arrival, the date of which no one

---

[1] *CJ*, iv. 632 and ff.; also, a letter from Ireland to Perceval, in HMC, *Egmont*, i. 304.

[2] 'A Letter from Kinsale', Thomason Tracts, BM, E. 354 (6).

[3] Inchiquin to Perceval, 28 Aug. 1646, HMC, *Egmont*, i. 306.

[4] Lord Lisle to Inchiquin, 5 Sept. 1646, HMC, *Egmont*, i. 312.

knew. Protestant Munster survived 1646, not as a consequence of assistance from the Parliament or its Lord Lieutenant, but as a result of a crucial split among the Irish.

The development of the Ulster rebellion of 1641 into a protracted and widespread war of resistance was basically the result of an unprecedented conjunction of discontents. The Ulster *enragés* would have been put down in a matter of months if they had not been joined in December by the Old English of the Pale. The tri-partite division of the population of Ireland into Native Irish, Old English, and New English, was essential to seventeenth-century English rule. The coalition of the two Catholic parties, whose historic enmity filled the better part of five centuries, converted an insurrection into a major challenge to Protestant and English rule. It was institutionalized in the general assembly of confederate Catholics which met in July 1642 at Kilkenny, and in its executive, the supreme council, which undertook to direct the war against the authority of English King, and Parliament, in Ireland, whether combined as at first, or separate. But if the open struggle between King and Parliament prevented and delayed English reconquest of Ireland, the more subterranean hostilities between Old English and Native Irish contributed to the failure of the Catholic cause to triumph. From September 1643, when a truce was signed with the Marquis of Ormond, commander of the King's forces in Ireland, a bitter debate ensued over the wisdom of this course. The papal legates, first Scarampi, then Rinuccini, urged a policy of uncompromising militancy as the only means of securing the Roman Catholic Church in Ireland. The more conservative, and largely Old English, elements of the confederation sought an accommodation with Charles I as the only practicable way of averting the ravages intended by a puritanical English Parliament.[1]

---

[1] The intricate and controversial history of the confederation is beyond the scope of this work. A modern, narrative, account exists in T. L. Coonan, *The Irish Catholic Confederation and the Puritan Revolution*, New York, 1954, a work which must be used with extreme caution. Written from an unapologetically *ex parte* position, it synthesizes the prejudices of 17th-century ultra-montanism with those of 19th-century Irish nationalism. For more objective guidance see J. C. Beckett, 'The Confederation of Kilkenny Reviewed', *Historical Studies*, ii, Michael Roberts, ed., London, 1959.

The Marquis of Ormond, on behalf of the King, concluded an uneasy peace with the confederate Catholics on 28 March 1646, and this at first gave rise to a fear among English Protestants that an amalgamated Irish army would sweep the Protestants out of Munster. But in August the legate Rinuccini organized a large-scale repudiation of the treaty among the clergy and several cities of the confederation, splitting it irrevocably into moderates (royalists) and zealots (opposed equally to Protestant parliaments and Protestant kings). Ormond's and Rinuccini's contest with each other for the loyalty of Catholic Ireland relieved the military pressure on Munster and actually allowed Inchiquin to improve his situation there during the autumn.

Ormond, faced with the prospect of losing Dublin to Rinuccini's party, indicated that he would, if necessary, save the city by surrendering it to Parliament. Commissioners were excitedly dispatched from Westminster to negotiate with him. This was an unhoped-for windfall and injected a temporary preoccupation with Dublin into Parliamentary policy. Inchiquin was suddenly asked to play the role of diverting Rinuccini's forces from Dublin, lest the place should fall to them before it could be taken over by Parliament.[1] Lord Lisle, who had previously been making slowly for Munster, asked Parliament in late October to redirect him to Dublin, where he could imagine a far more glorious entrée than in the province of a jealous Inchiquin.[2]

The prospect of the surrender of Dublin proved evanescent. In November the temporary defection of the Irish general Thomas Preston (later Viscount Tara) from the nuncio's party spared Ormond's Dublin for a few more months. In December the Lord Lieutenant's interest switched back to Munster, where a group of Anglo-Irish Protestants had recently called for him to begin the reconquest of Ireland. These propagandists began by dismissing Ulster as 'of no benefit or advantage [to Parliament]', despite the 8,000 British troops still in action there. Instead, they recommended that 'the safety of [Parliament's] parties and places in Munster be first taken into care'. There were already 4,000 foot and 300 horse in the Province, and they recommended that Lord Lisle should bring over an

[1] Committee of July 1 to Inchiquin, 16 Oct. 1646, BM Add. MS. 4769a, f. 28.
[2] *LJ*, viii. 547.

additional 8,000 foot and 1,800 horse. Most important, an increased assessment was to make available a steady supply of
money, Ireland being now too wasted to provide sustenance to
the armies fighting over her.[1]

The plan should have sounded attractive to the Munster
Protestants, but when Inchiquin heard of it he described it as
'a plot'.[2] Its authors were to become the principal members of
Lord Lisle's party. Sir John Temple was an old retainer of the
Sydneys, Sir Philip Sydney supposedly having died in the arms of
his father. Temple had served Lord Lisle's father, and probably
owed his election to Parliament for Chichester in 1645 to Sidney
influence.[3] When in 1646 Temple published his propagandist
history of *The Irish Rebellion*, his ultimate purpose may have
been to justify an imminent repression of Ireland by Lord Lisle
and to destroy any lingering basis for a negotiated settlement.
Walter Love, after examining the historiography of the Irish
massacre of 1641, pointed out that Temple's was the first
historical work to emphasize the 'massacre' rather than the
'rebellion' as the crime of Ireland : 'Of course, it is not necessary
to conclude that Temple had only in 1646 decided that a Bloody
Massacre had been committed back in 1641. The Lisle campaign
could have been the first occasion when it seemed necessary
and valuable to prove it. He was not, of course, the first person
to say a massacre had been committed, he was the first to try to
prove it by writing a history.'[4] Whereas the literature of 1641
and 1642 charged the Irish mainly with rebellion, after August
1642 rebellion was a less damning charge, coming from a
rebellious Parliament. Murder, rapine, and atrocity—con-
comitants of any seventeenth-century religious war—became
the only crimes which could justify the conquest and confiscation Temple had in mind.

Temple was joined in his authorship of the December letter
by Adam Loftus, Arthur Annesley, William Parsons, and

---

[1] The letter, dated 10 Dec. 1646, is in *Miscellaneous Papers and Letters from
the Southwell Collection*, BM, Egerton MS. 917, f. 25. It bears no address but
was undoubtedly directed to Lord Lisle.

[2] John Davies to Perceval, 13 Jan. 1646/7, HMC, *Egmont*, i. 355.

[3] I am indebted to David Underdown for pointing out this relationship in
his 'Civil War in Ireland: A Commentary', *EUQ*, Summer, 1966, p. 74.

[4] Ibid., p. 65.

Hardress Waller. Parsons, Lord Justice in the early days of the rebellion, had been among those most eager to exploit the Irish uprising by confiscation. Loftus, son of Adam Loftus, Viscount Loftus of Ely, stood squarely in the entrepreneurial tradition of the New English in Ireland, and was thought by Inchiquin to have written the slanderous pamphlet against him which appeared in the summer of 1646. Annesley was the son of Sir Francis Annesley, the famous victim of Strafford, whose cause and innocence had been championed by the Long Parliament. Hardress Waller was an exceptional member of the group, in that he alone had served under Inchiquin in Munster and had extensive landed interests in the Province. But Waller was a client of the Boyles, and there was bad blood between the Boyles and Inchiquin going back at least as far as 1642. Inchiquin had inherited effective military command over Protestant Munster from his father-in-law, the Lord President, Sir William St. Leger, when the latter died in the summer of 1642. Richard Boyle, the Great Earl of Cork, had long resented the role St. Leger played in Strafford's harassment of him—and sought briefly to have his eldest son, Richard, made Lord President in Inchiquin's stead. The move failed, but co-operation thereafter between Broghill (Cork's third son) and Inchiquin was rare, and in late 1646 both Broghill and Hardress Waller were edging towards co-operation with Lord Lisle.[1]

None of the framers of the December plan were adventurers. Few Anglo-Irish were; but at least two of the five (Annesley and Temple) were members of a new committee for Ireland which met at Derby House and took its name from that site. The committee was set up originally to exploit the situation created by Rinuccini's sabotaging of Ormond's truce in

---

[1] The relationship between Inchiquin and Broghill was a peculiarly cyclical one. When Inchiquin defected to Ormond and the royalists in 1648, Broghill made his separate way to Cromwell, whom he served loyally until the Protector's death. More than any man, Broghill was responsible for the triumph of Cromwellian arms in Munster, from which Inchiquin and the royalist Protestant forces were expelled in 1649 and 1650. Inchiquin joined Charles II on the Continent, returned to his native Catholicism, served the King in Tangiers, and returned to Ireland after the Restoration, where he spent the last years of his life as Vice-President of Munster under the presidency of his former subordinate and then foe, Broghill. See *DNB*, and also John A. Murphy, 'Inchiquin's Change of Religion', *JCHAS*, 1967, pp. 58–68.

August 1646. The records of the committee, which consisted of the English members of the old committee of both kingdoms with named additions, reveal that it operated as a handmaiden to Lord Lisle. Rarely was a supporter of Inchiquin in attendance, although his enemies, like Parsons and Loftus, joined the committee frequently.[1]

The committee's first task was to get Lord Lisle to Ireland. The major obstacles in his path were financial. No economic foundation had been laid for the expedition, by either taxation or confiscation. The figure of £30,000 was bruited as the amount the Lord Lieutenant would have at his disposal, but much of that amount was frittered away during months of waiting in England. Perhaps, however, there were political reasons for the delay as well. Lisle's father, the Earl of Leicester, recorded in his journal for 1 February 1647: 'My son, the Viscount Lisle went from London towards Bristol and from thence to his command in Ireland. So he went not away till the King was in the power of the Parliament, though he had been declared Lieutenant of that Kingdom by the Parliament somewhat more than a year before . . . and had his commission from the Parliament in April, 1646, so slow were their proceedings.'[2]

Sometimes (to paraphrase Marx) historic events occur *first* as farce and *then* as tragedy. Lord Lisle's expedition, finally launched in February 1647, was the curtain-raising farce to the uncomic Cromwellian conquest of two years later. Annesley, Sir Adam and Sir Arthur Loftus, and Sir Hardress Waller accompanied the Lord Lieutenant on his crossing from Bristol. Broghill had returned to Munster from England in December and had begun to lay the foundations for Lisle's arrival, with its inevitable challenge to Inchiquin's authority. A new kind of xenophobia appeared among the old Munster officers in anticipation of Lord Lisle's reported preference of English to Irish Protestants in positions of command. One officer lamented bitterly: 'It was decreed from the beginning [that] none allied or born [in Ireland] shall have command unless

---

[1] The committee's records are in S.P. 21/26, and are calendared in *CSPI, 1647–1660*, Addenda, pp. 726–86.
[2] HMC, *De L'Isle and Dudley*, vi. 561.

a time-server, back biter, a flatterer, and worse, or a relative to such.'[1]

Lord Lisle's expedition landed at Kinsale on 21 February 1647, and friction with Inchiquin was instantaneous. Lisle's party had come with strong preconceptions of mismanagement in Munster. Within two weeks Inchiquin could write: 'There appears but very little difference between the effects of [Lord Lisle's] access and those we might expect from being subdued by the rebels—the usage which hath been extended towards us who were on the place carrying with it the semblance rather of a conquest than a relief.'[2] The old Munster officers were removed from their commands and Inchiquin himself was excluded from the council of the Lord Lieutenant, who consulted only Broghill or the other members of his retinue. Inchiquin objected to Parliament that Lord Lisle was ignoring the tradition that the Lord President of any province was second-in-command when the Lord Lieutenant was in that province.[3] He professed surprise at Lord Lisle's hostility and could understand it only in terms of 'Independency', supposing that he was thought deficient in this religious sentiment which was then waxing in the House of Commons. Lord Lisle's party was composed of doctrinaire 'Independents' as far as Inchiquin was concerned.[4] This was a curious appellation for Annesley, Loftus, Parsons, and Temple. They were neither religious leaders, M.P.s, nor officers of the New Model Army, that seed-bed of Independency. What they had most in common was a New English background in Ireland, a virulent hatred of Catholicism, and, save Broghill, a lack of complicity in the cessation of 1643. They did not come in the name of the adventurers—or financed by them. They did not come for the Army, which in 1647 was increasingly hesitant to be tied up in Ireland while friction grew with the Parliament in England.

Lord Lisle was not so much an agent of the Army as a substitute for it, an *ersatz* Fairfax or Cromwell. His supporters were not the new men but the old. They were the old enemies of

[1] Richard Fitzgerald to Perceval, 13 Feb. 1646/7, HMC, *Egmont*, i. 360.
[2] Inchiquin to Alexander Pigott, 5 Mar. 1646/7, HMC, *Egmont*, i. 367.
[3] Inchiquin to the Earl of Manchester, 10 Mar. 1646/7, *LJ*, ix. 108.
[4] Inchiquin to Pigott, 5 Mar. 1646/7, HMC, *Egmont*, i. 367.

Strafford, or their sons; the opponents of compromise with the Celts and their religion; the self-styled avengers called for by Temple in his casebook of Irish atrocities published the year before. They were Parliament men for a mixture of reasons, but not least because co-operation with the King would have meant compromise with the Irish, and Parliament afforded them an organized programme for their anti-Irish sentiments. If they were in any sense Independents, it was not because of theological leanings in that vague direction, but because the Presbyterians after 1646 were equivocating on the question of tolerating Catholicism, as it became prerequisite to co-operation with the King. With a figurehead Lord Lieutenant, their expedition was little more than an exiles' return, a favourite gambit of meddlesome but parsimonious governments!

Lord Lisle's authority rested upon a foundation of shifting sand. He arrived in Ireland on 21 February 1647, but his commission as Lord Lieutenant expired on 9 April. He had precious little time to carry out the subjugation of an island which had been in rebellion for more than five years. This was Inchiquin's single consolation. As Sir Philip Perceval expressed it in late February, 'the party by whose powers . . . [Lord Lisle] was nominated is not the swaying party as they were then [in January 1646]'. But what *was* the party in the House of Commons which supported Lisle? And who *were* the friends of Inchiquin, and why? Perceval told Inchiquin no more than that he would find a friend in Denzil Holles and Lord Fairfax.[1]

The insecurity of Lord Lisle *vis-à-vis* both the House of Commons and the Army, together with the animosity between him and Inchiquin, prevented any worthwhile military activity in Munster. Inchiquin retained control of most of the 4,000 soldiers already in the province when Lisle arrived, and Lisle's harassment of the Lord President did little to deprive him of that influence. Instead of employing the most considerable agglomeration of soldiers and money yet to come into Munster, the leaders sat sulking in their tents or writing abusive letters to London. Each party begged to be unshackled from the other. Sir Arthur Loftus was sent back to England by Lisle to impeach

---

[1] 9 Mar. 1646/7, HMC, *Egmont*, i. 368.

the conduct of Inchiquin, and William Jephson of Mallow was sent by Inchiquin to answer him charge for charge.[1] Lisle's allies in England were unable to get his commission extended beyond 9 April, while Inchiquin's could offer him no other solace than that Lisle would soon be out of power.

A divided Parliament could not decide to renew Lord Lisle's commission—but neither could it decide what, if anything, to put in its place. In February 1647 Ormond re-opened negotiations for the surrender of Dublin, and by June it was firmly in the hands of Parliament forces under Michael Jones. Inchiquin was restored to the military command of Munster, under the supervision of a Parliamentary commission. One party in Parliament, of Presbyterian outlook, wished to entrust Colonel Edward Massey and Sir William Waller jointly with the Irish command. Another, closer to the Army and Independents, preferred Generals Cromwell and Skippon.[2] The Commons voted in April against the appointment of another Lord Lieutenant, and resolved that the civil and military government of Ireland should be divided, the former to be entrusted to two Lords Justices, the latter to be managed by a separate body of commissioners. A new Irish military command was created under the title of Field-Marshal, but was limited to the Provinces of Leinster and Ulster.[3]

When Sir William Waller was proposed for the new Field-Marshal command, the House of Commons divided against him, and the next day appointed Major General Philip Skippon (an adventurer for £250) to the command, with Sir Edward Massey to serve as his Lieutenant General of Horse.[4] This was a compromise appointment plan, Skippon, a mild Army man, being yoked with Massey, a City Presbyterian. More than anything else it was testimony of the powerlessness of Parliament to deal effectively with Ireland while it was divided against itself and at loggerheads with the Army. But while it failed to act, the total military cost of the repression steadily increased at the rate of £40,000 per month. Thus delay was a major contributor to the scale of the Cromwellian confiscations, for it,

---

[1] Inchiquin to Perceval, 13 Mar. 1646/7, HMC, *Egmont*, i. 374.

[2] Perceval to Inchiquin, 2 Apr. 1647, HMC, *Egmont*, i. 384.

[3] *CJ*, v. 131, 1 Apr. 1647.   [4] Ibid., and v. 133, for 2 Apr. 1647.

rather than any particular extravagance, expanded the cost of reconquest.

While factions within Parliament struggled over his successor, Lord Lisle played out the last days of his impotent lieutenancy. When his commission expired on 9 April, he argued tendentiously that Inchiquin's office lapsed simultaneously, and attempted to place Munster under the command of his brother, Algernon Sydney.[1] After this and several other expedients failed, Inchiquin literally embarked the Lord Lieutenant and most of his party at gun-point, and so dispatched them out of Munster.[1] Even if the highly coloured versions of the episode put out by Inchiquin's supporters are misleading, Lisle's expedition can scarcely be recorded as a triumph. Lisle's father noted that his son and his followers had left Ireland 'rather than stay under the command of the Lord of Inchiquin'. Of Lisle's party only Annesley had defected to Inchiquin's side and, 'as he had divers times before, loved his interest better than honesty'.[2] Driven from Munster by Inchiquin, Lisle had simultaneously been undermined in the House of Commons, where on 8 April even his commission to his brother for the command of Dublin was voided, in order to give it to the militarily distinguished Michael Jones.[3]

With the collapse of Lord Lisle's expedition, plans for a reconquest slumbered, and Inchiquin's troubles continued. With Michael Jones established in Dublin, Parliament could be more cavalier towards Munster, and relations with the Munster President gradually deteriorated. He commanded a substantially larger force after Lisle's departure than before his arrival—some seven to eight thousand, compared with four to five thousand— but he had no revenue equal to their £2,200 weekly cost. Many of the new soldiers, having come with Lord Lisle and been left behind, shared the Lord Lieutenant's suspicion of the Irish-born Lord President of Munster who now commanded them. They wrote letters critical of Inchiquin to London, where they were welcomed and publicized by the embittered supporters of Lisle.

---

[1] 'A True and Brief Relation', 30 Apr. 1647, Thomason Tracts, BM, E. 385 (13).

[2] HMC, *De L'Isle and Dudley*, vi. 566.   [3] Ibid., p. 565.

In the aftermath of Lisle's expedition London was filled with Munster officers quarrelling over Inchiquin's reputation. Having lost their case in Ireland, Lisle, Loftus, Broghill, and Temple carried it to the higher court in London, where they vigorously impugned the Lord President.[1] 'Unless the Parliament send over some commanders in chief, true, English-hearted men not interested here . . . many other commanders which came over with regiments out of England will have but a small comfort to stay here' wrote one of the disaffected soldiers from Munster.[2]

Parliament was diverted from mounting another expedition to Munster by both the surrender of Dublin and its own internal divisions. Skippon, whom it had chosen for the new Field-Marshal command, tried desperately to decline the post. When he finally accepted, he was little more successful than his Presbyterian adjutant, Massey, in persuading soldiers of the New Model to volunteer for Irish service. Their minds were on their own grievances and the better ordering of England. Ireland would have to wait, and Munster was no longer so exclusively the focus of Parliament strategy. The claims of Ulster, Connaught, and Leinster were again being heard in London after nearly two years of neglect.

Formal charges were brought against Inchiquin in June 1647 by Adam Loftus and Lord Broghill. It was alleged that the Lord President had been promiscuous in the distribution of custodiams, that his army was laden with royalists of one vintage or another, that he was known to express royalist sentiments himself, that he had been guilty of peculation with Parliament funds, and that he was, in general, too lenient with Catholics and Irishmen.[3] The publication of these charges coincided with proceedings of the New Model Army against the eleven Presbyterian M.P.s most obnoxious to it. Those men, finally forced on 26 June 1647 to withdraw from the House of Commons, were charged in the fourteenth article of their impeachment with having treasonably corresponded with Inchiquin

[1] Perceval to Inchiquin, 18 May 1647, HMC, *Egmont*, i. 405; and 'Two Letters from Lt. Col. Knight', Thomason Tracts, BM, E. 399 (23).

[2] Col. Francis Roe to Col. Henry Grey, 14 May 1647, HMC, *Egmont*, i. 403.

[3] 'Articles Exhibited to the Commons Against Inchiquin', Thomason Tracts, BM, E. 402 (19).

during Lord Lisle's residence in Munster.[1] Holles had certainly expressed his sympathies with Inchiquin. Several of the other impeached members—Stapleton, Clotworthy, Waller, and Massey—had been active in Irish policy, but whether they also opposed Lord Lisle is not otherwise apparent. Their removal from Parliament, however, was palpably a blow to Inchiquin.[2]

Several members of Lord Lisle's party, Broghill, Hardress Waller, Arthur Loftus, and Sir John Temple, insinuated themselves into the committee of the Lords and Commons for Irish affairs which met at Derby House. It was apparently to their popularity with the Army leaders that they owed their influence; and their popularity stemmed from their sympathy with the Army's reluctance to be thrown into the Irish cauldron while it was in the hands of an Irish chieftain like Inchiquin. Though the Presbyterians in Parliament were exhorting the Army to transport itself to Ireland and leave England in peace, Temple and Waller were, paradoxically, urging the Army commissioners to send nothing into Munster and only minimal reinforcements to Dublin. They advised that it was necessary only to *secure* the capital until the Army was able to send over a considerable force for the conquest of the kingdom.[3]

The advocates of the Munster expedition of early 1647 thus reversed their attitude and contributed to the strangulation of the larger military establishment which their expedition, however abortive, had helped to build.[4] Annesley, who had

---

[1] Inchiquin to William Pierpont, 11 Aug. 1647, HMC, *Egmont*, i. 447; and S. R. Gardiner, *History of the Great Civil War*, London, 1893, iii. 298.

[2] See Bottigheimer, op. cit., p. 223.

[3] Charles Howard, Third Earl of Nottingham, and Philip, Fourth Baron Wharton, to the Earl of Manchester, 29 July 1647 (correspondence addressed to Edward Montagu, Second Earl of Manchester, 1640–7, BM Add. MS. 34, 253, ff. 79–82).

[4] It seems impossible to show that the degree to which M.P.s favoured dispatch of the Army to Ireland in 1647 corresponded with the degree of their investment as adventurers. Indeed, those in the forefront of the disputes over Irish policy, Inchiquin, Lisle, Broghill, and Temple, were neither M.P.s nor adventurers. This is but another example of the 'displacement' of the adventurers from influence upon Irish policy. The dispute in 1647 was not principally between adventurers (advocating reconquest) and their opponents, but between the Army (advocating thorough settlement of England first) and *its* opponents. Irish policy was but a reflex or by-product of English internal affairs. See above, p. 72, n. 1, and David Underdown, 'Civil War in Ireland: Commentary', *EUQ*, Summer, 1966, pp. 75–6.

accompanied Lisle but come to side with Inchiquin, took a dim view of the access of his former colleagues, particularly Temple, to influence:

If it be observed whose counsels are taken for oracles concerning Ireland, and who have had and would still have the manage of those affairs, it is no wonder the expense hath been so great and the success so bad. . . . So long as Sir John Temple his motions may be credited, and they who support him . . . I look for no good for Ireland, for I know how he and his confederates came to their places, and they who buy, must sell.[1]

Munster became more and more disaffected, as Temple and his colleagues probably intended. Inchiquin thought he was being persecuted as a Presbyterian, and some of the Munster officers resolved to disobey all orders not authorized by the unpurged Parliament.[2] Colonel Robert Sterling, a Scot serving in Munster, wrote to the Earl of Leven of the devotion of Inchiquin and the Munster officers 'to the service of the Parliament in observance of the Covenant'.[3] The letters were intercepted by Parliament and contributed to growing suspicions of Inchiquin's loyalty.

In February 1648 Inchiquin entered into negotiations with the Irish which led in April to his final and permanent defection from Parliament. He had been forced into this action, he asserted, by the Independents in Parliament, to whom it appeared 'that to have the war finished . . . [in Ireland] before the perfection of their designs in England would prove . . . the greatest dissatisfaction in the world . . .'.[4] In his memoirs Denzil Holles detailed the disservices of the Independents to the Protestants of Ireland. 'Everybody knows', he wrote, 'the malice which is born them by that party which now bears sway [the Independents], what discouragements my Lord of Inchiquin has labored under and the small regard had of Col. [Michael] Jones.'[5]

---

[1] HMC, *Egmont*, i. 441.

[2] Inchiquin to Perceval, 17 Aug. 1647, HMC, *Egmont*, i. 452, and Inchiquin to Fairfax, 25 Aug. 1647, HMC, *Egmont*, i. 456-8.

[3] 30 Aug. 1647, *Tanner Letters*, pp. 259-65.

[4] Declaration of Inchiquin and the Protestant Army in Munster, printed late June 1648, Thomason Tracts, BM, E. 452 (10).

[5] *Memoirs of Denzil, Lord Holles*, London, 1699, p. 82.

It is certainly arguable that the crisis which brought Cromwell so ardently to Ireland—Ormond's new royalist alliance strengthened by the adherence of Inchiquin—was a by-product of Parliament policy, and in particular, of the Independents' refusal to support the Protestant cause in Ireland at its moment of need.

A final, futile, attempt had been made in November 1647 to raise additional money for Ireland from the adventurers. An ordinance of the 13th of that month, for raising £30,000, proclaimed that the terms of the doubling ordinance of 1643 should lapse on the 3rd of December.[1] That the response to the ordinance was less than enthusiastic is suggested by the Derby House committee's decision on 30 November to call together the adventurers 'in and about London', for the purpose of imparting to them something 'concerning their adventure and the advantage of the service of Ireland'.[2] When the adventurers met they established a sub-committee of forty-one members to deal with the Derby House committee.[3] But there are no records of subsequent negotiations between the two groups, and it seems unlikely that even as much as a few hundred pounds was raised from the disillusioned adventurers.

Parliament did not cease taking up loans for Ireland, but declined to secure them any longer upon Irish land. In May 1647, for instance, an ordinance was passed for securing a loan of £200,000 'for the service of this Kingdom and the Kingdom of Ireland' upon the grand excise and compositions made with delinquents.[4] An ordinance of 23 June 1647 called for a monthly assessment of £60,000 for the purposes of both England and Ireland, but another, of 16 February 1648, admitted that the 'exigencies of England' had not permitted any of that money to go to Ireland.[5] The old assessment of £80,000 p.a. exclusively for the uses of Ireland, first levied in October 1644, was apparently allowed to expire in October 1646. The last attempt to

---

[1] Firth and Rait, *Acts and Ordinances*, i. 1028.
[2] PRO, S.P. 21/26, f. 118.
[3] Ibid., f. 120.
[4] Firth and Rait, *Acts and Ordinances*, i. 928.
[5] Ibid., 958 and 1072.

raise money on Irish land was an ordinance of 3 January 1648. £50,000 was to be raised, and interest of 8 per cent per year to be paid upon it 'out of the moneys that shall be raised by a speedy sale of all the houses . . . [etc.] of the Irish Rebels' in Dublin, Cork, Kinsale, Youghal, and Drogheda, 'all of which are now in the present possession and power of the State'.[1] Not only the principal but the interest upon it was secured by Irish land. The investor would be repaid not in land but in money, with interest which the state obliged itself to raise from its acquired Irish assets. That the value and security of those assets was uncertain is further suggested by the fact that the ordinance provided the additional security of delinquent estates in England, 'until the sale be made of the said Rebels houses . . . and until payment be made to the said adventurers'.[1] We do not know how much money the ordinance succeeded in raising. Probably little, for, with Inchiquin's defection, property in Youghal, Cork, and Kinsale passed out of the 'present possession and power of the state'.[2]

It was in February 1648 that a scheme of promising magnitude was finally introduced. This was an assessment of £20,000 per month, to run for six months. Its announced purpose was 'to put that war to a happy and speedy period . . . with seasonable supplies, the want whereof hath hitherto hindered the completing of that work, notwithstanding that great sums have been at several times raised and spent for that service'.[3] This was the beginning of the financial build-up which, in the summer of 1649, carried Oliver Cromwell to Ireland.

The attempt to finance the Irish war with Irish land had been a failure. But it was as much a political as a fiscal failure. Substantial amounts of money were raised, and additional amounts could have been raised, had there been reasonable hope that they would be used in an unequivocal reconquest of Ireland. The civil war in England and the subsequent divisions between the Army and Parliament prevented that from happening. The logical alternative, a negotiated peace with the Irish rebels, was prevented first by the economic interest of the adventurers, for whom confiscation of Irish land was a necessity, and subsequently

---

[1] Firth and Rait, *Acts and Ordinances*, i. 1056.
[2] Ibid., p. 1147.   [3] Ibid., p. 1072.

by the insistence of the Independents that the Irish war should be won rather than merely ended.

It was Cromwell who translated that insistence into action. His triumph in Ireland was no less the result of fiscal policy than of strategy. According to W. C. Abbott, he could have sailed for Ireland in June 1649, but delayed until August, because 'if there was one lesson above all others which Irish affairs had taught, it was the absolute necessity for supplies of money as well as of men and war materials'.[1] The previous March he had asked for and received an assessment of £90,000 per month, a larger amount than the original assessment for Ireland (of October 1644) raised in a year.[2] Large loans were raised against the assessment, secured not by Irish land, for so long such elusive collateral, but by the tax revenue of the Commonwealth.[3] The history of the adventure proved, not that Ireland could not be made to pay the costs of rebellion, but rather that there was a limit to the amount of money which could be raised by the hypothecation of yet unconquered land. Once the public revenue was tapped to finance the actual conquest, confiscation became a policy of great potential. Public scepticism as to its worth placed a very real limitation on the amount of Irish land consumed by the adventure; but there was no natural limit to the amount of land the triumphant Commonwealth might confiscate in an effort to relieve itself of immense and unprecedented economic burdens, particularly in connection with the disbanding of the army. Hence the confiscatory policies which had failed to resolve the Irish problem in the 1640s were resurrected in the Cromwellian Settlement of the 1650s. The adventurers had become minor partners in that settlement. Their steady displacement from influence upon, and responsibility for, the Irish wars should probably be viewed as part of a larger process

---

[1] W. C. Abbott, *Writings and Speeches of Oliver Cromwell*, Cambridge, Mass., 1932–47, ii. 84.

[2] Firth and Rait, *Acts and Ordinances*, ii. 24–57.

[3] See PRO, S.P. 21/29, the Warrant Book of the Council of State, for the intricacies of gathering £100,000 to send with Cromwell to Ireland. £15,000 was more or less extorted from William Lenthall, Speaker of the House of Commons, and £150,000 from London's Common Council (Abbott, *Writings and Speeches of Oliver Cromwell*, ii. 86 and 93).

—the expanding competence of the state established by the Long Parliament and its Interregnum successors. By February 1649 Irish affairs had been removed from the tangle of Parliamentary and adventurers' committees which had handled them since 1641.[1] Henceforth they remained in the care of the executive, and the final Settlement of Ireland was worked out, not, primarily, for the benefit of those who had leapt in 1641 at the opportunity to acquire Irish land, but for the fiscal benefit of the Cromwellian state.

[1] *CSPD, 1647–1660*, p. xvi.

V

THE ENACTMENT AND
IMPLEMENTATION OF
THE CROMWELLIAN SETTLEMENT

T H E century of Plantation prior to 1641 provided the principles
which were selectively incorporated in the act for adventurers
of 1642. The lengthy continuance of the Irish wars after 1642,
and the immense expenses of reconquest after 1649, generated
economic pressure for the extensive application of the act, and
the exploitation of its implications. Had Ireland been conquered in late 1642 or early 1643 by an expedition financed by
the adventurers, a very different and much less drastic Settlement
would have resulted; one in which the adventurers rather than
the soldiers played the key role. In fact, even while the Settlement was being implemented in the years after 1653, the high
costs of administration and of maintaining a garrison in Ireland
were contributing to pressures for increasing confiscations.[1]
Time worked against land; the longer the Settlement took to
impose, the more land it consumed.

The act for adventurers had laid down the principle that the
costs of repressing the Irish rebellion could be defrayed by the
sale of confiscated Irish land, but it did not say *which* land, nor
did it designate what procedures were to be followed in trans-
ferring land from former owners to new ones. All such considerations necessarily awaited the forceful subduing of the
Irish. That process was begun by Cromwell, whose sizeable and
well-provided expedition reached Ireland in August 1649.
On the eve of his arrival a significant victory was achieved
by Michael Jones, commander of the Parliamentary garrison
holding Dublin since 1647. Dublin had been under siege by
the forces of the royalist alliance created by the Marquis of
Ormond, when, in January 1649, conservative influences again

---

[1] The total cost of the conquest is discussed above, pp. 55–6.

prevailed among the confederate Catholics. Jones launched a surprise attack on 2 August and left Ormond's forces in ruins. When Cromwell arrived two weeks later he was able to take the offensive, attacking royalist and Irish strongpoints with the vehemence and ruthlessness that gained him everlasting hatred in Ireland. When he left in May 1650, the spine of Irish resistance had been broken, but important areas remained unsubdued. Management of the war and military government was placed in the hands of Cromwell's son-in-law, Henry Ireton, until his premature death in November 1651, when it passed to Edmund Ludlow (until October 1652), Charles Fleetwood (until September 1655), and Henry Cromwell thereafter. Major conflict became infrequent by 1652, and in August of that year the Parliamentary commissioners for Ireland informed most of the military commanders that further organized resistance from the Irish was unlikely.[1]

The pressures to initiate the Settlement were such that, despite persistent guerilla-like activity, a piece of major legislation was prepared. This was the act for the settling of Ireland of 12 August 1652, and it found in its preamble that '. . . the Parliament of England, after the expense of much blood and treasure for suppression of the horrid rebellion in Ireland, have . . . brought that affair to such an issue, as that a total reducement and settlement of that nation may . . . be speedily effected'.[2]

The form which that Settlement would take had long been in contention, but it was increasingly evident that the adjective 'total', applied to it in the language of the preamble, was appropriate. In 1642, when rebellion rather than settlement was the preoccupation of Parliament, little was said about the *form* of the new Ireland. It was assumed that a major portion of Irish land would be escheated to the Crown (10,000,000 acres— or half of Ireland—proponents of the act for adventurers had estimated), and that 2,500,000 acres would suffice to repay the adventurers their hoped-for investment of £1,000,000. But since the ten-million-acre figure was itself entirely conjectural, no

---

[1] Bodleian MS, Firth C. 5, f. 131, cited in Kathleen Lynch, *Roger Boyle, First Earl of Orrery*, Knoxville, Tennessee, 1965, p. 83.

[2] C. H. Firth and R. S. Rait, eds., *The Acts and Ordinances of the Interregnum*, 3 vols., London, 1911, ii. 598.

formal consideration was given to the hypothetical seven and a half million acres which would remain after the adventurers were satisfied. There was, however, a consciousness by all parties of the immense amount of land likely to be available in Ireland upon the conclusion of the rebellion. It was well publicized that the adventurers had not subscribed anything like the £1,000,000 expected of them, and the ultimate accounting showed that they furnished only one-third of that amount. At the act rates, they would be entitled to less than a million Irish acres. The Cromwellian conquest resulted in the equivalent of unconditional surrender for the Irish. There were no negotiations. Ireland lay at the disposition of the Commonwealth 'like a patient etherized upon a table'. No obligation lay upon Parliament to confirm the loyal Catholics or even the loyal Protestants in their Irish lands. The severity of the acts of settlement would determine how much land was available for redistribution, and would create new classes of persons able to lay claim to it.

In the decade between 1642 and 1652 those facts had come to be appreciated, with the result that various sketches or blueprints of future settlement had been aired. Hints of them appear throughout the 1640s. The doubling ordinance of 14 July 1643 took the important step of writing the army into the eventual settlement by permitting 'officers and commanders in . . . the British armies in Ireland' to subscribe their pay or arrears for Irish land at the same rates as those available for the adventurers.[1] There is not much evidence that many of them chose to do so, but this was the beginning of a line of thought which would terminate in the settlement of 35,000 English soldiers on Irish land in lieu of paying their arrears in specie.[2]

---

[1] Ibid. i. 196.

[2] Land was also used to pay soldiers in England. 'But there was this difference between the position of the army in England and Ireland. In England the soldier's debenture was a promise to pay a certain sum of money for which the land was merely security. In Ireland the soldier's debenture expressly stated that the sum due was to be paid in land' (C. H. Firth, *Cromwell's Army*, Methuen edition of 1962, p. 202). An uncomputed number of English acres were claimed by holders of army debentures, but as these were largely confiscated Crown lands, they reverted to the King at the Restoration. Firth was moved to remark: 'In one country, therefore, the Cromwellian officers maintained their possessions and exerted a permanent influence on its later development; in the other, they returned to their original position' (ibid., p. 207). See also H. J. Habakkuk, 'The Parliamentary Army and the Crowns Lands', *Welsh History Review*, iii. 403–26.

In a pamphlet of early January 1646 the adventurers described a settlement in which they would *first* be satisfied out of the pool of confiscated Irish land, after which land for soldiers' arrears, and for foreign Protestant colonists, could be carved from the remainder.[1] Almost as an afterthought, 'full restitution' (but not compensation) was demanded for the Protestants of Ireland who had lost their estates through the wars, and for London merchants who had lost their debts there from the same cause. The adventurers obviously hoped that such a widening of the Settlement would involve multitudes of Protestants, because they argued that a 'mass' of Protestant freeholders would be the solution to the century-old threat of papist Ireland as a spearhead of the Counter-Reformation.

Further thoughts along such lines are to be found in the recommendations of 2 November 1648 to the House of Commons from the committee for Irish affairs at Derby House.[2] Among various proposals the committee called upon Parliament to enact that after disposition of the 2,500,000 acres of land intended for the adventurers 'all the residue of the lands forfeited by the rebels . . . be disposed of for the further prosecution of the war there, for advancing the revenues of the Crown, etc.'[3] The committee called also for an act of attainder against the rebels to insure the forfeiture of their estates.[4] These proposals suggest a resurrection, as it were, of the idea that Irish land should pay the full costs of Irish rebellion, and the recognition of the fact that the first attempt to make it do so—namely the adventure—had been a failure. The adventure had failed, first, to raise all or most of the £1,000,000 estimated necessary to finance the repression of Ireland. Secondly, it failed because those funds raised were almost immediately raided for domestic purposes, and thereafter were squandered piecemeal in Ireland without procuring the needed reconquest. Ultimately, it failed because of a common economic phenomenon, the classic example of which is the behaviour of the *assignat* during the French Revolution. Like the revolutionary government in

[1] 'The State of the Irish Affairs . . .', Thomason Tracts, BM, E. 314 (7).
[2] The history of the Derby House Committee may be found above, pp. 102–3.
[3] HMC, *Portland MSS.*, i. 502.
[4] Ibid. An ordinance to this effect was passed on 26 June 1657 (Firth and Rait, *Acts and Ordinances*, ii. 1250).

France, that in England possessed an important asset in confiscated land. The problem was to make maximum use of it. In
France this was done by issuing currency backed by the value
of the land, in England by making certain forms of government
indebtedness dischargeable in land at fixed rates. It happened,
however, that the market value of land fell, probably as a result
of Ireland's being ravaged by war, and because English capital
in search of land was reduced by confiscatory taxation and
economic dislocation. As land's market value fell, impatient
and disillusioned adventurers sold out at a loss, providing an
alternate and cheaper source of futures for those still interested
in buying them. The government readjusted its rates, offering
more land for less money (as in the doubling ordinance of 1643),
but thereby contributed to a downward spiralling of land
values which resulted in the constant deflating of the government's landed assets. The only solution to this dilemma was the
autocratic repaying of already existent debts at officially fixed
rates; and the fixed debt over which the government had the
greatest amount of control was that owed to the army. Soldiers
had little alternative to accepting their arrears in whatever form
the government paid them. They were, in effect, a captive class,
at least by 1653, when radical spirits like John Lilburne had
long been silenced. The army could be paid in Irish land at the
act rates long after the rate of land to money had ceased to attract
funds in the capital market. This is surely the reason why the
soldiers became the major partners in the Cromwellian Settlement of Ireland, and why, after 1647, Parliament made little
attempt to attract further adventure by offering Irish land at
cheaper rates.

It is difficult to determine at what point the government of
the Commonwealth determined to pay off the army in Ireland,
some 35,000 men, with Irish land. To do so, it had to convert
what began in 1643 as the *right* of a soldier fighting in Ireland
to receive his pay in Irish land, into an obligation to do so. By
1651 the Army clearly regarded itself as a legatee of Irish land
with a large stake in the imminent settlement, and by early 1652
the stage was set for a three-way dialogue between army,
adventurers, and Parliament over the exact form that settlement
would take. All that was certain was that Ireland had been

hypothecated for an immense but yet uncomputed amount of indebtedness, and that the adventurers were to be compensated at rates laid down in the act of 1642 and subsequent ordinances.

The first visible proposal for a settlement issued in January 1652 from the four Parliamentary commissioners for Ireland: Edmund Ludlow, John Jones, Miles Corbett, and John Weaver. The commissioners had been appointed in October 1650 for the purpose of establishing some sort of civil government, but, when the offices of Lord Lieutenant and Lord Deputy were abolished in November 1651, the commissioners became responsible for military as well as civil affairs.[1] The commissioners' main interest was in a settlement which would help to hold the land lately reconquered and provide for a speedy disbanding of the army. Accordingly, they called in January 1652 for a rapid casting of lots by the adventurers, 'to the end they may presently begin to plant, not withstanding the war is not ended, and may plant together and thereby be strengthened, which the act doth not provide for them. And to the end the Parliament may more freely dispose of the rest of their land to the public advantage.[2] The commissioners then proposed that sixteen Irish counties be divided into four 'allotments', one in the south-west, one in south Leinster, one in north Leinster and one in the north-west.[3] Each of the allotments, it asserted, would contain sufficient forfeited land to satisfy the adventurers, and they could therefore be conveniently settled in whichever of the four they drew.[4] After the adventurers had been satisfied in one of the four allotments, a new Pale was to be created 'by securing all the passes upon the [rivers] Boyne and . . . Barrow, and joining these two rivers in one entire line', an area which would include most of counties Meath, Dublin, Kildare, Wicklow, Carlow, and Wexford. But it was not at all clear who

---

[1] J. C. Beckett, *The Making of Modern Ireland, 1603–1923*, London, 1966, p. 105.

[2] 'Some Particulars Humbly Offered . . .', 8 Jan. 1651/2, Bodleian Carte MS, 67, f. 223. Printed in HMC, *Portland*, i. 624; and Robert Dunlop, *Ireland under the Commonwealth*, Manchester, 1913, p. 121.

[3] The named counties were as follows: in the first 'allotment', Limerick, Kerry, Clare, Galway; in the second, Kilkenny, Wexford, Wicklow, Carlow; in the third, Westmeath, Longford, Cavan, Monaghan; in the fourth, Fermanagh, Donegal, Leitrim, Sligo.

[4] Robert Dunlop pointed out that the scheme assigned 'some of the worst lands in Ireland' to the adventurers (*Ireland under the Commonwealth*, p. 121, fn.).

was to inhabit this area of maximum security. The adventurers would find a place in it only if they drew the second 'allotment', that containing Kilkenny, Wexford, Wicklow, and Carlow. Only the vaguest reference was made to satisfaction of the soldiers, who were to be 'fixed to their respective garrisons and quarters, and have lands assigned to them as well for their arrears, as in lieu (at least of part) of their present pay'.

The adventurers received these proposals with little enthusiasm. By an order of 30 January 1652 they had been enjoined to attend a meeting of a Parliament committee 'for public business', and were there ordered to propose what the body of adventurers conceived, concerning the government's desire for 'a speedy entering upon and planting of their several shares in order to the public interest'.[1]

On 6 April 1652 the committee of adventurers produced the requested proposals,[2] in the form of a petition to Parliament. It opened with a computation of the sums the adventurers had invested. These were probably derived from records which have since disappeared, for it would be exceedingly difficult to arrive at similar figures from the records that survive in the Public Records. The adventurers calculated that £293,062 had been adventured 'on the acts of Parliament for Ireland', a term which included the sea adventure ordinance of June 1642. A further £12,283 had been brought in by the doubling ordinance of 14 July 1643, and £1,363 for rebel houses in Limerick, Galway, Waterford, and Wexford under the same ordinance. According to the petition, £11,249 of the money raised under the 'acts' had already been repaid in the form of English 'Dean and Chapter Lands'.[3] The state owed the adventurers £281,813 collected under the acts, £12,283 under the doubling ordinance, and £1,363 for houses in the named towns. By a complicated

[1] 'Humble Petition of the Committee of Adventurers', 6 Apr. 1652, Carte MS. 67, f. 230. Printed in HMC, *Portland*, i. 639 and *CJ*, vii. 115.

[2] The committee was made up of twelve adventurers, who between them had invested about £8,000. They were Thomas Andrewes (£1,650), Cornelius Burges (£700), Charles Lloyd (£600), Richard Hutchinson (£250), John Greensmith (£300), Thomas Ayres (£200), Thomas Vincent (£1,300), John Brightwell (£785), William Hiccocks (£500), Samuel Avery (£400), Samuel Langham (£700), and George Almery (£800).

[3] This is the only reference I have found to such a procedure, but there is no internal reason to doubt it.

formulation the adventurers figured that it would require £73,698 to pay off the £12,283 paid in on the doubling ordinance.[1] Hence the sum to be satisfied was £281,813 plus £73,698 plus £1,363, or a total of £356,874.

To calculate how much Irish land this sum entitled them to, the adventurers divided by four the sum due to them under the act (£281,813). This gave them £70,453, the amount to be extracted in land from each of the four Provinces of Ireland. This was in accordance with the act of 1642, which had provided that the adventurers' land, as a whole, should be drawn equally from the four Provinces. It is also strong evidence that as late as April 1652 the adventurers were unaware of any attempt to move all the Irish to Connaught, a policy which would have required the new plantation to be limited to Munster, Leinster, and Ulster. By the rates provided in the acts, the adventurers calculated that £70,453 would require the use of 116,819 acres in Leinster, 156,551 in Munster, 228,831 in Connaught, and 352,255 in Ulster. The doubling ordinance allowed them to choose the province from which the lands in satisfaction of 'doubling' sums would be drawn, and they chose Munster, where 183,776 acres additional would be required to satisfy the £73,698 which they claimed in credit. Thus the adventurers called for a distribution of 1,038,232 acres to themselves, and further stipulated that these should be 'of profitable Irish measure, with bogs, woods and barren mountains cast in over and above'.[2]

Having stated their accounts in the manner most favourable to themselves and laid claim to over a million Irish acres (the equivalent of approximately 1,600,000 English acres) the adventurers balked at beginning the plantation—as the government and the Irish commissioners were so eager for them to do. 'It is impossible at this time', they wrote, 'to undertake and perform so great a work with hope of benefit, safety and honor

---

[1] By the ordinance of 1643 every new £1 advanced effectively doubled the sum of the new and old subscriptions as long as there was £4 of old subscription for every £1 of new. Thus £1 added to a £4 initial subscription resulted in a new credit of £10. Every pound of doubling adventure required £6 of land to repay it, and six times £12,283 is £73,698.

[2] All of the above derives from the 'Humble Petition of the Adventurers'. See above p. 121, note 1.

to the commonwealth, unless far greater encouragements than all the acts and ordinances do yet hold out, be granted of grace to the adventurers.'[1] In the continuing absence of such encouragements they hinted that they would prefer being repaid their adventure money in specie, with the addition of what they called 'reasonable interest' (8 per cent p.a. over a period, now, in most cases, approaching ten years). The adventurers had no right to demand repayment of their investments in specie, for the acts under which they invested offered them no such security or choice. The adventure, as we have already remarked, had certain characteristics of a 'lottery', and the loser in a lottery does not have the privilege of demanding the price of his ticket back. On the other hand, we can imagine with what chagrin the government would have faced the prospect of finding £356,874 and ten years interest upon it in order to repay the adventurers.

The adventurers, in the same document, made numerous suggestions as to how they might be encouraged to take over and plant their Irish property. All their lands might be set out in Munster and the contiguous parts of Leinster. 500,000 Irish acres might be gratuitously added to their due, and shared proportionately among them. Quit rents stipulated in the act of 1642 might be wholly remitted. Customs, excise, 'or any other impost or tax' might be indefinitely suspended, and all future keeping of order might be 'at the public charge of the commonwealth' and not of the adventurers in particular.[1]

To buttress these demands, the adventurers portrayed themselves—not altogether unconvincingly—as exhausted and bankrupted by their involvement with Ireland. They dwelt upon the length of the wars and the consequent length of time they had been without the use of their money. They would have been better off, they asserted, to have invested the money at the more normal 8 per cent, than to gamble it on Irish land. In 1642 they had been under the impression that their money would be used forthwith to repress the rebellion in Ireland. The 'conversion' of the first £100,000 raised (30 July 1642) 'for saving of England', and the remanding of Lord Wharton's brigade of horse and foot, intended for Munster but sent to Edgehill, made Parliament in their eyes responsible for the failure of the

[1] Ibid.

rebellion to be curbed immediately, and the failure of the adventurers, therefore, to be speedily planted on their lands. At all of this the adventurers hinted timorously. But their most persuasive arguments were practical rather than moral. If the intended plantation of the adventurers in Ireland now failed, the remainder of Ireland would become 'a wild, howling, wilderness'. That would doom the Protestant settlement as a whole:

It can hardly be found that ingenuous men of good estates have left their native soil (where they are well settled) for a foreign wilderness abounding with nothing but wants and dangers, upon condition to buy the land upon which they must plant: and in case they thrive, to be subject to all laws and ordinances of that state of which they purchase. . . . In foreign plantations (where the dangers have not been comparable to those in Ireland) they have not only their land free, but such large privileges and immunities (as to choose their own governor and he to be independent to make their own laws, etc.) as the adventurers out of love to the public and to the present government dare not seek or accept.[1]

Although it was a self-serving statement, the adventurers' warning was prophetic, and pointed to days not far off when the main friction between Ireland and England would be between English Protestants and Irish Protestant planters, the Celts having been reduced to several centuries of relative submission. The adventurers put their finger inadvertently on the dilemma of Ireland: that it was far enough removed from England to be treated as a colonizable area, but near enough to be governable by the English state in its own interests rather than be abandoned to the colonists and theirs. And yet it was not quite so simple a distinction, for the adventurers wanted, not so much to be left alone in the dangerous wilds of Ireland, as to be protected and coddled there by agencies of the English Commonwealth. And in Ireland, as distinguished from North America, they were able to view *themselves* as servants of the state, embarked on the vital mission of pacifying Ireland, and exposed to uncertainties and dangers for which broad acres were pitifully small reward.

On 20 April 1652 the House of Commons referred the adventurers' propositions to the Council of State, asking that it should

---

[1] The 'Humble Petition of the Adventurers'. See above p. 121, note 1.

prepare 'something . . . for the settling of the affairs of Ireland'. Further, it asked the Council to consider 'how the soldiers that have been or shall be disbanded in Ireland, and those officers there for whom there hath been no provision made here, may have reasonable satisfaction given to them in Ireland for their service'.[1] In the meantime Parliament was urged by the commissioners in Ireland not to truckle to the adventurers, but to insist that they should carry out their plantation on the originally agreed terms.[2]

An *ad hoc* committee of Parliament produced in early May what it hoped would be an acceptable compromise. The adventurers were to have all their land together in Munster, or Munster and southern Leinster, as they desired. An additional 500,000 acres were to be granted them in such places as Parliament saw fit. They were dispensed for seven years from paying customs on goods which they imported from England for the development of their properties, and for ten years from paying more than one-fifth the true yearly value of their land in taxes. But in return for these concessions the committee added the stringent requirement 'that such of the aforesaid lands as shall not be conveniently inhabited, and in some husbandlike manner managed, at the end of the said three years [i.e. 29 Sept. 1655] shall be forfeited to the Commonwealth'. If the adventurers hesitated to accept this compromise, the committee warned, Parliament would simply proceed to set forth their lands as stipulated by the former acts for adventure.[3]

The committee of adventurers wasted little time before replying to these proposals, which threw it into instant alarm. It rejected the supposed compromise, calling it pernicious and unfair. The adventurers saw harm even in what the committee

[1] J. T. Gilbert, *A Contemporary History of Affairs in Ireland*, Dublin, 1879, iii. 311.
[2] See 'Considerations to be offered to the Parliament by Mr. Weaver', 30 Apr. 1652, HMC, *Portland*, i. 644.
[3] There are several versions of this document. One printed in J. T. Gilbert, *A Contemporary History*, iii. 318, is dated 12 May 1652, and identified as coming from a MS. in the Royal Irish Academy, Dublin. Another version appears in Carte MS. 67, f. 255, is dated 11 May, and differs in certain minor details. Another copy of the same version is in HMC, *Portland*, i. 648. Copies of the 12 May document are also to be found in the Portland MSS., calendared ibid., and in the Carte Papers, 67, f. 256.

had intended as a concession. That the 500,000 additional acres to be granted them might not be adjacent to the rest, and that they had also to be settled within three years, the adventurers saw as vitiating their value. That exemption from customs was to last only seven years, and apply only to certain imported products and no exported ones, they saw as inadequate. Even in the suggested location of their lands they saw the hidden perils of bogs, woods, and mountains which would prevent them from planting close together. But on all these matters they were willing to negotiate. The real source of their alarm was the threat of confiscation if they did not settle within three years, or, indeed, within any fixed time. The lands, they stated forcefully, 'being their own by a dear purchase, they may plant and build for their own convenience at their own discretion, and that it is their liberty and birthright so to do'.[1]

It is interesting, this ability of Anglo-Saxons to summon up the indignation of Magna Carta whenever 'ancient liberties' are imperilled. The adventurers believed, with justification, that the Commonwealth was trying to foist the ravaged, still unpacified, wilds of Ireland upon them, and to make them into an unpaid army of occupation. But there was nothing in the acts for adventure guaranteeing the sound condition of Irish land, so that the state was within the letter if not the spirit of the law in demanding that the adventurers should accept it as they found it, without special compensations.

Another interesting aspect of the adventurers' reply was their response to a proposal, or concession, that no Irish whatever should be permitted to reside within the area of the plantation (still envisaged as one integral area of Ireland). The very fact that such a proposal was made at this time suggests that thoughts of removing the Irish from whatever areas were selected for English plantation were very much current, even though they had not yet eventuated in the policy of transplantation to Connaught. The adventurers displayed no enthusiasm for such a removal, entrusting the treatment of all the natives 'whether Protestants or others' to Parliament. Perhaps they were already aware, as English planters had learned in the past, that Irish

---

[1] 'Committee of the Adventurers to the Committee for Proposals', 14 May 6152, HMC, *Portland*, i. 649, and Carte MS. 67, ff. 257–60.

labour was cheap labour and that an exclusively English population meant higher costs and lower rents.[1]

Little more is to be learned about the conceptual development of the Settlement until the passage in August of the act for the settling of Ireland. The preamble of that act states that it was

not the intention of the Parliament to extirpate the whole [Irish] nation, but that mercy and pardon, both as to life and estate, may be extended to all husbandmen, plowmen, laborers, artificers, and others of the inferior sort, in manner as is hereafter declared; . . . And that others also of higher rank and quality may know the Parliaments intention concerning them, according to the respective demerits and considerations under which they fall.[2]

This conciliatory language, later regarded as irrefutable evidence of English hypocrisy, merely cloaked many months of struggle over the severity or lenity of the Settlement. The commissioners in Ireland had been debating, at least since January 1651, the terms on which the defeated Irish should be admitted to mercy.[3] Counsels of relative clemency were heard, if only because liberal conditions were convenient in persuading remaining Irish forces to surrender. In a memorable letter of 5 May 1652 to Parliament, the commissioners explained how they had finally triumphed over their own 'aptness to lenity'. Their saviour was the Scoutmaster-General, Henry Jones, the former Dean of Ardagh, and the first devoted student of the atrocities committed in Ireland in 1641.[4] Jones appeared before the commissioners in May 1652 with a lengthy abstract[5] of several thousand depositions of barbarous cruelty to Protestants in 1641 and after.[6] The commissioners professed 'they had never

---

[1] Ibid. [2] *Acts and Ordinances*, ii. 598.

[3] Dunlop, *Ireland under the Commonwealth*, p. 128, fn.

[4] Walter Love regarded Jones's *Remonstrance of Divers Remarkable Passages Concerning the Church and Kingdome of Ireland*, published in Mar. 1642, as the first report of the atrocities 'sufficiently detailed so as to seem a convincing portrayal of actual happenings, not a story', which by no means indicated Love's acceptance of its truth ('Appearances in Three Centuries of Historical Writing', *EUQ*, Summer, 1966, p. 59).

[5] This was subsequently printed as *An Abstract of Some Few of Those Barbarous, Cruell, Massacres and Murthers, of the Protestants, and English in Some Parts of Ireland, Committed since the 23 of October, 1641* (Thomason Tracts, BM, E. 149 (3)).

[6] The depositions were then in his possession, but were left at his death to Trinity College Library, where they remain bound in 33 volumes. Very little good use has ever been made of them.

formerly such full and particular knowledge and sense thereof, and indeed so deeply were . . . affected with the barbarous wickedness of the actors in these cruel murders and massacres' that they began to fear their 'behaviour towards this people may never sufficiently avenge the same'.[1] The commissioners then forwarded the abstract to Parliament, 'fearing lest others who are at a greater distance, might be moved to the lenity we have found no small temptation in ourselves'.[1] In the words of Walter Love, 'Jones had, with his new history, saved the settlement from moderation'.[2] Jones's 'abstract' was the moral equivalent of the Protocols of Zion. It revived, and, to a probably extensive degree, invented a moral justification for the expropriation of property. That it *caused* that expropriation seems less likely than that it clinched and rationalized what largely economic forces had made unavoidable: a massive confiscation.[3]

The very distinction in the act of 1652 between 'the inferior sort' and 'others . . . of the higher rank and quality', with more specific promise of clemency for the former, suggests that the act was 'land-minded', and that it was more concerned to establish the guilt of those who had something to confiscate than those who had not. Accordingly the act established categories or 'qualifications' of guilt, into one of which nearly every Irish Catholic and a good many Irish Protestants could, by triumphant judges, be fitted. Several hundred 'notorious' rebels were named in the act and excepted from pardon for life and estate, thus accomplishing indictment and conviction in a single stroke of the pen.[4] All Jesuits and priests were accorded a similar treatment, though not by name. All persons who participated either as principals or accessories in the acts of rebellion committed before 10 November 1642, or in the killing of any person (in a 'supposed' act of war) after 1 October 1642, constituted two

---

[1] Dunlop, *Ireland under the Commonwealth*, p. 179.

[2] 'Appearance in Three Centuries of Historical Writing', p. 68.

[3] By the time Vincent Gookin published his pamphlet, *The Great Case of Transplantation Discussed*, in 1655, the commissioners' hearts had already been well steeled against his arguments that this scheme was contrary to 'religion, profit, and safety'.

[4] Sometime in early Aug. 1651 the commissioners for Ireland sent to the committee of the Council of State for Irish affairs a list of 'the names of such persons as deserve (by the best inquiry we can make here) to stand excepted from pardon for life . . .' (Dunlop, *Ireland under the Commonwealth*, p. 28).

further classes exempted from pardon for life or estate. Those who refused within 28 days of the publication of the act to lay down arms were put into the same category. A lesser penalty, banishment and the loss of two-thirds of their estates, was reserved for those whose only offence was to have a position of command 'in the war against the Parliament or their forces'. Any papist who could slip through the sieve of these qualifications might yet be caught by another, entitling Parliament to confiscate one-third of the estate of those who could not prove 'constant good affection to the interest of the Commonwealth of England' between 1 October 1642 and 1 March 1650. A seemingly contradictory clause provided that persons whose total estates amounted to less than ten pounds might be left unharmed despite lapse from 'constant good affection' (though not despite inclusion in the other, more culpable categories), if they now subscribed an engagement to be faithful to the Commonwealth. Again, the preoccupation of the act was with land rather than guilt.

The act provided a canon by which the commissioners for Ireland were enabled to begin the complex task of judging the conquered. Its broad categories ensured that several times as much land would be confiscable as was owed to the adventurers, but it did not determine how much of that land would actually be confiscated, and considerable discretionary powers were left to the commissioners. Thus it did not resolve any disputes over the *form* the settlement would take. Neither did the act of 25 August 1652 for 'stating and determining the accompts of such officers and soldiers as are or have been imployed . . . in Ireland', which merely enacted machinery for ascertaining and certifying what was due to the soldiery, but made no attempt to translate those sums into specific acres of Irish land.[1]

Because of the requirement in the various acts and ordinances that the adventurers should be satisfied *first*, and because of the ignorance how much land would be confiscated, the whole settlement hung fire until the adventurers were satisfied; and the adventurers refused to be settled until the war was definitely ended. The war, unfortunately, was concluding fitfully rather than definitively. The Leinster army surrendered in May of

[1] *Acts and Ordinances*, ii. 603.

1652 upon articles drawn up at Kilkenny,[1] and the act of 12 August more or less asserted that the war was over; but the army of Ulster did not surrender until September.[2] Though it was the last formal army in the field, toryism—the special name for Irish brigandage—long survived its surrender, and order existed only within gunshot of the several hundred English garrisons. The army, therefore, came increasingly to view 'settlement' as the only possible alternative to years of expensive military occupation requiring a large garrison.

On 21 October 1652 a general council of officers serving in Ireland drew up recommendations that the settlement of the army should proceed forthwith and not await the satisfaction of the adventurers. They reasoned that if the adventurers were settled first, the land they occupied would have to be freed from the Irish assessment (otherwise they would not settle), and further funds from England would be necessary to make up the pay of the army. If, on the other hand, the army were settled first, and thereby reduced in size and cost, the reduction in the proceeds of the assessment would be matched by a corresponding diminution of expenses.[3]

All, however, was in the hands of Parliament, which by October had drawn up a draft act of 'satisfaction for adventurers and soldiers' and circulated it to the Parliamentary commissioners in Ireland. The commissioners' response was orally conveyed to Parliament by Sir Hardress Waller, and therefore, unfortunately, does not survive. We do know that the commissioners pleaded for haste in enactment of the matter.[4] A crucial decision was made in the Parliamentary committee considering the act and was ordered to be reported to Parliament on 23 December. It appears to have involved acceptance of a proposal of the army in Ireland that the heart of the settlement for both adventurers and soldiers should be the designation of ten Irish counties as the site of a new plantation. The ten counties, three in Munster, three in Ulster, and four in Leinster, were to be equally divided between adventurers and soldiers,

---

[1] J. P. Prendergast, *The Cromwellian Settlement of Ireland*, Dublin, 1875, p. 80, citing a document destroyed in the Record Office fire of 1922.

[2] Ibid., p. 81, citing no source.

[3] Dunlop, *Ireland under the Commonwealth*, p. 288.

[4] Ibid., pp. 290, 299, and 302; letters of 23 Oct., 3 Dec., and 9 Dec. 1652.

despite the probable need of the soldiers for a great deal more land. That was the army's principal concession. In return the common soldiers were to receive land at the same rates as had been established for adventurers.[1] The adventurers no longer considered those rates so favourable, but that was because the government had now had the use of their money for a decade or more. Soldiers' arrears rarely went back so far, and the 'act rates' were therefore considered of great value by the army. The adventurers were guaranteed their rates by the various acts and ordinances. The soldiers had no such protection. If, after the adventurers were settled, there proved to be less confiscable land left than would suffice to repay the soldiers at the act rates, then the rates would have to be revised upwards (more money for the same amount of land) in order to accommodate the entire army. The government did not attempt to make any alternative form of payment available, and the best the soldiers could hope for was maintenance of the act rates, an unlikely prospect.

The virtue of the 'ten-county' scheme was that it permitted, at least in theory, simultaneous settlement of the adventurers and the soldiers. An area of approximately 5,700,000 English acres (more than a quarter of the total acreage of Ireland) was to be set aside, half or 2,850,000 acres reserved for satisfaction of adventurers. It was supposed that after various exclusions (mainly of unprofitable and unforfeited lands) enough would remain to provide the adventurers the 1 to 1·5 million acres supposedly due to them. Secondly, the planting of the soldiers in the same counties with the adventurers was thought to offer some encouragement to the latter, who would know that able-bodied soldiers lay close at hand. The 'ten-county' scheme was reported to the Commons on 4 January 1653, whereupon the major elements of it were accepted.[2]

At this point the settlement of Ireland ran foul of the disorders in England. The Rump did not survive to enact the legislation on Ireland it had been preparing. On 20 April 1653 it was forcibly dissolved by Oliver Cromwell. For several weeks the future form of government was itself in doubt. In July Cromwell

[1] Carte MS. 67, f. 253. The ten counties were Armagh, Down, Antrim, Queens, Kings, Eastmeath, Westmeath, Limerick, Tipperary, and Waterford.
[2] *CJ*, vii. 242.

summoned a new assembly, composed of 140 men selected by
the army leaders from nominees of the Independent and
Baptist congregations. This unorthodox body, leavened by a
prepossessing contingent of religious enthusiasts, or 'saints',
took up the question of the settlement of Ireland where the
Rump had reluctantly left it. It is worth noting that the 'Barebones' Parliament made no changes in the 'ten-county' plan,
and, indeed, that the act as it was passed on 26 September 1653
bears no marks of saintly meddling or visionary impracticality,
except for its important insistence upon transplantation of the
Irish to Connaught.

For all that has been written about it, this odd assembly
remains an enigma, functioning at one moment like a sober heir
of the Long Parliament, and at another like a convention of wild-
eyed millenarians. Perhaps the clue, in the case of their Irish
policy, is that the real decisions were made by the Council of
State. Even before the Barebones Parliament convened, on
4 July, the Council of State had taken important steps toward
settlement. On 1 June it had appointed a committee to sit at
Grocers' Hall 'to regulate, order and dispose the drawing of
lots for the said adventurers where their dividents of land shall
be'.[1] On 22 June the Council of State empowered the Irish
Commissioners to 'cause all the lands (therein mentioned to be
forfeited to the Commonwealth) to be surveyed, in order to the
satisfying of adventurers for Ireland, and arrears of officers and
soldiers'.[2]

This was the inception of the 'gross survey', a first crude
attempt to determine how much land was at the disposal of
the Commonwealth for its various needs. The first drawings, or
lotteries, for Irish land among the adventurers were held in
London on 20 July, under the direction of the committee
appointed on 1 June. On 2 July the Council of State ordered
the commissioners to prepare the removal and transplantation
to Connaught, before 1 May 1654, of 'all persons in Ireland who
have right to articles [under the act of August 1652] for the

---

[1] *Acts and Ordinances*, ii. 723–39. The committee members were Methusaleh
Turner, Robert Hamon, Henry Brandiff, Nathaniel Manton, Elias Roberts,
Thomas Hubbard, Frances Blomer, George Gill, and Col. John Fenton. *CSPI,
Adventurers for Land, 1642–59*, p. 374.

[2] Thomason Tracts, BM, E. 1062 (3), and *Acts and Ordinances*, ii. 739.

better security of all those parts of Ireland which are now intended to be planted with English and Protestants'.[1] Crucial decisions were thus made, as we would almost expect in this period, in the absence of Parliament. No sooner was Parliament to assemble, however, than one observer could write: 'Our Parliament members of Ireland have been very active and are daily sitting in revising and finishing the adventurers' act, which I believe will be passed within this three weeks or month.'[2]

Particularly important was the Council of State's decision in favour of transplanting the Irish. This had been implicit in the 'ten-counties' idea, for the adventurers and soldiers were unlikely to smile upon the continuance of Irish neighbours in their plantations, unless with a servile, labouring, status. Furthermore, none of the ten counties was in or near Connaught (save Limerick, which was adjacent), a hint that Connaught had been considered for a special plantation for the Irish at least since late 1652. The order of 2 July, however, converted the implicit into the explicit, banishing all Irish, even those technically innocent under the act of 1652, to habitation west of the Shannon river.[3]

Thus the groundwork for the settlement was laid by executive order in the weeks between the dissolution of the Rump and the convening of the Nominated Parliament. The latter assembly passed an act of satisfaction on 26 September that confirmed the three executive orders of 1 June, 22 June, and 2 July 1653. The 'ten-county' scheme, with certain minor amendments, was formally promulgated, and the first half or 'moiety' was charged with the £360,000 claimed by the adventurers

[1] Thomason Tracts, BM, E. 1062 (4).

[2] William Dobbins to John Percival, July 1653, HMC, *Egmont*, i. 524.

[3] The complicated question of the transplantation was treated by S. R. Gardiner in an article, 'The Transplantation to Connaught', *EHR*, 1899, pp. 700–34. Gardiner was primarily concerned with the extent to which Cromwell was the author of the scheme, and the extent to which he allowed it to be implemented in the years after 1653. He agreed that its enunciation in the order of 2 July 1653 suggested Cromwell's 'unseemly haste' in the days immediately before the convening of the Nominated Parliament on 4 July. But, Gardiner argued, Cromwell had seen fit, as the new Parliament had not, to qualify the order for transplantation and to place in the hands of the commissioners discretionary powers which mitigated this harshest element of the Settlement.

as their due. The second moiety was charged with the arrears due to the soldiers 'at the act rate'; in theory, therefore, with another £360,000. In case the ten counties did not suffice to discharge all indebtedness to the adventurers and soldiers, Parliament provided that a surplus in one moiety could be used to satisfy those for whom land had not been found in the other. If both moieties were exhausted, confiscated land in the county of Louth could be drawn upon, and if the needs of the army were still unmet, as was virtually certain, additional surety was provided in designated portions of Sligo, Fermanagh, and Cork. Finally, all remaining confiscated land in whatsoever part of Ireland, save Connaught, was to be available first for the satisfaction of any portion of army arrears (since 5 June 1649) still unsatisfied, second for the payment of arrears which became due *before* 5 June 1649 for service in Ireland, and third 'for the just satisfaction of all such persons, their executors, administrators or assigns, bodies politic or corporate, as have lent monies upon the public faith'.[1]

The act of 1653 constituted the blueprint of what came to be called the Cromwellian Settlement. It derived neither from a demand for the punishment of the rebellious Irish, nor from an expansive force of Englishmen anxious to colonize Ireland. Its contours were principally determined by the fiscal exigencies of the Commonwealth, and the desire to disband a substantial portion of the English army in Ireland, where it would constitute less of a political and military threat to the fledgling Commonwealth.[2]

The implementation of the act was impossible without a precise notion of the amount and location of the 'profitable' land subject to confiscation. The framers of the act for adventurers had spoken loosely of 10,000,000 acres to be forfeited by the rebels, but there was no complete survey of Ireland to verify such a figure, and the government's creditors could only *hope* that the confiscations called for by the act of 1652 would be sufficient to discharge the obligations acknowledged by the act

---

[1] *Acts and Ordinances*, ii. 733.

[2] Prendergast commented: 'The Cromwellian design was wild in the extreme, for of all bodies an army is the worst to colonize with' (*The Cromwellian Settlement of Ireland*, p. 235).

of 1653.[1] In the absence of such knowledge it was necessary to establish priorities, so that the settlement could proceed even while surveys were being commissioned and carried out. By virtue of guarantees made to them in 1642 the adventurers were awarded first place. The ten half-counties assigned them by the act, plus the additional security of county Louth, were certain, even in the absence of a survey, to contain more land than the adventurers required. Furthermore, they were given control over disposition of this land among themselves. If, after satisfying all their members, the adventurers found additional land, they were obliged to return it to the state for the satisfaction of soldiers. Thus the adventurers enjoyed the lion's share, even though they had become, since 1642, a minority of those with an interest in the settlement. In round numbers they were 1,500 as against 35,000 soldiers. In pounds their share was but £360,000 out of more than £2,000,000 which the state intended to discharge out of Irish land. The adventurers could proceed immediately with their apportionment, confident that they would not exhaust the lands awarded them.

The soldiers' settlement was more cramped. Passage of the act of 1653 gave rise to immediate fears that insufficient land would remain for the army. The early returns of the 'gross survey' (because it did not distinguish profitable from unprofitable land) reportedly showed a total of 2,697,000 confiscable Irish acres in all of Leinster, Munster, and Ulster, 1,131,000 of them in the 'ten counties' to be divided between adventurers and soldiers.[2] As half the ten counties, approximately 565,000 acres were reserved for the adventurers, and an additional 404,000 acres lay in the counties of Dublin, Carlow, Kildare, and Cork, which were reserved for other uses of the government, only 1,727,500 acres remained for the discharge of military and logistical debts. In a letter of 16 December 1653 the commissioners in Ireland estimated those debts at £1,750,000:

---

[1] There had been earlier, partial surveys of Ireland, the most ambitious being Strafford's survey of Connaught (T. A. Larcom, ed., *The History of the Down Survey*, Dublin, 1851, p. 346).

[2] Dunlop, *Ireland under the Commonwealth*, p. 380. In fact, these estimates of Dec. 1653 were startlingly low. Abstracts of the gross survey in BM Egerton MS. 1762, f. 133, show the total contents of the ten counties to have been 2,065,224 Irish acres.

£1,550,000 in arrears to the army, and £200,000 in 'public faith bills' upon the Commonwealth.[1] The 1,727,500 acres at the commissioners' disposal would satisfy but £802,000 of that amount at the 'act rates'.[2] Thus, the commissioners estimated, on the basis of the information available to them, that £947,500 would have to be discharged from some source other than Irish land.[3]

Whether the commissioners' estimates of 16 December 1653 were correct or not, they accurately represented a widespread fear that there would be an insufficiency of land. But an army of 35,000 men, for which there was diminishing military need, could not be kept together until a thorough survey was completed. Under considerable pressure a general council of officers agreed in November 1653 to raise the rates applicable to the army, in order to initiate a distribution which would not threaten to exhaust the estimated land supply.[4] At the same time that the rates, in general, were increased, they were also adjusted to correspond more closely to the true agricultural worth of the land in the individual counties.[5] In some counties the army council more than doubled the rates, with the result that a

[1] Dunlop, op. cit., p. 380.

[2] The 'act rates' were £200 for every 1,000 acres of land in Ulster, £450 for every 1,000 in Munster, and £600 for every 1,000 in Leinster.

[3] The commissioners' letter is perhaps the most important single document concerning the Cromwellian Settlement, for it contains the only extant statement of the debt, additional to the adventurers', which the government intended to discharge with Irish land. These figures were expressed ambiguously by Prendergast when he wrote: 'The rest of Ireland, except Connaught, was to be set out amongst the officers and soldiers, for their arrears, amounting to £1,550,000, and to satisfy debts of money or provisions due for supplies advanced to the army of the Commonwealth, amounting to £1,750,000' (*Cromwellian Settlement*, p. 95); and they were completely misinterpreted by W. H. Hardinge, who took the *sum* of Prendergast's two figures as the estimate of the total debt. 'On Circumstances Attending the Outbreak of the Civil War in Ireland', *TRIA*, vol. 24 (Antiquities), p. 403. Even correctly interpreted, however, the commissioners' estimates are a slight basis upon which to construct a conceptual picture of the Cromwellian Settlement. Their figures for the gross survey are far below what that survey ultimately reported (see p. 135, n. 2). The estimates of government debt are likely to have been out in the same direction. Unfortunately, we can only conjecture as to the ultimate amounts of debt laid upon Irish land, but the squeeze which resulted is surely more a comment upon the magnitude of that sum than upon the restraint of the confiscators.

[4] Dunlop, *Ireland under the Commonwealth*, p. cxxxvii.

[5] All the counties outside Connaught were revalued; but, for purposes of illustration, the new rates in the ten counties were as follows:

soldier with £100 due to him in arrears would receive less than half the amount of land that an adventurer holding the same amount of debt would receive. In Antrim, for instance, an adventurer with £100 would obtain 500 acres, a soldier less than 200.

In January 1654 the first distribution was carried out among the soldiers. Over half a million acres was distributed to 4,711 soldiers in satisfaction of £282,209 in debts.[1] The soldiers consented only grudgingly to increased rates. For most of them, payment in land was an imposition rather than a desire, and the prospect of being fobbed off with less than the act rates promised was angering. In April 1654 the general council of officers voted to return to the act rates as a basis for further distributions.[2] According to one observer, the army was asking, in effect: 'Why should not England pay the remainder in money, or at least the adventurer[s], whose possession we have obtained?'[3]

In December 1654 the government contracted with William Petty, physician general to the army, for a survey of all lands appointed for the satisfaction of the army.[4] Preliminary findings caused Petty to estimate that there was enough land outside the adventurers' quarters to pay out only 12s. 6d. of each £1 owed to the army at act rates.[5] Despite the army's objections, subsequent disbandments in August 1655 and the summer

County	Act Rate for 1,000 acres £	Revised Army Rate for Same £
Kings	600	600
Queens	600	900
Westmeath	600	900
Meath	600	1,300
Waterford	450	800
Tipperary	450	1,000
Limerick	450	1,100
Antrim	200	520
Armagh	200	460
Down	200	520

(Prendergast, *The Cromwellian Settlement of Ireland*, pp. 213–14.)

[1] Dunlop, op. cit., p. cxxxviii, and pp. 422–3.
[2] Ibid., cliv.
[3] Thomas Birch, ed., *The Thurloe State Papers*, London, 1742, ii. 313, Thomas Sanford to Thurloe, 24 May 1654.
[4] Larcom, ed., *History of the Down Survey*, p. 23.
[5] Ibid., p. 63.

and autumn of 1656 were carried out on a fractional basis, the soldiers being promised that they would receive the remainder of their land if and when a surplus appeared in the settlement.[1]

The lands placed under the watchful eye of William Petty were surveyed and mapped with extraordinary accuracy. The adventurers, however, were given complete control over the settlement of their areas, and, according to Petty, made very poor use of them. Rather than await the results of an accurate survey, they rushed ahead with a distribution based upon the hurried gross survey carried out in late 1653 and early 1654 by Benjamin Worsley, the surveyor general. In the words of Petty:

> The survey made by the adventurers is not universal or even uniform, and is not even probably true. It has been discussed and exposed to much corruption since it was made. Little proof can be made that what is produced as the adventurers' survey is really such, much less that it is true. It wants so many of the essential features of an authentic survey that it is not one either in law or equity, either in matter or form.[2]

The majority of adventurers did not suffer from the gross survey's imperfections. Indeed, it resulted in most adventurers' being awarded more true acres of profitable land than were legally due to them. But a minority, those termed 'deficient', were at a disadvantage because the land in the ten demi-counties was alleged to be exhausted, when a true survey would have found much still available for them. The adventurers were divided among themselves over whether the settlement they had carried out on the basis of the gross survey should be preserved or brought into conformity with a better survey. The army strongly urged the latter course, for it justifiably suspected that if the adventurers submitted to a fair survey and settlement, additional land would be found in their share of the ten counties. The adventurers would not then require the security provided them in Louth, and that county, and any surplus in the ten counties, might be distributed to soldiers instead.

The Council in Ireland was anxious to settle the largest

---

[1] Dunlop, *Ireland under the Commonwealth*, clvi; and Prendergast, *The Cromwellian Settlement of Ireland*, p. 215.

[2] Propositions of 10 June 1658, *CSPI, Adventurers for Land, 1642–59*, p. 358.

number of claims with the least amount of land, but was power-less to force any course of action upon the adventurers. In May 1658 it sent Petty to London to convince the adventurers that a re-survey of their lands was in their own interests as well as that of the state.[1] Petty eventually prevailed with some, and this faction, perhaps a majority, requested the Council in Ireland to authorize Petty to proceed with a re-survey of the adventurers' lands.[2] Another faction contested this decision, arguing that the adventurers had full power over their ten half-counties, that the gross survey fulfilled the adventurers' obligations, and that 'the soldiery . . . [were] not entitled unto any surplusage upon the adventurers' moiety unless such surplusage do appear on the return of the gross survey, nor is there any power to make a general resurvey of the adventurers' moiety to find out a surplusage'.[3] Little is known about the outcome of this dispute, except that Petty was shortly thereafter employed in the work, and that it was allegedly completed by the end of 1658.[4] That there remained 'deficient' adventurers and soldiers seems certain, but the bulk of both are said to have been settled, if not physically, yet legally, upon their lands. Unfortunately, the records of Petty's settlement of the adven-turers, together with the records of the soldiers, do not survive and the resulting demographic pattern is therefore impossible to describe in any detail.

This is the ultimate frustration of assessing the Cromwellian Settlement and the adventurers' role within it. The accumulation of economic forces is perceivable, like static electricity in the clouds. The force of precedent, and the tendency of those economic forces to express themselves through the well-worn institutions of confiscation and plantation, is equally apparent. And yet at the moment in which lightning finally strikes, the records show nothing, and only the post-Restoration books of survey and distribution reveal that Ireland was monumentally transformed between 1653 and 1660. A drastic land revolution nearly escapes us, leaving only traces of its impact.

Petty's 'down survey' revealed that 11,000,000 of Ireland's

[1] Larcom, ed., *History of the Down Survey*, p. 229.
[2] Ibid., pp. 247–9.   [3] Ibid., p. 251.
[4] Lord Edmond Fitzmaurice, *The Life of Sir William Petty*, London, 1895, p. 64.

20,000,000 acres (English measure) were confiscated, and that 7,700,000 of those acres were regarded as profitable.[1] But it is impossible to know how much of its debt the revolutionary government in England managed to pay out of those lands, or to what extent it was paying the costs of revolution at home as well as repression abroad.

Some 35,000 soldiers were meant to be disbanded and settled in Ireland, but the surviving records do not show how many of them sold their shares to speculators and how many actually planted. With exceptions, the names of individual soldier-planters, and the extent and location of their lands, have also perished. By 1670 only some 8,000 soldiers and adventurers combined had had their estates confirmed to them by Charles II. Approximately 500 of them were adventurers. The other 7,500 may have been all that remained of the Cromwellian host.[2]

By the order of 2 July 1653 all Catholics, regardless of their guilt or innocence under the act of settlement, were subject to transplantation to Connaught, and 44,210 names were recorded on certificates of transplantation by 1 May 1654.[3] But how many Catholic proprietors or tenants were actually transplanted, or how many were left in the areas legally reserved for Protestants, remains unascertained. All that is known is that 700,000 Irish acres were ultimately (in the Cromwellian and Restoration Settlements) conveyed upon decrees of transplantation, an amount equivalent to 70 per cent of the profitable land of Connaught. The Cromwellian Settlement initiated an unalloyed Protestant plantation, but to what extent it succeeded remains an unanswered question.[4]

---

[1] Hardinge, 'On Circumstances Attending the Outbreak of the Civil War in Ireland', p. 418.

[2] The names are to be found in the Index of Names to the 'Inrolments of the Certificates for Adventurers, Soldiers, etc.', preserved in the office of the Chief Remembrancer of the Exchequer, Dublin, and printed in *Reports from the Commissioners of the Public Records for Ireland*, 15th Report (1821–5), pp. 403–33. The thirty rolls of 1767 vellum certificates to which this list was an index perished in the Irish Record Office fire of 1922, except for roll 29 and parts of rolls 7 and 30.

[3] Hardinge, 'On Circumstances Attending the Outbreak of the Civil War in Ireland', p. 395. His figures were based upon a manuscript epitome of the registers kept by the Lough Rea commissioners.

[4] William Petty, 'The Political Anatomy of Ireland', in *Tracts Relating to Ireland*, Dublin, 1769, p. 300. S. R. Gardiner's 'The Transplantation to Con-

Of the adventurers alone more is known. How much government debt they claimed to hold and how much land they were entitled to draw has been treated above. As they had first claim to Irish land, no question arose before 1660 of their accepting less than the full amount provided by the act rates. In particular the demographic character of the plantation they intended survives in the barony tables of 1654–8, and provides the subject of the next chapter. The names and acreages of the intended planters of every barony, quarter, and sub-quarter of the ten half-counties are contained in those records. Even the impact of the Restoration is known to some extent. Of 1,043 adventurers whose names appeared in the barony tables, approximately 500 were confirmed in their estates by Charles II.[1] And Petty noted, the adventurers survived the Restoration's acts of settlement with 390,000 of the 1,000,000 acres they had claimed.[2]

What is not known is what happened between the adventurers' own attempt at settlement and the Caroline acts; what effect Petty's re-survey had upon the adventurers' settlement, or even whether a re-settlement had been completed by the time of the Restoration. It appears very likely that time did not permit such extensive and difficult adjustments, and that Charles II inherited an Ireland caught in midstream, the ambitious Settlement of the Commonwealth far from complete. As late as March 1659 the Lord Deputy of Ireland, Henry Cromwell, was complaining to his brother Richard, the Protector, that 'there are many deficiencies of lands to adventurers, soldiers, and to persons transplantable by virtue of decrees, many public debts and engagements mentioned in the said act for satisfaction, besides what other public engagements lie upon the Commonwealth to be discharged thereout, which were contracted in the redeeming and reducing this poor land from the enemies thereof'.[3] And on 18 May 1659 we find notice that 'the

naught', *EHR*, 1899, is still the authoritative treatment of the subject, although it skims the quantitative and demographic aspects. A forthcoming work on the transplantation by Dr. R. C. Simington will undoubtedly advance understanding its nature and consequences.

[1] See p. 140, n. 2. To arrive at this figure I took a random sample of the names of 200 adventurers on the 1658 barony lists, and found 92 of them in the Index to names in the 'Inrolments of the Certificates . . .'.

[2] Petty, 'Political Anatomy of Ireland', p. 300.

[3] Dunlop, *Ireland under the Commonwealth*, p. 692.

whole business touching the settling the lands in Ireland on the adventurers and soldiers' was being considered in the restored and now violently anti-Cromwellian Rump Parliament, with a view to further legislation on the subject.[1] But nothing further of moment was enacted.

Everywhere there was chaos. The transplantation to Connaught was compromised by the discretionary powers placed in the commissioners' hands, and the continuance of members of 'the Irish nation' in Leinster, Munster, and Ulster was inevitable. The land situation was confused, because the continuous press of debts dischargeable in Irish land always threatened to force an over-all revision in the terms of the Settlement. Even where land was found for claimants, whether adventurers, soldiers, or creditors of the state, they too often hesitated to plant, and instead sold out to speculators more confident or hopeful of the future of Protestant Ireland. The Settlement conceived in the act for adventurers of 1642 never reached a conclusion. It grew great and complex, but like some gorged beast proved unable to digest what it had swallowed. Charles II had the opportunity to administer the needed digestive, for his Restoration in 1660 provided a political excuse for cutting away the undergrowth of claims upon Irish land. But the problems he encountered, which prevented him from managing to do so, must be the subject of another study.[2]

---

[1] Dunlop, *Ireland under the Commonwealth*, p. 696, and *CJ*, vii. 657.

[2] The most detailed study of the political geography of seventeenth-century Ireland remains that of Y. M. Goblet: *La Transformation de la géographie politique de l'Irlande au XVIIe siècle*, 2 vols., Paris, 1930. Its chapters on the Cromwellian Settlement, however, are based exclusively on printed sources.

VI

THE ANATOMY OF THE
ADVENTURERS' SETTLEMENT

Two basic types of statistical information are available regarding the adventurers: information regarding their subscriptions, and information regarding the attempted distribution to them of confiscated Irish land. In previous chapters we have examined the patterns of investment: the kinds of persons who invested, the schemes to which they were attracted, and the amounts that they actually subscribed. We now turn to the impact of that investment on the landed constitution of Ireland. We have sketched the history of the investment and the development of the legislation which attempted to define the settlement of Ireland. But the actual Settlement was a product of the interaction of that legislation with the adventurers' debt, as debt was translated by legal procedures into specific assignments or allotments of land. The act of 1653, recognizing that £360,000 in Irish land was due to the adventurers, called for £205,000 of that amount to be found in Leinster, £110,000 in Munster, and £45,000 in Ulster. Furthermore, it prescribed the maximum amount to be taken from the adventurers' half of each of the ten counties (see Table 2).[1]

In the interest of impartiality, lotteries were to be held by the adventurers in London, first to determine in what province an adventurer's share would fall; then in what county, barony, and quarter. A lottery was also held on 24 January 1654 to determine which baronies of each county would constitute the soldiers' half and which baronies the adventurers' half.[2] The committee of adventurers in London was simply to fill each county, like a

---

[1] There is no obvious explanation of how these sums were arrived at, as the earliest evidence of returns from the gross survey is in December 1653, two months after the passage of the act of satisfaction. Furthermore, the sums contained in the act originated in an order of the Council of State, later confirmed by the act, and probably issued on 1 June 1653.

[2] Robert Dunlop, *Ireland under the Commonwealth*, p. cxlii.

sack, to its appointed level. When the level was reached the county was 'full', and remaining adventurers were to be settled elsewhere. The acts and ordinances of 1642 relating to the adventure had established simple arithmetical principles—the 'act rates'—for the conversion of money lent into acres due in the various provinces of Ireland. The rates had never reflected very accurately the true value of the land and had become anachronisms after eleven years of war. Yet the adventurers insisted upon their right to them, fearing that any retreat would expose them to the fierce and massive competition of the soldiers for Irish land. Table 2 shows the amounts of profitable land (in Irish acres) necessary at the act rates to satisfy the sums appointed for the satisfaction of the adventurers in the ten counties. The mere facts, for instance, that £20,000 was set for Waterford, and that this amount converted to 44,444 Irish acres at the act rates, did not guarantee that so much confiscable, profitable land would be found in the adventurers' baronies of the county. Indeed,

TABLE 2[1]

Allocation of debt

Amount of debt allocated to the adventurers' halves of the ten counties, and the number of profitable Irish acres necessary to satisfy that debt at the act rates

Counties	Debt allocated	Acres necessary
	£	
Waterford	20,000	44,444
Limerick	30,000	66,666
Tipperary	60,000	133,332
Eastmeath	55,000	91,666
Westmeath	70,000	116,666
Kings	40,000	66,666
Queens	40,000	66,666
Antrim	15,000	75,000
Down	15,000	75,000
Armagh	15,000	75,000
	360,000	811,106

[1] The £ figures are taken from the act of 26 Sept. 1653 (Firth and Rait, *Acts and Ordinances of the Interregnum*, ii. 739). Conversion to acres simply requires application of the act rates appropriate to the various provinces.

since no known survey of these lands existed before late 1653 or 1654, that sum necessarily rested on even cruder estimates of the amount of land available there.

To add to the confusion, any of several standards of 'fullness' might be employed. In one sense, a county could be proclaimed 'full' if the £ limit set for it in the act was reached in the adventurers' accounts at Grocers' Hall. In another sense, the county might be 'full' if the number of acres allocated corresponded to the number of acres that amount of money would purchase at the act rates. Fullness in either of those two senses was highly theoretical and meant little more than compliance with statute. Whether there really existed sufficient land in any area to satisfy adventurers' claims upon it depended wholly upon surveys of

TABLE 3[1]

Returns of the gross survey for the ten counties

Counties	ACRES Confiscable, profitable, and unprofitable combined:	
	In county as a whole	In adventurers' baronies only
Waterford	153,110	not shown
Limerick	224,744	121,894
Tipperary	516,566	258,223
Eastmeath	185,917	92,983
Westmeath	130,386	65,136
Kings	138,080	71,039
Queens	153,654	76,424
Antrim	244,559	121,026
Down	230,230	101,543
Armagh	87,978	not shown
	2,065,224	

[1] The gross survey was ordered by instructions from the Council of State, dated 27 June 1653, and later incorporated in the act of 26 Sept. 1653. These sums are taken from an undated abstract of the gross survey in BM Egerton MS. 1762, f. 133, apparently a rare remaining fragment of the survey. A 'specimen sheet' of the survey for the barony of Dungannon in county Tyrone is reproduced in an appendix of T. A. Larcom, ed., *The History of the Survey of Ireland*, Dublin, 1851, p. 391.

the counties. The gross survey was providing crude barony totals of confiscable land by early 1654. Table 3 shows its only surviving estimate of the ten counties. As long as no more accurate survey was available, a county could also be thought full if the land allocated equalled the acreage reported in the gross survey.

The adventurers could, if they wished, exceed the act limits on the counties, if the gross survey suggested a greater supply of land. The ultimate standard for measuring fullness became available only in 1659, with the extension of Petty's Down survey to the adventurers' baronies. In the adventurers' baronies of Waterford, for instance, the Down survey found 40,526 acres of profitable land; in other words, nearly 4,000 acres less than the 44,444 theoretically required to plant £20,000 in adventure money. But the distributions of Irish land by the adventurers were carried out in the main between 1653 and 1658, that is to say, before the Down survey had been extended to their baronies. When we find, therefore, that by September 1658 they had planted £20,980 on 42,787 acres, we conclude that they exceeded the pound limit set for the county by the act, because the gross survey had reported so much more land to be available there (about 76,000 acres) than the necessary 44,444 acres. The whole settlement of Ireland depended upon knowledge of the amount of land subject to confiscation.

We should have expected a lengthy process, in which charges, under the act of 1652, would be brought against thousands of Irish (and some Protestant) proprietors covered by the qualifications of that statute, and that anything other than crude estimates of the amount of land available for redistribution would necessarily have awaited completion of such proceedings. But the commission of 27 June 1653 ordering the first survey demanded 'an exact and perfect survey and admeasurement of all . . . the honors, baronies, castles, manors . . . forfeited by force or virtue of all or any of the said acts . . .', as if such a determination could be easily made.[1]

It was assumed in the instructions joined to this commission that what was forfeit and what was not would be obvious to the surveyors. No procedures for making this distinction were

[1] *Acts and Ordinances*, ii. 742.

mentioned, except for provisions for Protestants to claim 'any right, title, or interest in, . . . the lands of any of the rebels in Ireland . . .' which they had held before the outbreak of the rebellion. How were the surveyors to know who was a rebel and who was not, which lands were confiscable and which were not? By the act of 1652 some persons were to lose all their estates, some two-thirds, and others only one-third. How were the surveyors to know how much, if any, of a given proprietor's land was confiscable? Nothing in the act of 1653 explains. Lord Edmond Fitzmaurice wrote in his *Life of Sir William Petty*: 'In the period between the end of the war and the year 1653 rough lists of the proscribed had been drawn up, and courts had been held to determine who could clear themselves of the charge of conspiracy in the late rebellion, and prove constant good affection.'[1] But if such lists existed, where are they now? who ever saw them? and by what procedures were the persons on them proscribed?[2] The absence of such evidence supports the contention that the confiscation of Irish land was a summary affair and that the surveyors simply classified as confiscable virtually all that had been Irish.

A comparison of the results of the gross survey with those of the later Down survey reveals substantial differences (see

[1] Lord Edmond Fitzmaurice, *The Life of Sir William Petty*, London, 1895, p. 27.

[2] There is considerable evidence of outlawries in the early years of the Rebellion, but no indication of how those rather summary lists were employed in the years following 1652. Examples of such lists are to be found in Richard Caulfield, ed., *The Council Book of the Corporation of Kinsale*, Guildford, 1879, Appendix B, and the publications of the commissioners for the Public Records of Ireland; see *Fifteenth Report, 1821–25*. Robert Dunlop rescued from the oblivion of the Record Office fire of 1922 a copy of an instruction, dated 16 Nov. 1653 and directed to the commissioners 'for examining the delinquency of Irish and other proprietors [in the precinct of Waterford] in order to the distinguishing of their respective qualifications, according to the act for settling Ireland'. But, according to the preamble, these instructions applied only to those Irish 'not being under any of the first five qualifications in the said act', that is to say, subject to loss of all their lands. Although from these instructions we have some idea of procedures used in Waterford, and probably elsewhere, to determine the guilt or innocence of those Irish not *automatically* excluded from future possession of land by the act, the instructions tell nothing about the procedures used for determining who fell *within* the five qualifications. Articles II and III were fairly precise. Article II excluded all Jesuits and priests. Article III named approximately 100 of the alleged chief rebels. But articles I, IV and V concerned conduct, and would seem to have required considerable adjudication. See Dunlop, *Ireland under the Commonwealth*, p. 378, and *Acts and Ordinances*, ii. 599.

TABLE 4[1]

*Returns in Irish acres of the gross and Down surveys for the
Adventurers' Baronies of the ten counties*

Moiety of:	Gross survey (1653–4)	Down survey (1658–9)	Down survey profitable (1658–9)
Waterford	approx. 76,000	64,413	40,526
Limerick	121,894	129,808	103,739
Tipperary	258,223	267,159	207,075
Eastmeath	92,983	121,150	106,554
Westmeath	65,135	102,989	75,520
Kings	71,039	57,832	30,635
Queens	76,424	57,392	42,472
Antrim	121,026	64,390	51,039
Down	101,543	70,558	47,386
Armagh	approx. 44,000	25,814	24,334
	1,028,267	961,505	729,280

Table 4). It reveals that the gross survey was erratic, and
that it tended, on the whole, to overestimate the amount of
confiscable land in the adventurers' baronies. Of course, the
adventurers in London knew that the gross survey included
unprofitable land, and it was in their power to discount a
proportion of the return and thereby achieve a closer estimate
of the amount of profitable. But what kind of formula would
have worked with equal accuracy in each of the ten counties?
In Down, Antrim, and Kings county the Down survey showed
that less than half the gross surveys' acreage for those counties
was actually available for distribution to adventurers as 'profitable'. In Armagh, Queens, and Waterford it was slightly more
than half. In Tipperary it was four-fifths and in Limerick five-
sixths, while in both Eastmeath and Westmeath the amount of
profitable land found by the Down survey *exceeded* by substantial
amounts the total of profitable and unprofitable, combined,
returned by the gross survey. If we regard the Down survey as

[1] Gross survey totals are from BM Egerton MS. 1762, f. 133. Separate totals
for the adventurers' baronies in Waterford and Armagh are not given there, and
my 'approximation' is simply half the total given for the county as a whole. Down
survey totals are taken from W. H. Hardinge, 'On Manuscript, Mapped, and
Other Townland Surveys in Ireland', *TRIA*, vol. 24 (Antiquities), pp. 100–24.

a standard of rectitude, we conclude that in the gross survey the adventurers had but a dim light to guide them in their plantation of a darkly labyrinthine Ireland. And yet the gross survey was the statistical basis for the entire plantation, and in 1658 some of the adventurers were to cling to it like drowning men to a raft.

The gross survey had even determined the lines along which the ten counties should be divided between soldiers and adventurers. The lottery held in January 1654 simply entailed the drawing by a representative of the army and a representative of the adventurers of two sets of baronies for each county. The acreage of the two sets was supposed in every case to be equal —something which could not have been determined without surveys of the respective baronies. That the gross survey was employed becomes evident when one notes that only by the standards of that survey are the two halves of each county equal. In Westmeath, for instance, the adventurers' baronies contained 65,135 acres, the soldiers' 65,251. In Queens and Eastmeath the division by the gross survey was equally neat, and very little less perfect in the remaining counties.[1]

Using the two tools of the gross survey and the limits to plantation in each county set by the act of 1653, the adventurers groped towards satisfaction of their members out of Irish land. The record of their attempt is found in the barony tables compiled at Grocers' Hall, London, between 1653 and 1658.[2] The barony tables reveal what the adventurers had done prior to the committing of the plantation to Dr. William Petty in late 1658. The tables are a list, by barony, of all the adventurers who drew land in Ireland, showing how many pounds of adventure they were credited with, and how many acres of Irish land they were allocated in repayment thereof. Table 5 shows the amounts of adventure money fixed upon the ten counties, and the number

[1] By the standard of the Down survey, the basic division of the ten counties between soldiers and adventurers was inequitable, the soldiers' half containing about 100,000 Irish acres more than the adventurers' half.

[2] There are three basic sets of these documents. The best known is found in PRO, S.P. 63/300. It was incompletely and, for statistical purposes, unsatisfactorily calendared in the volume, *CSPI, Adventurers for Land, 1642–1659.* A second set, in more perfect condition, survives in Marsh's Library, Dublin (Z.2.1.5), while a third set, an almost exact duplicate of the second, is in the Irish Record Office (R.O. 2A. 12. 43). My figures concerning the baronies are drawn from the second set, which is dated 26 Oct. 1658.

of profitable Irish acres thereby encumbered by the operation of the lottery to 26 October 1658.

TABLE 5[1]

*Debts assigned and acres encumbered in the ten counties by
26 October 1658*

Counties	Credit	Irish acres drawn
	£	
Waterford	20,980	42,787
Limerick	32,758	69,554
Tipperary	64,165	136,248
Eastmeath	52,221	84,338
Westmeath	41,385	62,695
Kings	39,991	63,845
Queens	38,557	62,319
Antrim	12,853	63,262
Down	14,147	70,425
Armagh	8,247	40,614
	325,304	696,087

It is clear that the adventurers had not, in total, exceeded the limits set to their activity by the act of 1653. But those limits were stated in pounds, not in acres, while the supply of land in the ten counties—and of profitable, confiscable, land especially— was a finite quantity. To satisfy approximately 90 per cent of the outstanding adventure money (£325,000, out of £360,000) the committee at Grocers' Hall had encumbered 70 per cent of the acreage reported by the gross survey (696,087 out of 1,028,267 acres), leaving, in theory, ample land. But the Down survey was to show in 1658 and 1659 that only 33,193 of those remaining acres were both profitable and confiscable (729,280—the total profitable in the ten counties minus 696,087, the total profitable allocated in London), and thus available for

---

[1] These figures represent totals derived from information in the barony tables. A computer card was made for each individual allotment specified in the tables. The card bore the name of the adventurer to whom the allotment was assigned, the acreage of the allotment, the amount of debt it was supposed to satisfy, and the location by barony, and province of the allotment. Barony, county, and provincial totals were thereafter computed electronically.

the use of unsatisfied adventurers and soldiers. In fact, over 95 per cent of the confiscable profitable land in the adventurers' half of the ten counties had been used up.

TABLE 6

Deficiencies and surpluses of land in the ten counties

Amount and value—at the 'act rates'—of lands allocated by the adventurers in London in comparison with the amount and value of lands reported by the Down survey

Counties	Acres deficient*	Acres surplus†	Pounds deficient‡	Pounds surplus‡
Waterford	2,000	..	900	..
Limerick	..	34,000	..	15,300
Tipperary	..	70,000	..	31,500
Eastmeath	..	22,000	..	13,200
Westmeath	..	13,000	..	7,800
Kings	33,000	..	19,800	..
Queens	20,000	..	12,000	..
Antrim	12,000	..	2,400	..
Down	23,000	..	4,600	..
Armagh	16,000	..	3,200	..
	106,000	139,000	42,900	67,800

* Acres allotted on barony lists minus acres profitable returned in Down survey. All acreages rounded to nearest thousand.

† Acres profitable returned in Down survey minus acres allotted on barony lists. Figures rounded to nearest thousand.

‡ At the act rates, 1,000 acres of Munster (first three counties) would satisfy £450 of adventure, 1,000 acres of Leinster (next four counties) £600, 1,000 acres of Ulster (last three counties) £200.

And yet the matter was not so simple, for the bag was not merely 95 per cent full. Instead, parts of it were under-full while others were overflowing. In Limerick, Tipperary, Eastmeath, and Westmeath the Down survey found 139,000 acres more profitable land than the adventurers had encumbered, while in the remaining six counties approximately 106,000 more acres had been encumbered than were revealed in the survey (see Table 6). Furthermore, because of the intricacies of the act rates, 'deficiencies' in one county were not necessarily compensable on an acre to acre basis by surplus in another. The value of the surplus acres minus the value of the deficient acres was approximately £25,000. That is to say £25,000 in adventure could be encumbered upon the adventurers' moieties of the ten counties in full compliance with the act rates, leaving only £10,000 of adventure to be satisfied from some other source or in some other way.

The discovery and utilization of that fact was largely the work of William Petty, who prevailed upon the adventurers in late 1658 to allow his survey to be extended to their lands, and their settlement to be redrawn in accordance with it. Petty, in his own writings, tells more about the methods he employed than about the results he achieved. The statistics above provide a picture only of what might have been done in the few months during which the adventurers' affairs were placed in his hands. By the application of the Down survey to the adventurers' halves of the ten counties Petty discovered that sufficient land remained to satisfy an additional £25,000 of adventure at the act rates. But the land was not necessarily put to that purpose. It may have been used instead to satisfy soldiers and officers, and others whose needs were greater and whose resources were less. About this aspect of the settlement little is known.

The barony tables provide the only statistical record of the Cromwellian Settlement that survives. No such picture survives of the lands planted by the soldiers. That the settlement described in the barony tables was relatively little changed before the Restoration remains a strong probability. Petty did not intend to stand the existing allocation on its head; only to squeeze it into a more compact form, and make use of the £25,000 worth of profitable land which his survey showed as remaining available. The adventurers' settlement, though untidy, was probably less atrocious than Petty proclaimed. The gross survey, though inaccurate and erratic, had over-estimated by less than 10 per cent the total confiscable land found by the Down survey in the ten half-counties (1,028,000 as against 961,000; see Table 4), and considering the rapidity with which it was carried out, provided a tolerably useful upper limit upon land allocation.

The barony tables show that 1,043 adventurers were allocated 696,294 Irish acres of profitable land, the equivalent of over 1,100,000 English acres, and an amount representing approximately 5 per cent of the total acreage of Ireland (profitable and unprofitable combined), or 17 per cent of the forfeited profitable land in the three Provinces of Ulster, Leinster, and Munster.[1] Even if Petty settled, in addition, the supposedly outstanding £35,000 of adventure, acreage figures would not increase more than 10 per cent. In the preceding chapter it was shown that the Cromwellian state intended to discharge at least £2,110,000 of its indebtedness with Irish land, and that only the first £360,000, or 17 per cent, was due to the adventurers. The adventurers' share of the debt fixed on Ireland (in 1653) was almost exactly the same as their share of the profitable land in the new, three-Province plantation. So exact a correspondence, given the many variables, is fortuitous—but it makes it possible to place, with some confidence, the role of 1,043 adventurers in the Cromwellian Settlement at less than 20 per cent, by acreage.

The average holding of each of these 1,043 settler-adventurers was a little less than 700 Irish acres, representing an average 'credit' for moneys lent to the state of something over £300. The average *settler*-adventurer was, therefore, a larger holder of shares than the average *original* investor, whose investment—as noted in Chapter III—was £220. Time and the vicissitudes of war served to boil down the investment, by causing small investors to sell out to larger ones. As so often in the history of the attempt to plant an English yeomanry in Ireland, small land-holders gave way to large ones, although a holding of 700 acres hardly made an adventurer into a Great Earl of Cork or a Marquis of Ormond, magnates whose holdings numbered in the tens of thousands of acres.

On the other hand, the average holding of 700 Irish acres should not blind us to the substantial number of very-large and very-small holdings among the 1,043 settler-adventurers. Among very large holders, for instance, Sir William Brereton, the Roundhead M.P. for Cheshire, appeared on the barony lists with 2,979 acres in Tipperary and 3,750 in Armagh. This was in compensation for 'credit' of £2,550. Brereton had originally subscribed £1,200 in adventure, but by 1653 had paid in only

[1] 1,100,000 out of 6,350,000 English acres. These figures are derived from W. H. Hardinge, 'On Circumstances Attending the Outbreak of Civil War in Ireland', *TRIA*, vol. 24 (Antiquities), p. 417.

£900 of that amount.[1] Of that £900, £50 belonged to Robert Blease, £50 to John Jones, £100 to Humphrey Kelsall, and £120 to Samuel Eaton, all of them friends of Brereton from Cheshire. Accordingly, in 1654 Brereton assigned those portions to his colleagues out of his acreage in Tipperary. But the names of the assignees do not appear on the barony tables—only Brereton's, with the undivided 'credit' and undivided acreage. In addition to the original subscription, Brereton had, on 24 December 1653, subscribed a further £300 under the terms of the act of satisfaction, which allowed adventurers to complete their original subscriptions—a pre-requisite to their being satisfied in Irish land at the act rates.[2] Thus he was nominally entitled to credit of £1,200, £320 of which he was obliged to assign to his Cheshire partners. But he had also purchased from one John Farley a share of adventure which Farley, in turn, had bought from Francis Ash, a London goldsmith who had advanced £200 under the original act and £50 under the doubling ordinance. Ash's share entitled him to a credit of £500, so that the £1,700 which the barony lists show Brereton drew in the barony of Iffa and Offa, in the county of Tipperary, undoubtedly derive from his own £1,200 investment plus the £500 credit from Ash. The list shows him with an additional £100 credit in Tipperary and £750 in the Ulster county of Armagh, but the adventurers' papers give no clue as to how he acquired these assets. Presumably he bought them from other adventurers, as he bought a £500 claim from John Farley. There is no sign of other partnerships, and the assignments to his Cheshire partners would have diminished his Irish estate by only some 710 acres, leaving him a quite comfortable 6,000.

Another giant of the barony lists was George Clarke, a London merchant. A modest original adventurer who invested £100 under the act of 1642, £100 under the ordinance for a sea adventure, and £25 under the doubling ordinance (total credit: £350), Clarke shows up on the barony lists with £5,617 in credit and 11,631 acres. For his original £350 of credit he drew 777 acres in Tipperary, and went on to draw an additional 7,114

---

[1] J. P. Prendergast, *Cromwellian Settlement of Ireland*, Dublin, 1875, Adventurer No. 28; and *CSPI, Adventurers for Land, 1642–1659*, p. 299.

[2] £1,216 was raised from 13 adventurers by this measure.

acres in that county, 2,581 acres in Eastmeath, and parcels in Kings county, Westmeath, and Down. He had bought up parcels large and small, for amounts unrecorded. From George Parker, a London merchant, he bought a £200 share; from Thomas Foote and Samuel Langham of London, grocers, £1,200 of original adventure and £200 in sea adventure; from other men, smaller shares. Clarke was probably buying shares at far less than the original owners had paid for them, on the expectation that they would eventually be of substantial value. His investment was a token in 1642, before the uncertainties and ill omens of the civil wars caused the price of Irish shares to plummet. Then he managed to buy in prodigious measure and accumulate a sizeable Irish estate.

A third tycoon of the barony lists was William Hawkins, merchant-tailor of London. Hawkins invested a substantial £1,250 under the original act, £1,000 under the sea ordinance, and £312 under the doubling ordinance—bringing his nominal credit to £4,124. He drew a small empire in county Down, 32,395 acres, nearly half of the total forfeited profitable land found in that county by the Down survey. More than a third of this acreage (12,815 acres) was acquired by purchasing the shares of other adventurers; but, unlike Clarke, Hawkins was expanding an original large investment rather than building an empire out of the foundering hulks of other men's financial hopes. In the language of modern financiers, he was 'averaging down', buying further after a price decline in order to benefit by that decline. Because land was cheap in Ulster, Hawkins's total credit of £6,687 bought the largest Irish estate described in the barony tables. In the total of pounds satisfied with Irish land, however, the London leather-seller Thomas Vincent led the list with £11,525. For that amount he drew 19,044 Irish acres in the more expensive Leinster counties of Eastmeath, Kings, and Queens. The same amount of land drawn in Ulster would have entitled him to more than 55,000 acres, nearly as much forfeit profitable land as was found in the whole county of Armagh. But Vincent's 19,000 acres in Leinster was no mean estate, and was nearly twice the 10,000-acre maximum which had been established (unsuccessfully) in the Elizabethan Plantation of Munster to prevent 'tituladoes' from gobbling up land intended for the support of a yeomanry. Vincent had begun as a fairly weighty adventurer, investing £300 under the act, and then £1,000 under the sea ordinance. Why the sea adventure had more appeal for him is difficult to say, although at the time it had hopes of lucrative privateering, which were probably only partially realized. Most of Vincent's £11,525 of credit came from other adventurers' shares. £300 was purchased from William Kendall of London, merchant tailor, in 1654; £600 from Sir John Evelyn, M.P. of Surrey, in December 1653; and £1,250 (£500 plus £125 doubling) from William Beeke of London, merchant tailor, in March 1654. Interestingly enough, most of the trading of Irish shares appears to have occurred not in the mid 1640s, when the vagaries of war rendered the value of the land incalculable, but in the mid 1650s, when the Irish had been defeated and the major uncertainties were administrative and agricultural ones.

A final representative of the barony-table magnates was the regicide, Gregory Clement. In March and July of 1642 Clement made substantial investments under both the act and the sea ordinance.[1] In 1646 he subscribed £600 under the doubling ordinance; and in 1653 drew £5,000 worth of land for 8,332 Irish acres in Kings county, and a further £50 for rebel houses in the town of Waterford. In April 1654 Cromwell wrote to the commissioners for Ireland to give order 'for the speedy surveying and setting forth the said lands unto him . . .', inasmuch as Clement had 'undertaken to transport near 100 families, who are also to go along with him for the planting of the said lands . . .'.[2] Clement's plantation did not proceed, but if all the adventurers' lands had been planted to an equal density with English families—that is to say, one family to each eighty acres—some nine or ten thousand English families would have been added to the Protestant population of Ireland. As it is, we know precious little about the actual plantation which the adventurer-settlers effected or even attempted. Brereton, Clarke, Hawkins, Vincent, and Clement are examples of the largest

[1] *CSPI, Adventurers for Land, 1642–1659*, p. 10. The exact amount of these investments is obscure, although I have credited him in Appendix A with £1,300 under the sea ordinance and £200 under the original act, following Prendergast's list (nos. 850 and 1313) in both cases.

[2] Dunlop, *Ireland under the Commonwealth*, p. 417.

adventurer-settlers, but of men who had credit for more than £1,000 of land there were approximately sixty and of men who drew more than 1,000 acres there were nearly 200.

At the other end of the scale were those who drew minuscule, or very small shares: Anthony Austin of Exeter, who drew 5 acres of land in Queens county; Edward Baglethole, who drew his father's £5 share of 6 acres in Limerick; or Anthony Fletcher, whose £6 drew 10 acres of Westmeath. Numerous small fry crowd the barony lists. Perhaps as many as 20 per cent of the settler-adventurers received credits of less than £50, and a smaller percentage drew lots of less than 50 Irish acres (remembering again that in Ulster a mere £10 credit would draw 50 acres). These numerous small adventurers are, in a sense, a puzzle. Were they, for the most part, original subscribers? and, if so, why had they not sold? Did they really intend to move to Ireland to cultivate their 40 acres? and if not, what did they intend to do with their lands? Many of the small subscribers do not appear at all in the adventurers' subscription papers—and the reason, in many cases, is that they subscribed through another, often wealthier, person. The subscription, then, was in the name of a 'front' man, who did not show up on the barony lists at all, or appeared with a smaller share than that to which his investment would nominally have entitled him. Sometimes the 'front' was not a person but a corporation. On Prendergast's list, for instance, the Barber Surgeons' Company is shown to have subscribed £50, but the company did not draw land in the lotteries of 1653–4, and it is likely that one or more members of the company had contributed this sum in 1642, and claimed it in 1653–4 under their own names.

The contributions of individuals and corporations were often enmeshed in a complicated way, particularly in the case of the four towns, Exeter, Dartmouth, Gloucester, and Great Yarmouth, which played so prominent a role in the subscription lists. Corporations were empowered to subscribe by an act of 1642 (16 Charles I, c. 35). In Great Yarmouth the investment was treated as a single, indivisible unit. £600 was subscribed by the corporation and paid in March and July of 1642.[1] The corporation held the shares and in the lotteries of 1653–4, drew

[1] *CSPI, Adventurers for Land, 1642–1659*, p. 14.

1,333 Irish acres in Tipperary. According to its records, this property was leased in 1714 for 1,000 years to one Richard Hamerton of Clonmel, Ireland, at a rent of £100 p.a.[1]

Gloucester was a slightly different case. That corporation advanced £1,350 in May and July of 1642,[2] and in 1653 drew 2,124 acres in Queens county. But, unlike that of Great Yarmouth, the Gloucester subscription was actually the composite of subscriptions by 24 individuals, 'each having the right to receive benefit in proportion to the amount he subscribes'.[3] The same pattern is observable in the Dartmouth subscription. £2,398 was paid in by 143 citizens of the town, apparently all in the name of the town.[4] Exactly how much was drawn is hard to calculate, because some of the lots were in the names of the individual investors and others in the name of the town. But approximately £1,571 was drawn in 1653 in the name of the corporation, and £1,079 in the names of 44 citizens of the town. All received their lots in the east quarter of the commodious Westmeath barony of Rathconrath, and it would be interesting to know to what extent that barony remained a preserve of Dartmouth men, and whether they generally held on to what, on the average, were quite small holdings.

By far the most important of the subscribing corporations was Exeter, but assessing its exact role in either the subscription or the plantation is difficult. In Prendergast's list 'The Mayor, Bailiffs, and Commonalty of Exon' are credited with a subscription of £9,890. But preceding this entry in the list (No. 1034) are the names and sums of 60 persons from Exeter and its environs, who cumulatively adventured £6,008 in addition to the sum advanced by the town as a corporation. This total of £15,898 from the town is supported by the reference in the Exeter city records to a sum of £15,728 paid for the city's lands in Ireland.[5] In the barony tables, however, we find that the city of Exeter was credited with only £1,883, which it drew for

---

[1] HMC, *Ninth Report*, Appendix, papers of the corporation of Great Yarmouth.
[2] *CSPI, Adventurers for Land, 1642–1659*, p. 38.
[3] S.P. 63/289, No. 174. Gloucester was also awarded property in the town of Galway to the value of £1,518 p.a. in accordance with a grant of £10,000, for services and losses, contained in the act of 26 Sept. 1653.
[4] *CSPI, Adventurers for Land, 1642–1659*, p. 254, and Prendergast, Adventure No. 891.   [5] HMC, *City of Exeter Records*, p. 329.

2,583 acres in Tipperary. The corporation subsequently sold this land for £1,500 in March 1656,[1] leaving us to wonder what became of the £14,000 remaining of Exeter investment. The 60 named Exonians on Prendergast's list are followed without difficulty. Charles Hopping (the first of them, no. 974, a fuller) drew 166 acres in Kings county. James White, merchant (no. 990), drew £300 for 666 acres also in Tipperary. Some sold out or died, and do not appear on the barony tables. In the adventurers' papers there are records of subscription by 132 West-Countrymen whose names do not appear in Prendergast's list. Their total contribution was £5,553, and it was probably the major component of Prendergast's £9,890 ascription to Exeter. The average subscription of these 132 'unnamed Exonians' was £42, while that of the 60 included in Prendergast's list was slightly over £100. It appears that Prendergast's list included the larger investors of the West Country, but lumped the more numerous small investors under the single Exeter entry.[2]

Unlike the Dartmouth adventurers, who all drew lots together in the barony of Rathconrath, the Exeter adventurers

---

[1] The buyers were Colonel Hierom Sankey, who had already bought 555 acres elsewhere in Tipperary, Sir Ames Amerideth, and Valentine Greatstakes (or Greatorex). HMC, *City of Exeter Records*, p. 329.

[2] The special difficulty of dealing with Exeter has resulted in the anomaly that it has *not* been included in Appendix A, along with the other investing corporations. Although there is no certificate of subscription for Exeter corporation in the State Papers, it would have been consistent with my procedures to have accepted Prendergast's figure of £9,890. An exception was made because it seemed probable that the role of Exeter would be overstated if it was credited with £9,890 in addition to the £5,553 credited to Exonians not named in Prendergast and the £6,008 credited to those named. It is possible, however, that Exeter has been done an injustice and that all or part of Prendergast's £9,890 should be added to Exeter's role, and to the sum raised by the adventurer, as a whole.
There were two other adventuring corporations, London and Taunton, but little is known about either. Taunton subscribed £1,360 between July 1642 and Mar. 1642/3, and drew that exact amount for 1,399 acres in Rathconrath, Westmeath. London's corporate adventure was insignificant in comparison with the investments of its individual merchants and citizens. £10,000 was paid in on 1 Aug. 1642 by Robert Bateman, Chamberlain of London, and the 'Companies of London' later drew £5,000 worth of land for 8,332 acres in the barony of Demmifore, Westmeath, and £2,500 for 4,166 acres in the barony of Skreene, Eastmeath (Meath). What became of the unaccounted-for £2,500 of adventure, or what use was made of the lands drawn, remains to be discovered.

were scattered about the ten counties. Clumps of them appear here and there, such as the 23 '1034s' (Exonians not mentioned by name in Prendergast's list, but presumably included in the Exeter venture, no. 1034) who drew together in the south-west quarter of Kenry in Limerick, but no single barony or set of baronies was dominated by colonists from the town. Only 65—slightly less than half—of the 132 '1034s' appear at all on the barony tables, and only 28 of the 60 West-Countrymen (nos. 974–1034) on Prendergast's list. Of course, their shares may have been taken over by other Exeter men, but the barony tables do not enable one to determine this, and the role of 'secondary' adventures is not ascertainable.

In general it would appear that the lottery system worked as it had been intended to work—to prevent the new settlers from grouping themselves together by their own choice of locations.[1] The London adventurers, for instance, had generated more than half of the total money subscribed and, had they not been prevented from doing so, could have taken over *en bloc* whole baronies and counties of Ireland. Their £171,000 of original investment could have secured all the available land in Leinster, or all of Ulster and Munster put together. This would have resembled the pattern of 1609, when the London companies, as a group, took over the Ulster county of Coleraine and made it into Londonderry. Exeter investors might have followed such a lead—as might Yorkshiremen, West-Countrymen, and so on. But such a pattern was not allowed, and beyond the associations of adventurers into relatively small groups, a random scattering of colonists was obtained. This fact may have contributed to the breakdown of the adventurers' settlement, for it obliterated an infra structure which might have lent to the ten counties the same kind of strength which corporate London had lent to Londonderry.

In commenting upon patterns of settlement perceivable in the barony tables, one is analysing an abstraction. Even if these tables looked little different after the adventurers' lands had

---

[1] The order of 1 June 1653, reaffirmed by the act of 26 Sept., allowed adventurers to join in the same lot, but only up to a limit of £10,000, i.e. an area of no more than 50,000 acres in Ulster, 22,222 acres in Munster, and 16,666 acres in Leinster (*Acts and Ordinances*, ii. 739).

been resurveyed and reallocated by Petty, what proof is there that they were ever actually settled along such lines? Did the adventurers named in the lists come over and plant? The surviving evidence, scanty as it is, suggests that many of them did not, and that the shortage of disposable land in the hands of the commissioners was paradoxically matched by a shortage of persons willing to settle the lands so much in demand. In March 1655 a messenger to Cromwell from the commissioners in Ireland was ordered 'to acquaint his Highness that the Adventurers for lands in Ireland, not coming over to take possession of their lands fallen to them by lot, the same generally lie waste . . .'[1] Samuel Avery, the London alderman, was at that time in Dublin demanding conditions prior to the adventurers taking up their lands. Those conditions included: prohibiting Protestant delinquents from compounding, as they had specifically been permitted to do in an act of 2 September 1654; voiding all leases for less than seven years made by the late commissioners of Parliament; placing immediately in the adventurers' hands all the land belonging to them in the ten counties; and voiding the numerous grants of lands to particular persons (not adventurers) by order of Parliament.[2] The terms of plantation had been laid down in an ordinance of 23 June 1654 'for the further encouragement of the adventurers for lands in Ireland, and of the soldiers and other planters there',[3] but the adventurers did not feel these terms were generous enough, or that they protected them from the competition of other special-interest groups. The two demands concerning leases and the immediate taking of possession by adventurers are of interest, for they reveal some of the complexities of land transfer. Throughout the wars military men, and later the commissioners, rented rebel lands as the enemy was driven off them. The rents from these 'custodiams' were among the few sources of revenue available to the forces in Ireland. Every effort was made to maintain them when the wars concluded, pending the occupation by adventurers and soldiers. The adventurers felt that their interest in the lands was often impaired by the existence of unfavourable leases which had to be honoured until their

---

[1] Dunlop, *Ireland under the Commonwealth*, p. 484.
[2] Ibid., p. 483. [3] *Acts and Ordinances*, ii. 924.

termination. They desired the profits of immediate possession but eschewed the obligation. The commissioners professed themselves unwilling and unable to meet the adventurers' demands.[1]

Even when the adventurers did attempt to enter upon their lands, they often faced serious impediments. If they were not among the earliest entrants into a barony, they frequently found that their predecessors 'do not only possess greater proportions than their lots will bear, but also take in, upon the account of barren and unprofitable, much profitable pasture and meadow, whereby not only the succeeding lots in those baronies are defeated, but also the Commonwealth is much prejudiced'.[2] Committees were appointed to adjust these differences and expedite the settlements, but the combination of the autonomy allowed the adventurers in London with the crudities of Worsley's gross survey made progress slow. The problems created by deficiencies were chronic by 1658, when the adventurers were finally persuaded to allow William Petty to resurvey and, where necessary, redistribute their lands. But even in 1659 there were surviving deficiencies, and it seems likely that the problem persisted into the Restoration.[3]

The disputes between the adventurers and the government certainly continued through the Interregnum. No evidence shows us how many of the adventurers actually went to Ireland and settled, though approximately half the persons listed on the barony tables had their Irish lands confirmed to them (after compounding) by the acts of settlement of Charles II. It seems unlikely that the fate of the others will ever be known.

In summary, the barony tables provide an approximation of the adventurers' settlement of Ireland. They are records of a settlement *in posse* rather than *in esse*, but they are an important reference point in the fragmentary statistical history of the expansion of the English colonial interest in Ireland.[4] They

---

[1] Dunlop, *Ireland under the Commonwealth*, pp. 509–14.

[2] Ibid., p. 487, Resolution of Lord Deputy and Council, 12 Mar. 1655. See the case of the adventurers of barony Slane in Eastmeath v. Sergeant-Major Edward Dendy (*CSPI, 1647–60*, pp. 596, 834).

[3] See comment of Henry Cromwell above, p. 141.

[4] A table of the adventurers' settlement in Dunluce, county Antrim, as of 15 Dec. 1662, shows virtually no change from the settlement described as of 1658 by the Marsh's Library table of that barony. This is further evidence that

demonstrate again the inadequacy of the adventure scheme as a means of Anglicizing Ireland. 1,043 planters, spread out over ten counties and averaging 700 Irish acres apiece, could hardly constitute a yeomanry equal to the work of stemming the tide of Irishry. Men in large numbers would be needed to work these properties, and where would they come from if not the native population, theoretically intended for banishment to Connaught? 1,043 men alone were entitled to plant one-half of the ten counties, while 35,000 others—the veterans of the Cromwellian army—attempted to crowd into the other. The adventure scheme which had introduced the policy of massive confiscation of Irish land into mid-seventeenth-century English policy was clearly unable to make good use of the resulting spoils.

the pattern created by the lotteries at Grocers' Hall was basically unchanged, and that the barony tables constitute an accurate picture of the adventurers' settlement (PRO, S.P. 63/311, No. 17).

CODES FOR APPENDICES A AND B

(a) CHRISTIAN NAMES

(Columns 4 (A) and (B))

AA	Anne, Anna	CT	Cuthbert
AB	Alban	CU	Cornelius
AC	Alice		
AD	Adam, Adoniram	DA	Daniel
AF	Alfred	DB	Darby
AG	Angelo	DD	David
AH	Ahasuerus	DE	Denbighe
AI	Adrian	DH	Dorothy
AM	Abraham	DK	Duncan
AN	Alan	DM	Dominick
AO	Arnold	DN	Dionisio
AR	Arthur	DV	Devoreux
AS	Ambrose		
AT	Augustine	ED	Edward
AW	Andrew, Andrea	EE	Ezechiel
AX	Alexander	EH	Edith
AY	Anthony	EL	Ellis, Ellen
		EM	Edmund
BB	Barnaby	EP	Ephraim
BE	Bernard	ET	Emott
BG	Bridget	EU	Eustace
BH	Bonham	EV	Evan
BJ	Benjamin	EZ	Elizabeth
BL	Blanche		
BM	Bertram	FD	Faith
BN	Brian	FM	Fitzwilliam
BP	Baptist	FO	Ferdinando
BR	Bernard	FR	Francis, Frances
BS	Basil	FT	Fortune
BU	Bulstrode	FU	Fulke
BW	Bartholomew	FX	Felix
		FW	Fleetwood
CA	Corporation of . . .		
CB	Caleb	GA	Geoffrey, Jeffrey
CC	Cecil, Cecilia	GB	Gabriel
CD	Caldwell	GC	Grace
CH	Charles, Christabel	GD	Godwin
CL	Clement	GE	George
CN	Clinton	GF	Griffin, Griffith
CO	Company of . . .	GG	Gregory
CP	Ciprian	GI	Giles
CR	Christopher	GL	Gilbert
CS	Constantine, Constance	GM	Gamaliel

GR	Gerard	MB	Mirabell
GT	Garrett	MC	Maurice
GU	Guy	MD	Marmaduke
GY	Godfrey	ME	Moses
		MG	Morgan
HA	Hannah	MH	Meredith
HB	Hubert	MI	Michael
HC	Hector	MK	Mark
HE	Henry	ML	Magdalene
HG	Hugh	MN	Miles
HK	Habbakuk	MO	Morris
HM	Herman	MR	Margery
HN	Helen	MS	Mascall
HO	Hogan	MT	Margaret
HR	Heritage	MV	Mathias
HS	Hercules	MW	Mathew
HT	Herbert	MX	Maximilian
HU	Humphrey	MY	Mary
HW	Howell		
		NA	Nathan
IB	Isabella	NI	Nicholas
IM	Ishmael	NL	Nathaniel
IR	Israel .		
IZ	Isaac	OB	Obadiah
		OC	Octavian
JA	James, Jane	OL	Oliver
JB	Joan	OS	Osmund
JC	Jacob	OT	Ottowell
JI	Jeremiah	OV	Overington
JL	Julius, Julia	OW	Owen
JM	Jerome		
JN	Jonah, Jonas	PA	Patrick
JP	Jasper	PC	Pierce, Piers
JO	John, Joan	PD	Periam
JR	Jervase, Gervase, Jarvis	PE	Peter
JS	Joseph	PF	Pauncefoot
JU	Joshua	PG	Peregrine
JV	Job	PH	Philip, Phillipa
		PL	Paul, Paula
KT	Katherine, Catherine	PN	Penning
		PR	Percival, Percy
LC	Lancelot, Lucy	PS	Priscilla
LK	Luke	PT	Patient
LL	Lionel	PU	Prudence
LN	Leonard		
LS	Lewis, Lewes	RA	Ralph
LT	Lambert	RC	Rice, Rees
LU	Laurence	RD	Roland
LV	Ludovico	RE	Radcliffe
LY	Lucy	RF	Randolph, Randall
		RG	Roger
MA	Martin	RI	Richard

RL	Reginald
RO	Robert
RR	Ross
RS	Rose, Rosamond
RW	Rowland

SA	Samuel
SB	Sebastian
SD	Savage
SF	Stafford
SG	Sigismund
SI	Simon
SL	Sidwell
SM	Solomon
SN	Susan, Suzanne
SP	Sampson
SR	Sarah
ST	Stephen
SV	Silvester

TB	Tobias
TH	Thomas
TK	Throckmorton
TR	Tristram
TS	Theophilus
TY	Timothy

| VC | Vincent |
| VL | Valentine |

WA	Walter
WD	Wilfrid
WK	Watkin
WL	Walsingham
WM	William
WN	Winifred

| ZY | Zachary |

(b) PLACE NAMES

(Column 6 (A))

English Counties

BD	Bedfordshire
BR	Berkshire
BU	Buckinghamshire
CA	Cambridgeshire
CH	Cheshire
CO	Cornwall
CU	Cumberland
DR	Derbyshire
DV	Devon
DO	Dorset
DU	Durham
EX	Essex
GL	Gloucestershire
HA	Hampshire
HF	Herefordshire
HT	Hertfordshire
HU	Huntingdonshire
KE	Kent
LA	Lancashire
LE	Leicestershire
LI	Lincolnshire
MX	Middlesex
MO	Monmouthshire
NF	Norfolk
NT	Northamptonshire
NO	Nottinghamshire

OX	Oxfordshire
RU	Rutlandshire
SA	Shropshire
SO	Somerset
ST	Staffordshire
SF	Suffolk
SR	Surrey
SX	Sussex
WA	Warwickshire
WE	Westmorland
WI	Wiltshire
WO	Worcestershire
YO	Yorkshire

Cities, Towns, Countries

LO	London
WM	Westminster
SK	Southwark
BS	Bristol
EN	Exeter
DT	Dartmouth
GY	Great Yarmouth
DB	Dublin
HD	Holland
IR	Ireland
SC	Scotland

Irish Provinces (Columns 19 (A) and 9 (B))

C	Connaught
L	Leinster
M	Munster
U	Ulster

Irish Counties (Columns 18 (A) and 8 (B))

AN	Antrim (U)
AR	Armagh (U)
DN	Down (U)
EM	Eastmeath (Meath) (L)
KI	Kings (L)
LI	Limerick (M)
QU	Queens (L)
WM	Westmeath (L)
WT	Waterford (M)
TP	Tipperary (M)
ZW	Waterford (alternative) (M)

Irish Baronies (Columns 17 (A) and 7 (B))

AR	Armagh (AR)
AD	Ards (DN)
BA	Ballybritt (KI)
BE	Belfast (AN)
CA	Carrickfergus (AN)
CL	Clanwilliam (TP)
CN	Connello (LI)
CO	Coshmore & Coshbride (ZW)
CU	Cullenagh (QU)
CY	Coonagh (LI)
DC	Decies (ZW)
DE	Deece (EM)

DM	Demmifore (WM)
DU	Dunluce (AN)
EG	Eglish (KI)
EL	Eliogarty (TP)
FE	Fartullagh (WM)
IK	Ikerrin (TP)
IL	Ileagh (TP)
IO	Iffa & Offa (TP)
JS	Geashill (KI)
KE	Kenry (LI)
KI	Kilkenny West (WM)
LE	Lecale (DN)
LS	Lismagh parish (KI)
LU	Lune (EM)
MA	Massereene (AN)
MD	Middlethird (TP)
MO	Morgallion (EM)
MR	Maryborough (QU)
MY	Moyashel (WM)
NA	Navan (EM)
ON	Oneilland (AR)
PB	Pubblebrien (LI)
PO	Portnahinch (QU)
RA	Rathconrath (WM)
SK	Skreene (EM)
SL	Slane (EM)
ST	Stradbally (QU)
SW	Slievemargy (QU)
TE	Tinnehinch (QU)
TU	Tiranny (AR)
UI	Upper Iveagh (DN)
ZW	Waterford (ZW)
ZL	Liberties of Waterford (ZW)

(c) PROFESSIONS

(Column 7 (A))

AL	Alderman
AM	Armorer
AP	Apothecary
AR	Artisan
BA	Baker
BL	Blacksmith
BO	Bowyer
BR	Brewer
BS	Barber-Surgeon
BT	Baronet
BU	Butcher

CA	Carpenter
CE	Clothier
CL	Cleric
CK	Cook
CO	Cordwainer
CP	Captain
CU	Cutler
CW	Cloth-worker
DR	Draper
DY	Dyer

EM	Embroiderer		PE	Pewterer
ES	Esquire		PH	Physician
			PL	Plasterer
FA	Factor		PS	Painter-Stainer
FE	Feltmaker			
FM	Fishmonger		SA	Salter
			SC	Scrivener
GE	Gentleman		SD	Sadler
GI	Girdler		SG	Sergeant at Law
GO	Goldsmith		SH	Shipright
GR	Grocer		SK	Skinner
			SO	Scholar or School-master
HA	Haberdasher		SR	Shoe-maker
HO	Horner		ST	Stationer
IK	Inn-keeper		TA	Tailor
IR	Iron-monger		TN	Tanner
			TC	Tallow-chandler
KN	Knight			
			UH	Upholder
LA	Lady		UP	Upholsterer
LD	Linen-draper			
LE	Leatherseller		VI	Vintner
LO	Lord			
LW	Lawyer		WC	Wax-chandler
			WE	Weaver
MA	Mariner		WH	White-baker
MC	Mercer		WL	Wool-merchant
ME	Merchant		WM	Wood-monger
MT	Merchant-tailor			
			YE	Yeoman
OF	Army Officer			

(d) MISCELLANEOUS

Sex, etc., (Column 5 (A))

M Male
F Female
W Widow
B Bachelor
S Spinster
R Widower
D Dowager

Additional Status (Column 8 (A))

1 Member of Parliament
2 Alderman
3 Sheriff
4 Member of Parliament according to Brunton and Pennington

Codes for Appendices A and B

Information Source (Column 9 (A))

1 Adventurer mentioned in S. P. 63, Prendergast's list, and Marsh's Barony Table.
2 Adventurer mentioned in S. P. 63 and Prendergast; NOT Marsh.
3 Adventurer mentioned in S. P. 63 and Marsh; NOT Prendergast.
4 Adventurer mentioned in Marsh and Prendergast; NOT S. P. 63.
5 Adventurer mentioned in S. P. 63 ONLY.
6 Adventurer mentioned in Marsh ONLY.
7 Adventurer mentioned in Prendergast ONLY.

In fact, there are no number '6's'. Adventurers mentioned only in Marsh's table appear in Appendix B.

Additional Investment Category (Column 14 (A))

1 Subscription under ordinance of 13 Nov. 1647 allowing non-adventurers to participate in the adventure at the rates of the doubling ordinance, by paying in the unpaid remainders of existing adventurers' subscriptions.
2 Subscription under ordinance of 30 Jan. 1642/3 allowing credit for goods (victuals, arms, powder, etc.) in lieu of money.
3 Subscription for houses in Waterford city under doubling ordinance of 14 July 1643.
4 Subscription of unpaid remainders of original adventures under act of 26 Sept. 1653.
5 Subscription of soldiers' pay under ordinance of 14 July 1643.

APPENDIX A

COMPOSITE LIST OF ORIGINAL INVESTORS IN IRISH LAND

THIS list was drawn from the three sources discussed in Chapter III above: The State Papers Relating to Ireland, the list of adventurers in Prendergast's *Cromwellian Settlement of Ireland*, and the manuscript barony tables in Marsh's Library, Dublin. No person, however, whose name appears only in the last of those sources is included here. Such persons will be found in Appendix B, an alphabetical compilation of Marsh's tables.

The list is a photo-copy of the computerized data used for all statistical calculations in this work. An error in the list, therefore, will be reflected in the calculations which treat that particular class of information. If Robert Adams (No. 2) was not from London but Suffolk, the role of Londoners in the adventure for Irish land is that much less than has been computed. With some editorial changes to improve legibility, the format of entries in the list corresponds to that of the 80 column computer cards which were employed to enter data.

In column 1 there appears a serial or identifying number, followed in column 2 by a card number from 1 to 9. With most adventurers it was possible to compress all relevant information on to one 80 column card, but in some cases supplementary information had to be recorded on subsequent cards. Thus, eight cards were necessary to record the numerous parcels of land which Thomas Vincent obtained in the lotteries of 1653–4. In column 3 is found the surname of the adventurer, followed in some cases by further identification such as JR or SR, or, in the case of Philip Herbert (No. 663) 4EP to indicate that this was, indeed, the fourth earl of Pembroke. Column 4 contains a two-letter code for Christian names. Some of the codes stand for more than one name. AW, for instance, could be Andrew or Andrea, but for a woman, sex being indicated by column 5, it would be Andrea (its commonness as a Christian name among male Italians notwithstanding). In a few cases, however (e.g., GF for Griffin or Griffith), subtle distinctions among first names will be lost.

Column 5 denotes sex, but includes marital status where that was recorded in the sources. Column 6, a residence code, must be used with caution. I have accepted uncritically whatever residence is attributed to an adventurer by the sources. In some cases they may err or refer to only one of an adventurer's several residences. The same hazards pertain to the information in column 7, a two-letter code describing the investor's profession or status. There may be errors here as well, though casual checking of the sources revealed relatively few. Column 8 identifies MPs, aldermen, and sheriffs, as well as MPs (according to Brunton and Pennington) who were not so described by the three sources. If a man was more than one, he was recorded under the lowest number (i.e., an MP if he was both that and an alderman, or that and a sheriff). Column 9 contains a code indicating which of the three sources, or what combination of them, provide information regarding a particular adventurer.

The subsequent columns indicate the amounts of money which an investor paid in under the various acts and ordinances: first (column 10), under the act of March 1642; then (column 11), under the sea adventure ordinance of June; thirdly (column 12), under the doubling ordinance of July 1643; and finally (column 13), under the various additional ordinances. The code in column 14 indicates under which specific ordinance the money recorded in column 13 was subscribed.

The remaining information describes the lands which the adventurer, or a relation of the same surname, drew in the lotteries at Grocer's Hall, and derives from the barony tables in Marsh's Library. Column 15 indicates the adventurer's 'credit', that is to say, the sum of the debentures which he possessed. This amount is not necessarily the same as the total of his investments (as observed in columns 10–13) because the operation of the doubling ordinance as well as the purchase of other adventurers' shares could increase his 'credit', while sales of his own shares could decrease it.

Column 16 shows the acreage (in Irish measure) necessary to satisfy the adventurer's 'credit' in the portion of Ireland he had drawn in the lottery, while columns 17, 18, and 19 indicate by barony, county, and province, the location of that portion. Additional cards describe additional parcels of land in diverse locations. If the adventurer drew several parcels all in the same barony, their acreage was summed and recorded on a single card.

Column 20 prints for adventurers who appear in Prendergast's list the serial number they occupy there. Most have only one such number, but some have two, for Prendergast's list included, as an addendum, a separate list of adventurers under the sea ordinance, many of whom also appear in the original list. Prendergast's numbers 1189–1360 pertain to the sea ordinance, and ordinarily appear in column 21 of this appendix. Number 1034 is applied to any adventurer who does not otherwise appear in Prendergast's list, but appears in the State Papers as a contributor from Exeter or its environs, the subscription of whose 'Mayor, Bailiffs, and Commonality' is described in Prendergast under that number.

Because this list is composite, information in it may not correspond exactly to data in any single source. In some cases conflicting data has had to be reconciled, and a relation of all the principles employed would impose unnecessarily upon the reader. An example, however, is that Prendergast may show an adventurer to have invested £100 under the original act and another £100 under the sea ordinance, while the documents in the State Papers may make no reference to the sea ordinance, but show an original subscription of £200 and a subscription of £50 under the doubling ordinance. In such a case (a very common one) I recorded that the adventurer in question had subscribed £100 under the original act, £100 under the sea ordinance, and £50 under the doubling ordinance. My reasons for doing so were that I discovered Prendergast a generally reliable source for sea adventure subscriptions, and the State Papers a generally reliable source for doubling ordinance subscriptions. It will be seen, however, that an element of personal judgement entered into the process of reducing the sources to useful data. Where Prendergast and the State Papers conflicted on the status, profession, or residence of an adventurer, I tended to follow the State Papers as a more primary source. On the other hand, in the complicated matter of the division among adventurers of partnerships, or group subscriptions, I more often followed Prendergast, a later list which reflects the adjudication of those questions in the 1650s and 1660s.

Some of the data is deductive, and in a sense, conjectural. The very act of giving an adventurer a unique serial number is an assertion of his identity. To take a particularly questionable case, the two William Adams (Nos. 4 & 5) who appear on the first page of Appendix A may well be the same man. One subscribed £200 under the original act and appears on Prendergast's list. The other subscribed £25 under the doubling ordinance, according to the State Papers, and appears nowhere else. One is described as a haberdasher, the other as a draper, and for that reason each has been given a separate serial number. But No. 5 was doubling someone's previous subscription, and it could well have been £100 of his own adventure here ascribed to another William Adams (No. 4).

Even more delicate is the connection between investors of money and drawers of land. Marsh's barony tables provide no distinguishing information about the adventurers they list, other than their

names, which are often spelled quite differently from the same names
in Prendergast and the State Papers. How can one be sure, then,
that the Francis Allen (No. 14), goldsmith of London and Member
of Parliament who appears in both the State Papers and Prendergast
as having adventured £200, is the same Francis Allen (No. 2008)
who received credit for £400 of adventure and drew 888 acres in
Tipperary? In the absence of supporting evidence, obviously one
cannot. But where there was circumstantial evidence within the
three sources linking a drawer of land with an investor of money,
either as the same person or as an heir of the same surname, I have
recorded a connection. Thus, John Pym (No. 1097) is shown in
Appendix A to have drawn 1000 acres in Meath, but the lotteries
were held ten years after his death. A look at Appendix B, under
Pym, shows that someone of that name drew £600, the exact amount
John Pym had subscribed; and it was, in this case, John Pym's son,
Alexander (No. 2747). Pym's case is more easily verified than most,
and the ascriptions of land drawn should be used with care and not
relied upon with reference to specific individuals, unless supported
by other evidence.

It cannot be too strongly stated that all information about the adventurers, with one exception, has been drawn exclusively from the
three named sources. That exception occurs in the identification of
members of parliament, a category of such importance that it has
been though necessary to indicate them even where the sources do
not.[1] Otherwise, all data upon which the three sources do not dis-
agree has been accepted uncritically, and no effort has been made to
consult other sources of contemporary biographical information.
The demands of consistency and practicality have made such a policy
all but inevitable. To have researched nearly 2000 persons would
have been the work of many years, while the admission of occa-
sional, external corrections would have destroyed the integrity of the
three sources as unreconstructed seventeenth-century documents.

[1] See codes for column 8.

KEY TO COLUMN HEADINGS

1 Serial number of adventurer
2 Card number
3 Surname
4 Code for Christian name
5 Code for sex and/or marital status
6 Code for principal place of residence
7 Code for profession or status
8 Code for additional status
9 Code for source or sources from which information regarding adventurer is derived
10 Amount of investment in pounds under original act for adventurers (March 1642)
11 Amount of investment in pounds under ordinance for sea adventure (June 1642)
12 Amount of investment in pounds under doubling ordinance (July 1643)
13 Amount of investment in pounds under subsequent miscellaneous ordinances
14 Code for specific ordinances under which amount in column 13 was subscribed
15 Amount of credit in pounds allowed adventurer in 1653–4 on the basis of alleged subscriptions under the act and ordinances for adventure
16 Amount of acreage (in Irish measure) due adventurer to satisfy credit (column 15) in portion of Ireland in which he had drawn (columns 17, 18, 19)
17 Code for barony in which adventurer's lot fell
18 Code for the county in which adventurer's lot fell
19 Code for the province in which adventurer's lot fell
20 First number given adventurer in appendix list printed in Prendergast's *Cromwellian Settlement of Ireland* (1875 and subsequent editions)
21 Second number given adventurer in Prendergast's list

1	2	3	4	5	6	7	8	9	10	11	12	13	14	15	16	17	18	19	20	21
1	1	ABDY	HU	M	OF			5				500	5							
2	1	ADAMS	RO	M	LO	MA		1	100					100	222	DC	ZW	M	226	
3	1	ADAMS	TH	M	LO		2	7	600										137	
4	1	ADAMS	WM	M	LO	HA		2	200										15	
5	1	ADAMS	WM	M	LO	DR		5			25									
6	1	ALCOCK	TH	M	LO	HA		1	300	100				500	1111	IO	TI	M	422	1237
7	1	ALCOCK JR.	WM	M	LO	MT		7	25										185	
8	1	ALDERSEY	MT	W	KE			5	60		50								724	
9	1	ALDERTON	JO	M	SR	DR		1	50					25	41	PO	QU	L	385	
10	1	ALEXANDER	JM	M				3			50			50		ZW	ZW	M		
11	1	ALFORD	JA	M	LO	GR		1	50					50	111	DC	ZW	M	548	
12	1	ALLANSON	WM	M	YO	KN	1	2	300		150								132	
13	1	ALLEINE	TB	M	EN			2	80										981	
14	1	ALLEN	FR	M	LO	GO	1	1	200					400	888	MD	TI	M	676	
15	1	ALLEN	JO	M		CL		1	100					100	222	DC	ZW	M	248	
16	1	ALLEN	RI	M	LO	GR		1	50	150				200	444	CL	TI	M	811	1295
17	1	ALLEN	TH	M	LO	GR		2	300										599	
18	1	ALLEN	WM	M	LO	VI		1	200	300				550	1222	EL	TI	M	478	1245
19	1	ALLEN	WM	M	LO	GR		2	300										599	
20	1	ALLEN	WM	M	DO			2	50										801	
21	1	ALLOTT	RI	M	LO	HA		2	50										420	
22	1	ALLWOOD	JO	M	DR			1	25					25	125	BE	AN	U	885	
23	1	ALMERY	GE	M	LO	GE		1	800					1300	2166	SW	QU	L	162	
24	1	ALMOND	WM	M	LO	PE		1	25					25	55	CL	TI	M	193	
24	2	ALMOND	WM	M	LO	PE								100	222	IO	TI	M		
25	1	ALSTON	ED	M	LO	PH		2	200										161	
26	1	ALSTON	JO	M	LO	ME		2	200		50								166	
27	1	ALSTON	PN	M	LO	GR		2	200		50								164	
28	1	ALURED	JO	M	YO	ES	1	2	100										1182	
29	1	AMYES	JO	M	LO			1	66					66	91	IO	TI	M	352	
30	1	ANDERSON	NL	M	MX	CL		2	100		25								267	
31	1	ANDREWES	MW	M	LO	GR		7	100										839	
32	1	ANDREWES	RI	M	LO	GI		5	150		93									
33	1	ANDREWES	TH	M	LO		2	1	675	500	374	100	1	1500	2500	8A	KI	L	155	1202
33	2	ANDREWES	TH											40		ZW	ZW	M	155	1202
34	1	ANNESLEY	ED	M	LO	AM		2	300		100								831	1310
35	1	ANTHONY	ED	M	EN	GO		1	100										1034	
35	2	ANTHONY	ED	M	EN			1	100					100	166	EG	KI	L	989	
36	1	ANTHONY	HA	W	EN			5	110										103	4
37	1	ARCHBOLD	ST	M				1	50					50	111	DC	ZW	M	289	
38	1	ARCHER	FR	M	LO	HA		3	58		8			383	638	SK	EM	L		
39	1	ARMYNE	WM	M	HU	KN	1	1	400					350	583	RA	WM	L	1075	
40	1	ARNOLD	GE	M	LO	GE		1	200					200	333	SW	QU	L	1147	
41	1	ARNOLD	JO	M				3	100					100	166	SL	WM	L		
42	1	ARNOLD	WM	M				3	100					100	166	SL	WM	L		
43	1	ARUNDEL	JO	M		MX		7	50										36	
44	1	ARUNDEL	WM	M		MX		7	50										36	
45	1	ARUNDELL	HE	M	MX	YE		1	150					150	250	RA	WM	L	34	
46	1	ASH	ED	M			1	1	400					400	888	CL	TI	M	3	
47	1	ASH	FR	M	LO	GO		2	200		50								143	
48	1	ASH	JA	M			1	2	400										3	
49	1	ASH	JO	M			1	1	400					800	1777	CL	TI	M	3	
50	1	ASH	MW	M	DR			1	25					25	125	BE	AN	U	885	
51	1	ASH	SI	M	LO	CL		1	100					100	222	IO	TI	M	847	
52	1	ASHETON	RA	M	LA	YE	1	2	50										1098	
53	1	ASHETON	WM	M	LA	CL		2	50										1098	
54	1	ASHLEY	JO	M	LO	FM		2	100										490	
55	1	ASHTON	MI	M	DR			1	20					20	61	UI	DN	U	798	
56	1	ASHURST	HE	M	LO	MT		2	50										418	
57	1	ASHURST	RI	M	LO	DR		1	100					100	750	SL	EM	L	362	
58	1	ASHWELL	WM	M	LO	ME		2	400										536	
59	1	ASTREY	FR	M				1	20					20	33	RA	WM	L	74	
60	1	ATKINS	A	M	SO			5	10										1034	
61	1	ATKINS	JO	M	SO			7	10										1126	
62	1	ATKINS	PE	M	DV			3	25					25	34	EL	TI	M	1034	
63	1	ATKINS	WM	M	SO			1	50					50	63	PB	LI	M	1125	
63	2	ATKINS	WM											10	10	EG	KI	L		
64	1	AUNGIER	PR	M	LO	GE		5			16									
65	1	AUSTEN	EM	M	LO	FE		1	100					100	166	DE	EM	L	908	
66	1	AUSTEN	HE	M	LO	FM		5			10									
67	1	AUSTIN	AY	M	EN			3	5					5	5	PO	QU	L	1034	
68	1	AUSTIN	GE	M		ME		1	600					600	2627	MA	AN	U	707	
69	1	AVERY	SA	M	LO	ME	2	3	300		100			1550	2764	CN	LI	M		
69	2	AVERY	SA											25		ZW	ZW	M		
70	1	AYNELL	JO	M	DV			5	60										1034	
71	1	AYRES	TH	M	LO	GE		7	200										666	
72	1	AYSCOUGH	ED	M	LI	KN	1	7	150										109	
73	1	BABB	WM	M	LO	FE		1	50					50	111	DC	ZW	M	262	

1	2	3	4	5	6	7	8	9	10	11	12	13	14	15	16	17	18	19	20	21
74	1	BABINGTON	AM	M	LO	DR		2	100	400									272	1216
75	1	BABINGTON	MI	M	LO			1	200					200	333	TE	WM	L	498	
76	1	BABINGTON	TH	M	LO			1	100					100	166	SK	EM	L	945	
77	1	BAGLEHOLE	ED	M	EN			3	5					5	6	KE	LI	M	1034	
78	1	BAILEY	TH	M	WI			2	150										875	
79	1	BAKER	JO	M	LO	WE		7	100										190	
80	1	BAKER	KT	W	BU			1	80					80	133	RA	WM	L	35	
81	1	BAKER	MY	W	KE			2	10										1056	
82	1	BALAM	WM	M	LO	GE		2	50										199	
83	1	BALL	SA	M	LO	SA		3	50		12			125	277	EL	TI	M		
84	1	BALL	WM	M	LO	CW		1	200					200	333	SL	EM	L	439	
85	1	BALL	WM	M	LO	LW		2	250										673	
86	1	BALLARD	JO	M	LO	SK		1	200					200	333	NA	EM	L	423	
87	1	BALLARD	TH	M	SX			1	25					25	25	DE	EM	L	969	
88	1	BALLARD	WM	M	LO	YE		1	200					200	333	NA	EM	L	393	
89	1	BAMFORD	PA	M	LO	MT		2	100										607	
90	1	BANCKS	JO	M	LO	GE		2	100										396	
91	1	BANCKS	TH	M	LO	GE		7	100										717	
92	1	BANNASTER	BJ	M	LO	AP		2	100										745	
93	1	BARBER	GB	M	HT	GE		1	200					200	333	MO	EM	L	833	
94	1	BARBER-SURGEONS	CA					7	50										188	
95	1	BARD	MX	M				5	200											
96	1	BARDOLPH	SI	M	SR	ME		2	100	200									809	1293
97	1	BARFOOTE	RO	M	LO	MT		1	100	150				100	166	MR	QU	L	10	1191
98	1	BARFOOTE	RO	M	LO	LE		1	25					25	41	ST	QU	L	690	
99	1	BARG	VC	M	GX	ES		2	20										1068	
100	1	BARKER	GE	M	SR			2	200										100	
101	1	BARKER	JO	M	WA		1	2	1200										125	
102	1	BARKER	MY	W	BS			2	1000										1133	
103	1	BARKER	WM	M	LO	ME		1	200					600	2330	UI	DN	U	637	
104	1	BARKSTEAD	JO	M	LO	GO		2	100										677	
105	1	BARLOW	HU	M	YO			3	62					62	192	ON	AR	U		
106	1	BARNARD	RI	M	SX	DR		1	200					200	333	PO	QU	L	967	
107	1	BARNARDISTON	NA	M	SF	KN	1	2	700					600	1000	CU	QU	L	21	
108	1	BARNARDISTON	TH	M	LO	ME	1	1	200	50	82			625	1388	IO	TI	M	207	1209
108	2	BARNARDISTON	TH											500	833	NA	EM	L	207	1209
109	1	BARNES	JA	M	LO	LW		2	400										30	
110	1	BARRETT	RO	M	LO	HA		1	50					100	137	CY	LI	M	400	
111	1	BARRINGTON	TH	M		KN	1	1	1200					1200	2000	SL	EM	L	20	
112	1	BARTLETT	BR	M	EN	ME		5	80										1034	
113	1	BARTLETT	JO	M	EN	CL		5	30										1034	
114	1	BARTLETT	WM	M				3	10					20	27	KE	LI	M	1034	
115	1	BARTON	WM	M	LO	ST		1	300					310	1550	AR	AR	U	503	
116	1	BARWICK	TH	M	LO	GR		1	100					100	500	LE	DN	U	457	
117	1	BASSETT	W	M	WS	O			1030					30 1	41	1K	EI	M	1112	
118	1	BATE	JO	M	LO	MT		2		200										1217
119	1	BATEMAN	JO	M		CL		2	50		6								699	
120	1	BATEMAN	JO	M		CL		2	50		6								699	
121	1	BATH	CA					7	25										1124	
122	1	BAYLIFF	JO	M	SO			5	10										1034	
123	1	BAYNTON	ED	M	WI		1	1	450										59	
124	1	BAYNTON	JA	M		ES		1	150										629	
125	1	BEADLE	TH	M	LO	TC		3	100					150	250	SK	EM	L		
126	1	BEALE	ST	M	LO	LE		2	100	1200									647	1264
127	1	BEALE	TH	M		TC		7	100										941	
128	1	BEALE	WM	M	LO	ME		2	187	506									810	1294
129	1	BEAPLE	RI	M	DV	ME		5	100										1034	
130	1	BEARD	MX	M	LO	GI		7	200										528	
131	1	BEARD	RO	M	EX			1	200					200	444	DC	ZW	M	346	
132	1	BEAUMONT	RI	M	LO	AP		1	30		8			100	166	LU	EM	L	261	
133	1	BECK	GB	M	LO	LW		1	300					600	1000	DM	WM	L	78	
134	1	BEDDINGFIELD	AY	M	LO	MC	1	2	400										82	
135	1	BEDDINGFIELD	HU	M	LO	GO		1	200					200	444	IO	TI	M	145	
136	1	BEEKE	WM	M	LO	MT		2	500	125									284	
137	1	BEIGHTON	RI	M	LO	SO		2	50										374	
138	1	BELFIELD	AY	M	HT			1	180					180	400	IO	TI	N	1158	
139	1	BELL	AG	M				1	50					50	51	SK	EM	L	702	
140	1	BELLERS	FU	M	WA	CL		7	25										1092	
141	1	BENCE	AX	M	SF	AL	1	1	600	150				1250	2777	IO	TI	M	81	
142	1	BENDISH	TH	M	EX	KN		7	400										645	
143	1	BENGOE	JA	M	LO	ME		2	25		6								381	
144	1	BENNETT	JO	M	DV			3	60					60	100	PO	QU	L	1034	
145	1	BENTLEY	JO	M	MX	GE		1	200					200	205	MO	EM	L	102	
146	1	BENYON	GB	M	LO	TC		3	100					225	375	ST	QU	L	936	
147	1	BERNARD	RI	M	LO	ES		1	200					200	333	DE	EM	L	79	
148	1	BERRY	JO	M	LO	CA		5	87											
149	1	BEST	SR	W	SR			2	20										1054	
150	1	BETSWORTH	WM	M	SX	BL		1	50					50	250	AR	AR	U	704	

1	2	3	4	5	6	7	8	9	10	11	12	13	14	15	16	17	18	19	20	21
151	1	BEWLEY	WM	M	LO	DR	2		100										520	
152	1	BEWLEY JR	TH	M	LO	DR	1		100					200	333	PQ	QU	L	519	
153	1	BEWLEY SR	TH	M	LO	DR	2		100										518	
154	1	BIDDLE	CR	M	LO	SH	1		25					25	41	PQ	QU	L	532	
155	1	BIDDOLPH	TS	M	LO	GR	1		200					100	222	CL	TI	M	606	
156	1	BIGG	AA	F	LO		5		200											
157	1	BIGG	JA	M	SO		7		7										1122	
158	1	BIGG	JO	M	KE	GE	2		100	1500									561	1256
159	1	BIGGS	JS	M		CL	1		50					50	111	DC	ZW	M	303	
160	1	BIGGS	MW	M		GE	7		200										413	
161	1	BIRCHE	TH	M	LI	GE	2		200										1099	
162	1	BIRD	JO	M	LO		2		10										956	
163	1	BISBY	WM	M	LO	SA	2		100		25								390	
164	1	BISCOE	JS	M	LO	AP	1		100		25			250	1250	UI	DN	U	686	
165	1	BISHOP	EP	M	SR	MC	1		20					20	27	IO	TI	M	1063	
166	1	BLACKBURROW	WM	M		LE	1		50					50	111	DC	ZW	M	294	
167	1	BLACKSMITHS	CO				5					23								
168	1	BLACKWELL	JC	M	LO	SC	1		234					300	666	IK	TI	M	556	
169	1	BLACKWELL	JO	M	LO		7		500										521	
170	1	BLACKWELL	JR	M	LO	SK	7		100										611	
171	1	BLACKWELL	JS	M	LO	BS	1		234					337	750	IL	TI	M	556	
172	1	BLACKWELL	TH	M	LO	MT	5					12								
173	1	BLAGE	NI	M	LO	ME	1		50					50	154	TU	AR	U	887	
174	1	BLAKE	EM	M	LO	ME	1		30					30	66	CY	LI	M	1150	
175	1	BLAKE	EZ	F		DV	2		10										1160	
176	1	BLAKE	GE	M			5					12								
177	1	BLAKESTONE	JO	M	NB		1	2	300		150	300	1						61	
178	1	BLATE	JO	M	LO	MT	7		100										280	
179	1	BLATT	EM	M			2		66										353	
180	1	BLATT	JA	M			1		66					133	182	IO	TI	M	351	
181	1	BLUNDEN	OV	M	LO		1		50					125	208	LS	KI	L	949	
181	2	BLUNDEN	OV											20		ZW	ZW	M	949	
182	1	BOATE	GR	M	LO	PH	1		80	100				468	847	IK	TI	M	865	1318
183	1	BOGGESTE	TH	M	LO		7		50										258	
184	1	BOGGIS	WM	M	SF	GE	2		50										791	
185	1	BOLT	NI	M	EN	WE	5		10										1034	
186	1	BOND	D	M	DO		1	2	2000										130	
187	1	BOND	JO	M	EN	CL	3		50					50	111	PB	LI	M	1034	
188	1	BOND	JO	M	SR		2		10										1048	
189	1	BOND	NI	M	LO	GE	1		100					100	222	MD	TI	M	688	
190	1	BONNER	NI	M		PS	2		50										246	
191	1	BOOLE	RO	M	EN		5		5										1034	
192	1	BOOLLE	JO	M	EN		5		10										1034	
193	1	BOONE	TH	M	DV	GE	3		600					600	1333	CN	LI	M	1034	
194	1	BOTTERELL	WM	M		SA	1		50					50	83	GA	KI	L	223	
195	1	BOULTON	E.	M		BS	7		25										444	
196	1	BOULTON	E.	M	LO	BS	7		100											1240
197	1	BOULTON	WI	M	LO	MT	2		100										402	
198	1	BOURCHER	NL	M		SX	7		4										973	
199	1	BOX	HE	M	LO		1		400					400	888	CL	TI	M	534	
200	1	BOYCE	HE	M	LO	TC	1		100	150				100	222	IO	TI	M	446	1242
201	1	BOYCE	JO	M	KE		1	3	100										666	
202	1	BOYNTON	MW	M	YO		1	2	1000										537	
203	1	BOYTE	JO	M	SO		5		10										1034	
204	1	BRADLEY	GE	M	LO	ST	1		100	50				100	222	DC	ZW	M	820	1303
205	1	BRADLEY	MK	M	LO	SC	1		100	50				100	222	DC	ZW	M	818	
206	1	BRACSHAW	EZ	W	LO		1		50					50	83	LS	KI	L	254	
207	1	BRAND	JS	M	LO	SA	1		200					600	617	KI	WM	L	500	
208	1	BRAND	MW	M		KN	3		200					200	206	KI	WM	L		
209	1	BREMBLECOMB	JO	M	DV		5		50										1034	
210	1	BRERETON	WM	M	KN		1	1	900			300	4	1700	2757	IU	TI	M	28	
210	2	BRERETON	WM	M										750	3750		AN	U	28	
210	3	BRERETON	WM	M										100	222	IO	TI	M	28	
211	1	BRETLAND	TH	M	DR		1		100					100	500	BE	AN	U	575	
212	1	BRETT	JO	M	LO	MT	2		700	300									283	1219
213	1	BREWER	CR	M	SO		7		3										867	
214	1	BREWSTER	ED	M	LO	ST	2		133					133	295	CL	TI	M	591	
215	1	BRICE	RI	M	BE		5					20								
216	1	BRICE	S.	M	SR		7		100										1061	
217	1	BRICE	WM	M	LO	CL	5					20								
218	1	BRICKDELL	JA	M	LO		7		10										1181	
219	1	BRIDGES	JI	M			7					25								1350
220	1	BRIDGES	JO	M	WA		1						300	1	1800	3999	CN	LI	M	1090	
221	1	BRIGGS	MN	M	LO	MT	1		50		12			125	208	DE	EM	L	427	
222	1	BRIGGS	TH	M	LO	ME	1		200										740	
223	1	BRIGHT	JO	M	SF		1		300	300				600	1333	CO	ZW	M	176	1205
224	1	BRIGHT	TH	M	SF	GF	2		200										892	
225	1	BRIGHTWELL	TH	M	LO	BQ	1		233	400	153			1583	3518	DC	ZW	M	504	1250

1	2	3	4	5	6	7	8	9	10	11	12	13	14	15	16	17	18	19	20	21
226	1	BRINLEY	LU	M	LO	ME		1	'250	200					450	750	FE	WM	L	856	1315
227	1	BRINLEY	NI	M	EN	ME		2	262										857	
228	1	BRINLEY	SR	F				7			50									1354
229	1	BRINLEY	TH	M	LO	ES		2	100										859	1316
230	1	BRISCOE	TH	M	LO	UH		3	50						100	222	CL	LI	M		
231	1	BRISTOW	HE	M	SX	YE		1	50						50	83	PO	QU	L	385	
232	1	BROCKET	JO	M	LO	CL		2	100											256	
233	1	BROCKETT	TH	M	LO	PE		1	50						50	83	ST	QU	L	910	
234	1	BROKING	NI	M	EN	ME		3	200						345	482	EG	KI	L	1021	
235	1	BROMLEY	MT	W	LE	LA		5			20										
236	1	BROMWICH	JO	M	LO			7	100											714	
237	1	BROOKE	WM	M		MT		7		200											1220
238	1	BROOMER	RI	M	LO			1	25						25	55	PO	QU	L	373	
239	1	BROWKER	TH	M	SA	GE		1	200						200	617	UI	DN	U	763	
240	1	BROWN	JO	M	LO			2	600											88	
241	1	BROWNE		M		CP		5	600												
242	1	BROWNE	GE	M	EX	YE		2	25											395	
243	1	BROWNE	HG	M				1		100					100	106	RA	WM	L		1337
244	1	BROWNE	HU	M	LO	GI		7	305											572	
245	1	BROWNE	JO	M	LO	LE		2	100											751	
246	1	BROWNE	JO	M	SO			2	75											772	
247	1	BROWNE	JO	M	DO	ES	1	7	450											117	
248	1	BROWNE	RI	M	LO	WM	4	7	600											711	
249	1	BROWNE	SA	M	LO	CU		2	50	50										863	1317
250	1	BROWNE	TH	M	LO			7	50	500										804	1251
251	1	BUCKLAND	JO	M	SO			1	37						50	51	MY	WM	L	1103	
252	1	BULLER	GE	M	CO		1	1	600						600	1333	ZL	ZW	M	110	
253	1	BUNCE	JA	M	LO	LE	2	2	600	200										710	1279
254	1	BUNSTON	WM	M	EN			3	25						25	41	LU	EM	L	1034	
255	1	BURGES	CU	M	HT	CL		1	700						700	1555	MD	TI	M	508	
256	1	BURGIS	JA	M	SO			7	10											1110	
257	1	BURKETT	MN	M	NT	CL		1	100						100	222	CO	ZW	M	1166	
258	1	BURLACE	JO	M		GE		7	25											921	
259	1	BURLACE	JO	M	BU			7	50											1035	
260	1	BURROUGHS	JI	M				2		100										1333	
261	1	BURTON	SI	M	LO	ST		1	50						50	111	DC	ZW	M	549	
262	1	BUTCHERS	CO					5				19									
263	1	BYE	TH	M	LO	TC		2	25											924	
264	1	BYFIELD	AD	M	LO	CL		2	50											1158	840
265	1	BYRD	WM	M	LO	PS		5				10									
266	1	CAGE	WM	M	SF		1	2	300											82	
267	1	CAMBELL	JA	M		ES	1	7	300											114	
268	1	CAMPHIELD	NA	M		CP		7	100											694	
269	1	CANNOCKT	AA	F	SR			7	25											1042	
270	1	CANTLIN	DA	M	LO	GR		1	25						25	42	SK	EM	L	265	
271	1	CARPENTER	JO	M				7	50											911	
272	1	CARPENTERS	CO		LO			3	36						72	122	CU	QU	L	514	
273	1	CARTER	ED	M	LO	GR		2	200											514	
274	1	CARTER	JO	M	LO	LE		1	50						50	83	JS	KI	L	245	
275	1	CARTER	RA	M	LO			2	100											425	
276	1	CARWITHEN	NI	M	EN	ME		2	50											995	
277	1	CARWITHEN	NI	M	EN			2	150											995	
278	1	CARYLL	JS	M	LO	CL		1	100						100	222	CO	ZW	M	860	
279	1	CASTELL	RI	M	LO	WL		2	120											322	
280	1	CATLIN	JO	M	HT	YE		2	25											269	
281	1	CAULIER	JA	M	LO	ME		2	200											1151	
282	1	CAVE	WM	M	EN			5	50											1034	
283	1	CAYCOTT	TH	M	SR			2	50			12								953	
284	1	CHAMBERLAIN	AM	M	LO	ME		1	300	500					625	1388	CN	LI	M	567	1258
285	1	CHAMBERLAIN	TH	M	LO	ME		1	300	500					975	2175	CN	LI	M	567	1258
286	1	CHAMBERS	HU	M	SO			7	3											866	
287	1	CHANDLER	RI	M	LO	HA		2	100											747	
288	1	CHAVENEY	HU	M	LE			1	100						100	137	IO	TI	M	669	
289	1	CHENEY	FR	M	BU			1	600						600	617	SW	QU	L	618	
290	1	CHESWICK	JA	M	YO			7	250											876	
291	1	CHEWNING	TH	M	LO	SK		1	100						245	544	IO	TI	M	318	
292	1	CHEYNEY	AA	W	LO			1	100						100	222	DC	ZW	M	249	
293	1	CHILD	JO	M	LO	WM		1	100						100	166	SL	EM	L	940	
294	1	CHILD	JO	M	SR			2	10											1051	
295	1	CHILD	RO	M				1	50						50	111	CO	ZW	M	406	
296	1	CHILLINGWORTH	RG	M	LO	FE		1	50						50	83	ST	QU	L	922	
297	1	CHURCH	MT	W	BR			5				30	3		30	41	CL	TI	M	1034	
298	1	CLAPHAM	JS	M	DV	ME		3	30						30	41	CL	TI	M	1034	
299	1	CLAPP	RI	M	DV	YE		7	200											1006	
300	1	CLARE	GL	M	EN	AR		5	10											1034	
301	1	CLARE	SF	M	LO	TC		1	50						50	83	ST	QU	L	354	
302	1	CLARKE	GE	M	LO	MT		1	100	100	25				350	777	IO	TI	M	8	1190
302	2	CLARKE	GE												650	1059	MO	EM	L		

1	2	3	4	5	6	7	8	9	10	11	12	13	14	15	16	17	18	19	20	21
302	3	CLARKE	GE											100	166	KI	WM	L		
302	4	CLARKE	GE											262	389	SK	EM	L		
302	5	CLARKE	GE											125	577	AD	DN	U		
302	6	CLARKE	GE											2200	4892	CL	TI	M		
302	7	CLARKE	GE											250	416	JS	KI	L		
302	8	CLARKE	GE											1000	2222	MD	TI	M		
302	9	CLARKE	GE											680	1133	LU	EM	L		
303	1	CLARKE	JA	M			1		200					200	205	DM	WM	L	494	
304	1	CLARKE	JA	M	MX	MC	2		100										403	1185
305	1	CLARKE	JO	M	SF	IR	1		300	200				1000	1666	SW	QU	L	177	1206
305	2	CLARKE	JO	M	SF									400	888	CO	ZW	M	177	1206
306	1	CLARKE	RA	M	DR		2		200										574	
307	1	CLARKE	RA	M		SK	7		75										1183	
308	1	CLARKE	RO	M	EN		5		50										1034	
309	1	CLARKE	SA	M	EN	ME	1	1	100					300	666	IO	TI	M	1010	
310	1	CLARKE	SA	M	WA	CL	7		25										1091	
311	1	CLARKE JR	CR	M	EN	ME	3		200					435	643	EG	KI	L	992	
311	2	CLARKE JR	CR	M	EN		5		75											
312	1	CLAY	RG	M	LO	FA	2		100										729	
313	1	CLAYDON	JO	M	LO		1		200					200	205	DM	WM	L	675	
314	1	CLEMENT	GG	M	LO	ME	1	1	200	1300	600			50		ZW	ZW	M	850	1313
314	2	CLEMENT	GG											2000		GA	KI	L		
314	3	CLEMENT	GG											3000		GA	KI	L		
315	1	CLOTWORTHY	JO	M		KN	1	1	1000					1120	5560	MA	AN	U	1170	
316	1	CLUTTERBUCK	RI	M	LO	MC	1		700	200				900	2000	MD	TI	M	314	1223
317	1	COBB	JO	M	LO	MT	1			50	12			125	208	EG	KI	L		1347
318	1	COCK	JO	M			1		100					100	500	ON	AR	U	480	
319	1	COCK	TH	M	LO	SA	1		100					200	333	NA	EM	L	312	
320	1	COCKS	JA	M	LO	MT	2		50										696	
321	1	COCKS	RI	M	LO	ME	2		50										769	
322	1	COFFIN	TH	M	LO	MT	5						15						1034	
323	1	COGAN	HU	M	DV	ME	5		100										1034	
324	1	COISH	RI	M	LO	SK	2		240	120		60,		600	1000	KI	WM	L	184	1208
325	1	COLBRON	HE	M	LO	SC	2		25										486	
326	1	COLCHESTER	OS	M	LO	MT	2			37		6							240	
327	1	COLE	FR	M	LO	ME	1			25		6		62	312	ON	AR	U	1164	
328	1	COLE	PE	M	LO		7		50										539	
329	1	COLE	TH	M	LO	MT	1		300			75		300	500	MY	WM	L	53	
330	1	COLES	HE	M			1		50					100	222	DC	ZW	M	288	
331	1	COLLETT	RI	M	LO	HA	2		100		25								9	
332	1	COLLIER	JS	M	LO	GR	1		50		12			125	208	ST	QU	L	944	
333	1	COLLINS	FR	M	LO	SK	1		100		50	37		412	687	BA	KI	L	625	1262
334	1	COLLOCOTT	WM	M	EN		5		5										1034	
335	1	COLTMAN	JO	M	LO	HA	2		100										683	
336	1	CONNOCK	AA	F	SR		5		50											
337	1	COOKE	CU	M		VI	7		100										904	
338	1	COOKE	ED	M	LO	AP	2		675		169								464	
339	1	COOKE	TH	M	LO	GO	1		300					300	500	LU	EM	L	684	
340	1	COOMB	JO	M	DV		7		37										901	
341	1	COOMB	TH	M	DV		7		20										977	
342	1	COOMBES	AS	M			2		25										377	
343	1	COOP	WM	M			7			50										1302
344	1	COOPER	AY	M			7		150										89	
345	1	COOPER	SA	M	LO	FM	1		100	50				100	500	DU	AN	U	659	1215
346	1	COOPER	WI	M	LO	HA	1		100					100	222	DC	ZW	M	819	
347	1	CORBETT	MN	M	NF	ES	1	1	200			50		150	217	MR	QU	L	122	
347	2	CORBETT	MN											100	166	PD	QU	L	122	
347	3	CORBETT	MN	M										700	1166	RA	WM	L		
348	1	CORDELL	JO	M	LO	KN	2	5					200							
349	1	COREY	TH	M	LO	LW	2		300										217	
350	1	CORNISH	JO	M			7		10										1123	
351	1	COULSON	JO	M	YO		2		200										855	
352	1	COXON	CL	M	LO	TA	1		50					50	111	DC	ZW	M	555	
353	1	CRANLEY	RI	M	LO		2			300										1340
354	1	CRESSY	SI	M	LO	GI	3		5					10	22	IK	TI	M		
355	1	GRESWICK	JA	M	YO		3		62					62	192	ON	AR	U		
356	1	CREW	AR	M	LO	HA	2		100										790	
357	1	CREW	JO	M			1	2	600										94	
358	1	CREW	RF	M			7		80										1188	
359	1	CREWE	AR	M	LO	HA	2		100										790	
360	1	CRICKNER	WM	M	SF	CE	2		600										178	
361	1	CRISPE	NI	M	LO	KN	1	1	900	1700				901	2002	CN	LI	M	138	1199
362	1	CRISPE	RI	M	KE	GE	1		600					600	1333	DC	ZW	M	563	1257
363	1	CRISPE	SA	M	LO	SA	2				850									1197
364	1	CROMWELL	OL	M	HU	GE	1	1	300	300				850	1257	EG	KI	L	72	1194
365	1	CROOKE	CH	M	BU	CL	1		225					225	500	IO	TI	M	239	
366	1	CROONE	HE	M	LO		2		200										585	
367	1	CROPLEY	ED	M	LO	ES	5				100									

N

1	2	3	4	5	6	7	8	9	10	11	12	13	14	15	16	17	18	19	20	21
368	1	CROSSING	PH	M	EN	ME	2		160										991	
369	1	CROSSING	TH	M	EN		2	5	100											
370	1	CROW	RI	M	SO		7		3										869	
371	1	CROWDER	TH	M	LO	MT	3		100						100	166	ST	QU	L		
372	1	CROWLEY	RO	M	LO	HA	1		75		25	25	1	250	1111	IL	TI	M	225	
373	1	CROWTHER	SA	M	LO	MT	7		100										931	
374	1	CULLEN	RI	M	EN		3	5	25										898	1034
375	1	CULMER	RI	M	KE	CL	1		200		50				250	416	LU	EM	L	1161	
375	2	CULMER	RI	M											250	416	SL	EM	L	1161	
376	1	CULPEPPER	JO	M	KE	KN	1	7	150										80	
377	1	CUNNINGHAM	TH	M			7			1800											1351
378	1	CURLE	JO	M			7		50										1114	
379	1	CURTIS	JO	M	SO		1		15		20		4	40	44	CL	TI	M	1106	
380	1	CURTIS	TH	M	SO		2		15		20		4						1106	
381	1	CUSTOM HOUSE					7		2000										1187	
382	1	DABBE	SA	M	LO	GR	1		75		25		4	100	102	EG	KI	L	186	
382	2	DABBE	SA	M											70	116	MO	EM	L		
383	1	DACRES	TH	M	KE	KN	1	2	600										95	
384	1	DANIELL	WM	M	LO	GO	1		100		8				100	222	IL	TI	M	144	
385	1	DARNELLY	RI	M	LO	HA	2		67		17								454	
385	2	DARNELLY	RI				2		100										454	227
386	1	DARTMOUTH	CA				1		2398						1518		RA	WM	L	891	
386	2	DARTMOUTH	CA												53	54	RA	WM	L	891	
387	1	DASHWOOD	FR	M			7		50										243	
388	1	DAVENPORT	HE	M		WM	2		25						25	41	ST	OU	L	305	
389	1	DAVES	JO	M	LO		7		6										451	
390	1	DAVEY	TH	M	SX		1		600						600	1333	MD	TI	M	438	
391	1	DAVIES	JO	M	LO	SK	5		6										891	
392	1	DAVIS	JP	M	LO		7		150										340	
393	1	DAVIS	TH	M			2		50										486	
394	1	DAVIS	WM	M	EN		3		10						10	10	PO	QU	L	1034	
395	1	DAVY	WM	M	NF	ME	1		150						200	333	CU	QU	L	1080	
396	1	DAWES	JO	M	LO	MC	1		100						400	888	EL	TI	M	259	
397	1	DAWES	RI	M	LO	PE	1		300						300	666	DC	ZW	M	300	
398	1	DAWES	RO	M	EX		1		300						300	666	CN	LI	M	214	
399	1	DAY	HE	M	LO	MC	1		200	200	25				350	777	IK	TI	M	235	1213
400	1	DEANE	TH	M	SO		3		20						20	27	PB	LI	M	1034	
401	1	DEANE	WM	M	SO		3		10						10	13	PB	LI	M	1034	
402	1	DEARDS	NA	M	LO	MT	2		50		12									244	
403	1	DELANOY	PE	M	LO	DY	1		100						100	166	ST	QU	L	768	
404	1	DELAWNE	G	M	LO	AP	5				50										
405	1	DELINE	PH	M	KE	CL	2		200											718	
406	1	DENNIS	AY	M	EN		3		40						40	41	PO	QU	L	1034	
407	1	DENNIS	SV	M	LO	DY	2		160										463	
408	1	DENNIS	TH	M	DV		3		50						50	68	MD	TI	M	1034	
409	1	DENT	GI	M	LO	SA	7		200										527	
410	1	DESKEENE	AM	M	LO	WE	7		200										440	
411	1	DETHICK	JO	M	LO	MC	1		200						200	333	SW	QU	L	550	
412	1	DIKE	WM	M	LO	IR	2		100										646	
413	1	DINGLEY	EZ	W	SR		1		60						60	100	PO	QU	L	1043	
414	1	DISNEY	TH	M	LO	GE	7		300										1146	
415	1	DITTON	MY	W	LO		7		100										890	
416	1	DOD	JO	M	LO	SA	2		200										389	
417	1	DOVER	GE	M	LO	AP	1		100		25				250	416	DM	WM	L	358	
418	1	DOVER JR.	DA	M	NF		7		50										1085	
419	1	DOVER SR.	DA	M	NF		7		200										1082	
420	1	DOWNE	AY	M	EN		5		53.										1034	
421	1	DOWNE	MK	M	EN	CL	5		50										1034	
422	1	DOWNING	CB	M	LO	CL	2		100										835	
423	1	DOWSE	AY	M	LO	HA	2		50										404	
424	1	DOYLEY	CH	M	LO	TC	2		100										397	
425	1	DRAKE	FR	M	BU	ES	1	1	200						200	206	KI	WM	L	121	
426	1	DRAKE	RG	M	PH		1		200		50				500	1111	IK	TI	M	897	
427	1	DRAKE	WM	M		KN	1	1	300										77	
428	1	DRAPER	MW	M	LO	ME	7		50										837	
429	1	DRING	AY	M	LO	MT	7		100										472	
430	1	DRING	RO	M			2		100										434	
431	1	DRING	SI	M	LO	IR	3		100						100	500	ON	AR	U		
432	1	DRURY	RI	M	LO		3				20				20		ZW	ZW	M		
433	1	DRYDEN	JO	M		KN	1	1	600						600	1000	EG	KI	L	123	
434	1	DUCANE	JO	M	LO		2		50										278	
435	1	DUKE	FR	M	WM		1		200						200	333	MO	EM	L	33	
436	1	DUN	SI	M	LO	IR	7		100										215	
437	1	DUPREE	DA	M	LO	ME	7		300										443	
438	1	DUQUESNE	PE	M	LO	ME	2		200										277	
439	1	DURRANT	WM	M	DV		5		5										1034	
440	1	DUTTON	MY	F	LO		5		100											
441	1	DYKE	JO	M	EN		3		10						10	10	PO	QU	L	1034	

1	2	3	4	5	6	7	8	9	10	11	12	13	14	15	16	17	18	19	20	21
442	1	DYKE	LS	M				7		5200										1352
443	1	EAMES	SA	M	LO	FA			2	100											734
444	1	EARLE	WA	M		KN	1		7	300											57
445	1	EAST	ED	M	LO	GO			1	100						100	166	MY	WM	L		685
446	1	EATON	JO	M	LO	MT			2	50												697
447	1	EDEN	TH	M	CA	LW	1		7	600												24
448	1	EDLIN	SA	M	MX	GE			1	100						100	166	SK	EM	L		32
449	1	EDWARDS	JO	M	LO	TA			2	40												1165
450	1	ELDRED	HE	M	LO	CW			2		100											1359
451	1	ELFORD	JO	M	DV				5	75												1034
452	1	ELIE	RO	M	LO	MC			7	100												649
453	1	ELLIOTT	SA	M	LO	ME			1	200						200	333	DE	EM	L		326
454	1	ELLIS	JO	M	EN				3	10						10	10	PO	QU	L		1034
455	1	ELLIS	RO	M	MC				2		300											1266
456	1	ELLISTON	JO	M	EX				7	100												1136
457	1	ELMSTON	HE	M	DV				3	20						25	55	MD	TI	M		1034
458	1	ELWILL	JO	M	EN	ME			5	32												1034
459	1	EMES JR.	JO	M	WA				7	25												1094
460	1	ENDERBY	DA	M	MX	TN			1	50						100	222	CO	ZW	M	38	405
460	2	ENDERBY	DA							50											38	405
461	1	ESTWICK	ST	M	LO	GI	2		1	100	100					800	1777	CN	LI	M		589
462	1	EVANS	JO	M	SR	PH			2	50												1062
463	1	EVANS	RI	M	EN				1	400						400	666	ST	QU	L		1018
464	1	EVELEIGH	NI	M	EN	ME			5	30												1034
465	1	EVELYN	EZ	F	SR				2	100												1041
466	1	EVELYN	JO	M	SR	KN	1		2	600												52
467	1	EWELIN	JO	M	LO	LW			7	600												105
468	1	EWER	GE	M	LO	FM			1	50						50	83	SK	EM	L		946
469	1	EYRES	TH	M	LO				3	100						200	444	MD	TI	M		
470	1	FALDO	HE	M	LO	HA			2	200												231
471	1	FANE	AY	M	SR				7	25												1040
472	1	FARMER	DV	M	NT				2	310												
473	1	FARMER	GE	M	LO	LW			1	600						600	617	KI	WM	L		622
474	1	FARRINGTON	CO	M	LO	ME			1	200						500	833	EG	KI	L		210
474	2	FARRINGTON	CD	M	LO	ME			5			50										
475	1	FARRINGTON	WM	M	LO	ME			2	200		50				500	833	EG	KI	L		206
476	1	FARTHING	JO	M	LO	CO			2	50		12										907
477	1	FARWELL	JO	M	BU	KN			7	100												308
478	1	FAWNE	LK	M	LO	ST			2	50												401
479	1	FEATHERSTON	HE	M	LO	ST			1	1200						1200	2000	SW	QU	L		557
480	1	FELL	WM	M	DV	ME			5	70												1034
481	1	FENTON	JO	M	LO				7	100												286
482	1	FERRIS	SA	M					2	160												1358
483	1	FEWSTER	WM	M	SR				1	150	50					150	750	UI	DN	U	624	1261
484	1	FIELD	JO	M	EX				1	50						50	111	CN	LI	M		779
485	1	FIELD	NI	M	DV				3	25						25	41	MY	WM	L		1034
486	1	FIENNES	NL	M			1		1	300						300	500	KI	WM	L		97
487	1	FIGG	VL	M	LO	AP			1	100						100	166	CU	QU	L		200
488	1	FINCH	FR	M	LO	CW			1	100						200	444	IO	TI	M		363
489	1	FISHER	JA	M	SR				1	25						25	42	SK	EM	L		264
490	1	FISKE	JO	M	SF				7	100												880
491	1	FISKE	WM	M	SF				2	200												879
492	1	FISSENDEN	GE	M	LO	ME			2	50												912
493	1	FLEMING	SN	F	EN				5	10												1034
494	1	FLETCHER	ED	M					2	100												304
495	1	FLETCHER	JA	M	LO	HA			1	200						200	444	IL	TI	M		329
496	1	FLETCHER	JO	M	LO	UP			2	120												320
497	1	FLETCHER	PL	M	DR				1	100						100	500	BE	AN	U		578
498	1	FLETCHER	WM	M	LO	CW			2	100												546
499	1	FLETCHER	WM	M	LO	FM			1	200	300					500	833	KI	WM	L	228	1211
500	1	FLOYD	RI	M	LO	GI			3	150		42				1050	1750	RA	WM	L		
501	1	FOLLIOT	DA	M	DV				7	10												1027
502	1	FOOT	RO	M	LO	GR			2		100											1328
503	1	FOOTE	TH	M	LO	GR			2	600	100										469	1243
504	1	FORD	FR	M	SO				7	6												1109
505	1	FORD	RI	M	LO	ME			5	100												
506	1	FOSTER	IZ	M	LO	GR			2	50		12										1145
507	1	FOUNTAIN	JO	M	LG				1	300							350	GA	KI	L		167
508	1	FOUNTAIN	TH	M	BU		1		2	200												66
509	1	FOWKE	JO	M	LO		2		1	600						600	1333	IK	TI	M		152
510	1	FOWLER	JO	M	LO	CW			2	200												604
511	1	FOWLER	RO	M	DV				2	60												1024
512	1	FOX	CH	M	LO	LE			1	50						50	83	SK	EM	L		948
513	1	FOXWELL	PH	M	EN				5	100												1034
514	1	FRANCIS	JO	M	SO				1	50						50	68	CL	TI	M		1127
515	1	FRANKLIN	JO	M	WI	KN	1		7	600												42
516	1	FREEMAN	TH	M					2	200												492
517	1	FRENCH	JO	M					3	67		17				600	1000	NA	EM	L		227

1	2	3	4	5	6	7	8	9	10	11	12	13	14	15	16	17	18	19	20	21
518	1	FRENCH	WM	M	CA	PH		2	50	150									799	1288
519	1	FRERE	TB	M	NF	ES		1	1000					1000	5000	LE	DN	U	1184	
520	1	FRITH	WM	M				5	67		17								227	
521	1	FRYER	FR	M	DV			3	15					15	15	EG	KI	L	1034	
522	1	GALLILEE	TH	M	LO			2	60		35								1140	
523	1	GALTON	GA	M	LO	ST		2	25										192	
524	1	GARDINER	RI	M				2	100										68	
525	1	GARDNER	JO	M	EX			1	50					50	111	CN	LI	M	783	
526	1	GARDNER	RO	M	LO	ES		7	150										644	
527	1	GARDNER	SA	M	WO		1	2	250										1174	
528	1	GARLAND	RO	M	LO	ME		3	275		200			750	1666	MD	TI	M		
529	1	GARNALL	RI	M	hA			7	25										1096	
530	1	GARNER	RO	M	LI			1	200					200	333	LU	EM	L	598	
531	1	GARNER	RO	M	LO	ME		7		400										1338
532	1	GARRARD	JC	M	KN		2	2	600										136	
533	1	GARTH	JO	M	SR			1	100					100	166	DE	EM	L	1039	
534	1	GASKELL	AD	M	LA	LD		1	50					50	111	CN	LI	M	1098	
535	1	GASTRELL	JS	M	OX	CL		7	7										1067	
536	1	GAUDEN	D.	M	LO			7		300										1265
537	1	GAY	JO	M	SO			1	25					25	77	DU	AN	U	1119	
538	1	GEARING SR	JC	M	LO	GR		2	75										531	
539	1	GERRARD	GL	M	MX	KN	1	1	600					600	1000	SL	EM	L	29	
540	1	GIBBES	RI	M	BU			2	200										141	
541	1	GIBBS	CR	M	LO	CW		1	50					50	83	EG	KI	L	913	
542	1	GIBBS	RO	M	EN			3	7					7	6	PO	QU	L	1034	
543	1	GIBBS	WM	M	LO	GO		1	200		50			500	1110	CO	ZW	M	146	
544	1	GIFFRY	R	W	EN			5	25										1034	
545	1	GILES	MS	M	SX	CL		2	50										972	
546	1	GILL	AX	M	IR			7	6										337	
547	1	GIPPS	GE	M	LE	CL		2	100										151	
548	1	GIPPS	RI					2	200										141	
549	1	GITTING	.MC	M	LO	MT		7	100										416	
550	1	GITTINGS	ED	M	LO	PS		2	100	100				100	100	ZL	ZW	L	667	1269
551	1	GLANVILLE	WM	M			1	2	600										83	
552	1	GLOUCESTER	CA					3	1350					1275	2124	ST	QU	L	893	
553	1	GOADE	CR	M	LO	CL		2	100	100									1155	1323
554	1	GODDARD	JO	M	LO	PH		1	100		25			100	166	MO	EM	L	666	
555	1	GODDARD	WM	M	LO	PH		1	100					100	102	EG	KI	L	757	
556	1	GODFREY	JS	M	LO			7	25										736	
557	1	GODFREY	TH	M	KE			5			50									
558	1	GODSDEN	HE	M	SR	MC		1	100					100	222	1K	TI	M	171	
559	1	GOMESDON	WM	M				7		300										1339
560	1	GOOD	EL	M	LO	HO		1	100					100	222	DC	ZW	M	652	
561	1	GOODIER	ME	M	CV	ME		7		200										1345
562	1	GOODING	WM	M	DV			5	20										1034	
563	1	GOODMAN	JO	M	LO			2	50					50	83	SL	EM	L	748	
564	1	GOODWIN	AR	M	LO		1	2	400										62	
565	1	GOODWIN	BJ	M	ES			3	300					525	875	KI	WM	L		
566	1	GOODWIN	JO	M	LO	CL		5	50											
567	1	GOODWIN	JO	M	LO			7	100										355	
568	1	GOODWIN	RO	M	ES		1	1	300					525	875	KI	WM	L	106	
569	1	GOSWELL	JO	M	EN	BS		2	50										985	
570	1	GOUCH	WM	M				7	100										882	
571	1	GOUGE	TH	M	LO	CL		7	600										661	
572	1	GOULD	IZ	M	LO	DR		1	100		50			400	666	LU	EM	L	428	
573	1	GOULD	JA	M	EN			2	200										1020	
574	1	GRANNOW	NL	M	LO	MT		7	25										376	
575	1	GRANT	HE	M	LO	DR		2	60		15								491	
576	1	GRANTHAM	WM	M	MX	IR		2	50		6								680	
577	1	GRAVES	RI	M	LO	GE		1	200					200	333	MU	EM	L	674	
578	1	GRAVES	WM	M	LO	BL		2	100										350	
579	1	GREENHILL	WM	M	LO	CL		1	100	100				100	500	UI	DN	U	705	1277
580	1	GREENINGS	WM	M	EN			3	5					5	5	PO	QU	L	1034	
581	1	GREENSMITH	JO	M	LO	MT		1	300					300	500	EG	KI	L	844	
582	1	GREENSMITH	PL	M	SX			2			50									1346
583	1	GREENWELL	RO	M	LO	GR		2	50										538	
584	1	GREGSON	GE	M	CW			2	50										292	
585	1	GREGSON	WM	M	MT			2	100										293	
586	1	GREY	CR	M	CV			3	20					20	33	ST	QU	L	1034	
587	1	GROCER	JA	M	BU	BU		5	54											
588	1	GROCER	JO	M	SF			1	100					100	222	CO	ZW	M	883	
589	1	GROVE	HG	M	SF			1	100		50			100	222	CO	ZW	M	179	1207
590	1	GULSON	HE	M	LO	PS		2	100										671	
591	1	GUNNING	JO	M	BS			1	1000					1000	1666	RA	WM	L	1171	
592	1	GUNSTON	WM	M	LO	FA		1	100					100	166	RA	WM	L	730	
593	1	GUPWELL	JO	M.	EN			5	10										1034	
594	1	GURDON	JO	M			1	2	1000										41	
595	1	GUY	JO	M	DV			3	100					100	166	JS	KI	L	1034	

1	2	3	4	5	6	7	8	9	10	11	12	13	14	15	16	17	18	19	20	21
596	1	GUY	NI	M				1	200					200	444	IL	TI	M	485	
597	1	HALES	ED	M		KN	1	1	1200					1199	5996	AR	AR	U	104	
598	1	HALES	RO	M	OX	GE		1	1200					1200	2000	KI	WM	L	566	
599	1	HALL	GY	M	LO	CO		1	50					50	83	RA	WM	L	748	
600	1	HALL	JO	M	SF			5			100									
601	1	HALL	NL	M	LO	SK		2	100	25									516	
602	1	HALL	TH	M	LO	CO		2	100										234	
603	1	HALLOWES	NA	M		DR	1	2	300										4	
604	1	HALSTEAD	LU	M	LO	ES	2	7	150										154	
605	1	HAMOND	JO	M		GE		3	200					200	206	KI	WM	L		
606	1	HAMPDEN	JO	M	BU		1	2	1000										44	
607	1	HAMPSON	HE	M	LO	MT		1	200					400	2000	ON	AR	U	610	
608	1	HAMPSON	TH	M	BU	KN		1	600					40	200	ON	AR	U	725	
609	1	HAMPTON	WM	M	SR	CL		1	100					100	222	CN	LI	M	616	
610	1	HANMER	JN	M	EN			3	26					26	27	PO	CU	L	1034	
611	1	HARDING	AC	F				2	100										636	
612	1	HARDING	GI	M	LO	BA		1	450	50				1065	2179	CN	LI	M	634	
612	2	HARDING	GI											950	2111	CY	LI	M		
613	1	HARDING	JO	M				7	100										1139	
614	1	HARDING	TH	M	LO	WH		1	200	100				970	2155	CY	LI	M	633	1138
615	1	HARDING	WM	M				1	100					280	622	CY	LI	M	635	
616	1	HARDY	NL	M	LO			7	50										959	
617	1	HARMAN	RI	M	NF		1	1	300					100	102	MR	QU	L	27	
618	1	HARPER	JO	M	LO	FM		5	100	25										
619	1	HARRIMAN	WM	M	LO	MT		2	100										181	
620	1	HARRINGTON	JA	F	LI	LA		1	50					150	154	NA	EM	L	870	
621	1	HARRINGTON	JA	M	LI			2	25			50	4						873	
622	1	HARRINGTON	JO	M		SO	1	1	400					200	444	ZL	ZW	M	1102	
623	1	HARRINGTON	WM	M	LI			2	25			50	4						874	
624	1	HARRIS	JO	M	LO	GI		2	100	50									821	1304
625	1	HARRIS	TH	M	LO	ME		2	100										533	
626	1	HARRIS	TH	M	LO	GR		2	100										545	
627	1	HARRISON	EM	M	LO	EM		1	200		50			600	1333	CY	LI	M	630	
628	1	HARRISON	JO	M	HT	KN	1	2	300					450	749	EG	KI	L	98	
629	1	HARRISON	WM	M	HT			1	150										99	
630	1	HARRISON	WM	M	LO			2	100										560	
631	1	HARSNETT	SA	M	LO	GR		2	25	150									805	1292
632	1	HART	A·	M	DV	MC		2	20										1025	
633	1	HART	SA	M	LO	IR		2	150										593	
634	1	HART	SR	F				2	50					50	110	CL	TI	M	594	
635	1	HARTFORD	H.	M	SR	CL		7	18										1046	
636	1	HARTOPP	TH	M		KN		5			200									
637	1	HARVEY	EM	M	LO	DR		2	150	100									241	1214
638	1	HARWELL	HE.	M	LO	HA		1	100					100	166	GA	KI	L	744	
639	1	HASLERIG	AR	M		KN	1	7	1000	600								.	76	1195
640	1	HASTINGS	HE	M	SR			2	100					100	102	MO	EM	L	339	
641	1	HATT	JO	M	LO	GE		1	300					600	1333	MD	TI	M	330	
642	1	HATTON	TH	M	LO	LW		7	10										760	
643	1	HAUGHTON	RO	M	LO			7	100										727	
644	1	HAULE	GE	M	KE	GE		1	250					250	555	DC	ZW	M	562	
645	1	HAWARD	NI	M	LO	GR		1	50					100	222	EL	TI	M	370	
646	1	HAWKES	HE	M	LO	TC		1	50		12			125	208	ST	QU	L	915	
647	1	HAWKINS	WM	M	LO	MT		1	1250	1000	312			1758	8793	AD	DN	U	709	1278
647	2	HAWKINS	WM											4929	23602	UI	DN	U	709	
648	1	HAYES	JA	M	LO	GR		1	100					100	222	EL	TI	M	311	
649	1	HAYES	RO	M	LO	AR		2	200										542	
650	1	HAYNES	WM	M	LO	WH		5			5									
651	1	HAYWARD	NI	M	LO			5	50											
652	1	HAZLEBURT	PE	M	NF			7	50										1083	
653	1	HEARD	JO	M	EN			3	20					20	20	PO	QU	L	1034	
654	1	HEARNE	JI	M	HT	CL		1	300					300	500	MR	QU	L	739	1232
654	2	HEARNE	JI	M	HT	CL													338	
655	1	HEATHCOTT	GC	M		DR		1	25					25	34	EL	TI	M	795	
656	1	HEATHCOTT	WM	M		DR		1	100					100	500	BE	AN	U	577	
657	1	HEATHER	WM	M	SR	YE		1	50		8			150	499	IK	TI	M	964	
657	2	HEATHER	WM	M										75		IK	TI	M	964	
658	1	HENLEY	GE	M	LO	ME		2	300										569	
659	1	HENLEY	HE	M	EN	ME		2	100										1029	
660	1	HENLEY	RO	M				7	300										570	
661	1	HENMAN	WM	M		MT		1	150					150	250	MY	WM	L	56.	
662	1	HENSON	ED	M	LO	GE		7	50										765	
663	1	HERBERT 4EP	PH	M	LO		1	7	600										135	
664	1	HERFORD	HR	M	SR			3	25					25	25	MO	EM	L		
665	1	HERMAN	RA	M	EN	GO	2	2	25										1034	
666	1	HERRING	MI	M	LO	HA	2	1	400	200				900	2000	EL	TI	M	843	1312
667	1	HEVENINGHAM	WM	M			1	1	600					600	1000	GA	KI	M	22	
667	2	HEVENINGHAM	WM						1200										23	
668	1	HICCOCKS	WM	M	LO	BR		1		400	100			602	1004	ST	QU	L	933	1320

Appendix A

1	*2*	*3*	*4*	*5*	*6*	*7*	*8*	*9*	*10*	*11*	*12*	*13*	*14*	*15*	*16*	*17*	*18*	*19*	*20*	*21*
669	1	HICKMAN	HE	M	LO	SA		2	200										540	
670	1	HIGGINS	JO	M	WO			2	40										884	
671	1	HIGGINS	RI	M	LO	CO		1	50		12			125	208	SK	EM	U	929	
672	1	HIGHGATE	ED	M				3	25					25	125	MA	AN	U		
673	1	HILDESLEY	MR	M	LO	VI		2	100										356	
674	1	HILL	HU	M	LO	MC		5			25									
675	1	HILL	RG	M	SO		1	2	200										1168	
676	1	HILL	RI	M	LO	CO		1	200					250	555	CL	TI	M	541	
677	1	HILL	RI	M	LO	ME		2		700										1336
678	1	HILL	RI	M	LO	DR		2	200										168	
679	1	HILL	WM	M	SR			7	25										655	
680	1	HIPPESLEY	ED	M	SO			7	6										1108	
681	1	HIPPESLEY	JO	M	SO			7	25										1128	
682	1	HIPPESLEY	RI	M	SO			7	6										1107	
683	1	HIPPESLEY	TH	M	SO			2	25										1105	
684	1	HITCHCOCK	WM	M	LO	MT		1	150					350	583	MY	WM	L	55	
685	1	HOARE	WM	M	WM			1	25			6		62	104	MO	EM	L	687	
686	1	HOBART	JO	M	NF	KN	1	7	600										1037	
687	1	HOBSON	WM	M	LO	HA		1	100		25			250	416	RA	WM	L	691	
688	1	HOBSON	WM	M	LO	GR		2	50		12								951	
689	1	HODGES	TH	M	LO	ME		1	600					600	1000	DE	EM	L	327	
690	1	HODGSON	ED	M	LO	GO		2	100		25								643	
691	1	HODILOW	JO	M	LO	BS		2	25										435	
692	1	HODILOW	RI	M	LO	GO		1	25					50	111	IO	TI	M	436	
693	1	HOLCOMBE	EZ	F	EN			5	5											
694	1	HOLLAND	CU	M		ES	1	1	600					300	666	CO	ZW	M	96	
695	1	HOLLAND	JO	M	LO	GE		1	400	100				1600	2666	BA	KI	L	163	
696	1	HOLLMAN	MA	M	DV			3	10					10	13	KE	LI	M	1034	
697	1	HOLMAN	GA	M	SR			2	100										617	
698	1	HOLMAN	RO	M	SR			2	100										615	
699	1	HOLT	PE	M	LA			2	50										1098	
700	1	HOLWILL	JO	M	EN			5	40										1034	
701	1	HONIWOOD	ED	M	LO	IR		2	100		25								845	
702	1	HONOR	JO	M	LO	PS		2	600		150			1500	2459	BA	KI	L	713	
703	1	HOPING	WM	M	EN			5	50										1034	
704	1	HOPPING	CH	M	EN	AR		1	100					100	166	EG	KI	L	974	
705	1	HORE	RO	M	DV			2	50										998	
706	1	HOTCHKIS	TH	M	hI	CL		2	20										1143	
707	1	HOUBELON	JA	M	LO	ME		2	600		50								274	
708	1	HOUBELON	JA	M	LO	DY		2	50										275	
709	1	HOUBLON	PE	M	LO	DY		2	200										279	
710	1	HOUGHTON	JO	M	LO	FM		5	10											
711	1	HOUGHTON	RO	M	LO	BR		2		400	80									1281
712	1	HOUSE	TH	M				7	50										270	
713	1	HOVELL	HG	M	LO	GR		2	200	100									605	1260
714	1	HOW	TH	M	EX	.		2	300										218	
715	1	HOXTON	JO	M	LO	SH		1	100					100	102	CU	QU	L	216	
716	1	HOYLE	TH	M	YO		1	2	450			150	4						128	
717	1	HUBBARD	WI	M	LO	MT		1	100					100	222	IK	TI	M	746	
718	1	HUDSON	GE	M	LO	HA			100					100	500	LE	DN	U	460	
719	1	HUDSON	PE	M	LO	UP		2	25					25	125	UI	DN	U	817	
720	1	HUDSON	TH	M	LO	SK		2	100										903	
721	1	HUGHES	GE	M	LO	CL		1	100					100	500	MA	AN	U	721	
722	1	HUMPHREY	JO	M	LO	EM		1	50					50	111	DC	ZW	M	943	
723	1	HUMPHRIES	ML	M	LO	IR		1	100					100	500	LE	DN	U	461	
724	1	HUNT	RI	M	LO	MC		1	600	100	58			1380	3065	CN	LI	M	229	1212
725	1	HUNT	RI	M	LO	SK		1	300		25			450	750	LU	EM	L	830	
726	1	HUNTER	JO	M				1	100					100	222	EL	TI	M	479	
727	1	HURST	JO	M	LO	CK		1	225					480	800	LS	KI	L	466	
728	1	HUSSEY	WM	M	DO			1	100					100	166	KI	WM	L	1176	
729	1	HUSSEY JR.	TH	M				2		200				433	764	ZL	ZW	M		1327
729	2	HUSSEY SEN	TH							200										1251
730	1	HUSSEY SEN.	TH	M	LO	GR	1	1	233	200				200	333	DM	WM	L	505	1327
731	1	HUTCHINS	TH	M	LO	ME		2	400					400	2000	LE	DN	U	544	
732	1	HUTCHINSON	RI	M	LO	IR		1	100	100	50			760	1466	IO	TI	M	825	1306
733	1	HYLAND	SA	M				7	50										955	
734	1	HYNDE	JO	M	LO	MT		2	25										375	
735	1	ILLINGWORTH	TH	M	LA			3	60					60	100	FE	WM	L		
736	1	INGHAM	NI	M	EX			5	40											
737	1	IRONS	RI	M				1	25					25	55	DC	ZW	M	296	
738	1	IRONS	TH	M	LO			1	60					60	133	DC	ZW	M	295	
739	1	ISAACK	NI	M	EN			2	100	100									894	1319
740	1	IVATT	TH	M	DV			2	450										900	
741	1	IVERY	SA	M	LO	ME		7	300										595	
742	1	JACKSON	AM	M		CL		2	300										189	
743	1	JACKSON	AX	M	LO	GO		1	100					100	166	NA	EM	L	150	
744	1	JACKSON	JS	M				4		100					100	106	RA	WM	L		1337
745	1	JACKSON	TH	M	LO	PE		1	100					100	222	IO	TI	M	836	

1	2	3	4	5	6	7	8	9	10	11	12	13	14	15	16	17	18	19	20	21
746	1	JAQUES	JS	M	LO	BR		1	300		75			750	1666	CL	TI	M	895	
747	1	JEFFERIES	JO	M	LO	GR		1	100					100	500	LE	DN	U	459	
748	1	JENKINS	ME	M	LO	CE		1	200	100				200	333	MY	WM	L	383	1234
749	1	JENNER	TH	M	LO	GR		1	10		2			25	55	CO	ZW	M	1177	
750	1	JENNY	CR	M	LO	DR		2	200										511	
751	1	JENNY	WM	M	LO	ME		1	200					200	333	NA	EM	L	509	
752	1	JESSON	JO	M	ES		1	7	75										127	
753	1	JESSON	WM	M	LO	MT	1	2	100		27	10	2						788	
754	1	JOHNS	AM	M	DV			3	10					10	13	KE	LI	M	1034	
755	1	JOHNS	WM	M	EN			3	10					.10	10	PO	QU	L	1034	
756	1	JOHNSON	JO	M	LO	MT		5	50											
757	1	JOHNSON	JO	M	WA			7	25										1095	
758	1	JOHNSON	TH	M	NF	ME		1	150					150	250	CU	QU	L	1078	
759	1	JONES	AX	M	LO	ME		2	200										467	
760	1	JONES	JO	M	EN	GE		2	100										861	
761	1	JONES	JO	M	LO	MT		7	200										664	
762	1	JONES	OW	M	LO	PE		1	100					100	222	DC	ZW	M	301	
763	1	JOSEPH	RO	M	KE			7	50										450	
764	1	JURIN	AM	M	LO	ME		2	100										431	
765	1	JURIN	IZ	M	LO	ME		1	100					100	222	CN	LI	M	430	
766	1	JURIN	JO	M	LO	ME		1	300	200				650	1444	CN	LI	M	429	1238
767	1	JUXON	AR	M	LO	SA		1	200					200	333	DE	EM	L	410	
768	1	JUXON	JO	M	SR	GE		1	200	200				200	333	DE	EM	L	411	1235
769	1	JUXON	TH	M	LO	MT		1	200					1075	1790	DE	EM	L	412	
769	2	JUXON	TH											200	333	NA	EM	L	412	
769	3	JUXON	TH											825	1327	CU	QU	L	412	
769	4	JUXON	TH											20		ZW	ZW	M	412	
770	1	KEEBLE	JS	M	LO	FM		5			10									
771	1	KENDALL	WM	M	LO	MT		5	300											
772	1	KENDRICK	JO	M	LO	GR		1	700					700	1555	IO	TI	M	453	
773	1	KENTISH	TH	M	HT	CL		2	200					200	444	CN	LI	M	770	
774	1	KERKHAM	RO	M	LO			1	50					50	111	EL	TI	M	345	
775	1	KERRIDGE	TH	M	LO	ME		1	400					400	888	EL	TI	M	535	
776	1	KEY	IZ	M	SF			5			12									
777	1	KEYNES	JO	M	WI			2	80										872	
778	1	KIDDERMINSTER	EM	M	LO	GE		1	100					100	500	LE	DN	U	456	
779	1	KILBY	JO	M	HT	YE		1	50					50	83	LU	EM	L	271	
780	1	KING	AR	M				1		100				100	106	RA	WM	L		1337
781	1	KING	AW	M	DV			3	10					10	50	BE	AN	U	1034	
782	1	KING	BJ	M	HT			2	25										266	
783	1	KING	JO	M	LO	HA		1	100	50				150	333	DC	ZW	M	224	1275
784	1	KING	JO	M	EX			1	75					75	166	CN	LI	M	774	
785	1	KING	JO	M	HT	CL		2	50		4								1135	
786	1	KING	JO	M	HT	CL		2	100										147	
787	1	KING	JO	M	LO			7	50										476	
788	1	KING	MT	F	LO			1	50					50	83	ST	QU	L	939	
789	1	KING	NA	M				1	25					25	125	MA	AN	U	653	
790	1	KING	TH	M	LO	CA		1	100					100	380	ON	AR	U	862	
791	1	KINGSTON	FX	M	LO	ST		1	100		8			150	250	LU	EM	L	627	
792	1	KNAPP	NI	M	SR	GE		2	100										103	
793	1	KNIGHT	CR	M	DV	TA		2	10										1026	
794	1	KNIGHT	JO	M	LO	SR		2	10		2								965	
795	1	KNIGHT	JO	M	NF	ME		2	150										1079	
796	1	KNIGHT	TH	M	CX	ES		2	200										71	
797	1	KNIGHT	TH	M	BU	ES		2	100										64	
798	1	KNIGHTLEY	WM	M	SR			7	10										1064	
799	1	KNOWLES	JA	M	SR			2	12										1047	
800	1	LACEY	NA	M				2		50										1276
801	1	LACEY	RI	M	LO	HA		2	100	50									692	1276
802	1	LAKE	JO	M	LO	SK		2	200										344	
803	1	LAMB	TH	M	LO	LE		7	50										359	
804	1	LAMBELL	GL	M	LO	ME		1	125	500				625	1388	IO	TI	M	792	1287
805	1	LAMBELL	RO	M	LO	GR		2	200	100									596	1259
806	1	LAMBERT	RG	M	LO	WM		1	100					300	581	EL	TI	M	424	
807	1	LAMBERT	WM	M	SR	YE		1	100					100	222	EL	TI	M	762	
808	1	LAMOTT	JO	M	LO	ES		2	600										202	
809	1	LANE	JO	M	LO			2	200										17	
810	1	LANE	JO	M	LO	GR		1	233	200				433	767	CO	ZW	M	506	1252
811	1	LANE	TH	M	LO	LW	1	2	400										14	
812	1	LANE	WM	M	SX			1	600					600	1000	DE	EM	L	970	
813	1	LANGDON	DD	M	EN			3	10					10	13	KE	LI	M	1034	
814	1	LANGE	HU	M	EN			3	5					5	5	PO	QU	L	1034	
815	1	LANGHAM	SA	M	LO	GR		2	600	100									470	1244
816	1	LANGLEY	PE	M	MX			2	700										764	
817	1	LANGWORTH	SA	M	DV			3	10					10	50	BE	AN	U	1034	
818	1	LASINBY	RG	M	LO	HA		1	100					100	222	CL	TI	M	864	
819	1	LAWRENCE	WA	M	EN			3	13					13	18	KE	LI	M	1034	
820	1	LEADER	DD	M	LO			2		100										1325

1	2	3	4	5	6	7	8	9	10	11	12	13	14	15	16	17	18	19	20	21
821	1	LEADER	RI	M	LO	ME		2	100		16									1325
822	1	LEAVER	RO	M	LA	CL		1	200					200	444		CN	LI	M	1137	
823	1	LEE	JO	M	LO	SA		1	100			25	1	250		555	DC	ZW	M	298	
824	1	LEE	JO	M	LO	EW		1	25					25			RA	WM	L	784	
825	1	LEE	WA	M	LO	HA		2	150											6	
826	1	LEET	WM	M	LO	CO		2	20											583	
827	1	LEGGETT	WM	M	LO	LE		1	100		8			125		278	PO	QU	L	626	
828	1	LEIGH	TH	M	LO	FA		2	100											735	
829	1	LENTHALL	TH	M				1	200					200		333	DM	WM	L	493	
830	1	LEVERING	JO	M	EN	ME		7	100											996	
831	1	LEVETT	JA	M	SR	GR		1	10					45		46	LU	EM	L	1050	
832	1	LEVITT	WM	M	LO	WM		2	25											367	
833	1	LEWELLIN	RO	M	LO	SA		7	25	200										445	1241
834	1	LEWIN	DA	M	HI			7	200											754	
835	1	LEWIN	EM	M		MT		7	400											753	
836	1	LEWIS	DA	M	LO	MT		2	200											201.	
837	1	LIFKINS	HE	M	LO	ME		2	37											522	
838	1	LINCOLN	TH	M	NF			1	100					100		222	CO	ZW	M	881	
839	1	LINE	SA	M	LO	CA		5	100												
840	1	LING	JO	M	LO	SA		1	100					100		222	CL	TI	M	512	
841	1	LIPINCOTT	FR	M	EN			5	50											1034	
842	1	LIPPIATT	CR	M	WI			1	50					50		250	ON	AR	U	530	
843	1	LISLE	JO	M			1	2	600											47	
844	1	LITEMAKER	ED	M	LO	BA		2	100											290	
845	1	LITTLER	RI	M	LO	AP		2	100											812	1296
846	1	LITTLETON	ED	M	ST	LO	1	7	150											134	
847	1	LLOYD	AR	M	LO	HA		2	50											641	
848	1	LLOYD	CH	M	LO	DR		1	600					1000		2222	CN	LI	M	554	
848	2	LLOYD	CH											125		208	SW	QU	L		
849	1	LLOYD	JU	M	BS	ME		2	50											641	
850	1	LLOYD	RI	M	LO	GI		7	300											388	
851	1	LOCKE	JO	M	LO	BL		1	100					300		500	FE	WM	L	12	
852	1	LOCKIER	NI	M	LO	CL		1	100			25		250		555	CN	LI	M	232	
853	1	LOMBARD	JO	M	SO			5	10											1034	
854	1	LOME	JO	M	EN			5	20											1034	
855	1	LONDON	CO		LO			1	5000					2500		4166	SK	EM	L	1186	
855	2	LONDON	CO		LO			1	5000					5000		8332	DM	WM	L	1186	
856	1	LONG	WA	M	ES		1	7	300											111	
857	1	LONGE	WM	M	SO	ES		7	50											1115	
858	1	LORD	GE	M	LO			2	37											285	
859	1	LORDELL	JO	M	LO	ME		2	100											432	
860	1	LORING	WM	M	LO	GO		2	200											515.	
861	1	LORRARD	JO	M						200											1330
862	1	LOTON	RI	M	LO	BR		1	100					762		1629	DC	ZW	M	334	
863	1	LOUP	WM	M	LO	BS		1	100	1000				200		333	SW	QU	L	815	1299
864	1	LOVE	CR	M		CL		3	100					100		500	AR	AR	U		
865	1	LOVERING	JO	M	EN	ES		3	600					600		1333	DC	ZW	M	1034	
866	1	LOWE	WM	M	HF	CL		1	100					100		137	ZL	ZW	M	222	
867	1	LUCAS	ED	M	LO	PL		2	50											379	
868	1	LUCAS	JO	M	NF	ME		7												660	
869	1	LUMLEY	MA	M	EX	CL	1	2	1200											92	
870	1	LUXON	GE	M	EN			3	6					6		6	PO	QU	L	1034	
871	1	LYON	TH	M	HT			2	50					50		111	CN	LI	M	781	
872	1	MABERLEY	TH	M	LO	WE		2	50											954	
873	1	MACKWORTH	HU	M	SA			1	1786			114	4	1700		1749	GA	KI	L	1100	
874	1	MACUMBER	TH	M	LO	IR		1	50					50		250	BE	AN	U	982	
875	1	MACY	GE	M	EN	ME		2	50											995	
876	1	MALLOCK	RI	M	DV			2	100											1023	
877	1	MALTHUS	RO	M	BR	CE		1	120					120		333	IK	TI	M	408	
878	1	MAN	WM	M	LO			5			12										
879	1	MANN	TH	M	LO	ES		2	300											600	
880	1	MARKS	NI	M	EN			5	25											1034	
881	1	MARLOW	MI	M				2	50		6									701	
882	1	MARRIOTT	JO	M	LO	MT		1	.150	500				225		327	GA	KI	L	252	1215
883	1	MARRIOTT	TH	M				2	100											253	
884	1	MARSHALL	JA	M	EN	ME		1	400					400		666	EG	KI	L	987	
885	1	MARTIN	HE	M	BR	ES	1	7	300											115	
886	1	MARTIN	JA	M	LO	FM		2	600											553	
887	1	MARTIN	JO	M	SR			2	50											385	
888	1	MASCALL	JO	M	LO	HA		2	100											313	
889	1	MASHAM	WM	M	KN		1	1	600					600		1000	SL	EM	L	91	
890	1	MASSEY	RO	M	SR			7	20											1052	
891	1	MATHEW	JO	W	LO			1	100					100		222	EL	TI	M	349	
892	1	MATHEW	TH	M	DV	ME		1	150					150		333	EL	TI	M	1016	
893	1	MATHEWS	RG	M	DT		1	2	300											133	
894	1	MATHEWS	TH	M	LO	ME		2	150											386	
895	1	MATHIAS	JO	M	EN			5	25					25			LU	EM	LI	O	34
896	1	MAUDIT	IZ	M	EN	ME		5	25											1034	

1	2	3	4	5	6	7	8	9	10	11	12	13	14	15	16	17	18	19	20	21
897	1	MAY	TH	M	LO	CW	1		50					50	111	EL	TI	M	1173	
898	1	MAY	WM	M	EN	AR	3		14					14		EG	KI	L	1034	
899	1	MAYNARD	JO	M			1	7	300					300	5CC	RA	WM	L	571	
900	1	MAYNE	EZ	F	EN		5		5										1034	
901	1	MAYNE	JO	M	EN		5		5										1034	
902	1	MAYNE	PU	M	EN		5		5										1034	
903	1	MAYNE	RI	M	EN		2		100										997	
904	1	MAYNE	SA	M	EN		5		5										1034	
905	1	MAYNE	TH	M	EN		5		5										1034	
906	1	MAYNE	ZY	M	EN		5		5										1034	
907	1	MEAD	RO	M	LO	ME	2		475										467	
908	1	MEAD	TH	M	LO	ME	2		600										738	
909	1	MEADE	PH	M	LO	FM	5		20		13									
910	1	MEARE	BB	M	LO	DR	1		100					100	166	DE	EM	L	419	
911	1	MEASEY	MI	M	LO		2		50										896	
912	1	MEGGOT	GE	M	LO	PE	7		25										935	
913	1	MELHUISH	TH	M	LO	FA	1		100	300				150	242	RA	WM	L	728	1282
914	1	MERCER	DA	M	LO	DY	2		200	50									950	1321
915	1	MEREDITH	CR	M	LO	ST	2		200										484	
916	1	MEREDITH	ED	M	LO	MT	2		25										619	
917	1	MERRICK	CR	M	LO	ME	1		200					200	333	SW	QU	L	602	
918	1	MERRICK	JO	M	LO	GE	1		100					100	166	TE	CU	L	758	
919	1	METHOLD	WM	M	LO	ME	1		700	400									853	1314
920	1	MICHELL	ED	M	LO	SC	2		50		12								203	
921	1	MICKLETHWAIT	NL	M	LO	FM	1		25					200	100C	ON	AR	U	473	
922	1	MILES	GB	M	LO	MC	2		800										160	
923	1	MILLER	GE	M	LO	ST	2		133					133	295	CL	TI	M	590	
924	1	MILLER	T.	M	LO	MT	7		200										414	
925	1	MILLINGTON	GL	M	NO		1	2	1275										129	
926	1	MILLS	PE	M	LO	AR	2		100										608	
927	1	MILLS	TH	M	LO	SK	7		50										343	
928	1	MINORS	RA	M	HT	SO	1		200					200	333	MO	EM	L	834	
929	1	MITCHELL	ED	M			7		25										773	
930	1	MOGGRIDGE	DH	F	EN		5		100										1034	
931	1	MOLINS	WM	M	LO	IK	2		150										251	
932	1	MONCKE	PS	W	EN		2		1C0										1C34	
933	1	MOODY	SA	M	SF		1		200	600				400	888	CO	ZW	M	174	12C4
934	1	MOORE	AY	M	EN		3		20					20	27	KE	LI	M	1034	
935	1	MOORE	DH	F	DB		2		150										712	
936	1	MOORE	GI	M	DV	YE	1		25					25	34	IO	TI	M	999	
937	1	MORELL	RI	M	LO	GO	1		100					100	222	CO	ZW	M	148	
938	1	MORETON	EZ	W	LO		2		50										538	
939	1	MORGAN	AY	M	LO		1		200					200	333	RA	WM	L	689	
940	1	MORLEY	HT	M	SX	ES	1	1	6C0					600	617	DE	EM	L	49	
941	1	MORLEY	WM	M	SX	KN	1	7	300										118	
942	1	MORRELL	RI	M	EN		5		7										1034	
943	1	MORRIS	JO	M	LO		2		100										905	
944	1	MORSE	GE	M	LO	MT	5		3C0											
945	1	MORTIMER	JO	M	EN	HA	2		100										858	
946	1	MORTON	TH	M	SR		2		200										471	
947	1	MOSYER	JO	M	LO		1		25					800	3888	DU	AN	U	1163	
948	1	MOUNDEFORD	EM	M	NF	KN	1	2	300										26	
949	1	MOUNSON	WM	M		LO	1	7	600										1157	
950	1	MOUNTAGUE	WM	M	LO	WH	2		25		6								380	
951	1	MOUNTNEY	CU	M	LO	HA	5		62											
952	1	MOUNTNEY	RI	M	LO	ME	2		250										336	
953	1	MOUNTNEY	ST	M	LO		2			100										1230
954	1	MOYER	SA	M	LO	ME	2		300	300									213	1210
955	1	MULES	EZ	W	EN		5		10										1034	
956	1	MUNDAR	AR	M	SO		3		20					20	27	PO	QU	L	1034	
957	1	MUNDAY	TH	M	SO		7		5										1111	
958	1	MUNDAY	WM	M	SR		1		50					25	41	PO	QU	L	385	
959	1	MURDOCK	JS	M	LO	SK	2		100										852	
960	1	MUSGRAVE	WM	M	DV		7		20										978	
961	1	MUSGROVE	PH	M	DV	TN	1		20					20	44	IO	TI	M	979	
962	1	NETTLE	WM	M	DV		7		100										1017	
963	1	NETTLESHIP	HG	M	LO	SA	1		150		50			450	750	LS	KI	L	260	
964	1	NEWMAN	FR	M	LO	HA	2		150	50									7	1189
965	1	NEWTON	RI	M	NT		1		300					300	666	IO	TI	M	299	
966	1	NICHOLAS	CR	M	LO	DY	2		100										357	
967	1	NICHOLLS	RG	M	MX		1		50					50	83	RA	WM	L	37	
968	1	NICHOLSON	CR	M	LO	FM	2		25										297	
969	1	NICOLLS	FO	M	EN		5		60										1034	
970	1	NOBBES	JO	M	LO	BO	1		37		12			156	260	ST	QU	L	96C	
971	1	NORRIS	HG	M	LO	ME	2		200										208	
972	1	NORTH	RI	M	SO		7		2										1118	
973	1	NORTHCOTT	IZ	M	DV		3		100					100	137	EL	TI	M	1034	
974	1	NORTHCOTT	JO	M		KN	1	7	225										120	

1	2	3	4	5	6	7	8	9	10	11	12	13	14	15	16	17	18	19	20	21
975	1	NORTHCOTT	SA	M	DV			3	50					50	68	MD	TI	M	1034	
976	1	NORTON	NI	M	LO	CW		7	300										947	
977	1	NOSEWORTHY	ED	M	EN	CL		3	20					20	20	DE	EM	L	1034	
978	1	NOSEWORTHY	WM	M	EN	SO		1	50					50	83	CU	QU	L	1033	
979	1	NUTKINS	WM	M				2	50		7								700	
980	1	OFFICIAL	WM	M	GY	ME		1	600					225	374	FE	WM	L	755	
980	2	OFFICIAL	WM											300	500	EG	KI	L	755	
981	1	OFFLEY	ST	M	LO	MT		2	50										341	
982	1	OLAND	ED	M	DV			3	12					12	20	RA	WM	L	1034	
983	1	OLDFIELD	JO	M	LO	FM		1	200		50			500	1111	CL	TI	M	237	
984	1	OLIVER	NI	M	EN			3	10					10	13	KE	LI	M	1034	
985	1	ONSLOW	RI	M		KN	1	1	400					400	548	CL	TI	M	116	
986	1	ORCHARD	TH	M	LO	PE		1	100		8			150	333	DC	ZW	M	191	
987	1	ORTON	NI	M	LO	CW		5	300		75									
988	1	OTGER	AM	M	LO	ME		2	600		150								409	
989	1	OVERING	ED	M	LO	SA		2	200										499	
990	1	OVERTON	HE	M	LO	ST		1	25		6			62	312	DU	AN	U	368	
991	1	OWEN	JO	M	LO	GR		7	200	200									749	1283
992	1	OWEN	PH	M				7	200										70	
993	1	OWEN	TH	M	EX			7	100										255	
994	1	OWER	MW	M	LO	GR		1	100					100	137	PB	LI	M	236	
995	1	OWFIELD	JS	M	EN	CL		5	50										1034	
996	1	OWFIELD	SA	M	SR	KN	1	1	250					250	416	TE	QU	L	75	
997	1	PACKER	JO	M	LO	ES		1	600					600	1000	GA	KI	L	87	
998	1	PAGE	ED	M	LO	HA		1	100					100	222	MD	TI	M	1148	
999	1	PAGE	TH	M	MX			2	100										31	
1000	1	PAGE	WM	M	LO	AP		2	100										706	
1001	1	PAINE	GE	M	SO			7	3										868	
1002	1	PAINTER	HE	M	EN	CL		5	50										1034	
1003	1	PALMER	DV	M	NT	ES		7	310										793	
1004	1	PALMER	PH	M	DV			3	5					5	6	KE	LI	M	1034	
1005	1	PANTER	JO	M	LO	MT		2	50										372	
1006	1	PARGITER	TH	M	LO	GR		1	100					100	222	CN	LI	M	11	
1007	1	PARKER	AY	M	SO	CL		2	60										886	
1008	1	PARKER	CH	M				7	100										1179	
1009	1	PARKER	GE	M	LO	ME		2	200										496	
1010	1	PARKER	GG	M	LO	HA		7	50										597	
1011	1	PARKER	JO	M	LO	DR		1	100										1179	
1012	1	PARKER	JO	M	LO	ME		1	700					575	958	NA	EM	L	183	
1013	1	PARKER	JO	M	LO	HA		2	50										584	
1014	1	PARKER	JO	M	OX			7	12										1069	
1015	1	PARKER	JS	M	LO	SK		1	200					100	166	SW	QU	L	552	
1016	1	PARKER	SR	W	LO			2	200										497	
1017	1	PARKES	ED	M	LO	MT		2	100										787	
1018	1	PARKHURST	JO	M	KE			7	7										1162	
1019	1	PARKHURST	RO	M	SR	KN	4	1	1000					600	1333	CN	LI	M	46	
1020	1	PARR	CR	M	LO	ME		3	100					100	137	PB	LI	M	1034	
1021	1	PARRIS	MA	M	DV			3	10					10	16	EG	KI	L	1034	
1022	1	PARRIS	TH	M	EN	ME		1	50					50	83	CU	QU	L	988	
1023	1	PARROTT	JO	M	LO	SK		2	100										547	
1024	1	PARRY	NI	M	LO			1	50					50	250	BE	AN	U	238	
1025	1	PARSONS	FR	M	LO	MT		1	60					40	124	MY	WM	L	324	
1026	1	PARSONS	HE	M	DV	MC		1	200					100	166	LU	EM	L	1003	
1027	1	PARSONS	HE	M	DV			7	100										1014	
1028	1	PARSONS	RO	M	LO	WE		1	50					50	111	CN	LI	M	926	
1029	1	PARTRIDGE	AX	M	LO			2	80										449	
1030	1	PARTRIDGE	ED	M	KE	KN	1	2	600										119	
1031	1	PATE	TH	M	LO	CU		2	200										501	
1032	1	PATTISON	ED	M	DV			3	30					30	30	DE	EM	L	1034	
1033	1	PAY	JO	M	DV	YE		7	100										1015	
1034	1	PEACOCK	LU	M	LO	MT		1	50					50	111	IO	TI	M	1154	
1035	1	PEACOCK	WM	M	LO	PS		2	200										1141	
1036	1	PEAKE	WM	M	LO	CW		2	100										766	
1037	1	PEARCE.	SA					7		100											1357
1038	1	PEARCE JR.	TH	M	DV			7	30										1013	
1039	1	PEARCE SR	TH	M	DV			1	30						30	NA	EM	L	1012	
1040	1	PEASE	WM	M	LO	SD		5		30										
1041	1	PECK	FR	M	LO	CL		5	50											
1042	1	PECK	FR	M	SR	CL		7	25										654	
1043	1	PECKETT	WM	M	KE	EL		1	200					200	1000	DU	AN	U	723	
1044	1	PEDDER	MW	M	BD			2	100										65	
1045	1	PEERES	ED	M	LO	GR		2	100										573	
1046	1	PENNINGTON	IZ	M	LO		1		1000										113	
1047	1	PENNOYER	SA	M	LO	ME		1		450				900	1500	BA	KI	L		1229
1048	1	PENNOYER	WM	M	LO	CW		2	150	350									332	1228
1049	1	PERIAM	JS	M	SO			5				12	4							
1050	1	PERRY	JO	M	LO	SK		1	50	50				949	4749	AR	AR	U	558	1255
1051	1	PETTIT	HE	M	LO	MT		2	200										609	

1	2	3	4	5	6	7	8	9	10	11	12	13	14	15	16	17	18	19	20	21
1052	1	PEYTON	TH	M	KE	KN	1	2	400										1074	
1053	1	PHEASANT	JP	M	DB			7	100										180	
1054	1	PHEASANT	ST	M	LO	LW		2	200										750	
1055	1	PHILLIPS	TH	M	LO	CW		1	40					40	71	CO	ZW	M	785	
1056	1	PICKERING	GL	M	NT		1	2	600										108	
1057	1	PIERCE	WM	M	LO			5			12									
1058	1	PIGGOTT	RI	M	LO	GR		2		300										1332
1059	1	PIKE	EM	M	LO	HA		1	100					100	222	DC	ZW	M	263	
1060	1	PINN	SA	M		CA		7	100										928	
1061	1	PITCHER	EM	M	LO	DR		1	100					100	500	BE	AN	U	737	
1062	1	PITCHES	L.	M				7			50									1356
1063	1	PITT	BJ	M	SO			1	50					50	83	CU	QU	L	1113	
1064	1	PITTS	JO	M	DV			3	100					100	222	IO	TI	M	1031	
1065	1	PITTS	JO	M				5	5											
1066	1	PITTS	PE	M	EN			5	10										1034	
1067	1	PLAYER	JO	M	KE	CL		1	25					25	55	CL	TI	M	1180	
1068	1	PLAYER	TH	M	LO	HA		2	200										849	
1069	1	PLUCKNETT	GE	M	LO	SC		1	100					100	166	EG	KI	L	743	
1070	1	POLLEN	JO	M	LO	WH		1	300					300	500	CU	QU	L	448	
1071	1	POOLE	JO	M	DV	KN		1	103					103	184	DC	ZW	M	1008	
1072	1	POOLE	PD	M	CV	GE		1	200					200	333	MR	QU	L	1019	
1073	1	POPHAM	FR	M	SO	KN	1	1	750			250	4	1000	1371	CL	TI	M	1101	
1074	1	PORDAGE	JO	M		PH		7	106										230	
1075	1	PORTER	RI	M	HT			1	200	400				600	1000	EG	KI	L	642	1263
1076	1	POTT	EM	M	LO	HA		2	200										16	
1077	1	POTTER	BJ	M	LO	SD		2	50										695	
1078	1	POTTS	JO	M	KN	NF	1	1	600										2	
1079	1	POULSTEAD	JO	M	LO	ME		3	600											
1080	1	POULSTED	HE	M	LO	ES		2	200		50								205	
1081	1	POULSTED JR	HE	M	LO	ME		2	200										211	
1082	1	POULTER	JO	M	LO	YE		1	70					50	83	JS	KI	L	40	
1083	1	POURDON	SA	M	EN			3	20					30	27	KE	LI	M	1034	
1084	1	POYNTINGTON	TH	M	DV			3	50					50	51	EG	KI	L	1034	
1085	1	PRESTLEY	WM	M	HT			2	146										1144	
1086	1	PRETTY	PG	M	LO	DR		1	200					200	444	CL	TI	M	510	
1087	1	PRIAULX	WM	M	SX	CL		2	50										559	
1088	1	PRICE	GE	M	SR		3	7	225										1038	
1089	1	PRICE	WA	M	HT			2	50				4						1134	
1090	1	PRIGG	HE	M	EN	WM		3	25					25	25	FE	WM	L	1034	
1091	1	PRINCE	PE	M	LO	TC		1	25	100				150	250	DM	WM	L	316	1225
1092	1	PRINCE	TH	M	LO	TC		2	25	100									315	1224
1093	1	PROCTOR	HE	M	LO	WE		1	100					100	166	DE	EM	L	366	
1094	1	PRYOR	GE	M	LO	GE		2	675										771	
1095	1	PULLER	AM	M	HT	CL		1	200					200	333	MO	EM	L	854	
1096	1	PYE	RO	M		KN	1	1	1000					1000	1666	GA	KI	L	19	
1097	1	PYM	JO	M	SO		1	1	600					600	1000	SL	EM	L	1	
1098	1	PYM	JO	M	BU			2	300										67	
1099	1	PYNNAR	TH	M	HF			2	100										221	
1100	1	PYTT	HE	M				1	300					300	500	KI	WM	L	97	
1101	1	QUINY	RI	M	LO	GR		1	100					200	333	GA	KI	L	741	
1102	1	RAINSBOROUGH	TH	M	LO	ME	1	2	100	400									715	1280
1103	1	RAINSBOROUGH	WM	M	LO	ME		2	100	400									715	1280
1104	1	RAND	JA	M				2	200										51	
1105	1	RANDALL	TH	M				2	50										426	
1106	1	RANDOLPH	TB	M	LO	CL		1	75			25	4	100	102	RA	WM	L	963	
1107	1	RATCLIFFE	AY	M	BU	ES		1	300					300	666	IK	TI	M	63	
1108	1	RATCLIFFE	HG	M	LO	HA		1	300					650	1444	IO	TI	M	5	
1109	1	RATCLIFFE	PE	M	DV	YE		7	25										1001	
1110	1	RATHBAND	WM	M	LO	CL		1	100					50	111	DC	ZW	M	663	
1111	1	RAY	GE	M	LO	ST		2	25										194	
1112	1	RAYMANT	JO	M	LO	WH		1	300					300	666	CL	TI	M	447	
1113	1	READ	EL	M	DV			2	20										1028	
1114	1	READ	SA	M	EX			7	12										657	
1115	1	READE	JO	M	LO	CA		2	50										961	
1116	1	REDFERNE	JO	M	SR			7	7										1049	
1117	1	REEVE	GY	M	LO	BA		1	100					50	83	ST	QU	L	287	
1118	1	REGEMORT	AH	M	LO	PH		1	400					100	222	MD	TI	M	169	
1119	1	RENDALL	WM	M	LO	ME		7	300										848	
1120	1	REYNOLDS	AY	M	LO	CL		2	30										1131	
1121	1	REYNOLDS	JO	M				1	25					25	41	ST	QU	L	307	
1122	1	REYNOLDS	JO	M	SX			7	12										971	
1123	1	REYNOLDS	RO	M	WI	ES	1	1	1200					1800	3000	BA	KI	L	18	1192
1124	1	REYNOLDS	WI	M	LO	MC		2	200										165	
1125	1	RICH	TH	M	LO	SO		5	100											
1126	1	RICHARDS	JO	M	EN			3	20					20	20	PO	QU	L	1034	
1127	1	RICHARDS	TH	M	LO	SO		7	100										842	
1128	1	RICHARDSON	CH	M	LO	FM		5			20									
1129	1	RICHARDSON	RI	M	LO	HA		2	25		6								378	

1	2	3	4	5	6	7	8	9	10	11	12	13	14	15	16	17	18	19	20	21
1130	1	RICHARDSON	WM	M	LO	ME		1	50					5050	111	IO	TI	M	613	
1131	1	RIDGES	WM	M	LO	SK	2	1	120					120	266	MD	TI	M	319	
1131	2	RIDGES	WM											150	205	IK	TI	M		
1131	3	RIDGES	WM											100	222	MD	TI	M		
1131	4	RIDGES	WM	M	LO	SK	2	5	60											
1132	1	RISBEY	WM	M	LO	DR		2	100										315	
1133	1	ROACH	HE	M				1		50									212	
1134	1	ROBERTS	JO	M	LO	HA		5	300					50	83	MO	EM	L		1272
1135	1	ROBERTS	WA	M		KN		7	100										1130	
1136	1	ROBINS	E	M	LO	ME		2	100	100										1267
1137	1	ROBINS	RO	M	EN			2	300										543	
1138	1	ROBINS	WM	M	SO			1	25					25	77	DU	AN	U	1120	
1139	1	ROBROUGH	HE	M	LO	CL		2		30										1348
1140	1	ROCHE	LY	S	CO			1	25					25	41	CU	QU	L	623	
1141	1	RODBEARD	TH	M	LO	FM		7	100	300									648	1269
1142	1	ROE	TH	M	LO	GI		1	50					50	111	CO	ZW	M	808	
1143	1	ROGERS	FR	M	SR			1	100					100	102	MO	EM	L	101	
1144	1	ROGERS	HU	M	hA			7	25										1097	
1145	1	ROGERS	RI	M	LO	GR		1	100	100	75			650	1444	EL	TI	M	310	1222
1146	1	ROGERS	TH	M	KE			2	100										195	
1147	1	ROGERS	TH	M	EX			2	25										394	
1148	1	ROGERS	WM	M	LO			1	25					50	111	IO	TI	M	621	
1149	1	ROLFE	JO	M	LO	GO		3	50		14	5	2	137	229	MY	WM	L		
1150	1	ROLLE	JO	M	DV		1	1	450					450	750	GA	KI	L	93	
1151	1	ROLLE	SA	M	KE	KN	1	1	1000					1000	1666	GA	KI	L	43	
1152	1	ROLLESTON	RO	M	LO	MT		2		100									1326	
1153	1	ROSEWELL	AY	M	SO			2	75										772	
1154	1	ROSS	TH	M	LO	TC		1	50					50	111	CO	ZW	M	863	
1155	1	ROSWELL	HE	M	DV	KN		7	200										902	
1156	1	ROTHEWELL	JO	M	LO	ST		2	50										399	
1157	1	ROUND	JO	M				7	50										197	
1158	1	ROUND	TH	M				7	50										196	
1159	1	ROVINS	E.	M	LO	MC		7	100										650	
1160	1	ROWE	HE	M		KN		2	300										600	
1161	1	ROWE	JO	M	DV			5	20										1034	
1162	1	ROYLEY	TS	M				7		50									1034	
1163	1	RUMNY	SI	M	SX			2	35										1156	1344
1164	1	RUSHLEY	JI	M	LO	SA		1	25					100	232	ST	QU	L	925	
1165	1	RUSSELL	JA	M	LO	DR		3			50			100	222	CO	ZW	M		
1166	1	RUSSELL	JO	M	SX	YE		1	250					250	416	DE	EM	L	968	
1167	1	RUSSELL	TH	M	NF			3	200					200	617	AD	DN	U		
1168	1	RUTTON	MV	M	LO			1	200					200	444	MD	TI	M	483	
1169	1	SADLER	GE	M	LO	ME		2	25			6							382	
1170	1	SADLER	JO	M				1	100					100	166	GA	KI	L	742	
1171	1	SAINTHILL	PE	M	DV			1	225										899	
1172	1	SALLOWAY	RI	M	LO	GR	1	2	1000										156	
1173	1	SALMON	HE	M	SO			7	12										1117	
1174	1	SANDERS	LU	M	LO	FA		1	100					150	242	RA	WM	L	731	
1175	1	SANDERSON	ED	M	YO	TN		3	62					62	192	ON	AR	U		
1176	1	SANDON	JO	M	LO	CO		2	50										916	
1177	1	SARES	RG	M		PE		2	100										639	
1178	1	SAVELL	ED	M	EX			1	50					50	111	CN	LI	M	780	
1179	1	SAVELL	JO	M	EX			1	75					75	166	CN	LI	M	775	
1180	1	SCARGILL	RO	M	YO			3	62					62	192	ON	AR	U		
1181	1	SCARLETT	IR	M	LO	AR		2	100										581	
1182	1	SCOBELL	HE	M	LO	LW		7	200										670	
1183	1	SCOTT	ED	M	KE	KN		1	200					200	274	CY	LI	M	1071	
1184	1	SCOTT	FR	M	LO	HA		2	120										323	
1185	1	SCOTT	GE	M	LO	GR		2	100		25								601	
1186	1	SCOTT	RO	M	KE	KN		1	200					200	274	CY	LI	M	1072	
1187	1	SEAGER	JO	M	DV	CL		1	150					200	444	IO	TI	M	994	976
1188	1	SEALE	WM	M				1	25					25	55	DC	ZW	M	291	
1189	1	SEAMEN	ED	M	LO	MA		5				10								
1190	1	SEARE	EM	M	LO			5	20										1034	
1191	1	SEARLE	CR	M	LO	DY		1	160	100				470	732	CU	QU	L	957	1322
1191	2	SEARLE	CR	M	LO	DY		5	40											
1192	1	SEARLE	JO	M	DV	CL		1	20					20	33	KI	WM	L	1011	
1193	1	SEARLE	RO	M	DV			2	30										1004	
1193	2	SEARLE	RO	M	DV			5	40											
1194	1	SEARLE	WM	M	DV			1	20					20	33	ST	QU	L	1005	
1195	1	SEDDON	PE	M	LA	YE		2	50										1098	
1196	1	SEDGWICK	ST	M	LO	BR		2	100										722	
1197	1	SEED	JO	M	LO	HA		1	200					200	444	IO	TI	M	586	
1198	1	SEELING	JO	M	LO	PE		5	100											
1199	1	SEWARD	JO	M	DV			5	50										1034	
1200	1	SHAKESPEARE	MY	M	LO			1	100					100	222	EL	TI	M	678	
1201	1	SHAXTON	RI	M	LO	FM		5				10								
1202	1	SHEAFE	EM	M	LO	MC		1	100					100	166	PO	QU	L	698	

1	2	3	4	5	6	7	8	9	10	11	12	13	14	15	16	17	18	19	20	21
203	1	SHEARES	WM	M	LE	YE		1	300					300	411	EL	TI	M	1088	
204	1	SHEBBER	WM	M	DV	YE		3	26					26	36	KE	LI	M	1034	
205	1	SHEERES	TH	M	DV			5	20										1034	
206	1	SHEFFIELD	SP	M				1	400	300	175			1750	2916	MR	QU	L	157	1203
207	1	SHEPARD	JO	M	NT	ML		3	150					150	750	TU	AR	U		
208	1	SHEPHEARD	WM	M	LO	GR		2	50										942	
209	1	SHEPPEY	WM	M	LO	WE		1	200		75			450	1000	DC	ZW	M	525	
210	1	SHERBROOKE	RI	M	LO	MT		1	300		75			300	500	MY	WM	L	54	
211	1	SHERLOCK	WM	M					100					100	222	DC	ZW	M	302	
212	1	SHINGLER	RI	M	LO	DR		2	100										433	
213	1	SHORT	JO					3	150		37			150	333	MD	TI	M		
213	2	SHORT	JO	M	LO	GE		3						225	5CC	MD	TI	M		
214	1	SHOWER	WM	M	EN			5	40											
215	1	SHUTE	RI	M	LO	ME		2	200	3OO									437	1239
216	1	SHUTE	TH	M				7	5										1121	
217	1	SHUTTLEWORTH	RI	M	LA		1	1	300			150	4	600	617	KI	hM	L	126	
218	1	SIBLAY	JO	M	BD			2	50										1159	
219	1	SIBLEY	JS	M	LO	TC		7	25										369	
220	1	SIBLY	SM	M	LO	SA		2	100										620	
221	1	SILLOBY	MY	W				7		10										1353
222	1	SIMMES	WM	M	SO			5	20										1034	
223	1	SIMPSON	MA	M	BR			2	50		12								703	
224	1	SKINNER	AT	M	KE	ES	1	7	100										131	
225	1	SKIPPON	PH	M			1	7	50	200									824	1305
226	1	SKRIMSHAW	WM	M				1	50					50	111	EL	TI	M	477	
227	1	SLADE	DA	M	DV			5	10										1034	
228	1	SLADE	SA	M	DV			5	20										1034	
229	1	SLADE	WM	M	LO	IR		3	50					50	83	ST	QU	L		
230	1	SLEIGH	EM	M	LO	MC		2	150	100									242	1214
231	1	SMALL	CR	M	DV			3	5					5	6	KE	LI	M	1034	
232	1	SMITH	ED	M	LO	SD		2	100		37			600	1OCO	LS	KI	L	281	
233	1	SMITH	EP	M	SR			2	10										1055	
234	1	SMITH	FR	M	LO			7	50										158	
235	1	SMITH	HE	M	LE	GR	1	1	200					200	444	CO	ZW	M	1087	
236	1	SMITH	HE	M	LO	GR		2	100										871	
237	1	SMITH	JA	M	LO	SA		1	200					200	1000	AR	AR	U	565	
238	1	SMITH	JO	M	LO	PL		1	10					10	22	DC	ZW	M	614	
239	1	SMITH	JO	M	LO	HA		2	50										468	
240	1	SMITH	JO	M	EN			5	30										1034	
241	1	SMITH	JS	M	LO			1	100					100	137	DC	ZW	M	582	
242	1	SMITH	RG	M	LE	KN		2	300		75								1086	
243	1	SMITH	RI	M	LO	PL		1	10					10	22	DC	ZW	M	614	
244	1	SMITH	RI	M	LO	GR		2	·100	200									489	1248
245	1	SMITH	RO	M	LO	GR		1	100	200									489	1248
246	1	SMITH	SI	M	LO	TC		2	100										·365	
247	1	SMITH	TH	M	LO	AP		1	100					100	222	ZL	QU	M	219	
248	1	SMITH	TH	M	EN			3	25					25	41	FE	WM	L	1034	
249	1	SMYTER	WM	M	LO			2	25										917	
250	1	SMYTH	KT	W	LO			2	100					3					846	
251	1	SNELL	GE	M	LO	GO		1	200		25			350	777	MD	TI	M	387	
252	1	SNELLING	GE	M	ME		1	7	100	100									906	1286
253	1	SNOW	JO	M	LO	HA		2	100										182	
254	1	SNOW	TH	M	LO	BA		2	100·										364	
255	1	SOAME	EZ	W	EX			1	300					300	666	EL	TI	M	628	
256	1	SOAME	TH	M	LO	KN	1	2	1000										60	
257	1	SOLSTED	JO	M	LO	MC		7	600										159	
258	1	SOUTH	GE	M				2	50										517	
259	1	SOWDON	JO	M	DV			2	25										1000	
260	1	SPARROW	JO	M	SF			1	50					50	111	CO	ZW	M	175	
261	1	SPARROW	PH	M	SF			1	50					50	111	CO	ZW	M	175	
262	1	SPELLER	JO	M	EX			1	50					50	111	CN	LI	M	777	
263	1	SPENCER	MI	M	YO			1	150					150	154	PO	QU	L	524	
264	1	SPRAGUE	JO	M				5	25										1034	
265	1	SPRAGUE	RO	M	LO	BU		5	25										1034	
266	1	SPRING	EM	M	NF			7	50										1084	
267	1	SPRINGATE	TH	M	SX			1	200					200	205	ST	QU	L	966	
268	1	SPRINGER	AY	M	LO			7	200										786	
269	1	SPURSTOWE	WM	M			1	2	400										50	
270	1	SQUIRE	WM	M	DV	GE		3	100					100	·222	MD	TI	M	1034	
271	1	ST.JOHN	OL	M	ES		1	7	300										58	
272	1	STACKHOUSE	RO	M				7	20										325	
273	1	STAINE	WM	M	PH			7	100											1329
274	1	STANDISH	HE	M	LO	CO		1	50					50	51	ST	QU	L	958	
275	1	STANTON	EM	M	CL			1	100					300	500	DE	EM	L	1044	
276	1	STAPER	RI	M	LO	GE		3	200		75	100	2	750	1666	MD	TI	M		
276	2	STAPER	RI	M										20		ZW	ZW	M		
277	1	STARKEY	WM	M		GE		7	75										632	
278	1	STARKY	PH	M	LO	CK		7	203										170	

1	2	3	4	5	6	7	8	9	10	11	12	13	14	15	16	17	18	19	20	21
1279	1	STARR	BR	M	EN	UP		2	100										984	
1280	1	STARR	GE	M	CO			2	150										80C	
1281	1	STATIONERS	CO					5			36									
1282	1	STAUNTON	RC	M	BD	ES		2		300	75									120
1283	1	STEANE	TH	M		TC		2	100										638	
1284	1	STEANE	TH	M		WC		5			64									
1285	1	STEDDE	WM	M		IR		7	50										932	
1286	1	STEDDERMAN	GE	M	SO	GE		7	25										1116	
1287	1	STEELE	JO	M	LO	SA		1	50					50	250	BE	AN	U	347	
1288	1	STEMING	JO	M	LO	LE		7	100										806	
1289	1	STEVENS	JO	M	DV			3	10					10	13	KE	LI	M	1034	
1290	1	STEVENSON	JO	M				1	50					50	83	SW	QU	L	306	
1291	1	STINT	TH	M	SR	GE		7	2										106C	
1292	1	STIPE	JO	M				7	100										442	
1293	1	STOCK	TH	M	LO	GR		1	200	400				600	1333	CL	TI	M	495	124
1294	1	STOCKLER	JO	M	SO			2.	13										1104	
1295	1	STONE	CH	W	EN			1	100					100	166	KI	WM	L	980	
1296	1	STONE	SA	M	LO	BR		2	50										716	
1297	1	STONE	TH	M	LO	HA		2	300	2C0									328	122
1298	1	STOREY	ED	M	LO	IR		1	50					50	111	CO	ZW	M	807	
1299	1	STORY	JA	M	LO			7	25	150									803	129
1300	1	STOUGHTON	AY	M	SR	GE		2	50										385	
1301	1	STOUGHTON	NI	M	SR		1	2	600		150								662	
1302	1	STRANG	JO	M	EN			3	50					50	51	PO	QU	L	1034	
1303	1	STRANGE	JO	M	LO	ME		2	300	2C0									526	125
1304	1	STRANGE	JO	M	LO	MT		2	3C0	200	50								526	125
1305	1	STRATTON	TH	M	LO	ME		1	37					100	126	LU	EM	L	348	
1306	1	STRICKLAND	WM	M	KN		1	1	600					600	823	CO	ZW	M	124	
1307	1	STRINGER	AY	M	LO	GE		5	150			50	4						107	
1308	1	STRODE	WM	M	DV	GE	1	2	600										107	
1309	1	STRODE	WM	M	SO		1	1	600					1300	2166	TE	QU	L		119
1310	1	STUBBER	PE	M	LO			7	100										257	
1311	1	STUBBINS	TH	M	LO	ME		1	200		50			500	833	EG	KI	L	209	
1312	1	STURDY	JO	M	LO	MT		1	25					25	125	BE	AN	U	475	
1313	1	STURGIS	TH	M	LO	GR		2	150	2C0									488	124
1314	1	STURMY	JU	M	SR			1	20					40	88	IU	TI	M	1053	
1315	1	SUELLING	JO	M	LO	PE		7	100										455	
1316	1	SUMMERS	RG	M	EN			5	30										1C34	
1317	1	SUMPNER	WM	M	EX			2	50										762	
1318	1	SUMPTER	GI	M	LO	FA		1	100					120	200	RA	WM	L	733	
1319	1	SURTEIS	RO	M	LO	BS		5	50										114	9
1320	1	SUTTON	RO	M	NO		1	2	200										112	
1321	1	SWAN	JO	M	KE	CL		2	50										1178	
1322	1	SWEETE	AC	W	EN			2	50										1022	
1323	1	SWEETE	PE	M	DV			3	10					10	10	EG	KI	L	1034	
1324	1	SWEETE	RI	M	EN	ME		1	250					250	530	PB	LI	M	1022	103
1325	1	SWYNOKE	RO	M	KE	GE		2	200										564	
1326	1	SYMONDS	RI	M	LO	BS		3	50					100	222	CL	LI	M		
1327	1	SYNTALL	EM	M	EN	WE		2	1C0										993	
1328	1	TABOR	JO	M	LO	GO		2	50										452	
1329	1	TABOR	RO	M	EX			2		50	12									134
1330	1	TACK	TH	M	EN	DR		5	22										1034	
1331	1	TALLOW-CHANDLERS	CO					5	69											
1332	1	TARLTON	JO	M		BR		7	50										934	
1333	1	TARRANT	LN	M	LO	YE		2	50		5	20	2						921	
1334	1	TAUNTON	CA					1	1360					1360	1399	RA	WM	L	1169	
1335	1	TAYLOR	ED	M	OX			2	200										1C66	
1336	1	TAYLOR	JO	M				3	75					75	125	NA	EM	L		
1337	1	TAYLOR	TH	M				3	75					75	125	NA	EM	L		
1338	1	TEMPLE	JO	M	WA			1	200					200	274	EL	TI	M	1089	
1338	2	TEMPLE	JO	M										100	166	KI	WM	L		
1339	1	TENDRING	F					7	25										658	
1340	1	TENNANT	MD	M	LO	CL		2		50										135
1341	1	TERRELL	JO	M	LO	MT		2	200					300	1500	MA	AN	U	72C	
1342	1	TERRY	RO	M	LO	DR		2.	50										927	
1343	1	THEWAR	JO	M	HT			2	25										268	
1344	1	THOMAS	GA	M	LO	MT		7	200										441	
1345	1	THOMAS	JO	M	EN			3	20					20	20	PO	QU	L	1034	
1346	1	THOMAS	RO	M	SR			2	25										1058	
1347	1	THOMASON	GE	M	LO	ST		1	700					700	1166	SW	QU	L	384	
1348	1	THOMPSON	GE	M	LO	ME	1	1	350	500	225			805	4030	TU	AR	U	335	123
1349	1	THOMPSON	IZ	M	KE	LD		2	50										198	
1350	1	THOMPSON	JO	M				1		200				1150	1916	MY	WM	L		133
1351	1	THOMPSON	MC	M	LO	ME		1	350	500	225			2150	10750	DU	AN	U	335	123
1351	2	THOMPSON	MC											805	4030	TU	AR	U	335	123
1352	1	THOMPSON	RO	M				7	100											133
1353	1	THOMPSON	WM	M	EX			1	50					50	111	CN	LI	M	776	
1354	1	THOMSON	WM	M	LO	SA		1	3C0	300	150								331	122

1	2	3	4	5	6	7	8	9	10	11	12	13	14	15	16	17	18	19	20	21
1355	1	THORNBURY·	WM	M	LO	GE		3	100						200		444	IK	TI	M		
1356	1	THOROLD	TH	M	LO	ME		2	600		150									187	
1357	1	THORPE	FR	M				2	10											1132	
1358	1	THRALE	RI	M	LO	ST		1	133					133	295	CL	TI	M		592	
1358	2	THRALE	RI											109		ZW	ZW	M		592	
1359	1	THROWGOOD	GE	M	LO			2	150											392	
1360	1	TICHBORNE	RO	M	LO	SK		2	200						200	333	SW	QU	L	551	
1361	1	TICKNEE	PE	M	DV			7	50											1032	
1362	1	TIFFEN	GC	F	SR			7	75											1057	
1363	1	TILLOTT	KT	W	LO			·5	50												
1364	1	TILLOTT	LN	M	LO	SA		2	100											789	
1365	1	TIL'SLEY	WM	M	LO			2	100											361	
1366	1	TIMME	JO	M	LO	GO		2	100											759	
1367	1	TIPPING	TA	M	OX		3	1	250						200	1000	DU	AN	U	1065	
1368	1	TOFTS	JO	M	NF	GR		2	50											1081	
1369	1	TOOLEY	TH	M	LI	ME		2	600											877	
1370	1	TOWNSHEND	GI	M	LO			1	200	100	67				650	1083	EG	KI	L	513	1253
1371	1	TOWSE	CR	M	LO	BA		1	100						100	222	MD	TI	M	679	
1372	1	TOWSE	JO	M	LO		2	2	700											139	
1373	1	TRACEY	JO	M	EN			3	10						10	13	KE	LI	M	1034	
1374	1	TRATTLE	RA	M	LO	FM		2	75											250	
1375	1	TRELAWNY	RO	M	DV		4	1	675						450	1000	EL	TI	M	878	
1376	1	TRENCHARD	JO	M	DO		1	2	600											84.	
1377	1	TRESCOTT	RO	M	EN	CW		3	85						85	87	EG	KI	L		
1378	1	TRIMBLETT	BE	M	LO	FA		1	100						150	242	RA	WM	L	732	
1379	1	TRIPLETT	KT		CX			2	20											1167	
1380	1	TRIPLETT	RA	M	LO	ST		1	300						310	1550	AR	AR	U	502	
1381	1	TROTMAN	TK	M	LO	ME		2	200		50									708	
1382	1	TUCKER	JA	M	EN		2	1	300						300	666	CN	LI	M	1009	
1383	1	TUCKER	WA	M	DV			5	100											1034	
1384	1	TUFFNAILE	EZ	W	LO			1	100											937	
1385	1	TUNBRIDGE	JS	M	EX			1	100						100	222	CN	LI	M	778	
1386	1	TURBRIDGE	RO	M	MX			5				300	1								
1387	1	TURLINGTON	JO	M	LO	SM		1	120						120	266	EL	TI	M	321	
1388	1	TURLINGTON	WM	M	LO·	ME		7	50											823	
1389	1	TURNER	AR	M		LW		1	200						200	333	SL	EM	L	462	
1390	1	TURNER	SA	M	LO	MT		2	200											415	
1391	1	TURNER SR	RI	M	LO			1	200	200					400	666	DE	EM	L	421	1236
1392	1	TUTTY	AA	W	LO			2	50											360	
1393	1	TUTTY	WM	M	HT	CL		2	25											474	
1394	1	TYFFIN	GL	W	SR			2	75											1057	
1395	1	TYLER	JO	M				7		75											1285
1396	1	TYLER	RI	M	LO	SA		3	75		25	25	1		250	1111	IL	TI	M		
1397	1	TYLER	TH	M				7		75											1285
1398	1	UNDERWOOD	ED	M	LO	GR		1	100						100	222	EL	TI	M	482	
1399	1	UNDERWOOD	RS	F				2	50											477	
1400	1	UNDERWOOD	WI	M	LO	GR	2	1	300	100					350	777	EL	TI	M	309	1221
1401	1	VALENTINE	TH	M	BU	CL		1	100						100	222	IO	TI	M	39	
1402	1	VASSAL	SA	M	LO		1	7	300											85	
1403	1	VAUGHAN	CH	M	DV		1	1	1000	100					2130	3530	ST	QU	L	827	1308
1403	2	VAUGHAN	CH	M	DV		1	1	630											827	1308
1404	1	VAUGHAN	ED	M	LO	GO	1	2	200	100			3							826	1307
1405	1	VAUGHAN	JS	M	LO	GO		2	100											828	
1406	1	VAUGHAN	NI	M	EN	GE		2	100											983	
1407	1	VAUGHAN	WM	M	LO	GR		2	300	100			3							829	1309
1408	1	VENNER	AX	M	LO			2		200										767	1284
1409	1	VENNER	RI	M	LO	BS		1	100	200					500	833	FE	WM	L	767	1284
1410	1	VERNON	RI	M	LO	PE		1	100						100	222	DC·	ZW	M	317	
1411	1	VICARIS	RI	M				1		100					100	106	RA	WM	L		1337
1412	1	VINCENT	TH	M	LO	LE		1	300	1000					300	500	LU	EM	L	282	1218
1412	2	VINCENT	TH												300	500	DE	EM	L		
1412	3	VINCENT	TH												600	1000	SL	EM	L		
1412	4	VINCENT	TH												4725	7874	BA	KI	L		
1412	5	VINCENT	TH												3550	5915	NA	EM	L		
1412	6	VINCENT	TH												200	205	ST	QU	L		
1412	7	VINCENT	TH												500	833	CU	QU	L		
1412	8	VINCENT	TH												1350	2217	PO	QU	L		
1413	1	VINER	TH	M	LO	GO		2	200											142	
1414	1	VINER	WM	M	LO	AR		2	100											529	
1415	1	VINER	WM	M	LO	GO		5			50										
1416	1	VOYSE	GM	M	LO	BR		1	50						50	51	ST	QU	L	914	
1417	1	VYE	JO	M	DV	YE		2	200											1002	
1418	1	WADE	WM	M	LO	ME		2	600											651	
1419	1	WADLAND	TH	M	EN			3	30						30	30	PO	QU	L	1034	
1420	1	WAGSTAFF	AY	M	DR			2	50											794	
1421	1	WAGSTAFF	EL	F	DR			2	50											796	
1422	1	WAGSTAFF	EM	M	DR			1	40						40	123	UI	CN	U	797	
1423	1	WAGSTAFF	JO	M	DR			2	50											794	

Appendix A

1	2	3	4	5	6	7	8	9	10	11	12	13	14	15	16	17	18	19	20	21
1424	1	WAGSTAFF	JS	M	LO	OF		1	25	100	12			312	520	DE	EM	L	813	1297
1425	1	WAGSTAFFE	WM	M	LO	MT		7	100						417					
1426	1	WALCOTT	RI	M	LO	ES		1	600					600	1000	RA	WM	L	580	
1427	1	WALDOE	DA	M	LO	CW		1	600					600	1333	CL	TP	M	756	
1427	2	WALDOE	DA											300	500	RA	WM	L		
1428	1	WALL	ME	M	LO	GE		1	200					200	333	RA	WM	L	73	
1429	1	WALLER	WM	M		KN	1	2	1000										45	
1430	1	WALLIN	PT	M	LO	BU		1	100		12			87	145	SW	QU	L	851	
1431	1	WALLINGTON	JO	M				7		25										1349
1432	1	WALLIS	RO	M	NO	CL		1	25					125	277	IK	TI	M	1172	
1433	1	WALLIS	WM	M	LO	MC		7		100										1343
1434	1	WALMESLEY	TH	M	BU			1	100					100	166	SW	QU	L	523	
1435	1	WALTER	HE	M	SX			2	100										888	
1436	1	WALTER	TH	M	EN			3	5					5	6	KE	LI	M	1034	
1437	1	WALTERS	TH	M	LO	CO			100					100	500	LE	DN	U	458	
1438	1	WARDELL	JO	M	LO	GR		7	150										204	
1439	1	WARING	RI	M	LO	GR		1	800		200			2000	4444	DC	ZW	M	487	1246
1440	1	WARNER	JO	M	LO			2	380										153	
1441	1	WARNER	SA	M	LO	GR		1	300	300	150			3000	5000	LU	EM	L	331	1227
1442	1	WARREN	GE	M	LO	DR		2	100			25	1						391	
1443	1	WATERHOUSE	FR	M	LO	FM		5	15											
1444	1	WATERHOUSE	TH	M	LO	FM		2	100		25								665	
1445	1	WATERTON	JO	M				7		50										1271
1446	1	WATKINS	DD	M	LO	KN		1	2025	375	600			3200	5332	MR	QU	L	25	1193
1446	2	WATKINS	DD											1800	3000	SK	EM	L		
1446	3	WATKINS	DD											1000	1666	CU	QU	L		
1447	1	WATSON	WM	M	LO	AP		1	50					50	111	CO	ZW	M	952	
1448	1	WEALE	JV	M	SR			1	373					373	511	SL	EM	L	173	
1449	1	WEBB	FR	M	LO	DY		7	12										656	
1450	1	WEBB	FR	M	LO	DY		7		1000										1268
1451	1	WEBSTER	JA	M	OR			1	100					50	68	CL	TP	M	579	
1451	2	WEBSTER	JA											100	222	CN	LI	M		
1452	1	WEBSTER	TH	M	MX	IK		2	50		12								681	
1453	1	WEBSTER	WM	M	SR	SA		1	100										726	
1454	1	WEBSTER	WM	M	LO	ME		1	150					300	666	MD	TI	M	386	
1455	1	WEED	JO	M	LO			2	200										586	
1456	1	WEEKS	OB	M	SR			1	50					100	222	CU	ZW	M	1045	
1457	1	WELLS	WA	M	HU	CL		2	250										1076	
1458	1	WENMAN	TH	M		LO	1	1	600					600	617	GA	KI	L	86	
1459	1	WEST	FR	M	LO	GR		1	200					200	1000	MA	AN	U	719	
1460	1	WEST	HE	M	LO	MA		1	200					200	444	DC	ZW	M	603	
1461	1	WESTROWE	TH	M	KE		4	1	300					300	308	MY	WM	L	1073	
1462	1	WHARTON	PH	D	YO	LA		2	200										1142	
1463	1	WHEATLEY	JO	M	LO	SC		1	25					125	277	IO	TI	M	371	
1464	1	WHETCOMBE	BJ	M						100				100	106	RA	WM	L		1337
1465	1	WHICHCOTT	CR	M	LO	ME		1	100					100	166	RA	WM	L	407	
1466	1	WHITE	ED	M	ST	MC		1	50					50	83	SK	EM	L	1152	
1467	1	WHITE	HE	M	LO	GR		1	50					50	83	ST	QU	L	962	
1468	1	WHITE	JA	M	EN	ME		1	300					300	666	IO	TI	M	990	
1469	1	WHITE	JO	M	EN	ME		2	200										975	
1470	1	WHITE	RI	M	DV	ME		1	400					133	296	PB	LI	M	1007	
1471	1	WHITE	ST	M	LO	GR		1	600					600	1333	CN	LI	M	273	
1472	1	WHITE	WM	M	LO	HA		2	50										693	
1473	1	WHITEAKER	HE	M		ME		1						200						1200
1474	1	WHITEHALL	RO	M	BU	CL		1	100					100	222	IO	TI	M	1036	
1475	1	WHITELOCKE	BU	M	BU		1	1	400					400	666	RA	WM	L	48	
1476	1	WHITING	JO	M	SF	MC		2	100	50									761	1360
1477	1	WHITSTON	FR	M	LO			7	50	150									476	1324
1478	1	WHITTINGHAM	HE	M	LO			2	200		50								1153	
1479	1	WICKES	NL	M	LO	CW		2	50										398	
1480	1	WICKES	TH	M	LO	CW		2	50										398	
1481	1	WILCOX	RI	M		HA		7	50										841	
1482	1	WILCOX	RO	M	WA			7	23										1093	
1483	1	WILD	JO	M		SG	1	2	200										13	
1484	1	WILDING	JO	M	LO	GO		2	50		12								923	
1485	1	WILKINS	SA	M	LO	TC		1	50		12			125	277	DC	ZW	M	918	
1486	1	WILKINSON	HE	M	LO	CL		5			10									
1487	1	WILLETT	RI	M	LO	MT		1	200	300	125	50	3	625	1041	MO	EM	L	832	1311
1488	1	WILLIAMS	JO	M	LO	FE		1	50					150	250	ST	QU	L	919	
1489	1	WILLIAMS	NI	M	LO	HA		2	100										752	
1490	1	WILLOUGHBY	WM	M	LO			1	150	50				200	333	LU	EM	L	672	1270
1491	1	WILSON	RI	M		GR		2	100										481	
1492	1	WINKFIELD	JO	M	LO	HA		1	40					40	66	ST	QU	L	587	
1493	1	WINSTON	RI	M	LO	GR		1	100	100									802	1289
1494	1	WINWOOD	RI	M			1	7	300										90	
1495	1	WITHAM	GE	M	LO	LE	2	1	300		100			750	1666	IO	TI	M	465	
1495	2	WITHAM	GE	M										25		ZW	ZW	M	465	
1496	1	WITHAM	NL	M	LO	BA		1	100					100	222	MD	TI	M	682	

1	2	3	4	5	6	7	8	9	10	11	12	13	14	15	16	17	18	19	20	21
1497	1	WITHAR	WM	M		ES	7		200										631	
1498	1	WOLFE	RI	M	LO	GI	2		20										1175	
1499	1	WOLLASTON	JO	M	LO	KN	2	2	900		225	25	3						140	
1500	1	WOOD	ED	M	LO	GR	1		175	500				675	1125	BA	KI	L	814	1298
1501	1	WOOD	JO	M	LO	ME	1			850				850	1416	EG	KI	L		1198
1502	1	WOOD	RI	M	DR		2		100										576	
1503	1	WOOD	RO	M	LO	HA	1		25	25				6		6	RA	WM	L		1341
1504	.1	WOOD	RO	M	SR		2		200										1059	
1505	1	WOOD	RO	M		TC	2		25										640	
1506	1	WOOD	TH	M	LO	MT	7		25										838	
1507	1	WOODCOCK	TH	M	LO	GR	1		100					100	222	IK	TI	M	342	
1508	1	WOODGATE	TH	M			7		.	200										1331
1509	1	WOODHEAD	WM	M	YO		1		220					230	383	LS	KI	L	107C	
1510	1	WOODHOUSE	WM	M	HT		1		100					100	166	SW	QU	L	247	
1511	1	WOODMAN	WM	M	LO		1		25					25	41	RA	WM	L	863	
1512	1	WOODROFFE	AM	M	LO		2			50										1274
1513	1	WOODWARD	CH	M	SF	CL	2		100										276	
1514	1	WOODWARD	EE	M	LO	GE	1		200					100	137	CL	TI	M	568	
1515	1	WOOLLEY	FR	M	LO	HA	1		67		17			166	370	IO	TI	M	149	
1516	1	WOOLNOUGH	JS	M	LO	MT	1		25	75	25			250	416	JS	KI	L	816	1300
1517	1	WORMELAYTON	FU	M	MX		2			50										1273
1518	1	WRIGHT	GE	M	LO	DR	1		50					50	83	EG	KI	L	612	
1519	1	WRIGHT	U.	F			7		50										1129	
1520	1	WRIGLEY	HE	M	LA		1		100					100	222	CN	LI	M	1098	
1521	1	WROE	RI	M	LA		2		50										1098	
1522	1	WYAN	TH	M	LO		2		100										69	
1523	1	WYMER	WM	M	NF.	ME	2		100										1077	
1524	1	YARD	GE	M	DV		7		50										986	
1525	1	YARD	JO	M	DV		3		25					35	57	LU	EM	L	1034	
1526	1	YARD	MT	F	DV		5		25										1034	
1527	1	YARMOUTH	CA.						600					600	1333	IO	TI	M	889	
1528	1	YATES	JO	M	HF	CL	1		100					100	222	ZL	ZW	M	220	
1529	1	YEO	JO	M	EN		5		25										1034	
1530	1	YONGE	JO	M	DV		5				25								1034	
1531	1	YOUNG	JO	M	LO	DR	1		100										172	
1532	1	YOUNG	MW	M	LO	BR	2		50		.								507	
1533	1	YOUNG	TH	M	LO	ME	1		100		25			250	416	ST	QU	L	822	

O

APPENDIX B

ADVENTURERS WHO DREW IRISH LAND

INTRODUCTION

In contrast to Appendix A, this list is not composite. It is, in fact, merely an alphabetized, slightly rearranged, and coded version of the manuscript barony tables in Marsh's Library, Dublin (Z. 2. 1. 5), which are described in detail in Chapter III above. The codes for Christian and place names are the same as those used for Appendix A, but in this list there is no biographical information and no information about investment. Nor is there information about sources, as only one source was employed. The list shows the names of the men who drew Irish land in the adventurers' lotteries held at Grocers' Hall, London, in 1653 and 1654; the credit in pounds which they were allowed by virtue of their investments under the various acts and ordinances pertaining to adventurers, the number of Irish statute acres to which this credit entitled them in the province in which they drew, and the barony, county, and province in which their allotments fell. This information has not been published previously, although *CSPI Adventurers for Land, 1642–1659*, prints without credit or acreage figures the very similar table surviving in the State Papers. Columns 10 and 11 represent respectively the sums of columns 5 and 6 on each card for each adventurer. Thus, the sum of the pounds credited to Francis Bellers (No. 2098) appears in column 10 of his last card, in this case the fifth. The sum of acres drawn by him is adjacent in column 11.

KEY TO COLUMN HEADINGS

1 Serial number of adventurer
2 Card number
3 Surname
4 Code for Christian name
5 Amount of credit in pounds claimed by adventurer (and allowed) for subscriptions under the act and ordinances for adventure
6 Amount of acreage (in Irish measure) due adventurer to satisfy credit (column 5) in portion of Ireland in which he had drawn (columns 7, 8, 9)
7 Code for barony in which adventurer's lot fell
8 Code for county in which adventurer's lot fell
9 Code for province in which adventurer's lot fell
10 Amount in pounds of sum of adventurer's credit
11 Amount in Irish acres of sum of adventurer's lands

1	2	3	4	5	6	7	8	9	10	11
2001	1	ADAMS	NL	-100	222	DC	ZW	M	100	222
2002	1	ADDYE	TH	361	802	IO	TP	M	361	802
2003	1	ALCOCKE	CH	500	1111	IO	TP	M	500	1111
2004	1	ALDERMAN	CR	20	27	DC	ZW	M	20	27
2005	1	ALDERTON	JO	25	41	PO	QU	L	25	41
2006	1	ALEXANDER	JM	50	Q	ZW	ZW	M	50	0
2007	1	ALFORD	JA	50	111	DC	ZW	M	50	111
2008	1	ALLEN	FR	400	888	PD	TP	M	400	888
2009	1	ALLEN	JO	100	222	DC	ZW	M	100	222
2010	1	ALLEN	RI	200	444	CL	TP	M	200	444
2011	1	ALLEN	WM	550	1222	EL	TP	M.	550	1222.
2012	1	ALLWOOD	JO	25	125	BE	AN	U		
2012	2	ALLWOOD	JO	25	125	BE	AN	U	50	250
2013	1	ALMERY	GE	1300	2166	SW	QU	L	1300	2166
2014	1	ALMOND	WM	100	222	IO	TP	M		
2014	2	ALMOND	WM	25	55	CL	TP	M	125	277
2015	1	AMYES	JO	66	91	IO	TP	M	66	91
2016	1	ANDREW	BJ	1225	2722	CN	LI	M	1225	2722
2017	1	ANDREWES	NL	200	333	BA	KI	L	200	333
2018	1	ANDREWES	TH	750	1250	BA	KI	L		
2018	2	ANDREWES	TH	40	0	ZW	ZW	M	790	1250
2019	1	ANOLL	JO	60	100	EG	KI	L	60	100
2020	1	ANTHONY	ED	100	166	EG	KI	L	100	166
2021	1	ARCHBOLD	ST	50	111	CC	ZW	M	50	111
2022	1	ARCHER	FR	383	638	SK	EM	L	383	638
2023	1	ARMYNE LADY		350	583	RA	WM	L	350	583
2024	1	ARNERIDETH	JO	14	14	RA	WM	L	14	14
2025	1	ARNOLD	GE	200	333	SW	QU	L	200	333
2026	1	ARNOLD	JO	100	166	SL	EM	L	100	166
2027	1	ARNOLD	WM	100	166	SI	EM	L	100	166
2028	1	ARUNDELL	HE	150	250	RA	WM	L	150	250
2029	1	ASH	ED	400	888	CL	TP	M	400	888
2030	1	ASH	JO	800	1777	CL	TP	M	800	1777
2031	1	ASH	JO	25	125	BE	AN	U		
2031	2	ASH	JO	25	125	BE	AN	U	50	250
2032	1	ASH	L.	100	222	IO	TP	M	100	222
2033	1	ASHTON	MI	20	61	UI	DN	U	20	61
2034	1	ASHURST	RI	100	750	SL	EM	L	100	750
2035	1	ASTRAY	FR	20	33	RA	WM	L	20	33
2036	1	ATKINS	BJ	50	111	EL	TP	M	50	111
2037	1	ATKINS	PE	25	34	EL	TP	M	25	34
2038	1	ATKINS	WM	10	10	EG	KI	L		
2038	2	ATKINS	WM	50	63	PB	LI	M	60	73
2039	1	AUSTEN	EM	100	166	DE	EM	L	100	166
2040	1	AUSTIN	AY	5	5	PO	QU	L	5	5
2041	1	AUSTIN	ED	1000	2222	EL	TP	M	1000	2222
2042	1	AUSTIN	HE	380	1893	MA	AN	U		
2042	2	AUSTIN	HE	220	729	MA	AN	U	600	2622
2043	1	AVERY	SA	1550	2764	CN	LI	M		
2043	2	AVERY	SA	25	0	ZW	ZW	M	1575	2764
2044	1	BABB	WM	50	111	DC	ZW	M	50	111
2045	1	BABINGTON	MI	200	333	TE	WM	L	200	333
2046	1	BABINGTON	TH	100	166	SK	EM	L	100	166
2047	1	BAGLETHOLE	WM	5	6	KE	LI	M	5	6
2048	1	BAKE	B.	12	20	RA	WM	L	12	20
2049	1	BAKER	KT	80	133	RA	WM	L	80	133
2050	1	BAKER	WM	150	250	KI	WM	L	150	250
2051	1	BALL	SA	125	277	EL	TP	M	125	277
2052	1	BALL	WM	200	333	SL	EM	L	200	333
2053	1	BALLARD	AA	200	333	NA	EM	L	200	333
2054	1	BALLARD	TH	25	25	DE	EM	L	25	25
2055	1	BANISTER	TH	50	111	DC	ZW	M	50	111
2056	1	BARBOR	GB	100	166	MO	EM	L	100	166
2057	1	BARBOR	JO	50	83	MO	EM	L	50	83
2058	1	BARBOR	JS	50	83	MO	EM	L	50	83
2059	1	BAREFOOT	RO	25	41	ST	QU	L	25	41
2060	1	BAREFOOTE	B.	100	166	MR	QU	L	100	166
2061	1	BARKER	TH	50	68	EL	TP	M	50	68
2062	1	BARKER	WM	400	2330	UI	DN	U		
2062	2	BARKER	WM	200	2330	UI	DN	U	600	4660
2063	1	BARKHAM	ED	600	1000	MR	QU	L	600	1000
2064	1	BARLOWE	FR	62	192	CN	AR	U	62	192
2065	1	BARNABYE	AM	25	55	IO	TP	M	25	55
2066	1	BARNARD	JO	200	333	PO	QU	L	200	333
2067	1	BARNARDISTON	AR	600	1000	CU	QU	L	600	1000
2068	1	BARNARDISTON	MI	20	0	ZW	ZW	M	20	0
2069	1	BARNARDISTON	SA	100	166	CU	QU	L	100	166
2070	1	BARNARDISTON	TH	625	1388	IO	TP	M		

1	2	3	4	5	6	7	8	9	10	11
2070	2	BARNARDISTON	TH	500	833	NA	EM	L	1125	2221
2071	1	BARNES	JO	12	13	RA	WM	L	12	13
2072	1	BARNES	RO	.25	25	RA	WM	L	25	25
2073	1	BARNES	WM	25	25	RA	WM	L	25	25
2074	1	BARRETT	CH	163	207	MR	QU	L	163	207
2075	1	BARRETT	JO	300	666	CY	LI	M		
2075	2	BARRETT	JO	200	444	CN	LI	M	500	1110
2076	1	BARRETT	PE	162	207	MR	QU	L	162	207
2077	1	BARRETT	RO	100	137	CY	LI	M	100	137
2078	1	BARRINGTON	JO	1200	2000	SL	EM	L	1200	2000
2079	1	BARROWE	RO	250	1250	AD	DN	U	250	1250
2080	1	BARTLETT	WM	20	27	KE	LI	M	20	27
2081	1	BARTON	WM	310	1600	AR	AR	U	310	1600
2082	1	BARWICK	TH	100	500	LE	DN	U	100	500
2083	1	BASSETT	WM	300	411	KE	LI	M	300	411
2084	1	BATEMAN	AA	600	3000	LE	DN	U	600	3000
2085	1	BATES	RI	100	166	SK	EM	L	100	166
2086	1	BAYBEARE	NI	133	296	PB	LI	M	133	296
2087	1	BAYLY	JO	10	10	EG	KI	L	10	10
2088	1	BEACH	MT	50	83	JS	KI	L	50	83
2089	1	BEADLE	HE	150	250	SK	EM.L		150	250
2090	1	BEAKE	RI	337	750	DC	ZW	M	337	750
2091	1	BEALE	MY	100	222	DC	ZW	M	100	222
2092	1	BEAMOUNT	RI	100	166	LU	EM	L	100	166
2093	1	BEARD	RO	200	444	DC	ZW	M	200	444
2094	1	BECK	GB	600	1000	CM	WM	L	600	1000
2095	1	BEDDINGFIELD	HU	200	444	IO	TP	M	200	444
2096	1	BELFIELD	AY	180	400	IC	TP	M	180	400
2097	1	BELL·	A.	50	51	SK	EM	L	5	51
2098	1	BELLERS	FR	100	500	CN	AR	U		
2098	2	BELLERS	FR	250	352	RA	WM	L		
2098	3	BELLERS	FR	50	83	SL	EM	L		
2098	4	BELLERS	FR	600	1000	SL	EM	L		
2098	5	BELLERS	FR	850	1416	FE	WM	L	1850	3351
2099	1	BENCE	AX	1250	2777	IC	TP	M	1250	2777
2100	1	BENNIT	MT	60	100	PC	QU	L	60	100
2101	1	BENTLEY	JO	200	205	MO	EM	L	200	205
2102	1	BENYON	GB	225	375	ST	QU	L	225	375
2103	1	BERNARD	RI	200	333	CE	EM	L	200	333
2104	1	BETSWORTH	RI	50	250	AR	AR	U	50	250
2105	1	BEWLEY	TH	200	333	PO	QU	L	200	333
2106	1	BIDDLE	JO	25	41	PO	QU	L	25	41
2107	1	BIDDOLPH	TS	100	222	CL	TP	M	100	222
2108	1	BIGG	FR	100	222	IO	TP	M		
2108	2	BIGG	FR	200	444	CN	LI	M		
2108	3	BIGG	FR	100	166	LU	EM	L	400	832
2109	1	BIGG	JS	50	111	DC	ZW	M	50	111
2110	1	BIGG	MW	300	500	DE	EM	L	300	500
2111	1	BIRD	WA	9	9	RA	WM	L	9	9
2112	1	BIRKENHEAD	TS	100	222	CL	TP	M	100	222
2113	1	BIRKETT	MN	100	222	CO	ZW	M	100	222
2114	1	BISHOP	EP	20	27	IC	TP	M	20	27
2115	1	BLACKBURROW	WM	50	111	DC	ZW	M	50	111
2116	1	BLACKWELL	JS	337	750	IL	TP	M	337	750
2117	1	BLACKWELL	SA	38	84	CL	TP	M		
2117	2	BLACKWELL	SA	200	274	CL	TP	M	238	358
2118	1	BLACKWELL JR	JO	1350	2914	IK	TP	M	1350	2914
2119	1	BLACKWELL SR	JO	300	666	IK	TP	M	300	666
2120	1	BLADEN	TH	100	500	TU	AR	U	100	500
2121	1	BLAGE	JO	50	154	TU	AR	U	50	154
2122	1	BLAKE	EM	30	66	CY	LI	M	30	66
2123	1	BLANDE	JA	200	444	CL	TP	M	200	444
2124	1	BLATT	JA	133	182	IO	TP	M	133	182
2125	1	BLIGH	JO	600	1000	MC	EM	L	600	1000
2126	1	BLINCKHORNE	JO	50	83	GA	KI	L	50	83
2127	1	BLUNDEN	OV	20	0	ZW	ZW	M		
2127	2	BLUNDEN	OV	125	208	LS	KI	L	145	208
2128	1	BOALE	JO	10	10	PO	QU	L	10	10
2129	1	BOALE	RO	5	5	PO	QU	L	5	5
2130	1	BOATE	GR	468	847	IK	TP	M	468	847
2131	1	BOATE	KT	156	282	IK	TP	M	156	282
2132	1	BOND	JO	50	111	PB	LI	M	50	111
2133	1	BOND	NI	100	222	MO	TP	M	100	222
2134	1	BOONE	TH	6	6	RA	WM	L		
2134	2	BOONE	TH	50	83	RA	WM	L	56	89
2135	1	BOONE	TH	600	1333	CN	LI	M	600	1333
2136	1	BOSSEVILLE	WM	400	888	IO	TP	M	400	868
2137	1	BOTTERELL	WM	50	83	GA	KI	L	50	83

1	2	3	4	5	6	7	8	9	10	11
2138	1	BOUGHTON	RI	115	435	IL	TP	M		
2138	2	BOUGHTON	RI	92	202	IL	TP	M	207	637
2139	1	BOX	HE	400	888	CL	TP	M	400	888
2140	1	BOYCE	JO	10	10	EG	KI	L		
2140	2	BOYCE	JO	100	222	IO	TP	M	110	232
2141	1	BOYCE	RO	50	83	FE	WM	L	50	83
2142	1	BRADLEY	GE	100	222	DC	ZW	M	100	222
2143	1	BRADLEY	MK	100	222	DC	ZW	M	1CO	222
2144	1	BRADSHAW	EZ	50	83	LS	KI	L	50	83
2145	1	BRAMPTON	M.	100	102	MR	QU	L	100	102
2146	1	BRAND	JS	200	333	MO	EM	L	200	333
2147	1	BRAND	MW	200	206	KI·	WM	L	200	206
2148	1	BRANDON	NI	45	75	LU	EM	L	45	75
2149	1	BRERETON	WM	1700	2757	IO	TP	M		
2149	2	BRERETON	WM	350	1750	AR	AR	U		
2149	3	BRERETON	WM	400	2000	CN	AR	U		
2149	4	BRERETON	WM	100	222	IO	TP,	M	2550	6729
2150	1	BRETLAND	TH	100	500	BE	AN	U	100	500
2151	1	BREWSTER	DA	100	223	CL'	TP	M	100	223
2152	1	BREWSTER	SA	100	222	CL	TP	M	100	222
2153	1	BRIDGES	JO	1800	3999	CN	LI	M	1800	3999
2154	1	BRIGGS	MN	125	208	DE	EM	L	125	208
2155	1	BRIGHT	JO	600	1333	CC	ZW	M	600	1333
2156	1	BRIGHTWELL	TH	1583	3581	DC	ZW	M	1583	3581
2157	1	BRIGSTOCK	GE	450	750	SL	EM	L	450	750
2158	1	BRINLEY	LU	450	750	FE	WM	L	450	750
2159	1	BRISCOE	JS	250	1250	UI	DN	U	250	1250
2160	1	BRISCOE	TH	100	222	CL	TP	M	100	222
2161	1	BRISTOW	HE	50	83	PO	QU	L	50	83
2162	1	BROCKETT	SR	50	83	ST	QU	L	50	83
2163	1	BROCKHOVEN	JO	800	4000	DU¡	AN	U	800	4000
2164	1	BROGHTON	AW	100	222	EL	TP	M	100	222
2165	1	BROKING	NI	145	149	EG	KI	L		
2165	2	BROKING	NI	200	333	EG	KI	L	345	482
2166	1	BROOMER	RI	25	111	PO	QU	L	25	111
2167	1	BROWKER	TH	200	617	UI	DN	U	200	617
2168	1	BROWNE	JO	6	10	RA	WM	L	6	10
2169	1	BROWNE	JS	75	125	RA	WM	L	75	125
2170	1	BROWNE	RI	600	1000	SK	EM	L	6CC	1000
2171	1	BROWNEJOHN	JO	100	166	SK	EM	L	100	166
2172	1	BRUMSKELL·	OL	20	44	IK	TP	M	20	44
2173	1	BUCKLAND	JO	50	51	MY	WM	L	¡50	51
2174	1	BULLER	MY	600	1333	ZL	ZW	M	600	1333
2175	1	BUNCHE	JO	100	222	CO	ZW	M	100	222
2176	1	BUNSTON	WM	25	41	LU	EM	L	25	41
2177	1	BURCH	TH	200	333	EG	KI	L	200	333
2178	1	BURGES	CU	700	1555	MD	TP·	M	7CO	1555
2179	1	BURIE	RI	325	722	KE	LI	M		
2179	2	BURIE	RI	325	722	KE	LI	M		
2179	3	BURIE	RI	25	56	KE	LI	M		
2179	4	BURIE	RI	325	722	KE	LI	M		
2179	5	BURIE	RI	80	177	KE	LI	M		
2179	6	BURIE·	RI	200	205	EG	KI	L	1280	2604
2180	1	BURMAN	WM	100	500	LE	DN	U	100	500
2181	1	BURTON	HE	100	166	NA·	EM	L	100	166
2182	1	BURTON	SI	50	111	DC	ZW	M	50	111
2183	1	BURTON	WM	350	583	MY	WM	L	350	583
2184	1	BUSHELL	ED	400	2000	LE	DN	U	4CO	2000
2185	1	CADOGAN	WM	400	411	NA	EM	L	400	411
2186	1	CALECOTT	EZ	5	6	KE	LI	M	5	6
2187	1	CANTLIN	DA	25	42	SK	EM	L	25	42
2188	1	CAREY	LC	26	27	RA	WM	L	26	27
2189	1	CAREY	RI	200	0	EG	KI	L	200	0
2190	1	CARPENTERS	CO	73	122	CU	QU	L	73	122
2191	1	CARROLL	JS	100	222	CC	ZW	M	100	222
2192	1	CARTER	R.	50	83	JS	KI	L	50	83
2193	1	CARY	WM	132	220	RA	WM	L	132	220
2194	1	CASTLE	RI	120	200	NA	EM	L	120	200
2195	1	CHAMBERLAIN	AM	625	1389	CN	LI	M	625	1389
2196	1	CHAMBERLAIN	TH	625	1388	CN	LI	M		
2196	2	CHAMBERLAIN	TH	350	777	CN	LI	M	975	2165
2197	1	CHAMPNIES	JO	100	166	SW	QU	L	100	166
2198	1	CHANDLER	RI	100	166	EG	KI	L	100	166
2199	1	CHAVENY	PE	100	137	IO	TP	M	100	137
2200	1	CHENEY	CH	600	617	SW	QU	L	600	617
2201	1	CHEWNING	TH	245	544	IO	TP	M	245	544
2202	1	CHEYNEY	AA	100	222	DC	ZW	M	100	222
2203	1	CHILD	JO	10	10	LU	EM	L	10	10

1	2	3	4	5	6	7	8	9	10	11
2204	1	CHILD	MV	50.	83	SL	EM	L	50	83
2205	1	CHILD	MY	50	83	SL	EM	L	50	83
2206	1	CHILD	RO	50	111	CO	ZW	M	50	111
2207	1	CHILLINGWORTH	RI	50	83	ST	QU	L	50	83
2208	1	CLAPHAM	R.	30	41	CL	TP	M	30	41
2209	1	CLARE	MY	25	42	ST	QU	L	25	42
2210	1	CLARKE	CR	360	566	EG	KI	L		
2210	2	CLARKE	CR	75	77	EG	KI	L	435	643
2211	1	CLARKE	GE	650	1059	MO	EM	L		
2211	2	CLARKE	GE	100	166	KI	WM	L		
2211	3	CLARKE	GE	262	389	SK	EM	L		
2211	4	CLARKE	GE	125	577	AD	DN	U		
2211	5	CLARKE	GE	2200	4892	CL	TP	M		
2211	6	CLARKE	GE	250	416	JS	KI	L		
2211	7	CLARKE	GE	1000	2222	MD	TP	M		
2211	8	CLARKE	GE	680	1133	LU	EM	L		
2211	9	CLARKE	GE	350	777	IO	TP	M	5617	11631
2212	1	CLARKE	JA	200	205	DM	WM.L		200	205
2213	1	CLARKE·	JA	100	222	CO	ZW	M	100	222
2214	1	CLARKE	JO	1000	1666	SW	QU	L		
2214	2	CLARKE	JO	400	888	CO	ZW	M	1400	2554
2215	1	CLARKE	JS	50	51	EG·KI	L		50	51
2216	1	CLARKE	RI	200	1000	BE	AN	U	200	1000
2217	1	CLARKE	SA	300	666	IO	TP	M	300	666
2218	1	CLARKE	TH	100	166	MO	EM	L	100	166
2219	1	CLARKE	WM	6	6	RA	WM	L	·6	6
2220	1	CLARKE CO	SI	300	500	EG	KI	L	300	500
2221	1	CLAY	JO	60	133	IO	TP	M	60	133
2222	1	CLAYDON	JO	200	205	DM	WM	L	200	205
2223	1	CLELAND	BJ	25	25	RA	WM	L	25	25
2224	1	CLEMENT	GG	3000	0	GA	KI	L		
2224	2	CLEMENT	GG	2000	0	GA	KI	L		
2224	3	CLEMENT	GG	50	0	ZW	ZW	M	5050	0
2225	1	CLIFTON	JS	115	113	IO	TP	M	115	113
2226	1	CLOTWORTHY	JO	750	3749	MA	AN	U		
2226	2	CLOTWORTHY	JO	370	1811	MA	AN	U		
2226	3	CLOTWORTHY	JO	1134	5671	DU	AN	U	2254	11231
2227	1	CLUTTERBUCK	RI	900	2000	MD	TP	M	900	2000
2228	1	COBB	JO	125	208	EG	KI	L	125	208
2229	1	COCK	JO	100	500	ON	AR	U	100	500
2230	1	COCK	TH	200	333	NA	EM	L	200	333
2231	1	COISH	E.	600	1000	KI	WM	L	600	1000
2232	1	COLE	FR	62	312	ON	AR	U	62	312
2233	1	COLE	TH	300	500	MY	WM	L	300	500
2234	1	COLEBY	RO	225	308	DC	ZW	M	225	308
2235	1	COLES	HE	100	222	DC	ZW	M	100	222
2236	1	COLLIER	BJ	125	208	ST	QU	L	125	208
2237	1	COLLIER	EZ	25	41	ST	QU	L	25	41
2238	1	COLLINS	FR	412	687	BA	KI	L	412	687
2239	1	COLLINS	WM	162	812	CN	AR	U	162	812
2240	1	COMBE	TH	20	27	IO	TP	M	20	27
2241	1	CONSTANTINE	J.	150	247	SW	QU	L	·150	247
2242	1	COOKE	EZ	100	222	IO	TP.M		100	222
2243	1	COOKE	TH	300	500	LU	EM	·L	300	500
2244	1	COOPER	SA	50	250	DU	AN	U	50	250
2245	1	COOPER	WM	100	222	DC	ZW	M	100	222
2246	1	CORBETT	MN	100	166	PO	QU	L		
2246	2	CORBETT	MN	700	1166	RA	WM	L		
2246	3	CORBETT	MN	150	217	MR	QU	L	950	1549
2247	1	COULSON	JO	200	1000	LE	DN	U	200	1000
2248	1	COURAGE	JA	50	83	PO	CU	L	50	83
2249	1	COURAGE	SN	50	83	PO	QU	L	50	83
2250	1	COVE	WM	50	·83	MY	WM	L	50	83
2251	1	COX	·JA	100	166	GA	KI	L	100	166
2252	1	COXON	CL	50	111	DC	ZW	M	50	111
2253	1	CRAWLEY	RO	250	1111	IL	TP	M	250	1111
2254	1	CRESSEY	L.	10	22	IK	TP	M	10	22
2255	1	CRESWICK	AA	62	192	CN	AR	U	62	192
2256	1	CRISPE	EL	1075	1791	MY	WM	L	1075	1791
2257	1	CRISPE	NI	181	402	CN	LI	M·		
2257	2	CRISPE	NI	720	1600	CN	LI	M	901	2002
2258	1	CRISPE	RI	600	1333	DC	ZW	M	600	1333
2259	1	CROMWELL	OL	850	1257	EG	KI	L	850	1257
2260	1	CROOKE	CH	225	500	IO	TP	M	225	500
2261	1	CROSSING	RI	250	390	KI	WM	L	250	390
2262	1	CROWDER	TH	100	166	ST	QU	L	100	166
2263	1	CUBITT	JS	25	25	RA	WM	L	25	25
2264	1	CULMER	RI	250	416	LU	EM	L		

1	2	3	4	5	6	7	8	9	10	11
2264	2	CULMER	RI	250	416	SL	EM	L	500	832
2265	1	CURRER	WM	1225	2722	CN	LI	M		
2265	2	CURRER	WM	200	333	MY	WM	L	1425	3C55
2266	1	CURTIS	JO	40	44	CL	TP	M	40	44
2267	1	DABBE	SA	70	116	MO	EM	L		
2267	2	DABBE	SA	100	102	EG	KI	L	.170	218
2268	1	DANIEL	SN	50	111	IL	TP	M	50	111
2269	1	DANIEL	TH	50	111	IL	TP	M	.50	111
2270	1	DARTMOUTH	CA	1518	0	RA	WM	L		
2270	2	DARTMOUTH	CA	53	54	RA	WM·	L	157	54
2271	1	DAVEY	MY	4	4	RA	WM	L	4	4
2272	1	DAVEY	MY	600	1333	MD	TP	M	600	1333
2273	1	DAVIS	WM	10	.10	PO	QU	L	10	10
2274	1	DAVY	WM	150	250	CU	CU	L		
2274	2	DAVY	WM	50	83	CU	QU	L	200	333
2275	1	DAWES	RI	300	666	DC	ZW	M	300	666
2276	1	DAWES	RO	300	666	CN	LI	M	300	666
2277	1	DAWLING	JO	115	404	IL	TP	M		
2277	2	DAWLING	JO	90	202	IL	TP	M	205	606
2278	1	DAWSON	JO	600	1333	CL	TP	M		
2278	2	DAWSON	JO	300	496	IO	TP	M	9CC	1829
2279	1	DAY	HE	350	777	IK	TP	M	350	777
2280	1	DEACON	RI	37	38	MO	EM	L	37	38
2281	1	DEANE	TH·	20	27	PB	LI	M	20	27
2282	1	DEANE	WM	10	13	PB	LI	M	10	13
2283	1	DELANOY	PE	100	166	ST	QU	L	100	166
2284	1	DELAWNE	HE	100	500	CA	AN	U	100	500
2285	1	DENNIS	AY	40	41	PO	QU	L	40	41
2286	1	DENNIS	TH	50	68	MD	TP	M	50	68
2287	1	DIKE	JO	10	10	PO	QU	L	10	10
2288	1	DINGLEY	EL	60	100	PO	QU	L	60	100
2289	1	DOE	CH	1134	5672	DU	AN	U	1134	5672
2290	1	DOLMEY	EZ	200	333	ST	QU	L	200	333
2291	1	DOVER	DA	300	500	CU	QU	L	300	500
2292	1	DOVER	GE	250	416	DM	WM	L	250	416
2293	1	DRAKE	FR	200	206	KI	WM	L	200	206
2294	1	DRAKE	RG	500	1111	IK	TP	M	500	1111
2295	1	DRING	SI	100	500	CN	AR	U	100	500
2296	1	DRURY	RI	20	0	ZW	ZW	M	20	0
2297	1	DRYDON	JO	600	1000	EG	KI	L	6CC	1000
2298	1	DUCANE	BJ	50	111	CN	LI	M	50	111
2299	1	DUKE	FR	200	333	MO	EM	L	200	333
2300	1	DURANO	PE	200	333	ST	QU	L	200	333
2301	1	DURANT	EZ	15	20	CN	LI	M	15	20
2302	1	EARLSTONS	WM	200	333	LU	EM	L	200	333
2303	1	EAST	ED	100	166	MY	WM	L	100	166
2304	1	EDLIN	SA	100	166	SK	EM	.L	100	166
2305	1	EDWARDS	JA	1100	5117	DU	AN	U		
2305	2	EDWARDS	JA·	63	313	CU	AN	U	1163	5430
2306	1	ELDRED	RO	100	222	MD	TP	M	100	222
2307	1	ELLIOTT	SA	200	333	DE	EM	L	200	333
2308	1	ELLIS	FR	62	104	SW	QU	L	62	104
2309	1	ELLIS	JO	10	10	PC	QU	L	10	10
2310	1	ELMSTON	HE	25	55	MD	TP	M	25	55
2311	1	ENDERBY	DA	100	222	CO	ZW	M	100	222
2312	1	ESCOTT	EP	4	4	RA	WM	L	4	4
2313	1	ESTWICK	ST	800	1777	CN	LI	M		
2313	2	ESTWICK	ST	750	1250	BA	KI	L	155C	3027
2314	1	EVANS	RI	400	666	ST	QU	L	400	666
2315	1	EWER	GE	50	83	SK	EM	L	50	83
2316	1	EXETER	CA	1883	2583	MD	TP	M	1883	25E3
2317	1	EYRES	TH	200	444	MC	TP	M	200	444
2318	1	FARELTON	JO	50	83	ST	QU	L	50	83
2319	1	FARMER	GE	600	617	KI	WM	L	600	617
2320	1	FARRINGTON	AY	500	833	EG	KI	L	500	833
2321	1	FARRINGTON	CD	500	833	EG	KI	L	500	833
2322	1	FARWELL	CH	100	500	CA	AN	U	100	500
2323	1	FEIBYAN	WM	6	10	RA	WM	L	6	10
2324	1	FETHERSTON	H.	1200	2000	SW	QU	L	1200	2000
2325	1	FEWSTER	EZ	150	750	UI	DN	U	150	750
2326	1	FIELD	JO	50	111	CN	LI	M	50	111
2327	1	FIELD	NI	25	41	MY	WM	L	25	41
2328	1	FIELD	TH	600	1000	SL	EM	L		
2328	2	FIELD	TH	40	41	SL	EM	L	640	1041
2329	1	FIELD	WM	50	83	ST	QU	L	50	83
2330	1	FIENNES ·	NL	300	500	KI	WM	L	300	500
2331	1	FIGG	VL	100	166	CU	QU	L	100	166
2332	1	FILLINGHAM	MY	50	83	EG	KI	L	50	83

1	2	3	4	5	6	7	8	9	10	11
2333	1	FINCH	FR	200	444	IO	TP	M	200	444
2334	1	FISHER	JA	25	41	SK	EM	L	25	41
2335	1	FISHER	JO	25	55	IC	TP	M	25	55
2336	1	FISHER	JO.	150	750	DU	AN	U	150	750
2337	1	FISKE	JO	3,00	666	CC	ZW	M	3CO	666
2338	1	FISKE	TH	200	444	CG	ZW	M	200	444
2339	1	FITCHBORNE	HE	37	38	RA	WM	L	37	38
2340	1	FLARR	WM	50	'83	EG	QU	L	50	83
2341	1	FLEETWOOD	CH	300	500	SW	QU	L	300	500
2342	1	FLEMING	JO	10	10	MY	WM	L	10	10
2343	1	FLETCHER	AY	6	10	RA	WM	L	6	10
2344	1	FLETCHER	BJ	500	833	KI	WM	L	500	833
2345	1	FLETCHER	JA	2CO	444	IL	TP	M	200	444
2346	1	FLETCHER	PL	100	500	BE	AN	U	100	500
2347	1	FLOYD	RI	750	1250	RA	WM	·L		
2347	2	FLOYD	RI	300	500	RA	WM	L	1050	1750
2348	1	FOLLOTT	AY	9	9	RA	WM	L	9	9
2349	1	FOSTER	CR	100	222	CL	TP	M	100	222
2350	1	FOUNTAINE	MY	210	350	GA	KI	L	210	350
2351	1	FOWKE	JO	600	1333	IK	TP	M	600	1333
2352	1	FOWLER	M.	100	102	MR	QU	L	100	102
2353	1	FOWLER	MY	60	133	PB	LI	M	60	133
2354	1	FOX	CH	50	83	SK	EM	L	50	83
2355	1	FRANCIS	A.	25	34	CL	TP	M	25	34
2356	1	FRANCIS	EZ	25	34	CL	TP	M	25	34
2357	1	FRENCH	JO	600	1000.	NA	EM	L	600	1000
2358	1	FRERE	TB	800	4000'	LE	DN	U		
2358	2	FRERE	TB	200	1000	LE	DN	U	100C	50C0
2359	1	FRYE	JO	200	333	LU	EM	L	200	333
2360	1	FRYER	FR.	15	15	EG	KI	L	15	15
2361	1	GARDNER	JO	50	111	CN	LI	M	50	111
2362	1	GARDNER	RO	87	145	SW	QU	L	87	145
2363	1	GARLAND	MY	375	833	MD	TP	M	375	833
2364	1	GARLAND	RO	375	833	MD	TP	M	375	833
2365	1	GARNER	RO	200	333	LU	EM	L	200	333
2366	1	GARTH	JO	100	166	DE	EM	L	100	166
2367	1	GARTON	WM	62	104	PO	QU	L	62	1C4
2368	1	GASKELL	AD	50	111	CN	LI	M	50	111
2369	1	GAY	EZ	100	102	EG	KI	L,	100	102
2370	1	GERRARD	GL	600	1000	SL	EM	L	600	1000
2371	1	GIBBS	CR	50	83	EG	KI	L	50	83
2372	1	GIBBS	RO	7	6	PG	QU	L	7	6
2373	1	GIBBS	WM	500	1110	CO	ZW	M	500	1110
2374	1	GLASCOCK	MT	50	83	ST	QU	L	50	83
2375	1	GLOUCESTER	CA	1275	2124	ST	QU	L	1275	4
2376	1	GODDARD	JO	100	166	MO	EM	L	100	166
2377	1	GODFREY	JO	100	500	ON	AR	U	100	5C0
2378	1	GODSEN	HE	100	222	IK	TP	M	100	222
2379	1	GOLD	IZ	200	333	LU	EM	L	200	333
2380	1	GOLD	JO	262	436	SL	EM	L	262	436
2381	1	GOOD	EL	100	222	DC	ZW	M	100	222
2382	1	GOODWIN	BJ	525	875	KI	WM	L	525	875
2383	1	GOODWIN	RO	525	875	KI	WM	L	525	875
2384	1	GOODYEARE	TH	20	33	JS	KI	L	20	33
2385	1	GOWER	TH	138	0	ZW	ZW	M		
2385	2	GOWER	TH	99	0	ZW	ZW	M		
2385	3	GOWER	TH	600	1333	CL	TP	M	837	1333
2386	1	GRAVES	RI	200	333	MO	EM	L	2C0	333
2387	1	GRAY	CR	20	33	ST	QU	L	20	33
2388	1	GRAY	JO	25	77	DU	AN	U	25	77
2389	1	GREENINGS	WM	5	5	PO	QU	·L	.5	5
2390	1	GREENSMITH	JO	300	500	EG	KI	L	300	500
2391	1	GREGORY	JN	200	333	MC	EM	L	200	333
2392	1	GROCER	JN	100	222	CC	ZW	M	100	222
2393	1	GROVE	HG	100	222	CO	ZW	M	100	222
2394	1	GUNNING	JO	1000	1666	RA	WM	L	1000	1666
2395	1	GUNSTON	WM	100	166	RA	WM	L	100	166
2396	1	GUY	JO	100	166	JS	KI	L	100	166
2397	1	HADDILOWS	RI	50	111	IO	TP	M	50	111
2398	1	HALES	JO	350	583	ST	QU	L		
2398	2	HALES	JO	400	666	ST	QU	L	750	1249
2399	1	HALES	RO	1200	2000	KI	WM	L	1200	2000
2400	1	HALFRED	TH	50	51	RA	WM	L	50	51
2401	1	HALL	GY	25	42	RA	WM	L	25	42
2402	1	HALL	JO	25	41	RA	WM	L	25	41
2403	1	HALLS	GE	125	278	DC	ZW	M	125	278
2404	1	HALLS	SA	125	277	DC	ZW	M	125	277
2405	1	HAMOND	EZ	200	206	KI·	WM	L	200	206

1	2	3	4	5	6	7	8	9	10	11
2406	1	HAMOND	RO	3C0	500	TE	QU	L		
2406	2	HAMOND	RO	143	319	IC	TP	M		
2406	3	HAMOND	RO	140	700	LE	DN	U		
2406	4	HAMOND	RO	60	300	LE	DN	U	643	1819
2407	1	HAMOND	TH	100	166	KI	WW	L	100	166
2408	1	HAMPDON	RI	31	51	KI	WM	L	31	51
2409	1	HAMPSON	HE	4C0	2000	ON	AR	U	400	20C0
2410	1	HAMPSON	TH	40	200	CN	AR	U	40	200
2411	1	HAMPTON	WM	100	222	CN	LI	M	100	222
2412	1	HANNER	JO	26	27	PC	QU	L	26	27
2413	1	HAPLEHILL	GL	12	13	RA	WM	L	12	13
2414	1	HARDING	GI	50	111	CN	LI	M		
2414	2	HARDING	GI	220	388	CN	LI	M		
2414	3	HARDING	GI	20	33	MY	WM	L		
2414	4	HARDING	GI	795	1680	CN	LI	M		
2414	5	HARDING	GI	95C	2111	CY	LI	M	2035	4323
2415	1	HARDING	TH	970	2155	CY	LI	M	97G	2155
2416	1	HARDING	WM	2E0	622	CY	LI	M	280	622
2417	1	HARFORD	AY	27	44	RA	WM	L	27	44
2418	1	HARMER	RI	100	500	CN	AR	U	100	500
2419	1	HARMON	RA	100	137	PB	LI	M	100	137
2420	1	HARMON	RI	100	102	MR	QU	L	1C0	1C2
2421	1	HARRINGTON	JO	200	444	ZL	ZW	M	200	444
2422	1	HARRINGTON	L.	150	154	NA	EM	L	150	154
2423	1	HARRIS	CH	6C0	1000	BA	KI	L	600	1CCC
2424	1	HARRISON	EM	600	1333	CY	LI	M	600	1333
2425	1	HARRISON	JO	450	749	EG	KI	L	450	749
2426	1	HART	JO	100	222	CL	TP	M	1C0	222
2427	1	HARVES	JO	650	3250	DU	AN	U	650	3250
2428	1	HARWELL	HE	100	166	GA	KI	L	100	166
2429	1	HATT	JO	600	1333	MD	TP	M	600	1333
2430	1	HAWARD	NI	1C0	222	EL	TP	M	100	222
2431	1	HAWES	JO	400	888	EL	TP	M	400	888
2432	1	HAWKES	HE	125	208	ST	QU	L	125	208
2433	1	HAWKINS	WM	1200	6000	AD	ND	U		
2433	2	HAWKINS	WM	558	2793	AC	DN	U		
2433	3	HAWKINS	WM	44	228	UI	ON	U		
2433	4	HAWKINS	WM	15B0	7550	UI	DN	U		
2433	5	HAWKINS	WM	1580	7550	UI	DN	U		
2433	6	HAWKINS	WM	145	724	UI	DN	U		
2433	7	HAWKINS	WM	1580	7550	UI	DN	U	6687	32355
2434	1	HAYES	JA	100	222	EL	TP	M	100	222
2435	1	HAYES	PH	25	25	RA	WM	L	25	25
2436	1	HEARD	JO	20	20	FC	QU	L	20	20
2437	1	HEARNE	JI	300	500	MR	QU	L	300	5C0
2438	1	HEATHCOTT	BJ	50	250	BE	AN	U	50	250
2439	1	HEATHCOTT	GC	25	34	EL	TP	M	25	34
2440	1	HEATHCOTT	JS	50	250	BE	AN	U	50	250
2441	1	HEATHER	WM	50	277	IK	TP	M		
2441	2	HEATHER	WM	75	0	IK	TP	M		
2441	3	HEATHER	WM	100	222	IK	TP	M	225	499
2442	1	HENLY	JO	300	500	RA	WM	L	3C0	500
2443	1	HENMAN	WM	150	250	MY	WM	L	150	250
2444	1	HERFORD	HR	25	25	MO	EM	L	25	25
2445	1	HERRING	MI	900	2000	EL	TP	M	900	2000
2446	1	HEVENINGHAM	WM	600	1000	GA	KI	L	600	1000
2447	1	HEYDON	RI	125	208	SW	QU	L	125	208
2448	1	HICCOCKS	WM	602	1004	ST	QU	L	602	1004
2449	1	HIGHGATE	EM	25	125	MA	AN	U	25	125
2450	1	HILDERSEY	MT	210	349	RA	WM	L	210	349
2451	1	HILL	ED	175	388	CY	LI	M	175	388
2452	1	HILL	FR	150	282	RA	WM	L	150	282
2453	1	HILL	RI	250	555	CL	TP	M	250	555
2454	1	HILL	RW	250	555	MO	TP	M	250	555
2455	1	HILL	WM	200	333	RA	WM	L	200	333
2456	1	HITCHCOCK	WM	350	583	MY	WM	L	350	583
2457	1	HOARE	DD	62	104	MO	EM	L	62	1C4
2458	1	HOBSON	WM	250	416	RA	WM	L	250	416
2459	1	HODGES	TH	600	1000	DE	EM	L	60G	1000
2460	1	HOFTER	IZ	125	208	ST	QU	L	125	208
2461	1	HOLLAND	CU	300	666	CO	ZW	M	300	666
2462	1	HOLLAND	JO	1600	2666	BA	KI	L	1600	2666
2463	1	HOLLYGROVE	JO	25	25	RA	WM	L	25	25
2464	1	HOLSMAN	MA	10	13	KE	LI	M	10	13
2465	1	HOME	SA	50	83	RA	WM	L	50	83
2466	1	HONLEY	HE	100	102	RA	WM	L	100	102
2467	1	HONOR	HE	750	1249	BA	KI	L	75C	1249
2468	1	HONOR	JO	750	1250	BA	KI	L	750	1250

1	2	3	4	5	6	7	8	9	10	11
2469	1	HOODHAM	WM	750	1250	KI	WM	L	750	1250
2470	1	HOPPING	CH	100	166	EG	KI	L	100	166
2471	1	HORMAN	RO	200	444	CN	LI	M	200	444
2472	1	HORSWILL	EM	4	4	RA	WM	L	4	4
2473	1	HORWOOD	RI	25	25	RA	WM	L	25	25
2474	1	HOUBLON	PE	200	333	ST	QU	L	200	333
2475	1	HOUBTON	JA	900	2000	CN	LI	M	900	2000
2476	1	HOXTON	JO	100	102	CU	QU	L	100	102
2477	1	HUBBARD	WM	100	222	IK	TP	M	100	222
2478	1	HUDSTON	GE	100	500	LE	DN	U	100	500
2479	1	HUGHES	GE	100	500	MA	AN	U	100	500
2480	1	HUMPHREY	JO	50	111	DC	ZW	M	50	111
2481	1	HUMPHRIES	NL	100	500	LE	DN	U	100	500
2482	1	HUNT	JS	450	750	LU	EM	L	450	750
2483	1	HUNT	RI	1250	2777	CN	LI	M		
2483	2	HUNT	RI	130	288	CN	LI	M	1380	3065
2484	1	HUNTER	JO	100	222	EL	TP	M	100	222
2485	1	HURST	JO	480	800	LS	KI	L	480	800
2486	1	HUSSEY	WM	100	166	KI	WM	L	100	166
2487	1	HUSSEY SR	TH	200	333	DM	WM	L	200	333
2488	1	HUSSEY JR	TH	433	764	ZL	ZW	M	433	764
2489	1	HUTCHINSON	D.	500	705	NA	EM	L	500	705
2490	1	HUTCHINSON	RI	760	1466	IO	TP	M	760	1466
2491	1	ILLINGWORTH	TH	60	100	FE	WM	L	60	100
2492	1	INGLE	TH	25	41	ST	QU	L	25	41
2493	1	INGRAM	L.	1000	1371	IO	TP	M	1000	1371
2494	1	INNSWORTH	SR	50	83	FE	WM	L	50	83
2495	1	IRISH	SA	12	20	RA	WM	L	12	20
2496	1	IRONS	RI	25	55	DC	ZW	M	25	55
2497	1	IRONS	TH	60	133	DC	ZW	M	60	133
2498	1	JACKSON	AX	100	166	NA	EM	L	100	166
2499	1	JACKSON	TH	100	222	IO	TP	M	100	222
2500	1	JAGOE	RO	6	10	RA	WM	L	6	10
2501	1	JAGOE	WM	50	83	RA	WM	L		
2501	2	JAGOE	WM	6	6	RA	WM	L	56	89
2502	1	JAQUES	JS	750	1666	CL	TP	M	750	1666
2503	1	JEFFERIES	JO	100	500	LE	DN	U	100	500
2504	1	JENKINS	ME	200	333	MY	WM	L	200	333
2505	1	JENNER	TH	25	55	CO	ZW	M	25	55
2506	1	JENNEY	WM	200	333	NA	EM	L	200	333
2507	1	JESOPP	WM	310	318	KI	WM	L	310	318
2508	1	JOHNS	SA	10	13	KE	LI	M	10	13
2509	1	JOHNS	WM	10	10	PC	QU	L	10	10
2510	1	JOHNSON	TH	150	250	CU	QU	L	150	250
2511	1	JONES	G.	100	222	CC	ZW	M	100	222
2512	1	JURIN	IZ	100	222	CN	LI	M	100	222
2513	1	JURIN	JO	50	111	CN	LI	M		
2513	2	JURIN	JO	650	1444	CN	LI	M	700	1555
2514	1	JUXON	AR	200	333	DE	EM	L	200	333
2515	1	JUXON	JO	200	333	DE	EM	L	200	333
2516	1	JUXON	TH	20	0	ZW	ZW	M		
2516	2	JUXON	TH	750	1250	CU	QU	L		
2516	3	JUXON	TH	75	77	CU	QU	L		
2516	4	JUXON	TH	200	333	NA	EM	L		
2516	5	JUXON	TH	25	41	DE	EM	L		
2516	6	JUXON	TH	700	1166	DE	EM	L		
2516	7	JUXON	TH	350	583	DE	EM	L		
2516	8	JUXON	TH	25	41	DE	EM	L	2145	3491
2517	1	KENDRICK	JO	700	1555	IO	TP	M	700	1555
2518	1	KERKHAM	RO	50	111	EL	TP	M	50	111
2519	1	KERRIDGE	TH	400	888	EL	TP	M	400	888
2520	1	KIDDERMINSTER	EM	100	500	LE	DN	U	100	500
2521	1	KILBY	JO	50	83	LU	EM	L	50	83
2522	1	KING	AW	10	50	BE	AN	U	10	50
2523	1	KING	HA	25	125	MA	AN	U	25	125
2524	1	KING	JO	75	166	CN	LI	M	75	166
2525	1	KING	JO	150	333	CC	ZW	M	150	333
2526	1	KING	TH	100	380	ON	AR	U	100	380
2527	1	KINGSTON	JO	150	250	LU	EM	L	150	250
2528	1	KITTLEBUTTON	RI	25	34	IO	TP	M	25	34
2529	1	KNIGHT	CR	10	13	PB	LI	M	10	13
2530	1	KNIGHT	JO	200	333	CU	QU	L		
2530	2	KNIGHT	JO	50	83	CU	QU	L	250	416
2531	1	KNOWLING	ST	25	41	RA	WM	L	25	41
2532	1	LAKE	JO	200	444	EL	TP	M	200	444
2533	1	LAMBELL	GL	625	1388	IO	TP	M	625	1388
2534	1	LAMBERT	RG	300	581	EL	TP	M	300	581
2535	1	LAMBERT	WM	100	222	EL	TP	M	100	222

1	2	3	4	5	6	7	8·9	10	11
2536	1	LAND	TR	12	13	RA	WM L	12	13
2537	1	LANDON	JO	50	83	ST	QU:L	50	83
2538	1	LANE	JO	433	764	CO	ZW M	433	764
2539	1	LANE	WM	600	1000	DE	EM L	600	1000
2540	1	LANGDON	BL	12	13	RA	WM L	12	13
2541	1	LANGDON	DD	10	13	KE	LI M	10	13
2542	1	LANGE	HU	5	5	PO	QU L	5	5
2543	1	LANGHAM	HE	340	755	IO	TP M	340	755
2544	1	LANGWORTH	SA	10	50	BE	AN U	10	50
2545	1	LASINBY	RG	100	222	CL	TP M	100	222
2546	1	LATTIMER	TH	62	138	CN	LI M	62	138
2547	1	LATTYMER	HG	125	208	EG	KI L	125	208
2548	1	LAWRENCE	WA	13	18	KE	LI M	13	18
2549	1	LAWSON	JO	20	33	NA	EM L	20	33
2550	1	LAWSON	WM	100	166	SK	EM L	100	166
2551	1	LEARLETT	EZ	50	51	MR	QU L	50	51
2552	1	LEARLETT	JO	50	51	MR	QU L	50	51
2553	1	LEARS	RG	100	222	IO	TP M	100	222
2554	1	LEAVER	TH	20	33			20	33
2555	1	LEAWARD	JO	50	51	EG	KI L	50	51
2556	1	LEE	GE	25	25	RA	WM L	25	25
2557	1	LEE	JO	250	555	DC	ZW M	250	555
2558	1	LEE	JO	25	55	CO	ZW M	25	55
2559	1	LEGATT	WM	150	111	PO	QU L	150	111
2560	1	LENDALL	JA	50	83	LU	EM L	50	83
2561	1	LENTHALL	TH	200	333	DM	WM L	200	333
2562	1	LEVER	RO	200	444	CN	LI M	200	444
2563	1	LEVITT	JA	45	46	LU	EM L	45	46
2564	1	LEWIN	EM	877	4380	AR	AR U		
2564	2	LEWIN	EM	322	1616	AR	AR U	1199	5996
2565	1	LIBBEY	L.	100	166	JS	KI L	100	166
2566	1	LIDSTONE	TH	6	6	RA	WM L	6	6
2567	1	LINCOLN	TH	100	222	CO	ZW M	100	222
2568	1	LING	BJ	25	25	MC	EM L	25	25
2569	1	LING	JS	100	222	CL	TP M	100	222
2570	1	LIPPIAT	CR	50	250	ON	AR U	50	250
2571	1	LIPPINCOT	FR	100	166	EG	KI L	100	166
2572	1	LISLE LORD		600	1000	KI	WM L		
2572	2	LISLE LORD		1800	3000	SW	QU L	2400	4000
2573	1	LIVINOCK	EZ	125	278	IL	TP M	125	278
2574	1	LIVINOCK	SR	125	277	IL	TP M	125	277
2575	1	LLOYD	CH	125	208	SW	QU L		
2575	2	LLOYD	CH	1000	2222	CN	LI M	1125	2430
2576	1	LOBB	RI	250	416	RA	WM L	250	416
2577	1	LOBNIS	RO	400	633	DC	ZW M	400	633
2578	1	LOCKE	JO	300	500	FE	WM L	300	500
2579	1	LOCKIER	NI	250	555	CN	LI M	250	555
2580	1	LOELING	JO	106	109	JS	KI L	106	109
2581	1	LOMBARD	JO	10	13	PB	LI M	10	13
2582	1	LOME	JO	20	20	DM	WM L	20	20
2583	1	LOMER	JO	4	4	RA	WM L	4	4
2584	1	LONDELL	JA	50	111	CN	LI M	50	111
2585	1	LONDON	CA	5000	8332	DM	WM L		
2585	2	LONDON	CA	2500	4166	SK	EM L	7500	12498
2586	1	LOTON	RI	381	815	DC	ZW M	381	815
2587	1	LOUP	WM	200	333	SW	QU L	200	333
2588	1	LOVE	CR	100	500	AR	AR U	100	500
2589	1	LOVERING	JO	600	1333	DC	ZW M	600	1333
2590	1	LOWDON	JO	25	25	RA	WM L	25	25
2591	1	LOWE	JO	20	20	EG	KI L	20	20
2592	1	LOWE	WM	100	137	ZL	ZW M	100	137
2593	1	LOYE	NI	100	102	RA	WM L	100	102
2594	1	LUCAS	JO	50	250	DU	AN U		
2594	2	LUCAS	JO	100	222	CO	ZW M	150	472
2595	1	LUCAS	L.	400	666	LU	EM L	400	666
2596	1	LUMNEY	L.	95	112	IO	TP M	95	112
2597	1	LUXON	GE	6	6	PO	QU L	16	6
2598	1	LYNN	SA	75	125	ST	QU L	75	125
2599	1	LYON	TH	50	111	CN	LI M	50	111
2600	1	LYTON	FR	78	130	ST	QU L	78	130
2601	1	MACKWORTH	HU	1700	1749	GA	KI L	1700	1749
2602	1	MACUMBER	TH	50	250	BE	AN U	50	250
2603	1	MALLEW ·	WM	1000	1029	SL	EM L	1000	1029
2604	1	MALTHUS	RO	150	333	IK	TP M	150	333
2605	1	MAN	JO	250	555	CL	TP M	250	555
2606	1	MANSOTT	JO	100	222	DC	ZW M	100	222
2607	1	MANTON	NL	180	135	PB	LI M		
2607	2	MANTON	NL	542	1032	PB	LI M	722	1167

1	2	3	4	5	6	7	8	9	10	11
2608	1	MARKS	NL	500	833	KI	WM	L	500	833
2609	1	MARRIOTT	JO	225	327	GA	KI	L	225	327
2610	1	MARRYMAN	WM	100	137	PB	LI	M	100	137
2611	1	MARSHALL	GL	2625	5833	CN	LI	M	2625	5833
2612	1	MARSHALL	JA	400	666	EG	KI	L	400	666
2613	1	MARSHALL	WM	25	41	LU	EM	L	25	41
2614	1	MARTIN	JO	250	389	KI	WM	L	250	389
2615	1	MARTIN	JO	100	166	PC	QU	L	100	166
2616	1	MASHAM	WM	600	1000	SL	EM	L	600	1000
2617	1	MASTERS	RI	300	308	DE	EM	L	3CC	308
2618	1	MATHEW	JA	100	222	EL	TP	M	100	222
2619	1	MATHEW	TH	150	333	EL	TP	M	150	333
2620	1	MATHEWES	JO	12	20	RA	WM	L	12	20
2621	1	MAY	WM	14	14	EG	KI	L	14	14
2622	1	MAYFIELD	WA	5	6	RA	WM	L	5	6
2623	1	MAYNARD	JO	300	500	RA	WM	L	300	500
2624	1	MAYNARD	L.	250	555	CO	ZW	M	250	555
2625	1	MAYNE	JO	230	511	DC	ZW	M	230	511
2626	1	MAYNE	RO	6	6	RA	WM	L	6	6
2627	1	MEARES	BB	100	166	DE	EM	L	100	166
2628	1	MEGGOTT	GE	50	83	ST	QU	L	50	83
2629	1	MELHUISH	MY	150	282	RA	WM	L	15C	282
2630	1	MERRICK	CR	200	333	SW	QU	L	200	333
2631	1	MERRICK	JO	100	166	TE	QU	L	100	166
2632	1	MICKLETHWAIT	NL	1C0	500	ON	AR	U		
2632	2	MICKLETHWAIT	NL	600	1000	SL	EM	L		
2632	3	MICKLETHWAIT	NL	850	1416	FE	WM	L	1550	2916
2633	1	MIDDLETON	SI	1200	2666	IK	TP	M	1200	2666
2634	1	MILLER	AM	100	222	CL	TP	M	100	222
2635	1	MILLER	WM	25	111	PO	QU	L	25	111
2636	1	MINORS	RA	200	333	MG	EM	L	200	333
2637	1	MINRATT	RI	100	222	CC	ZW	M	100	222
2638	1	MOODY	SA	400	888	CG	ZW	M	400	888
2639	1	MOORE	AS	800	1333	MG	EM	L		
2639	2	MOORE	AS	400	666	NA	EM	L	1200	1999
2640	1	MOORE	AY	20	27	KE	LI	M	20	27
2641	1	MOORE	GI	25	34	IO	TP	M	25	34
2642	1	MOORE	TH	150	333	MO	TP	M		
2642	2	MOORE	TH	300	411	MO	TP	M	45C	744
2643	1	MORELL	G.	100	222	CO	ZW	M	1C0	222
2644	1	MORGAN	AY	200	333	RA	WM	L	200	333
2645	1	MORLEY	HT	600	617	DE	EM	L	600	617
2646	1	MORRIS	EZ	27	44	RA	WM	L	27	44
2647	1	MORRIS	SA	125	208	MC	EM	L	125	208
2648	1	MOSELEY	ED	600	3000	MA	AN	U	600	3000
2649	1	MOSYER	JO	800	3888	DU	AN	U		
2649	2	MOSYER	JO	100	137	IL	TP	M	900	4025
2650	1	MOULSWORTH	RO	600	1000	LU	EM	L		
2650	2	MOULSWORTH	RO	6C0	1000	MO	EM	L		
2650	3	MOULSWORTH	RO	300	500	MG	EM	L	1500	2500
2651	1	MUDD	DH	25	25	RA	WM	L	25	25
2652	1	MULLNIS	WM	450	1000	DC	ZW	M	45C	1000
2653	1	MUNDAY	AR	20	27	PB	LI	M	20	27
2654	1	MUNDAY	WM	25	41	PO	QU	L	25	41
2655	1	MURDOCK	GE	100	166	EG	KI	L	100	166
2656	1	MUSGROVE	PH	20	44	IO	TP	M	20	44
2657	1	MUSGROVE	WM	20	27	IO	TP	M	20	27
2658	1	NARY	JO	400	666	MG	EM	L	400	666
2659	1	NETTLES	JO	200	444	CO	ZW	M	200	444
2660	1	NETTLESHIP	HG	450	750	LS	KI	L	450	750
2661	1	NEWCOMEN	B.	62	104				62	104
2662	1	NEWTON	RI	300	666	IO	TP	M	300	666
2663	1	NICHOLLS	RG	50	83	RA	WM	L	50	83
2664	1	NOBBS	JO	156	260	ST	QU	L	156	260
2665	1	NOBLON	PE	450	750	ST	QU	L	450	750
2666	1	NOEL	MA	1040	2311	EL	TP	M	1040	2311
2667	1	NORTHCOTT	JU	100	137	EL	TP	M	100	137
2668	1	NORTHCOTT	SA	50	68	MD	TP	M	50	68
2669	1	NOSEWORTHY	ED	20	20	DE	EM	L	20	20
2670	1	NOSEWORTHY	JO	50	83	CU	QU	L	5C	83
2671	1	NOTLEY	WM	100	222	DC	ZW	M	100	222
2672	1	NUBERRY	R.	25	56	PB	LI	M	25	56
2673	1	OFFICIAL	WM	225	374	FE	WM	L	225	374
2674	1	OLAND	ED	12	20	RA	WM	L	12	20
2675	1	OLIVER	NI	10	13	KE,	LI	M	10	13
2676	1	ONSLOW	RI	400	548	CL	TP	M	4C0	548
2677	1	ORCHARD	TH	150	333	DC	ZW	M	150	333
2678	1	OSBORNE	JO	100	166	SK	EM	L	100	166

1	2	3	4	5	6	7	8	9	10	11
2679	1	OSBORNE	WM	133	296	PB	LI	M	133	296
2680	1	OVERTON	NL	62	312	DU	AN	U	62	312
2681	1	OWER	MW	100	137	PB	LI	M	100	137
2682	1	OWFIELD	JO	500	1111	CL	TP	M	500	1111
2683	1	OWFIELD	WM	250	416	TE	QU	L	250	416
2684	1	PACKER	PH	600	1000	GA	KI	L	600	1000
2685	1	PAGE	AA	20	33	EG	KI	L	20	33
2686	1	PAGE	MY	50	111	MC	TP	M	50	111
2687	1	PALMER	CL	25	25	RA	WM	L	25	25
2688	1	PALMER	E.	612	1020	MG	EM	L	612	1020
2689	1	PALMER	PH	5	6	KE	LI	M	5	6
2690	1	PARGITER	TH	100	222	CN	LI	M	100	222
2691	1	PARKER	EZ	100	166	SW	QU	L	100	166
2692	1	PARKER	JO	25	0	EG	KI	L	25	0
2693	1	PARKER	JO	575	958	NA	EM	L	575	958
2694	1	PARKHURST	RO	600	1333	CN	LI	M	600	1333
2695	1	PARR	CR	100	137	PB	LI	M	1CC	137
2696	1	PARRIS	MA	10	16	EG	KI	L	10	16
2697	1	PARRIS	TH	50	83	CU	QU	L	50	83
2698	1	PARRY	NI	50	250	BE	AN	U	50	250
2699	1	PARSONS	FR	90	124	MY	WM	L	90	124
2700	1	PARSONS	HE	100	166	LU	EM	L	100	166
2701	1	PARSONS	RO	50	111	CN	LI	M	5C	111
2702	1	PARTRIDGE	JO	200	333	DE	EM	L	200	333
2703	1	PATTISON	ED	30	30	DE	EM	L	30	30
2704	1	PEACOCK	GE	600	823	PB	LI	M	600	823
2705	1	PEACOCK	LU	50	111	IO	TP	M	50	111
2706	1	PEARCE	CB	15	20	MD	TP	M	15	20
2707	1	PEARCE	JU	15	21	MD	TP	M	15	21
2708	1	PECKETT	WM	200	1000	DU	AN	U	200	1000
2709	1	PEIRCE	TH	30	30	NA	EM	L	30	30
2710	1	PENDARVIS	TH	66	10	RA	WM	L	66	10
2711	1	PENDLETON	MI	100	166	EG	KI	L	100	166
2712	1	PENNOYER	SA	900	1500	BA	KI	L	900	1500
2713	1	PENNY	HE	6	6	RA	WM	L	6	6
2714	1	PEPYS	TH	33	166	CA	AN	U	33	166
2715	1	PERRY	JO	72	362	AR	AR	U		
2715	2	PERRY	JO	877	4387	AR	AR	U	949	4749
2716	1	PERRY	SA	20	44	CC	ZW	M	20	44
2717	1	PHILLIPS	JA	200	444	EL	TP	M	200	444
2718	1	PHILLIPS	TH	40	71	CO	ZW	M	40	71
2719	1	PIDOCKE	TH	800	1333	MC	EM	L	800	1333
2720	1	PIKE	ED	100	222	DC	ZW	M	100	222
2721	1	PITCHER	WM	100	500	BE	AN	U	1C0	500
2722	1	PITT	MW	50	83	CU	QU	L	50	83
2723	1	PITTS	JO	100	222	IO	TP	M	100	222
2724	1	PLANLEIGH	JO	100	102	RA	WM	L	100	102
2725	1	PLAYER	JO	25	55	CL	TP	M	25	55
2726	1	PLUCKNETT	GE	100	166	EG	KI	L	10C	166
2727	1	POLLYNE	JA	300	500	CU	QU	L	300	500
2728	1	POOLE	HE	50	111	CN	LI	M	50	111
2729	1	POOLE	JO	103	184	CC	ZW	M	103	184
2730	1	POOLE	P.	100	167	MR	QU	L	100	167
2731	1	POOLE	T.	100	166	MR	QU	L	1C0	166
2732	1	POPHAM	AX	1000	1371	CL	TP	M	1000	1371
2733	1	PORTER	RI	600	1000	EG	KI	L	600	1000
2734	1	POTTS	CH	600	617	LU	EM	L	600	617
2735	1	POULSTED	HE	1000	2222	CY	LI	M	1000	2222
2736	1	POULTER	JO	50	83	JS	KI	L	50	83
2737	1	POURDON	SA	30	27	KE	LI	M	30	27
2738	1	POYNTINGTON	TH	50	51	EG	KI	L	50	51
2739	1	PRATT	JO	300	500	DE	EM	L	300	500
2740	1	PRICE	RO	100	222	IO	TP	M	100	222
2741	1	PRIGG	HE	25	25	FE	WM	L	25	25
2742	1	PRINCE	PE	150	250	DM	WM	L	150	250
2743	1	PRITTIE	PG	200	444	CL	TP	M	200	444
2744	1	PROCTOR	JO	100	166	DE	EM	L	1C0	166
2745	1	PULLER	IZ	200	333	MC	EM	L	200	333
2746	1	PYE	JO	1000	1666	GA	KI	L	1000	1666
2747	1	PYM	AX	600	1000	SL	EM	L	600	1000
2748	1	PYNNAR	ED	100	222	ZL	ZW	M	100	222
2749	1	PYTT	HE	300	500	KI	WM	L	300	500
2750	1	QUINEY	RI	200	333	GA	KI	L	200	333
2751	1	RANDOLPH	MW	300	500	SK	EM	L	300	500
2752	1	RANDOLPH	TB	100	102	RA	WM	L	100	102
2753	1	RATCLIFFE	HG	650	1444	IO	TP	M	650	1444
2754	1	RATCLIFFE	PE	25	55	IO	TP	M	25	55
2755	1	RATHBAND	WM	50	111	DC	ZW	M	50	111

1	2	3	4	5	6	7	8	9	10	11
2756	1	RAWLINSON	JO	100	166	BA	KI	L	100	166
2757	1	RAYMANT	JO	300	666	CL	TP	M	3CC	666
2758	1	READ	MY	75	125	ST	QU	L	75	125
2759	1	REEVE	GY	50	83	ST	QU	L	50	83
2760	1	REGEMORT	AH	1C0	222	MC	TP	M	100	222
2761	1	REYNOLDS	JO	25	41	ST	CU	L	25	41
2762	1	REYNOLDS	RO	1800	3000	BA	KI	L	1800	300G
2763	1	RICH	JO	4	4	RA	WM	L	4	4
2764	1	RICHARDS	JO	20	20	PC	QU	L	20	20
2765	1	RICHARDSON	WM	50	111	IO	TP	M	50	111
2766	1	RIDGES	WM	100	222	MD	TP	M		
2766	2	RIDGES	WM	150	205	IK	TP	M		
2766	3	RIDGES	WM	120	266	MD	TP	M	370	693
2767	1	ROACH	HE	50	83	MO	EM	L	5C	83
2768	1	ROACH	LY	25	41	CU	QU	L	25	41
2769	1	ROBERTS	EL	250	0	ZW	ZW	M		
2769	2	ROBERTS	EL	350	777	ZL	ZW	M		
2769	3	ROBERTS	EL	1400	3111	MD	TP	M	2000	3888
2770	1	ROBINS	WM	25	77	DU	AN	U	25	77
2771	1	ROGERS	FR	100	102	MO	EM	L	10G	102
2772	1	ROGERS	RI	650	1444	EL	TP	M	650	1444
2773	1	ROGERS	WM	50	111	IC	TP	M	50	111
2774	1	ROLFE	JO	137	229	MY	WM	L	137	229
2775	1	ROLLE	JO	450	750	GA	KI	L	450	750
2776	1	ROLLE	SA	1000	1666	GA	KI	L	1000	1666
2777	1	ROSSE	TH	50	111	CC	ZW	M	50	111
2778	1	ROWE	TH	50	111	CC	ZW	M	50	111
2779	1	RUDDLE	AR	50	83	RA	WM	L		
2779	2	RUDDLE	AR	300	500	RA	WM	L		
2779	3	RUDDLE	AR	12	13	RA	WM	L		
2779	4	RUDDLE	AR	25	25	RA	WM	L	387	621
2780	1	RUSHLEY	JI	50	166	ST	QU	L		
2780	2	RUSHLEY	JI	50	166	ST	CU	L	100	332
2781	1	RUSSELL	FR	54	270	GN	AR	U	54	270
2782	1	RUSSELL	JA	100	222	CO	ZW	M	100	222
2783	1	RUSSELL	JO	250	416	DE	EM	L	250	416
2784	1	RUSSELL	TH	200	617	AD	DN	U	200	617
2785	1	RUTHORNE	JS	250	555	CL	TP	M	250	555
2786	1	RUTTON	MV	200	444	MD	TP	M	200	444
2787	1	SADLER	JO	100	166	GA	KI	L	100	166
2788	1	SAMPFORD	CR	100	222	DC	ZW	M	100	222
2789	1	SANDERS	LU	150	242	RA	WM	L	150	242
2790	1	SANDERSON	ED	62	192	CN	AR	U	62	192
2791	1	SANKEY	JM	50	111	IG	TP	M		
2791	2	SANKEY	JM	200	444	IG	TP	M	25C	555
2792	1	SAVELL	AA	50	111	CN	LI	M	50	111
2793	1	SAVELL	JO	75	166	CN	LI	M	75	166
2794	1	SCARGILL	RO	62	192	ON	AR	U	62	192
2795	1	SCOTT	ED	200	274	CY	LI	M	200	274
2796	1	SCOTT	RO	200	274	CY	LI	M	200	274
2797	1	SEAGER	JO	200	444	IC	TP	M	200	444
2798	1	SEALE	WM	25	55	DC	ZW	M	25	55
2799	1	SEARLE	CR	470	732	CU	QU	L	470	732
2800	1	SEARLE	JO	20	33	KI	WM	L	20	33
2801	1	SEARLE	WM	20	33	ST	QU	L	20	33
2802	1	SEED	JO	20C	444	IC	TP	M	200	444
2803	1	SEUTT	RI	250	555	PB	LI	M	250	555
2804	1	SEYMOUR	RO	200	333	NA	EM	L	200	333
2805	1	SHAKESPEARE	MY	100	222	EL	TP	M	100	222
2806	1	SHEAFE	SP	1C0	166	PC	QU	L	100	166
2807	1	SHEARES	WM	300	411	EL	TP	M	300	411
2808	1	SHEBBER	MY	25	50	PB	LI	M	25	50
2809	1	SHEBBER	WM	26	36	KE	LI	M	26	36
2810	1	SHEFFIELD	JA	1750	2916	MR	QU	L	1750	2916
2811	1	SHELBURY	RI	50	83	RA	WM	L	50	83
2812	1	SHEPCOTT	AA	50	111	MC	TP	M	50	111
2813	1	SHEPHEARD	JO	150	750	TU	AR	U	150	750
2814	1	SHEPPARD	JU	25	41	RA	WM	L	25	41
2815	1	SHEPPEY	JO	775	1722	CN	LI	M	775	1722
2816	1	SHERBROOKE	RI	300	500	MY	WM	L	300	500
2817	1	SHERLEY	SN	25	34	KE	LI	M	25	34
2818	1	SHERLOCK	WM	100	222	CC	ZW	M	100	222
2819	1	SHEWELL	JO	10	16	ST	QU	L	10	16
2820	1	SHORT	JO	225	500	MD	TP	M	225	500
2821	1	SHORT	RI	62	104	SW	QU	L	62	104
2822	1	SHORT	SR	150	333	MD	TP	M	150	333
2823	1	SHUTTLEWORTH	RI	600	617	KI	WM	L	600	617
2824	1	SIMMES	WM	20	27	PB	LI	M	20	27

1	2	3	4	5	6	7	8	9	10	11
2825	1	SKRIMSHAW	WM	50	111	EL	TP	M	50	111
2826	1	SLADE	WM	50	83	ST	QU	L	50	83
2827	1	SMALL	AA	5	6	KE	LI	M	5	6
2828	1	SMART	IH	100	222	ZL	ZW	M	100	222
2829	1	SMITH	E.	200	1000	CN	AR	U		
2829	2	SMITH	E.	1150	5750	AD	DN	U		
2829	3	SMITH	E.	300	666	CL	TP	M		
2829	4	SMITH	E.	1345	2988	CL	TP	M	2995	10404
2830	1	SMITH	ED	351	585	LS	KI	L		
2830	2	SMITH	ED	248	414	LS	KI	L		
2830	3	SMITH	ED	56	0	ZW	ZW	M		
2830	4	SMITH	ED	100	222	DC	ZW	M	755	1221
2831	1	SMITH	HE	200	444	CO	ZW	M	200	444
2832	1	SMITH	JA	200	1000	AR	AR	U	200	1000
2833	1	SMITH	JO	10	22	DC	ZW	M	10	22
2834	1	SMITH	JS	100	137	DC	ZW	M	100	137
2835	1	SMITH	RI	10	22	DC	ZW	M	10	22
2836	1	SMITH	TH	25	41	FE	WM	L	25	41
2837	1	SMITH	TH	100	222	ZL	ZW	M	100	222
2838	1	SNELL	GE	350	777	MD	TP	M	350	777
2839	1	SOAME	JO	300	666	EL	TP	M	300	666
2840	1	SOMERS	RO	30	30	EG	KI	L	30	30
2841	1	SPARKE	RO	12	13	RA	WM	L	12	13
2842	1	SPARROW	JO	50	111	CO	ZW	M	50	111
2843	1	SPARROW	PH	50	111	CO	ZW	M	50	111
2844	1	SPELLER	JO	50	111	CN	LI	M	50	111
2845	1	SPENCER	MI	150	154	PC	QU	L	150	154
2846	1	SPILMAN	CL	128	213	SK	EM	L		
2846	2	SPILMAN	CL	100	166	SK	EM	L		
2846	3	SPILMAN	CL	200	333	NA	EM	L		
2846	4	SPILMAN	CL	30	50	NA	EM	L		
2846	5	SPILMAN	CL	100	166	SK	EM	L	558	928
2847	1	SPILMAN	M.	100	102	MR	QU	L	100	102
2848	1	SPOURWAY	ED	25	25	RA	WM	L	25	25
2849	1	SPRING	EM	50	83	CU	QU	L	50	83
2850	1	SPRINGATE	AY	200	205	ST	QU	L	200	205
2851	1	SQUIBB	AR	300	372	MO	EM	L	300	372
2852	1	SQUIRE	WM	100	222	MD	TP	M	100	222
2853	1	STANDISH	HE	50	51	ST	QU	L	50	51
2854	1	STANTON	EM	300	500	DE	EM	L	300	500
2855	1	STAPER	RI	750	1666	MD	TP	M		
2855	2	STAPER	RI	20	0	ZW	ZW	M	770	1666
2856	1	STARKEY	GE	200	444	IL	TP	M	200	444
2857	1	STEELE	JO	50	250	BE	AN	U	50	250
2858	1	STEPHENS	JO	10	13	KE	LI	M	10	13
2859	1	STEPHENSON	JO	50	83	SW	QU	L	50	83
2860	1	STOCK	TH	600	1333	CL	TP	M	600	1333
2861	1	STONE	WM	100	166	KI	WM	L	100	166
2862	1	STONMAN	RO	9	9	RA	WM	L	9	9
2863	1	STOREY	ED	50	111	CC	ZW	M	50	111
2864	1	STRANG	GE	50	51	PO	QU	L	50	51
2865	1	STRATTON	TH	100	126	LU	EM	L	100	126
2866	1	STRICKLAND	WM	600	823	CO	ZW	M	600	823
2867	1	STRODE	WM	750	1250	TE	QU	L		
2867	2	STRODE	WM	550	916	TE	QU	L	1300	2166
2868	1	STUBBINS	TH	500	833	EG	KI	L	500	833
2869	1	STURDY	JO	25	125	BE	AN	U	25	125
2870	1	STURMY	JU	40	88	IO	TP	M	40	88
2871	1	SUMPNER	WM	50	111	CN	LI	M	50	111
2872	1	SUMPTER	GI	120	200	RA	WM	L	120	200
2873	1	SUTTON	ED	75	375	CN	AR	U	75	375
2874	1	SWEETE	PE	10	10	EG	KI	L	10	10
2875	1	SWEETE	RI	50	86	PB	LI	M		
2875	2	SWEETE	RI	200	444	PB	LI	M	250	530
2876	1	SWEETING	JO	400	666	GA	KI	L	400	666
2877	1	SWIFT	TH	40	200	ON	AR	U	40	200
2878	1	SWIFT	TH	350	583	MY	WM	L	350	583
2879	1	SYMONS	RI	100	222	CL	TP	M	100	222
2880	1	TALEBOYS	AA	75	125	JS	KI	L	75	125
2881	1	TANDY	PH	150	250	NA	EM	L		
2881	2	TANDY	PH	250	416	DE	EM	L	400	666
2882	1	TAUNTON	CA	1360	1399	RA	WM	L	1360	1399
2883	1	TAYLOR	JO	75	125	NA	EM	L	75	125
2884	1	TAYLOR	TH	75	125	NA	EM	L	75	125
2885	1	TAYLOR	WM	6	10	RA	WM	L	6	10
2886	1	TEMPLE	JO	100	166	KI	WM	L		
2886	2	TEMPLE	JO	200	274	EL	TP	M	300	440
2887	1	TEMPLE	TH	450	750	KI	WM	L	450	750

1	2	3	4	5	6	7	8	9	10	11
2888	1	THOMAS	ED	100	222	CC	ZW	M	100	222
2889	1	THOMAS	JO	20	20	PO	QU	L	20	20
2890	1	THOMASON	GE	700	1166	SW	QU	L	700	1166
2891	1	THOMPSON	FR	100	102	MO	EM	L	100	102
2892	1	THOMPSON	GE	805	4030	TU	AR	U	805	4030
2893	1	THOMPSON	JO	1150	1916	MY	WM	L	1150	1916
2894	1	THOMPSON	MO	806	4031	TU	AR	U		
2894	2	THOMPSON	MO	287	1437	TU	AR	U		
2894	3	THOMPSON	MO	2150	10750	DU	AN	U	3243	16218
2895	1	THOMPSON	WM	50	111	CN	LI	M	50	111
2896	1	THORNBURY	WM	200	444	IK	TP	M	200	444
2897	1	THRALE	RI	100	222	CL	TP	M		
2897	2	THRALE	RI	109	0	ZW	ZW	M	209	222
2898	1	THYNN	TH	25	125	UI	DN	U	25	125
2899	1	TIBBS	WM	1102	2418	IO	TP	M		
2899	2	TIBBS	WM	40	66	NA	EM	L	1142	2484
2900	1	TIGH	RI	425	708	RA	WM	L		
2900	2	TIGH	RI	900	1500	BA	KI	L		
2900	3	TIGH	RI	600	617	SW	QU	L	1925	2825
2901	1	TILLOTT	JO	100	166	NA	EM	L	100	166
2902	1	TILSLEY	WM	100	222	EL	TP	M	100	222
2903	1	TIPPING	TH	200	1000	DU	AN	U	200	1000
2904	1	TIRRELL	JO	300	1500	MA	AN	U	300	1500
2905	1	TITCHBORNE	HE	50	51	LU	EM	L		
2905	2	TITCHBORNE	HE	50	83	LU	EM	L		
2905	3	TITCHBORNE	HE	100	500	LE	DN	U	200	634
2906	1	TITCHBORNE	RO	200	333	SW	QU	L	200	333
2907	1	TOWNE	HU	1200	2666	IO	TP	M		
2907	2	TOWNE	HU	600	1333	IO	TP	M	1800	3999
2908	1	TOWNSHEND	GE	650	1083	EG	KI	L	650	1083
2909	1	TOWSE	CR	100	222	MC	TP	M	100	222
2910	1	TRACEY	JN	10	13	KE	LI	M	10	13
2911	1	TRELAWNY	JO	150	333	EL	TP	M	150	333
2912	1	TRELAWNY	RO	450	1000	EL	TP	M	450	1000
2913	1	TRESCOTT	RO	85	87	EG	KI	L	85	87
2914	1	TRIMBLETT	BR	150	242	RA	WM	L	150	242
2915	1	TRIPLETT	RA	310	1550	AR	AR	U	310	1550
2916	1	TUCKER	TH	300	666	CN	LI	M	300	666
2917	1	TUFFNAILE	AM	200	205	MO	EM	L	200	205
2918	1	TUNBRIDGE	JS	100	222	CN	LI	M	100	222
2919	1	TURLINGTON	JO	120	266	EL	TP	M	120	266
2920	1	TURLINGTON	R.	25	41	CU	QU	L	25	41
2921	1	TURNER	ED	200	333	SL	EM	L	200	333
2922	1	TURNER	TH	200	333	DE	EM	L	200	333
2923	1	TURNER JR	RI	400	666	DE	EM	L	400	666
2924	1	TWOLEY	TH	450	750	LU	EM	L	450	750
2925	1	TYLER	RI	250	1111	IL	TP	M	250	1111
2926	1	UNDERHILL	TH	78	130	ST	QU	L	78	130
2927	1	UNDERWOOD	BJ	50	111	EL	TP	M	50	111
2928	1	UNDERWOOD	GE	100	222	EL	TP	M	100	222
2929	1	UNDERWOOD	WM	350	777	EL	TP	M	350	777
2930	1	UPTON	AR	50	83	RA	WM	L		
2930	2	UPTON	AR	100	166	RA	WM	L	150	249
2931	1	VALENTINE	TH	100	222	IO	TP	M	100	222
2932	1	VAUGHAN	CH	2130	3530	ST	QU	L	2130	3530
2933	1	VEALE	PH	5	6	KE	LI	M	5	6
2934	1	VENNER	RI	500	833	FE	WM	L	500	833
2935	1	VERNON	RI	100	222	DC	ZW	M	100	222
2936	1	VINCENT	TH	1350	2217	PO	QU	L		
2936	2	VINCENT	TH	500	833	CU	QU	L		
2936	3	VINCENT	TH	200	205	ST	QU	L		
2936	4	VINCENT	TH	3550	5915	NA	EM	L		
2936	5	VINCENT	TH	4725	7874	BA	KI	L		
2936	6	VINCENT	TH	600	1000	SL	EM	L		
2936	7	VINCENT	TH	300	500	DE	EM	L		
2936	8	VINCENT	TH	300	500	LU	EM	L	11525	19044
2937	1	VOYSE	GM	50	51	ST	QU	L	50	51
2938	1	VOYSEY	L.	100	102	RA	WM	L	100	102
2939	1	VRING	FR	6	10	RA	WM	L	6	10
2940	1	WADE	BJ	25	125	CN	AR	U	25	125
2941	1	WADE	NL	25	125	CN	AR	U	25	125
2942	1	WADE	RI	25	125	CN	AR	U	25	125
2943	1	WADE	TY	25	125	CN	AR	U	25	125
2944	1	WADLAND	TH	30	30	PO	QU	L	30	30
2945	1	WAGSTAFF	EM	40	123	UI	DN	U	40	123
2946	1	WAGSTAFF	WM	312	520	DE	WM	L	312	520
2947	1	WALCOTT	RI	600	1000	RA	WM	L	600	1000
2948	1	WALDOE	DA	300	500	RA	WM	L		

1	2	3	4	5	6	7	8	9	10	11
2948	2	WALDOE	DA	600	1333	CL	TP	M	900	1833
2949	1	WALLEY	TH	381	814	DC	ZW	M	381	814
2950	1	WALLIN	PT	87	145	SW	QU	L	87	145
2951	1	WALLIS	RO	125	277	IK	TP	M	125	277
2952	1	WALLIS	TH	50	111	MD	TP	M	50	111
2953	1	WALLS	ME	200	333	RA	WM	L	200	333
2954	1	WALMESLEY	TH	100	166	SW	QU	L	100	166
2955	1	WALTER	TH	5	6	KE	LI	M	5	6
2956	1	WALTERS	TH	100	500	LE	DN	U	100	500
2957	1	WAMENRIGHT	JA	1700	2833	NA	EM	L	1700	2833
2958	1	WARING	RI	2000	4444	DC	ZW	M	2000	4444
2959	1	WARNER	SA	777	1295	LU	EM	L		
2959	2	WARNER	SA	2223	3705	LU	EM	L	3000	5000
2960	1	WARPLE	GE	50	250	ON	AR	U	50	250
2961	1	WATKINS	DD	1000	1666	CU	QU	L		
2961	2	WATKINS	DD	1800	3000	SK	EM	L		
2961	3	WATKINS	DD.	1600	2666	MR	QU	L		
2961	4	WATKINS	DD	1600	2666	MR	QU	L	6000	9998
2962	1	WATSON	DH	.50	83	CU	QU	L	:50	83
2963	1	WATSON	SA	50	111	CO	ZW	M	50	111
2964	1	WATSON	TH	100	166	MO	EM	L	100	166
2965	1	WATTS	B.	4	4	RA	WM	L	4	4
2966	1	WATTS	WM	300	666	MD	TP	M		
2966	2	WATTS	WM	100	222	MD	TP	M		
2966	3	WATTS	WM	500	1111	MD	TP	M	900	1999
2967	1	WEALE	JU	373	511	SL	EM	L	373	511
2968	1	WEBB	AA	625	1041	MO	EM	L	625	1041
2969	1	WEBB	WM	50	0	ZW	ZW	M	50	0
2970	1	WEBSTER	JA	50	68	CL	TP	M		
2970	2	WEBSTER	JA	100	222	CN	LI	M	150	290
2971	1	WEBSTER	WM	300	666	MD	TP	M	300	666
2972	1	WEEKS	OB	100	222	CO	ZW	M	100	222
2973	1	WELLS	.JO	28	63	DC	ZW	M	28	63
2974	1	WENMAN LORD		600	617	GA	KI	L	600	617
2975	1	WERKES	JO	50.	83	MR	QU	L	50	83
2976	1	WEST	HE	200	444	DC	ZW	M	200	444
2977	1	WEST	JO	200	1000	MA	AN	U	200	1000
2978	1	WESTERN	RO	628	1046	CU	QU	L		
2978	2	WESTERN	RO	240	401	CU	QU	L	868	1447
2979	1	WESTON	WM	100	222	DC	ZW	M	100	222
2980	1	WESTROWE	N.	300	308	MY	WM	L	300	308
2981	1	WHALLEY	HE	1200	6000	AD	DN	U	1200	6000
2982	1	WHARTON	H.	25	41	ST	QU	L	25	41
2983	1	WHARTON	JA	646	1077	KI	WM	L		
2983	2	WHARTON	JA	100	166	KI	WM	L	746	1243
2984	1	WHARTON	TH	200	333	SL	EM	L	200	333
2985	1	WHARTON	TH	400	666	DE	EM	L	400	666
2986	1	WHEATLEY	JO	125	277	IC	TP	M	125	277
2987	1	WHEELER	LU	25	25	RA	WM	L	25	25
2988	1	WHERLER	CR	12	20	RA	WM	L	12	20
2989	1	WHETCOMBE	BJ	500	833	RA	WM	L	500	833
2990	1	WHITE	BW	300	666	IO	TP	M	300	666
2991	1	WHITE	ED	50	83	SK	EM	L	50	83
2992	1	WHITE	EL	25	42	ST	QU	L	25	42
2993	1	WHITE	RI	133	296	PB	LI	M	133	296
2994	1	WHITE	SR	25	41	ST	QU	L	25	41
2995	1	WHITE	ST	600	1333	CN	LI	M	600	1333
2996	1	WHITE	TH	300	500	CU	QU	L	300	500
2997	1	WHITE	TH	115	404	IL	TP	M		
2997	2	WHITE	TH	90	202	IL	TP	M	205	606
2998	1	WHITEAKER	HE	200	333	TE	QU	L	200	333
2999	1	WHITEAKER	WM	50	83	ST	QU	L	50	83
3000	1	WHITEHALL	RO	100	222	IC	TP	M	100	222
3001	1	WHITELOCK	BU	400	666	RA	WM	L	400	666
3002	1	WHITWAY	JO	325	722	KE	LI	M		
3002	2	WHITWAY	JO	325	722	KE	LI	M		
3002	3	WHITWAY	JO	25	55	KE	LI	M		
3002	4	WHITWAY	JO	325	722	KE	LI	M	1000	2221
3003	1	WILLETT	RI	625	1041	MC	EM	L	625	1041
3004	1	WILLIAMS	JO	150	250	ST	QU	L	150	250
3005	1	WILLKINS	SA	125	277	DC	ZW	M	125	277
3006	1	WILLOUGHBY	FR	200	333	LU	EM	L	200	333
3007	1	WINKFIELD	TB	40	66	ST	QU	L	40	66
3008	1	WINSPEARE	JO	75	166	EL	TP	M	75	166
3009	1	WINSTON	DH	28	62	DC	ZW	M	28	62
3010	1	WINSTON	EZ	28	62	DC	ZW	M	28	62
3011	1	WINSTON	JO	85	190	DC	ZW	M	85	190
3012	1	WINSTON	RI	28	62	DC	ZW	M	28	62

1	2	3	4	5	6	7	8	9	10	11
3013	1	WITCHROTT	CR	100	166	RA	WM	L	100	166
3014	1	WITHAM	ED	220	366	RA	WM	L	220	366
3015	1	WITHAM	GE	25	0	ZW	ZW	M		
3015	2	WITHAM	GE	750	1666	IO	TP	M	775	1666
3016	1	WITHAM	NL	100	222	MD	TP	M	100	222
3017	1	WITTERONGE	JO	600	1000	MY	WM	L	600	1000
3018	1	WOLLEY	E.	12	13	RA	WM	L	12	13
3019	1	WOOD	ED	675	1125	BA	KI	L	675	1125
3020	1	WOOD	JO	773	1296	TE	QU	L		
3020	2	WOOD	JO	850	1416	EG	KI	L	1623	2712
3021	1	WOOD	JO	62	312	DU	AN	U	62	312
3022	1	WOOD	MY	50	250	UI	DN	U	50	250
3023	1	WOOD	RI	100	500	BE	AN	U	100	500
3024	1	WOODCOCK	TH	100	222	IK	TP	M	100	222
3025	1	WOODHEAD	WM	230	383	LS	KI	L	230	383
3026	1	WOODHOUSE	WM	120	200	TE	QU	L		
3026	2	WOODHOUSE	WM	100	166	SW	QU	L	220	366
3027	1	WOODMAN	WM	25	41	RA	WM	L	25	41
3028	1	WOODWARD	ED	600	1000	KI	WM	L	600	1000
3029	1	WOODWARD	H.	100	137	CL	TP	M	100	137
3030	1	WOOLLEY	FR	166	370	IO	TP	M	166	370
3031	1	WOOLNOUGH	JS	250	416	JS	KI	L	250	416
3032	1	WOOLTON	WM	9	9	RA	WM	L	9	9
3033	1	WORTH	ZY	100	222	CL	TP	M	100	222
3034	1	WRENN	TH	5	6	KE	LI	M	5	6
3035	1	WRIGHT	JN	50	83	EG	KI	L	50	83
3036	1	WRIGLEY	HE	100	222	CN	LI	M	100	222
3037	1	YARD	JO	25	42	LU	EM	L		
3037	2	YARD	JO	10	16	LU	EM	L	35	58
3038	1	YARD	MV	25	41	LU	EM	L	25	41
3039	1	YARMOUTH	CA	600	1333	IO	TP	M	600	1333
3040	1	YATES	JA	400	718	MD	TP	M	400	718
3041	1	YATES	JO	100	222	ZL	ZW	M	100	222
3042	1	YEATES	DH	100	166	ST	QU	L	100	166
3043	1	YOUNG	JO	10	16	LS	KI	L	10	16

APPENDIX C

DISTRIBUTION OF LAND CONFISCATED IN THE CROMWELLIAN SETTLEMENT

THE adjacent map is based upon the digest of Irish land surveys published by W. H. Hardinge (*TRIA*, vol. 24 (Antiquities), p. 104). It illustrates the percentages of lands found forfeit in the various counties in the course of the Cromwellian Settlement. In the most heavily shaded counties 80 per cent or more of all land (profitable and unprofitable combined) was forfeit. In the unshaded counties less than 20 per cent of all land was forfeit. The three intermediary shadings, going from light to dark, distinguish counties in which 20–39, 40–59, and 60–79 per cent of all land was forfeit.

The map illustrates which areas felt Cromwellian confiscations most heavily, but it will not support the inference that areas of high confiscation necessarily became areas of heavy Protestant colonization. Connaught, by far the most heavily confiscated province, was for the most part turned back, not to its original owners, but to 'innocent' Catholics transplanted there from the other three provinces. Very few native Catholics of Connaught could have been left among them, at least as proprietors.

A secondary, but perhaps more important, use for the map is to suggest percentages of Catholic ownership in the various counties as of 1641. It does this approximately rather than exactly, because it includes in its percentages land forfeit by Protestants not 'of constant good affection' to the Parliament of England. Thus, the county of Tipperary, where 77 per cent of all land was forfeit, was less a county of markedly heavy Catholic proprietorship, than a county in which the royalist Earl of Ormond held extensive estates. The amount of land forfeited by Protestants in the Cromwellian Settlement has never been exactly calculated, but Ormond was probably one of relatively few sufferers. The transgressions of most Protestants were forgiven, so that areas of heavy forfeiture were, by and large, areas of extensive Catholic ownership. Less ambiguous maps of proportions of land held by Catholics in 1641, 1688, and 1703 will be found in J. G. Simms, *The Williamite Confiscations in Ireland*, London, 1956, p. 196.[1]

According to Hardinge's figures for the amounts of forfeit and non-forfeit land, the percentage of land confiscated in each county in accordance with the acts of 1652 and 1653 was as follows:

[1] See also Dr. Simms, 'Land owned by Catholics in Ireland in 1688', *IHS*, VII (1950–1).

Galway	91	Wexford	60	Antrim	41
Clare	80	Kerry	59	Leitrim	39
Mayo	80	Sligo	58	Monaghan	38
Tipperary	77	Kilkenny	58	Wicklow	35
Meath	76	Limerick	57	Armagh	34
Westmeath	75	Waterford	52	Down	26
Carlow	72	Kildare	49	Fermanagh	15
Roscommon	68	Dublin	46	Londonderry	14
Louth	65	Kings	46	Donegal	11
Cork	65	Cavan	43	Tyrone	4
Longford	61	Queens	43		

Percentage of land confiscated

less than 20% □
20%-39% ▢
40%-59% ▤
60%-79% ▨
80% and over ■

SELECT BIBLIOGRAPHY

I. BIBLIOGRAPHIES

HAYES, R. J., *Manuscript Sources for the History of Irish Civilization*, 10 vols., Boston, 1965.

JOHNSTON, EDITH M., *Irish History: a Select Bibliography*, London, The Historical Association, 1969.

MULVEY, HELEN F., 'Modern Irish History since 1940: a Bibliographical Survey (1600–1922)', in E. C. Furber, ed., *Changing Views on British History*, Cambridge, Mass., 1966.

SIMMS, J. G., 'Thirty Years' Work in Irish History: Seventeenth-Century Ireland', *IHS*, 1967.

II. MANUSCRIPTS

Individual manuscripts are cited and described in footnotes

Bodleian Library: Carte, Clarendon, Rawlinson, and Tanner MSS.

British Museum: Additional, Cotton, Egerton, and Sloane MSS.

Marsh's Library, Dublin.

National Library of Ireland.

Public Record Office, London.

Record Office, Dublin.

Trinity College, Dublin.

III. PRINTED SOURCES

ABBOTT, W. C., ed., *Writings and Speeches of Oliver Cromwell*, 4 vols., Cambridge, Mass., 1937–47.

BIRCH, THOMAS, ed., *Thurloe State Papers*, 7 vols., London, 1742.

Calendar of State Papers, Domestic Series.

Calendar of State Papers Relating to Ireland.

CAULFIELD, RICHARD, ed., *Council Book of the Corporation of Kinsale*, Guildford, 1879.

CLARENDON, EARL OF. See Hyde.

COATES, WILLSON H., ed., *The Journal of Sir Simonds D'Ewes*, New Haven, Conn., 1942.

DUNLOP, ROBERT, ed., *Ireland under the Commonwealth*, 2 vols., Manchester, 1913.

FIRTH, C. H. and RAIT, R. S., eds., *Acts and Ordinances of the Interregnum*, 3 vols., London, 1911.

GARDINER, S. R., ed., *Constitutional Documents of the Puritan Revolution*, Oxford, 1906.

GILBERT, J. T., ed., *A Contemporary History of Affairs in Ireland*, 6 vols., Dublin, 1879–80.

GOOKIN, VINCENT, *The Great Case of Transplantation Discussed*, London, 1655.

GROSART, A. B., ed., *The Lismore Papers*, 10 vols., London, 1886–8.

Historical Manuscripts Commission:
  Fifth Report
  Ninth Report
  Twelfth Report
  De L'Isle and Dudley
  Buccleuch and Queensberry
  Egmont
  Exeter City
  House of Lords
  Ormonde
  Portland

HOLLES, DENZIL, *Memoirs of*, London, 1699.

HYDE, EDWARD, Earl of Clarendon, *History of the Rebellion and Civil Wars in Ireland*, London, 1719, Dublin, 1720.

—— *Life* [by himself, 1759], being a Continuation of the *History of the Rebellion in England*, 2 vols., Oxford, 1857.

Journals of the House of Commons [England].

Journals of the House of Lords [England].

KAVANAGH, Revd. STANISLAUS, ed., *Commentarius Rinuccinianus*, 6 vols., Dublin, Irish Manuscripts Commission, 1932–49.

LARCOM, T. A., ed., *History of the Survey of Ireland*, Dublin, 1851.

McNEILL, CHARLES, ed., *Tanner Letters*, Dublin, Irish Manuscripts Commission, 1943.

MAXWELL, CONSTANTIA, ed., *Irish History from Contemporary Sources, 1509–1610*, London, 1923.

MAY, THOMAS, *History of the [Long] Parliament*, London, 1647, Oxford, 1854.

MORLEY, H., ed., *Ireland under Elizabeth and James I*, London, 1890.

PETTY, WILLIAM, 'The Political Anatomy of Ireland', in *Tracts Relating to Ireland*, Dublin, 1769 or *Economic Writings of Sir William Petty*, C. H. Hull, ed., 2 vols., Cambridge, 1899.

[Reports from the] Commissioners for the Public Records for Ireland, *Fifteenth Report, 1821–25*.

RUSHWORTH, JOHN, ed., *Historical Collections*, 7 vols., London, 1659–1701.

SIMINGTON, R. C., ed., *Books of Survey and Distribution*, Dublin, Irish Manuscripts Commission: *Roscommon*, 1949, *Mayo*, 1956, *Galway*, 1962, *Clare*, 1967.

SPEDDING, JAMES, ed., *Collected Works of Sir Francis Bacon*, 14 vols., London, 1857–74.

Statutes of the Realm.

Thomason Tracts, British Museum.

IV. LATER WRITINGS

ASHLEY, MAURICE, *Financial and Commercial Policy under the Cromwellian Protectorate*, 2nd edn., London, 1962.

BAGWELL, RICHARD, *Ireland under the Stuarts*, 3 vols., London, 1909–16.

—— *Ireland under the Tudors*, 3 vols., London, 1885–90.

BECKETT, J. C., 'The Confederation of Kilkenny Reviewed', *Historical Studies*, ii, Michael Roberts, ed., London, 1959.

—— *A Short History of Ireland*, New York, 1968.

—— *The Making of Modern Ireland, 1603–1923*, London, 1966.

BONN, M. J., *Die Englische Kolonisation in Irland*, 2 vols., Stuttgart, 1906.

BOTTIGHEIMER, K. S., 'English Money and Irish Land: the "Adventurers" in the Cromwellian Settlement of Ireland', *JBS*, 1967.

BRUNTON, D. and PENNINGTON, D. H., *Members of the Long Parliament*, London, 1954.

BUTLER, W. F. T., *Confiscation in Irish History*, 2nd edn., London, 1918.

CARTE, THOMAS, *Life of James, First Duke of Ormonde*, 6 vols., Oxford, 1851.

CLARKE, AIDAN, *The Old English in Ireland, 1625–1642*, London, 1966.

CLODE, CHARLES M., ed., *London during the Great Rebellion*, London, 1892.

COONAN, T. L., *The Irish Catholic Confederation and the Puritan Revolution*, New York, 1954.

COOPER, J. P., 'Wentworth and the Byrnes County', *IHS*, 1966.

CURTIS, EDMUND, *A History of Ireland*, London, 1936.

DUNLOP, ROBERT, *Ireland from the Earliest Times to the Present Day*, Oxford, 1922.

—— 'The Plantation of Leix and Offaly', *EHR*, 1891.

—— 'The Plantation of Munster, 1584–1589', *EHR*, 1888.

—— 'Sixteenth-Century Schemes for the Plantation of Ulster', Scottish Historical Review, 1925.

EDWARDS, R DUDLEY and MOODY, T. W., 'The History of Poynings' Law, 1494–1615', *IHS*, 1941.

FIRTH, C. H., 'Account of Money Spent in the Cromwellian Reconquest and Settlement of Ireland, 1649–1656', *EHR*, 1899.

—— *Cromwell's Army*, Methuen Paperback edn., London, 1962.

FIRTH, C. H., *The Last Years of the Protectorate*, 2 vols., London, 1909.

FITZMAURICE, LORD EDMOND, *The Life of Sir William Petty*, London, 1895.

FROUDE, J. A., *The English in Ireland*, 3 vols., London, 1881.

GARDINER, S. R., 'The Transplantation to Connaught', *EHR*, 1899.

—— *History of the Commonwealth and the Protectorate*, 4 vols., London, 1903.

—— *History of England, 1603–1642*, 10 vols., London, 1883–4.

—— *History of the Great Civil War*, 4 vols., London, 1893.

GLOW, LOTTE, 'Political Affiliations in the House of Commons after Pym's Death', *Bulletin of the Institute of Historical Research*, 1965.

GOBLET, Y. M., *La Transformation de la géographie politique de l'Irlande au XVIIᵉ siècle*, 2 vols., Paris, 1930.

HABAKKUK, H. J., 'The Parliamentary Army and the Crown Lands', *Welsh History Review*, 1967.

—— 'Public Finance and the Sale of Forfeited Property during the Interregnum', *EcHR*, 1962.

HARDINGE, W. H., 'On Circumstances Attending the Civil War in Ireland', *TRIA* (Antiquities), vol. 24.

—— 'On Manuscript, Mapped and Other Townland Surveys in Ireland', Ibid.

HAZLETT, HUGH, 'The Financing of British Armies in Ireland, 1641–49', *IHS*, 1938.

—— 'The Recruitment and Organization of the Scottish Army in Ulster', in *Essays in British and Irish History in Honour of James Eadie Todd*, H. A. Cronne, T. W. Moody, and D. B. Quinn, eds., London, 1941.

HEXTER, J. H., *The Reign of King Pym*, Cambridge, Mass., 1941.

HILL, GEORGE, *An Historical Account of the Plantation of Ulster, 1608–10*, Belfast, 1877.

KEARNEY, HUGH F., *Strafford in Ireland*, Manchester, 1959.

LOVE, WALTER, 'Civil War in Ireland: Appearances in Three Centuries of Historical Writing', *EUQ*, 1966.

LOWE, JOHN, 'Charles I and the Confederation of Kilkenny, 1643–49', *IHS*, 1964.

LYNCH, KATHLEEN, *Roger Boyle, First Earl of Orrery*, Knoxville, Tenn., 1965.

MACCORMACK, J. R., 'The Irish Adventurers and the English Civil War', *IHS*, 1956.

MAXWELL, CONSTANTIA, 'The Colonization of Ulster', *History*, 1916.

MOODY, T. W., *The Londonderry Plantation, 1609–1641*, Belfast, 1939.

MURPHY, JOHN A., 'Inchiquin's Change of Religion', *JCHAS*, 1967.

O'BRIEN, GEORGE, *The Economic History of Ireland in the Seventeenth Century*, Dublin, 1919.

OTWAY-RUTHVEN, A. J., *A History of Medieval Ireland*, London, 1968.

PEARL, VALERIE, *London and the Outbreak of the Puritan Revolution*, Oxford, 1961.

—— 'Oliver St. John and the "middle groups" in the Long Parliament', *EHR*, 1966.

—— 'The "Royal Independents" in the English Civil War', *Transactions of the Royal Historical Society*, 1968.

PRENDERGAST, J. P., *The Cromwellian Settlement of Ireland*, Dublin, edn. of 1875.

QUINN, D. B., 'A Discourse of Ireland (*circa* 1599)', *Proceedings of the Royal Irish Academy*, XLVII, Section C, No. 3 (1942).

—— 'The English Interpretation of Poynings' Law', *IHS*, 1941.

—— *The Elizabethans and the Irish*, Ithaca, New York, 1966.

—— 'Ireland and Sixteenth-Century Expansion', *Historical Studies*, I, T. Desmond Williams, ed., London, 1958.

—— 'The Munster Plantation: Problems and Opportunities', *JCHAS*, 1966.

—— 'Sir Thomas Smith and the Beginnings of English Colonial Theory', *Proceedings of the American Philosophical Society*, vol. 89.

RABB, THEODORE K., *Enterprise and Empire: Merchant and Gentry Investment in the Expansion of England, 1575–1630*, Cambridge, Mass., 1967.

RANGER, T. O., 'Richard Boyle and the Making of an Irish Fortune', *IHS*, 1957.

—— 'Strafford in Ireland: a Revaluation', *Past and Present*, 1961.

SCOTT, W. R., *The Constitution and Finance of English, Scottish and Irish Joint Stock Companies to 1720*, 3 vols., Cambridge, 1912.

SIMMS, J. G., *The Williamite Confiscations in Ireland, 1690–1703*, London, 1956.

TREVOR-ROPER, H. R., 'The Fast Sermons of the Long Parliament', in *Essays in British History Presented to Sir Keith Feiling*, H. R. Trevor-Roper, ed., London, 1964.

UNDERDOWN, DAVID, 'Civil War in Ireland: a Commentary', *EUQ*, 1966.

—— 'The Independents Again', *JBS*, 1968.

WHITE, DEAN G., 'The Reign of Edward VI in Ireland', *IHS*, 1965.

WILLSON, D. H., *James VI and I*, London, Cape Paperback edn., 1963.

V. UNPUBLISHED THESES

BOTTIGHEIMER, K. S., 'The English Interest in Southern Ireland, 1641–50', University of California, Berkeley, Ph.D., 1965.

LANG, R. G., 'The Greater Merchants of London in the Early Sixteenth Century', Oxford, D.Phil., 1963.

LOWE, JOHN, 'The Negotiations between Charles I and the Confederation of Kilkenny', London, Ph.D., 1960.

RANGER, T. O., 'The Career of Richard Boyle, First Earl of Cork in Ireland, 1588–1643', Oxford, D.Phil., 1958.

WHITE, D. G., 'The Tudor Plantations in Ireland before 1571', Trinity College, Dublin, Ph.D., 1968.

INDEX

Abbott, W. C., 113
Act for adventurers, 40–2
Adams, Thomas, 61
Anglo-Saxons, 3, 4, 6
Annesley, Arthur, later 1st Earl of Anglesey, 102, 103, 104, 107, 109
Antrim, colonization of, 23
Ash, Francis, 154
atrocities, reports of, 1641, 34, 42
Austin, Anthony, 154
Avery, Samuel, 161

Bacon, Sir Francis, 17
Baglethole, Edward, 157
Barber Surgeons' Company, 157
'Barebones' Parliament, 132
Barker, Alderman William, 74
Bateman, Robert, 159
Beckett, Professor J. C., 3
Beeke, William, 156
Blease, Robert, 154
Bond, Dennis, 71
Borlase, Sir John, 35
Boyle, Richard. See Cork, 1st and 2nd Earls of
Boyle, Roger. See Broghill, Baron
Brehon Law, 19
Brereton, Sir William, 153
Bristol, 21; adventurers from, 65
Broghill, Roger Boyle, Baron, 91, 97, 102, 103, 104, 108, 109
Bruce, Edward, 4
Buckinghamshire, adventures from, 65
Burghley, William Cecil, Lord, 13
Butler, James. See Ormond, 1st Duke of
Butler, W. F. T., 9

Carew, Sir Peter, 9, 10
Castlehaven, James Touchet, 3rd Earl of, 91, 92
Catholics, confederate, 86, 99, 100
Charles I, 24, 32, 36, 37, 43, 44, 76, 83, 99
Charles II, 140, 141, 142, 162
Chatterton, Thomas, 14
Chichester, Sir Arthur, 17, 18, 24

Clanricarde, Ulick de Burgh, 5th Earl of, 25, 81
Clarendon, Edward Hyde, 1st Earl of, 43
Clarke, George, 154, 155
Clement, Gregory, 71, 156
Clontarf, Battle of, 4
Clotworthy, Sir John, 89, 91, 109
committee of both kingdoms, 87, 88, 90
Commons, English House of, 36, 39, 40, 47, 95
Corbett, Miles, 120
Cork, Richard Boyle, 1st Earl of, 12, 28, 46, 49, 102, 153
Cork, Richard Boyle, 2nd Earl of, 90, 102
Counter Reformation, 5
Crispe, Sir Nicholas, 52, 71, 81
Croft, Sir James, 9
Cromwell, Henry, 116, 141
Cromwell, Oliver, 70, 96, 106, 111, 112, 115, 116, 131, 133, 156, 161
Cromwell, Richard, 141
Cumberland, adventurers from, 65
Cunningham, Thomas, 74

Danes, 3
Darnelly, Richard, 61
Dartmouth, 157, 158, 159
Davies, Sir John (1569–1626), 16, 17, 19
Davies, John, 97
Derby House Committee, 102, 109, 111, 118
Derbyshire, adventurers from, 65
Desmond, Rebellion of, 10, 11, 12
Devon, adventurers from, 65
D'Ewes, Sir Simonds, 33, 36, 38, 50, 78
Dorset, adventurers from, 65
doubling ordinance, 62, 85, 90, 93, 95, 111, 117, 119, 121
Down, colonization of, 23
Down survey, 147, 150, 151
Dunlop, Robert, 14, 42

Durham, adventurers from, 65
Dyke, Lewis, 74

East India Company, 22
Eaton, Samuel, 154
Edgehill, Battle of, 80, 123
Edward VI, 6, 9
Elizabeth I, 6, 14, 20
Essex, adventurers from, 65
Essex, Walter Devereux, 1st Earl of, 15
Evelyn, Sir John, 156
Exeter, 62, 65, 66, 157, 158, 159, 160

Fairfax, Thomas, 3rd Baron, 92, 96, 98, 105
fasts, 33
Fenton, Sir Geoffrey, 17
Fitzgeralds, 10
Fitzmaurice, Lord Edmond, 147
Fleetwood, Charles, 116
Fletcher, Anthony, 157
Foote, Thomas, 155
Forbes, Alexander, Lord, 81
French, John, 61
Frith, William, 61

Gardiner, S. R., 32, 33
gentry, investment of, 66, 69
Gilbert, Humphrey, 9
Gloucester, adventure from town of, 157, 158
Goodwin, Sir Robert, 91
Grand Remonstrance, 36, 39, 44
Great Yarmouth, adventure from town of, 157, 158
Grenville, Sir Richard, 9
Grocers' Hall, London, Committees at, 92, 93, 95

Halstead, Laurence, 61
Hamerton, Richard, 158
Hamilton, James, 1st Viscount Claneboye, 23
Hampden, John, 70
Haselrigge, Sir Arthur, 61, 70
Hawkins, William, 95, 155
Henry II, 4
Henry VII, 5
Henry VIII, 5, 6
Herbert, Philip. See Pembroke, 4th Earl of
Herbert, Sir William, 13

Hertfordshire, adventurers from, 65
Holland, 51
Holles, Denzil, 70, 105, 109, 110
Hopping, Charles, 159

Inchiquin, Murrough O'Brien, 1st Earl of, 81, 86, 88, 89, 91, 94, 96, 97, 98, 100, 102, 103, 104, 105, 106, 107, 108, 109, 110, 111, 112
Independency, 104
'Independents', investments of, 71–3
Ireton, Henry, 116
Irish Society, the, 22, 23

James I, 18, 24
Jephson, William, 91, 106
Jones, Henry, Bishop of Clogher (1645), and of Meath (1661), 46, 47, 48, 49, 127, 128
Jones, John, 120, 154
Jones, Michael, 107, 110, 115, 116

Kearney, Professor Hugh F., 26
Kelsall, Humphrey, 154
Kendall, William, 156
Kent, Henry Grey, 9th Earl of, 91
Kinsale, Battle of, 25
Knightley, Richard, 91

Lancashire, adventurers from, 65
Lang, R. G., 67
Langham, Samuel, 155
Leicester, Philip Sydney, 3rd Earl of, 35, 37, 40, 78, 97, 103
Leix, Plantation of, 7–9, 11, 26
Leven, Alexander, 1st Earl of, 97, 110
Lisle, Robert Sydney, Viscount, 97, 98, 100, 101, 102, 103, 104, 105, 106, 107, 108, 109, 110
Littleton, Edward, 1st Baron, 69
Loftus, Sir Adam, 102, 103, 104, 108
Loftus, Sir Arthur, 103, 105, 109
London, City of, 19, 20, 21, 22, 23, 32, 36, 38, 39, 51, 52, 64, 65, 66; adventure of, 79, 81, 83, 159, 160
Londonderry, Plantation of, 20–4, 38, 55, 67, 70
Long Parliament, 70
Lords, House of, 36, 39
Love, Walter, 34, 46, 101, 128
Ludlow, Edmund, 116, 120

MacCormack, J. R., 48, 50, 51, 63, 64, 71, 72
MacMahon, Hugh Roe, 14, 17
Massachusetts Bay Company, 22
Massey, Colonel Edward, 106, 108
merchants, 38, 67, 69
Middlesex, adventurers from, 65
Millington, Gilbert, 63
Montgomery, Hugh, 23
Moody, Professor T. W., 20, 21, 22, 38
Mounson, William Lord, 69
Mountjoy, Charles Blount, 8th Baron of, 78
Munster, Plantation of, 9–14, 26

Naseby, battle of, 95
New Model Army, 92, 96, 108
Norfolk, adventurers from, 65
Normans, 4
North America, colonization of, 3, 75
Northumberland, Algernon Percy, 10th Earl of, 88

O'Carroll, Ely, 24
O'Connor, 7, 8
O'Doherty, Cahir, 18
O'Ferrall, 24
Offaly, plantation of, 7–9, 11
Old English, 5, 7, 24, 99
O'More, 7, 8
O'Neil, Phelim, 43
Ormond, James Butler, 1st Duke of, 86, 99, 100, 103, 104, 106, 111, 115, 116, 153

Parker, George, 155
Parsons, Sir William, 35, 102, 103, 104
Pembroke, Philip Herbert, 4th Earl of, 61, 69
Penn, Admiral William, 92
Perceval, Sir Philip, 38, 96, 97, 105
Perrot, Sir John, 10
Petty, William, 137, 138, 139, 141, 149, 152, 153, 161
Philips, Sir Thomas, 21
Plantations, Miscellaneous: Longford, 24; Leitrim, 24; Wexford, 24; Kings County, 24; Connaught, 24, 26, 27
Portland, Jerome Weston, 2nd Earl of, 90

Poynings, Sir Edward, 5
Prendergast, J. P., 59, 60, 61
Presbyterians, investments of, 71–3
Preston, Thomas, later 1st Viscount Tara, 100
Providence Company, 22
Pye, Sir Robert, 38
Pym, John, 32, 36, 37, 48, 51, 70, 78, 84
Pynnar, Captain Nicholas, 23

Quinn, Professor D. B., 2, 10, 15, 16

Rabb, T. K., 55, 67
Raleigh, Sir Walter, 9, 12
Rebellion of 1641, 28, 30, 31
Restoration settlement, 3, 62, 140, 141, 142, 162, 163
Rigby, Alexander, 91
Rinuccini, Giovanni Battista, Archbishop of Fermo, 99, 100, 103
Romans, 3, 14

St. John, Oliver, 61, 70, 88
St. Leger, Sir Anthony, 7
St. Leger, Sir William, 102
Scarampi, Pietro Francesco, 99
Scotland, 32
Scots, 23, 36, 40, 86, 87, 88, 96
Scott, W. R., 44
Sea adventure, 52, 65, 81–2, 91, 121
Skippon, General Philip, 106, 108
Smith, Sir Thomas, 14, 15
Somers Island Company, 22
Somerset, adventurers from, 65
Spain, 10
Spencer, Edmund, 13
Stapleton, Philip, 88, 109
Star Chamber, 22
Sterling, Colonel Robert, 110
Strafford, Thomas Wentworth, 1st Earl of, 25, 26, 28, 102, 105
Suffolk, adventurers from, 65
Surrender and Regrant, 6, 7
Surrey, adventurers from, 65
Sussex, adventurers from, 65
Sussex, Thomas Radcliffe, 3rd Earl of, 14
Sydney, Algernon, 107
Sydney, Philip. *See* Leicester, 3rd Earl of
Sydney, Robert. *See* Lisle, (Viscount)

Taunton, 159
Temple, Sir John, 101, 104, 108, 109, 110
theatres, closing of, 33
Thomond, O'Brien Earls of, 25
Trevor-Roper, Professor H. R., 30
Tyrconnell, Rory O'Donnell, 1st Earl of, 16
Tyrone, Hugh O'Neill, 1st Earl of, 16

Ulster, plantation of, 14–24, 67

Vane, Sir Henry (the elder), 88
Vassal, Samuel, 61
Vincent, Thomas, 155, 156
Virginia Company, 22, 45, 55

Waller, Sir Hardress, 96, 102, 103, 109, 130

Waller, Sir William, 106
Wallop, Robert, 88
Warner, John, 61
Warwick, Robert Rich, 2nd Earl of, 45, 49
Watkins, Sir David, 73
Weaver, John, 120
Wenman, Thomas, 2nd Viscount, 69
Wentworth, Thomas. *See* Strafford
Weston, Jerome. *See* Portland
Wharton, Philip, 4th Baron, 79; brigade of, 80, 92, 93, 123
White, James, 159
Whitehead, Richard, 91
Whitelocke, Bulstrode, 48
Windsor, Treaty of (1175), 4
Worsley, Benjamin, 138, 162